The Flash Usability Guide

Guide

Interacting with Flash MX

Chris MacGregor
Crystal Waters
David Doull
Bob Regan
Andrew Kirkpatrick
Peter Pinch

The Flash Usability Guide

Interacting with Flash MX

© 2002 Apress

Originally published by friends of ED in 2002

First Printed August 2002

Trademark Acknowledgements

friends of ED has endeavored to provide trademark information about all the companies and products mentioned in this book by the appropriate use of capitals. However, friends of ED cannot guarantee the accuracy of this information.

Extracts from adidas websites are reproduced by consent of adidas International B.V. adidas, the adidas logo and the three stripe trade mark are registered trade marks of the adidas-Salomon group.

ISBN 978-1-59059-201-4   ISBN 978-1-4302-5465-2 (eBook)
DOI 10.1007/978-1-4302-5465-2

The Flash Usability Guide

Interacting with Flash MX

Credits

Authors
Chris MacGregor
Crystal Waters
David Doull
Bob Regan
Andrew Kirkpatrick
Peter Pinch

Commissioning Editor
Ben Renow-Clarke

Graphic Editor
Ty Bhogal

Cover Design
Katy Freer

Editors
Paul Thewlis
Dan Squier
Alan McCann

Author Agent
Gaynor Riopedre

Project Manager
Richard Harrison

Indexer
Simon Collins

Technical Reviewers
Marco Baraldi
Eng Wei Chua
Clifton Evans
Steve Kirby
Vibha Roy
Eric Vardon

Proofreaders
Ben Renow-Clarke
Simon Collins
Richard Harrison
Fiona Murray
Paul Thewlis

Managing Editor
Ben Huczek

The Flash Usability Guide

Chris MacGregor   **www.macgregor.net**

Chris is an Interaction Designer with MacGregor Media in Houston, Texas. He consults with clients across the world to improve the usability of their Flash projects. In addition to his award-winning work, he is recognized as a leading proponent of Flash and usability. He is the publisher of Flazoom.com, a popular Flash critique site and author of a number of articles focusing on deploying usable Flash content. In 2001 Macromedia published his Flash usability white paper entitled "Developing User-Friendly Flash Content."

Crystal Waters   **www.typo.com**

Crystal has been writing about consumer-oriented technology since the 80s, back when 5MB hard drives were a novel upgrade. She is author of two books, *Web Concept & Design*, and *Universal Web Design* (New Riders), and of many, many articles. She has been an editor at a number of magazines and was director of MFWeb conferences, among other roles, and is a long-distance charity cyclist and avid kayak-fisherman. She lives and fishes with her boyfriend Dwayne (who took this photo) and dog Nellie (pictured) in Vermont. Her sites are typo.com and girlbike.com. She likes parentheses (obviously)—and, erm, dashes.

David Doull   **www.artifactinteractive.com.au**

David is an Australian freelance developer specializing in building applications in Flash. He's based in Adelaide and is best known for his sites smallblueprinter.com, urbanev.com and artifactinteractive.com.au.

Author Biographies

Bob Regan

Bob is the senior product manager for accessibility at Macromedia. In that role, he works with designers, developers, and engineers from around the world to communicate existing strategies for accessibility as well as develop new strategies. He works with engineers and designers within Macromedia to develop new techniques and improve the accessibility of Macromedia tools.

Bob has a Masters degree from Columbia University in Education. He is currently a doctoral student in Education at the University of Wisconsin, Madison where he lives now. Bob spent six years as a teacher and technology leader in Chicago and New York City.

Andrew Kirkpatrick

Andrew is Project Manager for the Access to Rich Media Project at the CPB/WGBH National Center for Accessible Media (NCAM) in Boston. He is focused on Web accessibility, with emphasis on streaming and interactive media accessibility. Andrew is involved with NCAM's work with the accessibility efforts of companies such as Macromedia and AOL, and is on the development team for NCAM's software for creating captions and audio descriptions, MAGpie. Andrew's work creating an online resource for developers interested in making accessible rich media can be accessed at http://ncam.wgbh.org/richmedia.

Peter Pinch

Peter is Director of Technology for Interactive Content at WGBH Interactive, part of the WGBH Educational Foundation in Boston. WGBH Interactive produces educational web sites, DVDs, and Interactive Television for programs such as *This Old House*, *NOVA*, *Arthur* and many others. Peter's most recent Flash project was "Zoot Suit Culture" for the PBS program *American Experience*. Peter has taught Flash labs at Yale and Harvard, and currently teaches Educational Web Design at Marlboro College.

The Flash Usability Guide

Choosing usability   4

Showing users respect   8

The Flash Usability Guide

Offline Flash

11

User testing

12

Appendix: Resources and Articles on the Web

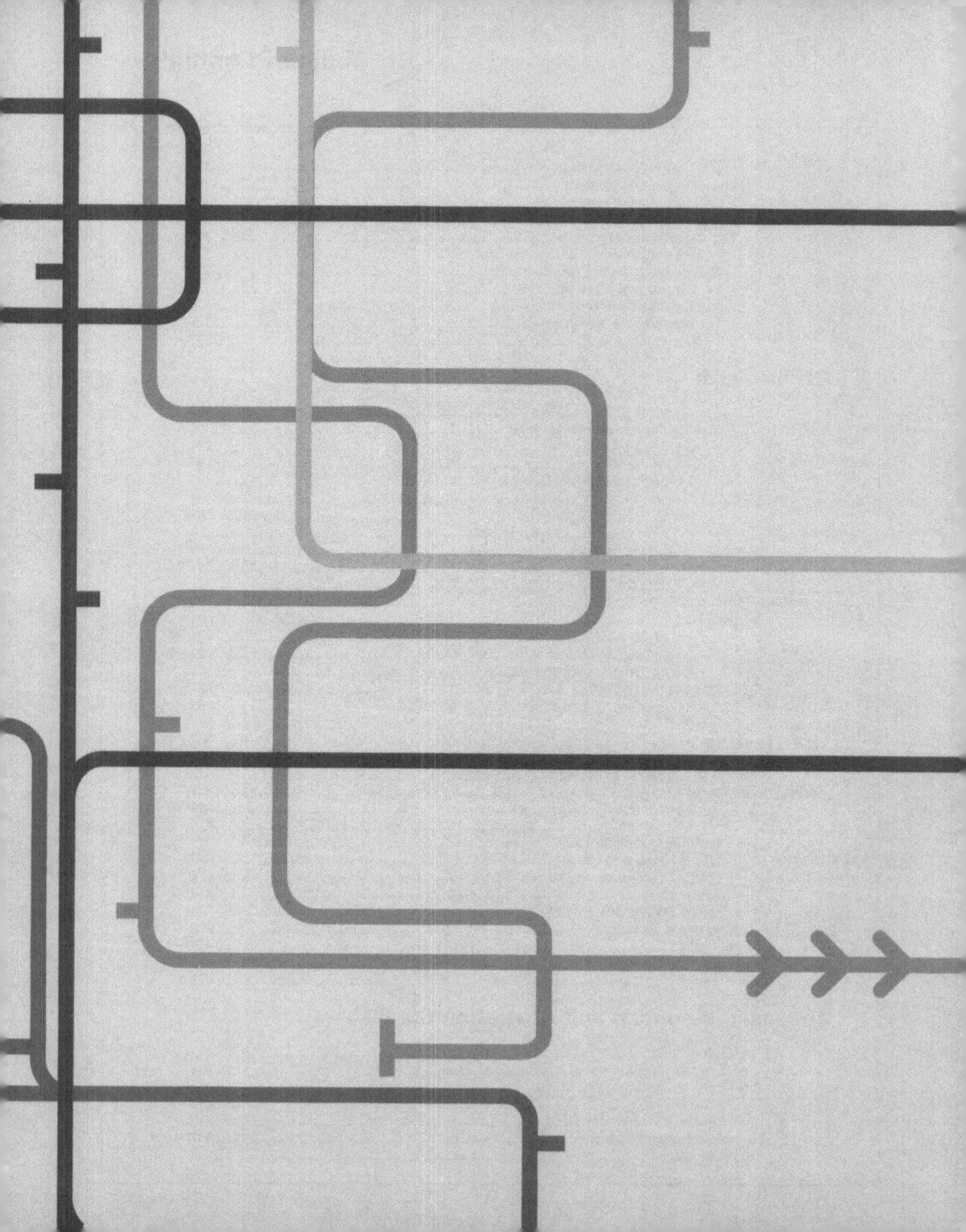

Introduction

As the Web matures, more and more designers are realizing the potential of Macromedia Flash. For many people Flash has been a godsend, and there are now some truly remarkable Flash creations out there that have made the Web a more exciting and visually stimulating place. But as the initial excitement about Flash has died down over the last couple of years, we're beginning to find out that there's more to this powerful piece of software than just making things look great.

It's now commonplace to find entire web sites built in Flash. A growing number of designers (and developers) are even using Flash to create complex applications – both integrated into their site designs and standalone. This adds a new dimension to the art and science of Flash authoring: **usability**.

Many influential web pundits and commentators are beginning to speak out on this important issue. They believe it's time for the design community to think about their work within a broader paradigm, one that embodies the aesthetic *and* the usable. It's no longer good enough for designers to publish a cutting-edge piece of electronic art and expect it to be embraced by their audience simply because it looks so fantastic. If the users can't do what they came to the site to do, then no matter how cool it looks, the project is a failure.

No one's suggesting that we ditch all vestiges of artistic flair in our work - a really usable web site can also look stunning. It's just time to stop and think about what we're doing. Are we really achieving what we should be with a web design project if our users can't navigate the site because the buttons are camouflaged against the background of a beautifully presented interface?

What this book is about

This book is about getting designers who use Flash to start thinking about usability. We want to raise awareness of this important and topical issue. We're not aiming to give a definitive, fail-safe process for creating usable

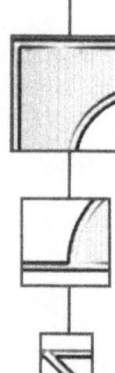

Flash content. What we are hoping to do is present guidelines that can be applied to a wide variety of Flash projects.

Topics covered in the book include:

- History of the debate about Flash design versus usability

- What usability means in practice

- Why usability is important

- Why we should ensure that Flash is the right tool for the job in hand

- How understanding our users is integral to implementing usability

- Structuring Flash content to optimize usability

- Using Macromedia Flash MX to improve accessibility

- Establishing design conventions that aid usability

- The importance of user testing

It's important to bear in mind that the implementation of web usability is an evolving science and as such many of its core hypotheses are still under debate. Some of the views and opinions of the authors in this book may provoke a certain amount of controversy amongst the Flash community and we at friends of ED hope that they do. While you may not initially agree with everything you read, we hope that it gives you some food for thought and helps you stand back from your work with a slightly more objective eye.

What we expect you to know

We expect most readers of this book to be experienced Flash designers who want to expand their skill-set beyond the purely technical. There are many non-technical skills that are essential to your success as a Flash designer; one of those is understanding and implementing usability.

You won't find very much code in the book or too many hands-on tutorials. This is because we expect you to already have the technical knowledge to implement the usability techniques that are suggested.

How the book looks

We've tried to keep the book as clear and as easy to follow as possible, so we've only used a few layout styles:

- When you come across an important word or phrase, it will be in **bold type**.

- We'll use a different font to emphasize words and phrases that appear on the screen, `code`, `filenames`, and URLs (e.g. www.friendsofed.com)

- When there's some information that we think is really important, we'll highlight it like this:

> *This is important stuff – make sure you're paying attention!*

- Worked exercises are laid out like this:

Tutorial

1. Open up Flash
2. Save your file as `usability.fla`
3. And so on

■ Caption text that relates to screenshots and other images looks like this:

> This is a caption. It tells you all about the pictures you're looking at.

■ Throughout the book we'll be using a case study to demonstrate some of the usability theory you'll be learning. You can easily spot case study pages because they have a different border.

Feedback and support

friends of ED books aim to be easy to follow and error-free. However, if you run into problems, don't hesitate to get in touch – our crack team of reader support professionals will have you back on the straight and narrow in no time!

You can reach us at support@friendsofed.com, and we'd love to hear from you, even if it's just to make suggestions for future books or tell us how much you loved this one!

> *To tell us a bit about yourself and make comments about the book, why not fill out the little reply card at the back and mail it to us?*

You can also check out our web site for news, more books, downloads, and, of course, our packed message boards! Point your browser at www.friendsofed.com.

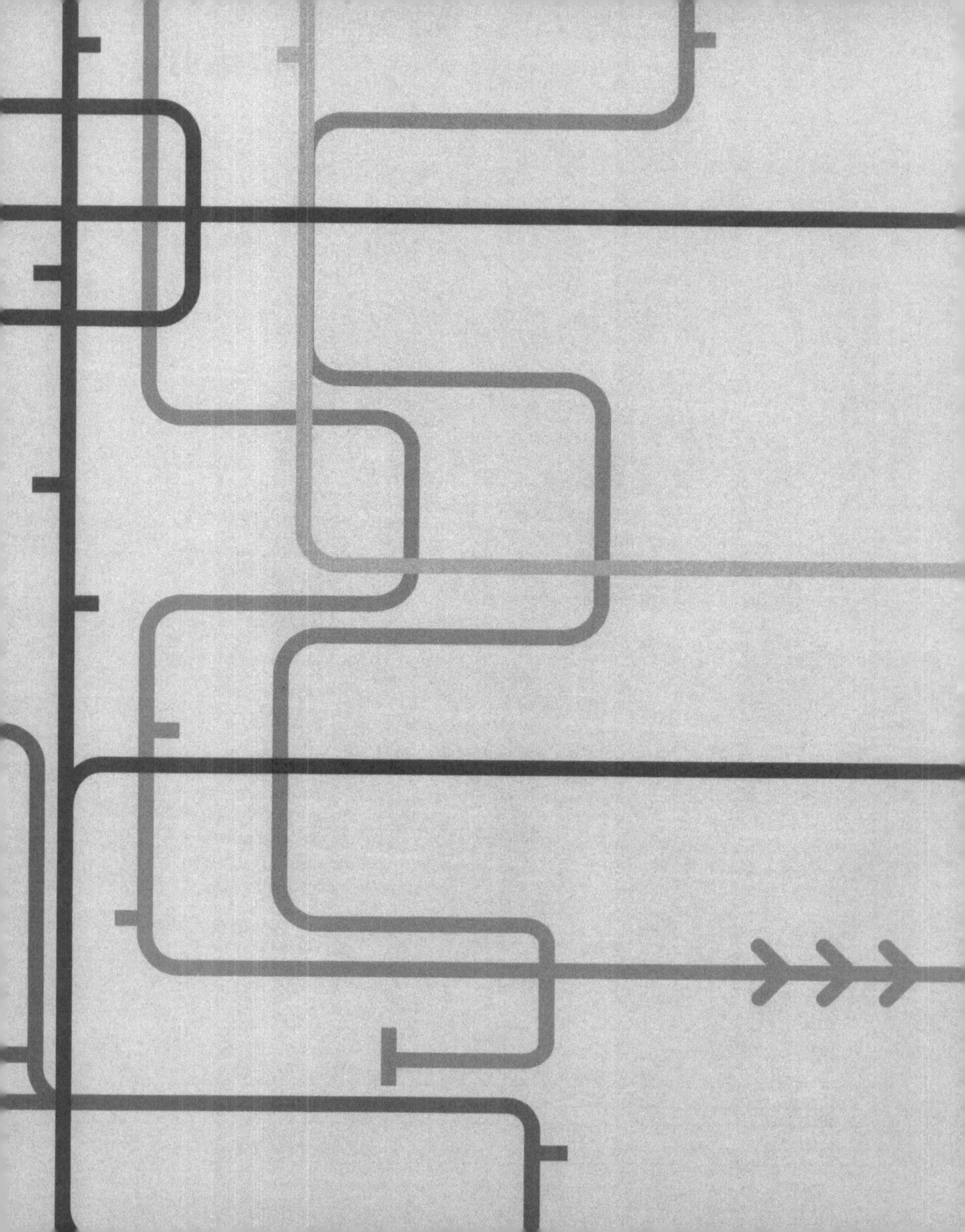

Flash vs. Usability

If you're relatively new to the world of Flash design, you may wonder why so many folks seem to make such a fuss about this mysterious, intangible thing known as **usability**. Wherever you look, there are web sites, books (like the one you are reading now), training CDs, and white papers that are all dedicated to improving the usability of Flash content. So, what's all the fuss about?

Well, **usability** itself is a fairly simple notion. It's defined as the ease with which someone can use (or interact with) a system, whether it's a Flash movie, a plain old HTML web site, or something completely different like a VCR or washing machine. Ideally, the user doesn't have to put any great effort into figuring out which button to push, what information to feed in, which link to click on, or which spin cycle to use for their brand new Levi's. A usable system will make things as clear as possible, so that the user can apply nothing more complex than common sense to get the results they want right away.

The trouble is, when it comes to this sort of thing, Flash content (particularly on the Web) has a bad reputation. It's a reputation with its roots firmly planted in movies that annoy their users with lengthy downloads, unwanted introductions, and confusing interactions. It's a reputation for sites that frustrate their users with overly complex interfaces, and it's a reputation that deserves to be changed.

In this opening chapter, I'm going to talk about the history of Flash's all too stormy relationship with the science of usability. We'll look at some of the ways in which Flash designers have been poorly implementing Flash for clients and their customers. We'll also see what usability gurus such as Jakob Nielsen have had to say about Flash, and how it's relevant to what we're developing today. Finally, we'll take a quick look at how Flash MX starts helping us to address the criticisms of the past.

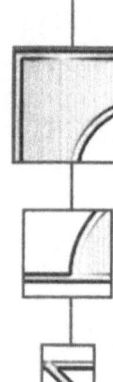

Flash in control

Yes, Flash is a pretty darned powerful piece of software. Part animation tool and part interactive content development tool, it offers everything that stressed-out web designers could ask for and more. After years of frustration dealing with coding HTML web sites for different browsers and platforms, Flash came along and offered us **complete control** over all that the user saw and experienced. Of course, it didn't take long for us to start using this power to try and change the face of the Web.

However, by mid-2000, Flash had begun to outlive its initial welcome. Designers were attracting attention for the excesses of their sites, and web usability pundits were eager to point out the potential for damage that such excesses lead to. For web surfers, visiting an all-Flash site almost certainly meant large files and confusing interactions.

Indeed, most Flash sites seemed to offer the user little more than a long wait and, well, Flash. By the end of 2000 the most vocal critic on the Web weighed in on Flash content, and it wasn't good. "Flash: 99% Bad!" said Jakob Nielsen (the guru of web usability) about the tool that we had all come to love. And then, in less than one thousand words, Jakob pulled the plug on the Internet's greatest design renaissance. The Flash bubble popped, and reality started creeping back into the design specs for Flash projects.

There are three main reasons that Flash acquired such a poor reputation for usability on the Web:

- Because it's such a powerful piece of software, it's capable of extending the Web experience far beyond what most users find comfortable

- Flash designers have tended to be too experimental and self-referential when designing and developing Flash content for the Web

- Clients have placed more value on 'cool' and 'edgy' sites instead of favouring ones that are useful to their customers and users

Of course, none of these problems were insurmountable. Unfortunately though, they lent enough weight to statements like "Flash: 99% Bad" that many clients grew reluctant to use Flash on their sites at all – even if it was the best solution for a particular project.

It's only now (mid-2002 at time of writing) that we're starting to see light at the end of the tunnel. The release of Flash MX, and the announcement that Jakob Nielsen's very own usability consulting group is to work with Macromedia in developing "best practice guidelines" for Flash on the Web, demonstrate that Macromedia is taking this usability thing very seriously indeed. Let's follow their example, and try to understand what went wrong the first time around.

Too much power?

It was in December 1996 that Jonathan Gay handed over FutureSplash Animator to Macromedia, and Flash 1.0 was born. Of course, as soon as Flash was in the hands of us designers, we started to explore its potential. Empowered by the abilities of Flash to create unheard of interactivity on the Web, designers ran amuck. Flash became the new `<blink>` tag of the Web.

Interactions within HTML are fairly straightforward and simple: If a user clicks a link or button, they are taken to a new page. If a user wants to copy some text, they only have to highlight and copy it. If they want to see the source for a page, it's available and more recent browsers allow users to scale text on the fly, making even the tiniest typefaces larger and easier to read. HTML offers the user many options for how they use the content on a page.

Because the interactions within HTML are fairly similar from site to site, users have become used to these interactions.

> *Users have developed a set of expectations based on how HTML pages work on the Web, and they bring those expectations to every site that they visit.*

Flash, on the other hand, has very few interaction conventions that dictate it behavior from site to site. Until the release of Flash MX there were no standard user interface elements that would work the same way across all sites. Flash designers had to build their own scroll-bars, their own radio buttons and their own checkboxes. The result was that the interactions on a Flash site were only as good as the skills of the designer.

Any user who visits Flash sites needs to continually readjust their expectations on how the interface will work. Each interface element has a period of trial and, more often than not, error. On one Flash site the up arrow scrolls the text up, and on the next Flash site the up arrow scrolls the text down. This leads to confusion for the user.

> *The site for German Networking Company, Toptronix (www.toptronix.de) is a good example of how Flash designers can confuse users by offering inconsistent navigation controls. In the 'network', 'direct marketing' and 'database management' sections, there are up and down arrow buttons on the right-hand side of the screen, but they don't scroll. Instead, you have to click and drag the scroll bar, which even lets you scroll the content right off the screen! Meanwhile, the news section (which pops up in a mini-window) has scroll arrows, but no scroll bar – and no news either when I looked...*

While HTML-based content doesn't offer the ability to create new interface elements with the ease of Flash, that's not always a bad thing. Designers adding scrollable content using HTML know that the user's experience when scrolling that content will be the same as every other HTML site they visit. Ideally, Flash interfaces that present Flash-built versions of standard HTML UI controls should mimic the behavior and general appearance of the HTML version.

A Flash site that does offer a good example of a UI component that mimics its commonly experienced HTML counterpart is www.aldoshoes.com. Go to the section called 'Aldo Central' and select 'About Aldo'. You'll be presented with a box of scrolling text featuring an easy-to-recognize, easy-to-use scroll bar that looks and behaves like its HTML counterpart.

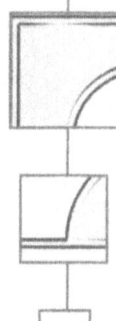

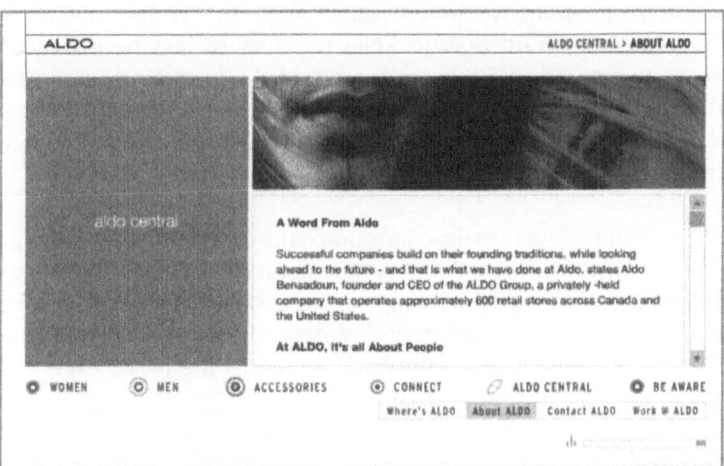

Too little restraint?

Flash gets a bad rap from many web pundits, and in many cases the bad reputation is justly deserved. Too many designers focused on making things 'cool' instead of making the Web easier to use.

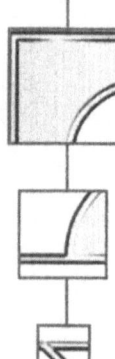

When Macromedia Flash first hit the Web it was marketed as offering streaming and small file sizes. We could design a Flash menu that would load faster than a bunch of JavaScript rollover GIF files, and it would start to play as soon as enough content was downloaded. Flash offered us solutions to many of the problems with HTML.

As Flash became more powerful, we started to explore the potential of the program. We found techniques for making more complicated interfaces, better sound integration, and more complex animations. The Flash content that we were deploying on the Web started to grow in file size, and decrease in usability. We started to abuse our users with feature-laden Flash sites that were more about showing off our skills than meeting the users' needs.

Now, just a few years later, the art of streaming Flash content is all but forgotten. It seems we would rather make our visitor wait for a 200Kb+ download than learn how to keep our files within the download stream. What is worse, some Flash designers tout the program as a replacement to HTML (along with DHTML, XHTML and other web standards) like there was something wrong with it. HTML is still a far better medium for much of the content on the Web than Flash is!

When Flash reached version 4, ActionScript started to come of age. Instead of implementing interactions that would be familiar to the user, Flash designers started experimenting with new styles of interface. When Flash 5 came out, with even more powerful ActionScript abilities, designers started creating interactions that were totally alien to the user's experience of the Web.

Flash designers started to experiment with the new capabilities of Flash, and share their experiments online. Some absolutely beautiful Flash art was created, blending technical mastery of ActionScript with creative design skill. These experiments showed designers what Flash was capable of, and soon all Flash web sites started having more in common with experimental Flash art than the HTML Web that the user was familiar with.

Flash designers, in a rush to adopt the latest cutting-edge interaction that Flash is capable of, forgot their accountability to the client and the user. Instead the Flash designer community was engrossed with a race to keep up with the most creative designers. Creating experimental interactions is fun, and we designers get a great sense of accomplishment when we are able to get our computer to do something that it has never done before.

Sites across the Web started to replace their HTML designs with Flash interfaces. Online retailers like Boo.com employed Flash content to create a richer experience for their users. Every web design company seemed to be developing their own all-Flash portfolio site. The Web at large was getting impatient with Flash content that was big and slow. Users were frustrated with the valueless animations, the confusing interfaces, and the loss of user control.

While the user's frustration with Flash content was growing, we were enjoying the renaissance that Flash brought to web design. Finally we had control over the presentation of content online. Integration of sound, animation, and interactivity was easy to build, and we didn't have to learn a complex programming language to do so.

The major design awards didn't help the issue either. Many Flash sites that featured a confusing, frustrating user experience garnered awards from top competitions. The prestige of design awards overtook any thoughts about usability. Flash designers stoked their egos fueled by their design awards and fawning clients. They forgot that our job is to deliver effective communication.

All-Flash sites sometimes present interactions in such a complex way that the designers find they need to add a 'help movie' with visual cues as to how to use the site. Even with a help movie, interactions on a site like www.barneys.com grew so complex that many users had a hard time figuring out what was going on!

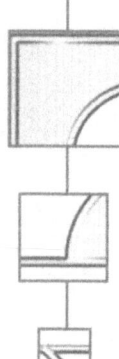

Whose computer is it anyway?

People's computers play an important part in their lives: they reflect work habits, entertainment choices, and – in these and many other ways – reflect our overall personality. While a CD or DVD may promise a largely passive experience, the Web is a different beast altogether: you expect to be in control to a much greater extent.

Most users have quite fixed expectations of the content they receive via the Web. All web users are barraged with virus warnings and hoaxes, so it's no great surprise that they tend to mistrust anything on the Web that doesn't behave as expected. The more control a site appears to wield over their computer, the more vulnerable they're likely to feel.

Some Flash-only sites use interfaces that have more in common with an operating system than they do with a web page. EgoMedia's site (www.egomedia.com), for example, presents a full-screen Flash movie that appears to completely replace the user's desktop. Impressive as it is, many users find this quite alarming – when the familiar 'close window' button disappears from the top of their browser, they can lose a sense of control over what's being shown on their computer screen.

> *Offering up web content that acts like nothing they've seen before is a great way to grab the user's attention, but it's not an experience that's going to make them feel particularly comfortable.*

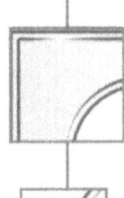

EgoMedia certainly developed some very impressive content, which would have been perfectly at home on a CD-ROM or the like. But web users generally want to see their environment (the browser, the menu bar, the desktop, and so on) respected. Because their site disregarded just about every convention of web design, it inevitably caused confusion and anxiety to many of its users. Its unfamiliar behavior was more likely to alienate the average web user than it was to impress them.

> *It's important to consider how your Flash content impinges on a user's environment, and how it might challenge their expectations of what web content should and should not be able to do.*

The sense of control that a user has over their computer and its behavior is an almost sacred thing. Think about your own personal computer for a minute. I bet you have the preferences tweaked to suit your own particular needs. After all, it's *your* computer – not mine, not Barneys' and not EgoMedia's.

When a web site takes control of the computer away from the person who's using it, they're quite likely to resent it. "Who does this designer think he is opening a new window on my screen?" they may well ask. If you do need to break with convention, the least you can do is to check with the user first – ask permission, and you're putting them back in control. Just be sure to allow for the possibility they'll say, "No!"

Designers use the Web differently

Designers like to win awards and see their work featured in the design journals and web sites. It's the narcotic of our profession. We see incredibly cool work from other designers and think to ourselves, "I wish I could design like that", or, "I wish I had clients who would pay for something like that".

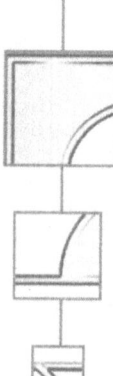

If the truth be told, I think most of us prefer to design without the restraint of clients, markets, and focus groups. We'd love to be creating that amazing work that every designer will be talking about. The personal web sites of designers are definitely the place to go to see cutting edge web and Flash design. We like to design for those who appreciate the same values that we appreciate in design, and thus our design becomes self-referential.

The problem is that as designers, we're trained to make complex collections of information simple. When a designer is presented with a complex interface, he or she automatically starts to deconstruct it. Because we're trained to do this as part of our job, designers prefer to have more challenging designs presented to them. And, we prefer to be free to design complex interfaces ourselves.

Unfortunately, this doesn't hold true for the average user. While a designer may be able to understand the visual language of a site like www.2Advanced.com, your average web surfer is going to have a hard time understanding what is important on the page. There's a simple lesson to be learned:

> *As a designer, you're not designing Flash content for yourself – you're doing it for the users.*

Experimentation, breaking conventions, and pushing the envelope are all admirable goals, but they're rarely the things that make a client's money worth spending. There's nothing wrong with creating an abstract, experimental Flash site – just don't use it as the basis for your client's e-commerce interface, or they may go bust and turn litigious when none of their users can figure out how to buy anything!

Web surfers want to be able to quickly understand the basic structure of a page. They want to take a quick look and say to themselves, "Ok, that's the information I was looking for," or, "That button should take me to the page I need".

That's not to say that complex interactions have no place on a web site. Some features will require a small learning curve for users to engage in. The point is this: *where* should that learning curve take place? Okay, maybe the site's online flight simulator needs one or two non-standard interactions to be viable – but should you really be asking users to go study a manual if all they want to do is check the time, the weather, and the sports results?

> *If complex interactions are justified, it's best to keep them removed from the needs of the casual user. As visitors return to the site for its core content, they may dabble with more complex features, and they can face the learning curve with a better understanding of what the effort involved may be worth to them. This doesn't just apply to Flash – an excellent example in pure HTML can be found at* www.google.com, *where the world-famous search engine offers basic search facilities to every passing web surfer, while more complex features (including localized searches and translation) are available on a separate page.*

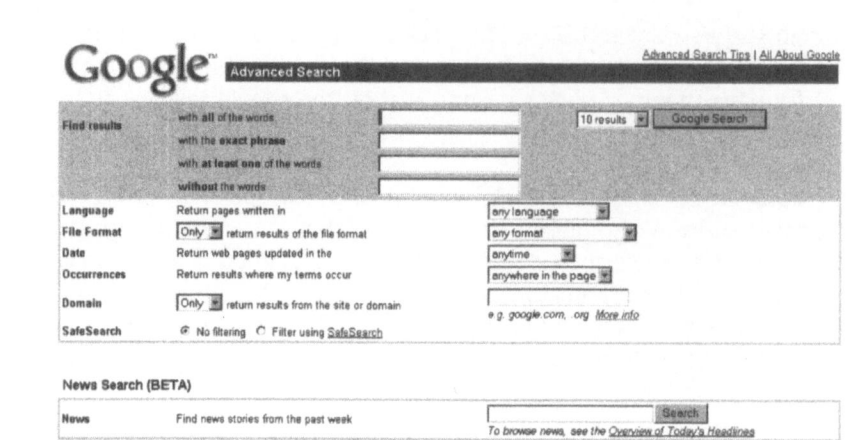

Who has the need for speed?

In just a few short years Macromedia took a great little animation package and beefed it up to include all the features web designers wanted. With the release of Flash 4 the potential for creativity was turned up to eleven. Designers were handed the most powerful development tool the Web had ever seen with a note saying, "Have Fun!"

Imagine yourself behind the wheel of a top-of-the-line Porsche 911 Turbo on a deserted stretch of road. The car, according to Porsche's web site, has a top speed of 189mph (305km/h). Now, how fast do you want to go?

The power that Flash offers designers is like the engine of that sports car. With Flash, designers can accomplish much more than any other technology on the Web today. We can build content that seamlessly integrates video, sound, animation, databases and more, all running on the souped-up engine of Flash.

Designers quickly got drunk on the power that Flash offered. We started to forget the lessons of web design and do the things that we had learned to avoid. Splash screen? Just wait until you get a load of this 45-second, 300K, intro movie! Annoyed by the blink tag? Take a look at this mouse chaser. We were delivering sites that had the gas pedal welded to the floor.

When you use Flash to create a web site, you're creating a user experience. You can compare that experience to the speed at which our Porsche travels. When the user interacts with Flash, their experience can be that of a friendly, leisurely drive through town or it can be a terrifying breakneck race along a twisty mountain road. The difference is, the sites and content that we designers build are going to be driven by someone else: the user.

Now imagine your grandmother behind the wheel of that same Porsche 911 turbo. How fast do you think she would like to go down that same stretch of deserted road? Do you think your grandmother would like to be in a car that could do 189 mph?

The experience of the user relates to the control they have over the operation of the content. By keeping interactions simple and straightforward, you allow the user to control more of their experience. The *user's* foot – and *not* the designer's – should be on the gas pedal.

Biting the hand that feeds

Not all the blame for Flash's poor usability reputation falls on the shoulders of the designers. Sure designers have been pushing the Web to unheard of extremes and selling our experiments as suitable interfaces, but someone has been paying for all this. The **clients** who hire designers to create sites that break every usability guideline share just as much blame as the designers who create them.

If you've worked for any length of time designing content for the Web then you've probably realized that many of the people holding the purse strings have little idea about what their customers need from the web sites they're

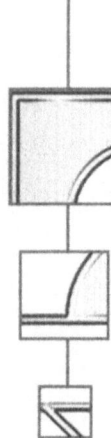

paying for. It seems that clients looking for web design have reached the pinnacle of being uninformed about what they're buying.

Clients don't care how their content works

For the past seven years I've been designing web sites and Flash content for the Web. In all those years and all those meetings and all those clients, I don't think that I've worked on one single project where the client didn't ask for the design to be either 'cool' or 'edgy'.

Clients have been shopping for design the way that they would shop for a sports car. They focus on the color and the styling, and rarely look under the hood. I've worked on projects where the entire design of the site was dictated by the client's favorite color and preferred typeface.

But Flash content is not a sports car – at least not the client's sports car. The Flash that the client is paying for is for their customers, their users, and their business. Remember that the user is final arbiter of whether the site works, and not the client, nor the designer.

Ignoring the user

Client-focused design leads to many usability issues with a number of Flash sites on the Web. Everything from intro movies to soundtracks to mouse chasers to experimental interfaces, these needless bits of content that come with too many Flash sites are all approved by clients. While the extra features may be very impressive to show off, they're also likely to put off users who come to a site. And you can bet that a user visiting a site with a purpose is more likely to be a potential customer.

While writing this book I found that late night sessions of research and writing were significantly improved with the popular energy drink 'Red Bull'. Being the 'infoholic' that I am, I wanted to find out just what was in the Red Bull I had been drinking. It didn't take me long to point my browser at www.RedBull.com, but once there, I was greeted by the unfortunate experience of branding gone haywire.

Once I made it past a broken Flash detection script, I found a home page with nothing more than a 162K Flash file containing eleven links. That's nearly 15K per link! Can you imagine trying to get client approval for a page consisting of nothing more than eleven 15K animated GIFs? No, me neither – and for good reason! So, why do they seem to think it's okay to do it with Flash?

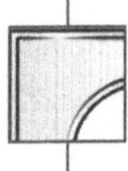

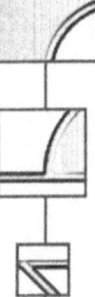

To make matters worse, it took a total of 30 seconds for all eleven links to show up on the screen – that's *after* the entire Flash file loaded. Now, I don't know about you, but I'm not usually the type of person who wants to wait 30 seconds to make a decision about where to click on a web page. And it wasn't like the 30 seconds was filled with an impressive 'rich-content' experience. All that happened was a series of animated cartoon bulls appeared with the buttons that formed the menu. That was it.

So, I clicked on the first button that looked feasible, but that link didn't have the type of information that I needed (although it was to an HTML page). The second button I chose was wrong too, and at that point I stopped my interaction and went off to ask Google for an answer.

The end result of my interaction was a change in my purchasing habits. Until I visited www.RedBull.com I was a budding loyal customer. After suffering the user experience of the site I'm back to coffee and Diet Dr. Pepper to assist in late night writing!

When I see sites like this, I can't help but wonder how the development meetings for the site went. Is this a case of client-focused development (make the client happy) or a case of designer-focused development (make the designer look cool). It certainly doesn't look like a case of user-focused design!

I wonder if the designers were as frustrated as I am with clients who insist on letting superficial issues drive site development. All too often I speak with fellow Flash designers who comment on a usability issue with Flash content they built by saying, "That's what the client wanted, and they pay the bills".

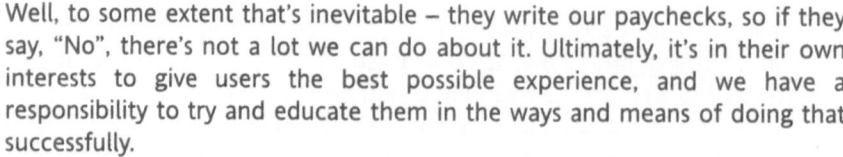

Well, to some extent that's inevitable – they write our paychecks, so if they say, "No", there's not a lot we can do about it. Ultimately, it's in their own interests to give users the best possible experience, and we have a responsibility to try and educate them in the ways and means of doing that successfully.

A little bit of thought and consideration for the user goes a long way when you're designing something as fundamental as a site's navigation. In my opinion Red Bull have got it wrong for all the reasons I've mentioned above. They've neglected the user in favor of a quirky navigation. But you can use Flash to design really useful navigations that are beyond the capabilities of HTML. Chronicle Books use a really nice hierarchical menu structure on their Flash site (www.chroniclebooks.com) that's intuitive, logical and above all usable:

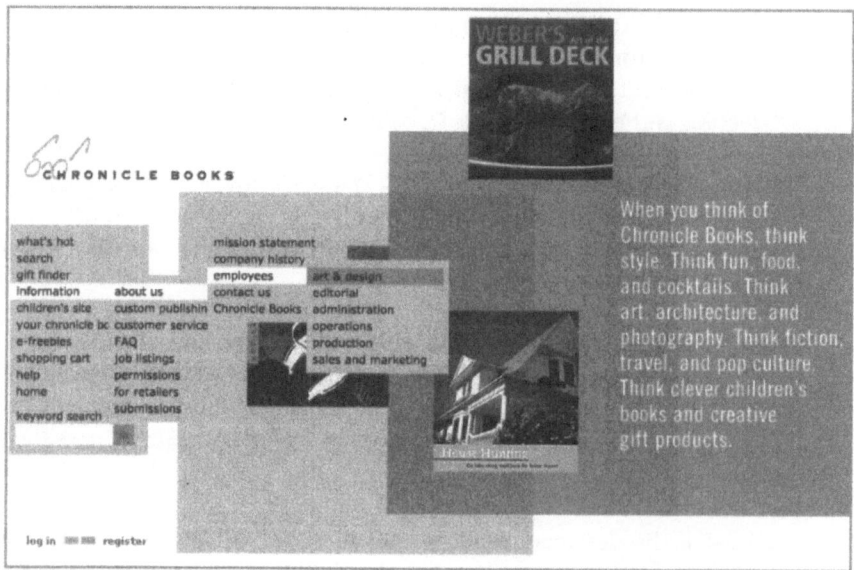

It's easier to buy something cool than it is to buy something useful

It's easy to understand why clients want to make the easy decisions like typefaces and colors. Everything else requires thinking, effort, and work. The Web is meant to be fun!

When clients come to fancy web design shops with their pachinko machines and foosball tables, they see the design firm as a place to get away from the heavy thinking of their corporate life, kick back, and have fun. They're not there to think about customers – they're there to be creative!

All too often, the end result is an amazingly cool-looking web site in the client's favorite color and typeface, but one that's virtually impossible to use. While naming a section of the content 'Bling Bling' may have seemed a good idea in the development meeting, users may actually find 'Financial' more useful when they're hunting about for a link to their stock prices.

Year 2000: the Flash backlash

When Boo.com folded in early 2000, online retailers were already pretty wary of using Flash for their sites. A Flash designer working for one of the big name dot-com retailers at the time reported that management put out a memo effectively killing all Flash development, period. In May of that year, the online magazine, *Salon*, put it like this:

> "In the year 2000, there is no excuse for any professional web site that expects to reach a wide audience of users to put on its home page an animation that requires a browser plug-in..."

October saw Jakob Nielsen sink the final nail in the coffin of the first Flash wave. In his widely read **Alertbox** column (www.useit.com/alertbox/20001029.html), the Web's most vocal usability critic wrote:

> "About 99% of the time, the presence of Flash on a website constitutes a usability disease."

He went on to outline three major reasons why Flash was bad for the Web:

- Flash encourages design abuse

- Flash content breaks with the Web's fundamental interaction principles

- Flash distracts attention from the site's core value

While his arguments weren't exactly watertight, the impact that this column had on the Flash development community was far-reaching. Flash projects were stopped in mid-production, new projects were halted, and clients started asking their designers for much better justification before even considering the further use of Flash content.

Addressing the critics

The points Nielsen raised regarding Flash itself hit home – when Macromedia shipped Flash MX in 2002 it became clear that they'd taken many of these criticisms to heart. They did a good job of resolving them too, as witnessed by Nielsen himself in a recent addendum to his infamous column:

> "The version of Flash introduced in 2002 (Flash MX) has solved many of the technical usability problems in previous versions of Flash."

All in all, Flash MX presents us with a better environment than ever for creating highly usable Flash content. Here's a quick summary of how it responds to Nielsen's main criticisms:

Criticism	Response
Flash encourages design abuse.	Flash MX offers a number of UI components which serve the double purpose of speeding up development time and making Flash UI elements behave the same across different designers' content.
Flash content breaks with the Web's fundamental interaction principles.	Flash MX is integrated with the browser 'back' and 'forward' buttons for the majority of web users. Flash MX offers improved accessibility through the integration of screen reader technology. Flash MX has a font object, which designers can integrate in our Flash content allowing users to re-size text to suit their needs.
Flash distracts attention from the site's core value.	Flash MX offers multiple new ways to integrate Flash with back-end publishing technologies including better XML support, support for database interactivity and Flash remoting. This allows Flash interfaces to deliver richer and more robust information to users with lower development costs.

Of course, that's not the whole story. Nielsen's original column also raised a number of issues concerning the way designers produce and deploy their Flash content. Even once the majority of users have upgraded to the latest Flash plug-in, it still takes an informed Flash designer to implement these new features in an effective manner.

Let's take a look at the charges Nielsen leveled at Flash designers back in October 2000 in more detail, and see if they're still pertinent to us today.

Charge #1: "Flash encourages design abuse"
Nielsen argues that the application Flash encourages Flash intros, gratuitous animation, non-standard GUI controls, and reduces the amount of user control over the content. He speaks of the Flash application like it was a malignant force, corrupting designers by seducing them with its power.

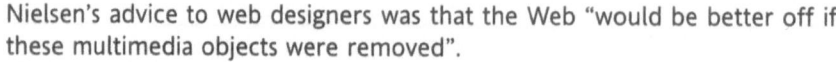

Nielsen's advice to web designers was that the Web "would be better off if these multimedia objects were removed".

When the Alertbox column was written there were a number of sites that included Flash intro-movies. Users visiting those sites would experience the same frustrations as visiting an HTML site with an intro-tunnel: Unnecessary and large content sent to the user before they could get to the information that they were looking for. In many cases the content on these Flash sites was passive in nature, and users want the Web to be anything but passive.

Nielsen also states in his column that, "Flash encourages **gratuitous animation**". Well, I'd argue that Flash doesn't *encourage* animation – it simply makes it much easier to create the stuff. Of course, when animation suddenly became easy to create and deliver, designers felt no great need to hold back. Just as the over-abundance of animated GIFs annoyed web users in the mid-90s, enthusiasm for Flash designers' long animated sequences was not shared across the Web.

Blaming Flash for the excesses of designers is not a valid reason to remove it from the Web. Flash did remove many of the limitations to animation on the Web. Prior to Flash, animation on the Web consisted of animated GIFs with up to 256 colors, or in more extreme cases, server push technology that never seemed to work smoothly. You don't hear critics calling for the removal of all GIFs on the Web just because you can animate them.

> *Nielsen's main issue here seems to be that we designers were incorporating Flash into our sites very poorly. Fortunately that's a trait that we can easily fix, by educating ourselves about creating user-friendly Flash content.*

The argument that Flash reduces the user's control over the content is a valid issue that we need to address when creating user-friendly Flash content. As Nielsen states:

> "Flash designers decrease the granularity of user control and revert to presentation styles that resemble television rather than interactive media."

The argument certainly applies to intro-movies and animated content (cartoons like the wonderful "Radiskull & Devil Doll!" series) but it hardly applies to the majority of Flash content available. In many cases the types of interactions that Flash designers were unleashing on web users offered too *much* control. By saturating the user with options like background images, soundtracks, draggable windows and other bells and whistles, designers made their sites unnecessarily complex.

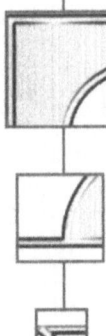

Flash content offers a number of interaction methods that differ from the more static experience of an HTML web page. Flash content can present information in a predetermined sequence, or it can present an interface for the user to interact with the content. Entire applications can be built in Flash offering the user more control over the content than HTML can offer.

Of course, Nielsen's comment about non-standard GUI controls is less of an issue with Flash MX. We now have access to a toolbox of common UI elements including scroll-bars, pull-down menus, radio buttons and more. We just need to use them!

Charge #2: "Flash does not work with established web fundamentals"

The way users normally interact with content on the Web will not always apply to Flash. In 2000, issues like use (or rather, uselessness) of the browser's 'back' button, link colors, font scaling and accessibility were all issues that Flash was just not ready to deal with.

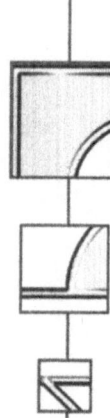

With the release of Flash MX, the majority of Nielsen's points have been addressed. Flash MX is now integrated with the browser's 'back' and 'forward' buttons through the use of Anchors.

Accessibility

The latest version of Flash also offers improved accessibility through integration of screen reader technology. Users interacting with Flash MX content can load special software that 'speaks' the content through the user's speakers. This new feature opens Flash MX content to a host of sight-impaired users, but only when designers have taken the time to develop their content with the new accessibility features in mind.

Flash MX has a font object, which designers can integrate with Flash content, allowing users to resize text to suit their needs. Users who have a hard time reading small type in a Flash interface can now be given tools to control the font size.

Modified links

The issue of links not showing the history of the user's interaction was quickly solved by a number of Flash designers. Flash resource sites like www.flashkit.com quickly addressed this issue with a number of creative solutions.

Flash MX also lets us modify the appearance of visited links. What's more, this doesn't just apply to text links, but to graphical buttons as well, something that HTML has yet to achieve.

Plug-ins

When it comes to the plug-in issue, I think Julie Meloni put it best in her Webmonkey article 'Tipping Jakob's Ladder' (http://hotwired.lycos.com/webmonkey/01/26/index1a.html?tw=commentary):

"With this plug-in installed in over 95 percent of the browsers in use today, exactly what else does a technology have to do to become a 'standard'?"

Internationalization and localization

Nielsen also states that internationalization and localization of Flash content is complicated. Well, internationalization and localization of HTML content is complicated too! There's nothing easy about taking content developed for one culture and translating it for another.

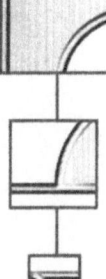

Fred Sharples of Orange Design has this to say about internationalization and localization of Flash content in the book *Flash Enabled*:

> "One of the ways that we saved money and time in the Star Wars Starfighter™ project was when we decided to localize into other languages. Imagine all the labor involved in localization using traditional console UI design. In the Flash user interface for Star Wars Starfighter™, we created versions for French, German, Italian and Spanish in just one week."

This particular project involved creating a user interface for a PlayStation game, but the same basic rules apply to creating alternate language versions of Flash content for the Web. The main cost and labor factor is still that of translation. Content created in Flash does not present any additional barriers to internationalization and localization.

Charge #3: "Flash content distracts from a site's core values"

In my opinion, Nielsen's last argument is his weakest. He states that developing Flash content takes resources away from improving the site's core values of:

- Frequently updating content (Flash content tends to be created once and then left alone)

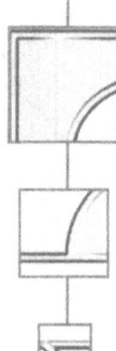

- Providing informative content that answers users' key questions at all depth levels (Flash content is typically superficial)

- Identifying better ways to support customers by task-analyzing their real problems (Flash is typically created by outside agents who don't understand the business)

All these issues are related to the **management** of a site. The value of the content and responsibility for keeping it updated is the publisher's, not the designer's. We all have experience of projects that are held up or cut back because the client isn't able to deliver the content the site needs.

Using Flash on a web site doesn't automatically mean that it will never be updated. All-Flash sites like www.FlashMagazine.com are updated with new information weekly. The ability to interact with server-side languages such as ColdFusion and PHP, along with Flash MX's super-fast XML parser means that it's becoming easier and easier to create Flash sites that incorporate dynamic content:

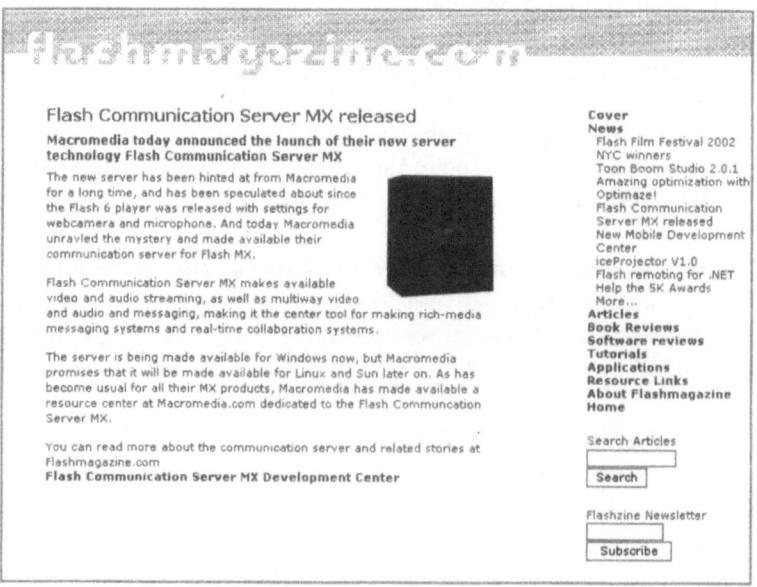

> *Flash designer Samuel Wan*
>
> (www.samuelwan.com/mainmenu.swf) *has even created a Flash interface for MovableType – a very popular software package used for publishing online diaries.*

Nielsen's last point is that Flash projects are typically developed by outside agents who don't understand the business. Again, this is a problem whose source lies with the management of a project. Blaming Flash for the shortcomings of a project manager is not a reason to cease the use of Flash on the Web. If nothing else, it seems quite ironic for a consultant to raise this issue!

Summary

So, is Flash no longer 99% bad? Well, the impact of Nielsen's column is still resonating in the Flash designer community. Our clients are still more than a little wary of using Flash, and in the long run, that's no bad thing. We need to become better at judging if Flash is the best solution for the project. We need to improve the way we build Flash content. We need to strive to create user-friendly Flash content.

Is Flash 99% bad for users? No. Flash offers users new ways of interacting with the Web. Thoughtful implementation of Flash can improve a complicated user experience. Flash can offer users a richer, more intuitive way of interacting with content.

That's what this book is for, 'a guide to improving the usability of your Flash content'. Now that we know Flash's history, and why Flash has a reputation for poor usability, we can avoid making the same mistakes of the past. We can start to learn about usability, and how to apply it to our Flash content.

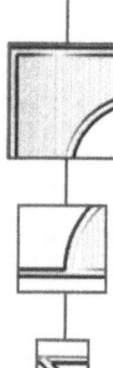

Flash development has been focusing on the cool, the edgy and the experimental for too long. We need to move away from creating web content that drives like a monster truck, and start building useful content that helps our users. Flash has extraordinary abilities to improve the user experience online, but we haven't been applying Flash that way.

Instead, Flash designers and our clients have been pushing the envelope so far away from how our users want to experience the Web that they're afraid to come back and try our Flash content again. Users have been bitten before, and as designers we need to start showing them that Flash can actually make their online experience easier.

The announcement that Macromedia and the Nielsen Norman Group (the usability consulting company founded by Jakob Nielsen and Donald Norman) are joining forces to develop "best practice guidelines for creating usable rich Internet applications with Macromedia Flash MX" is truly fantastic news. It highlights just how much the success of Flash depends on a community of designers who understand and appreciate the principles that underlie good usability. Sure, the days of long intro movies may be quickly fading, but that doesn't mean that Flash sites will cease to exist. There are still many compelling reasons to choose Flash for sites on the Web, and the more that we Flash designers can learn about usability, and how to apply it to our Flash content, the better.

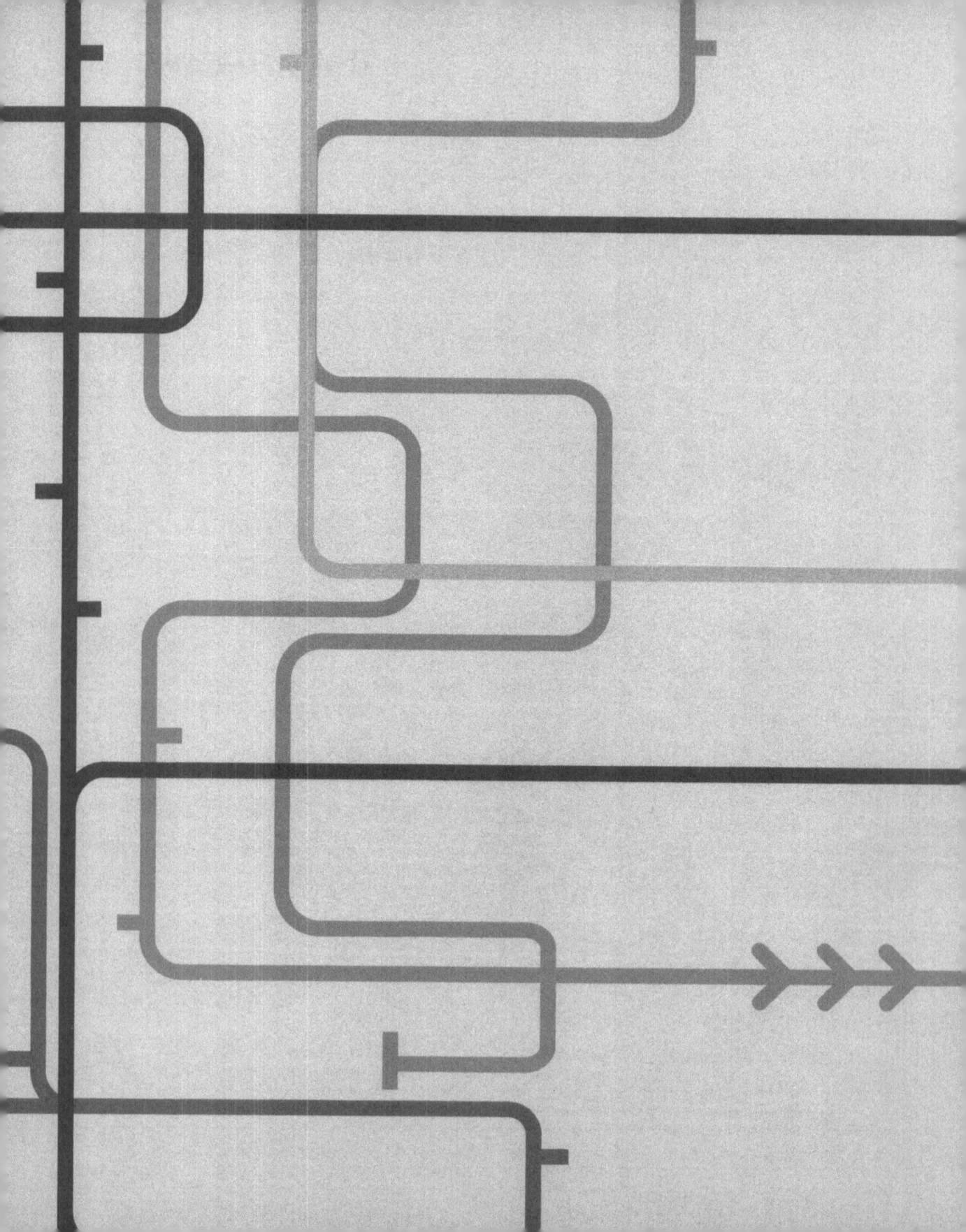

Whose contribution counts where?

One of the most important concepts for a Flash designer to grasp when applying usability to a project is that his goal must always be to focus on the end user of the completed site. Getting to the real meat of site usability starts with two simple guidelines:

- You, the designer, are *not the user*

- The client for whom you're building the site is *not the user*

Both client and designer are crucial to the creation of a great site, providing the informative content, the cool aesthetics, and so on. This is precisely why neither one is qualified to represent the target audience when it comes to judging the site's usability. They're simply too close to the project to be objective, even if the rest of your personal demographics match the average expected site visitor.

A good site should influence users' behaviors in a way that makes the client happy (for example, the visitors purchase goods, spend a lot of time reading articles, visit high-paying advertisers' sites, and so on). At the same time, it should give users a satisfying experience, giving them what they want, when they want it. It's the designer's job to find a workable balance between these two goals.

So how do you, as a designer, create a site that's usable, accessible and successful for users you've never met? Not to mention, a site that makes your client extremely pleased with your work? You must tackle this problem the moment your work begins.

> *You're not the user, the client isn't the user - but you both have invaluable experience and information that will make the user experience better.*

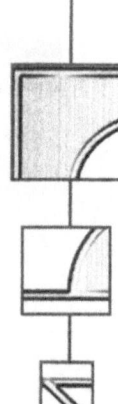

In this chapter, we'll take an overview of what we're striving for when trying to make a site usable. We'll attempt to figure out just who these 'users' we keep talking about are, what your role is in the mix, and what the client's function and responsibilities are. Finally, we'll talk about how it all merges into smart Flash development.

Taking it easy, making it easy

Where does the word 'usability' come from? I was hoping to find an alternative word to use in this book once in a while instead of having to write out 'usability' hundreds of times, so I turned to Microsoft Word's thesaurus. For some reason, instead of giving synonyms for 'usability', it suggested that I had misspelled the word 'urchin'. Not a very usable result.

The terms 'usability' and 'accessibility' are often used interchangeably, and while in some cases that works out fine for a site's audience, it's important to note the difference:

- Usability is generally used to describe the overall audience's capability for using a site as the client and developer intended.

- Accessibility *can* mean the same (the success level of an audience in reaching the content it desires), but it also addresses potential limitations or barriers to those with visual, hearing, cognitive, and mental impairments and how to bridge these limitations so that as many people as possible can access the content of any site they want to.

The usability of a site often seems to imply nothing more than how easy it is to use. But in reality, it goes beyond that. It's not just about how easy it is, but also about how satisfying the experience of the site is, and how effectively a user can accomplish their goals, whether they're passively watching Flash-based animation, or wanting to engage in an interactive discussion on research treatments for uterine abnormal cell growth with medical professionals and patients around the world.

So it looks like the word 'easy' is itself too simple an explanation. When we talk about making a site easy to use, we're certainly not implying that it should be as simplistic as a *See Jane Run* book or that you should only use one-syllable words. Rather, we're concerned with how straightforward it is for someone to come to the site and learn how to get around and get what they want.

One major factor in this concerns how the site *assists* users in achieving their goals. If the target audience is made up of kindergarten students, then one-syllable words and primary colors, large menu buttons with immediate visual and audio feedback, goofy music, and simple directives will all help. For researchers intent on finding up-to-the-minute papers and images showing surgery techniques or cell growth patterns, any gratuitous or extraneous Flash content just gets in the way. The look, feel, presentation, and development of these sites are totally different, but your goal remains the same – to help the user get what they want.

What's intuitive for you may not be intuitive to them

As a Flash designer, when you visit a web page that uses Flash, the chances are you recognize the Flash content right away. At the very least, you recognize that Flash is being used, even if you're not quite sure what the extent of that use is.

On a Flash-intensive site, designed with a unique, custom navigation system, you probably don't have too much trouble picking up new interaction methods and leaving your HTML preconceptions at the door. You have plenty of experience with simple Flash interactions, so they're not going to freak you out too much. If there's something truly strange going on, you're probably going to be curious about how the designer implemented it.

> *As a Flash designer, you recognize that the interactions within the Flash content may not act the same as interactions on an HTML page. You probably don't need to think about it, and can make the mental switch quite intuitively.*

I know I find a break from the norm is often welcome when finding a site or page with its navigation designed in an unusual, non-standard fashion. I've been a judge for Flash design and development competitions, and I can attest that the sites that do something completely unexpected, and even goofy or laughable can be a welcome sight.

This is why I have to remember that while I may embrace a weirdly designed infrastructure as a mentally stimulating oasis among thousands of entries, it's not what the average person may greet with enthusiasm. The weirdly designed infrastructure may win an award for 'innovative use of Flash' but not an award for navigational consistency and intuitive design.

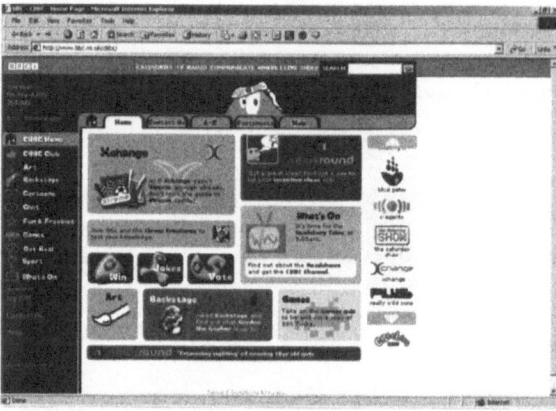

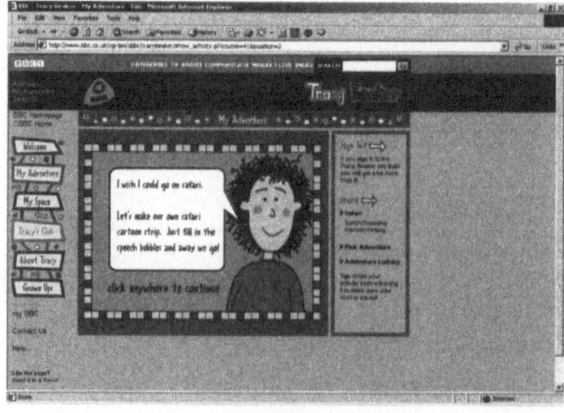

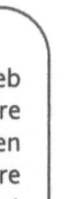

The BBC has done a great job of mixing familiar HTML-based web site layout with elements of Flash on their children's site. Where Flash is used to present content or as a navigational tool (and even while loading), suitable, concise guidance and instructions are provided. While Flash animation is used generously, it's not gratuitous, which works perfectly for this entertainment-oriented site. A visitor may never know that Flash has anything to do with the creation of this site, nor do they have to.(www.bbc.co.uk/cbbc)

The average web user may not recognize that Flash content is deployed on a web page, nor should they have to.

Someone coming to your site shouldn't be expected to have your intuition or curiosity about a new way to navigate. They might try to interact with

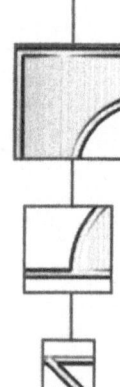

Flash content as if it were an HTML-based page. They may not know that it's Flash – they just know it's not doing what they expect it to.

What is an average user?

As of May 2002, Nielsen/NetRatings (www.nielsen-netratings.com) estimate there are some 450 million people in the world with access to the Internet, almost half of whom live in the US. On average they spend roughly 10 hours per month browsing, with about 45 seconds on each page, and a session time running just a touch over 32 minutes.

eMarketer (www.emarketer.com) gives an even higher estimate of global users for 2002: 529 million, and estimate that nearly 200 million more will go online by 2004.

According to Global Reach (http://glreach.com) a consultancy in San Francisco that specializes in driving web traffic from other countries to those in the US, 228 million people who access the web speak English, and 339 million speak 'non-English', some of whom overlap because they browse the Web in two or more languages.

Try this experiment. Go into a mega-bookstore, perhaps one at your local university that has a variety of titles, subjects, and books in various languages. Without any particular book or product in mind, plan to spend a half hour there. Pay attention to your actions; take notes (at least mental ones) of where you go and what you do. When you're done, come back and ask yourself the following questions:

- When you walked in, where did you go?

- Were you attracted to brightly colored book covers, sale signs, or the information booth?

- Did you find books that interest you, but disregarded books that match your interest, written in a language you can't read?

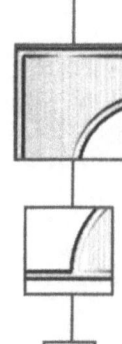

- What about newly published books versus ones in the cutout bin? Which did you look through for more up-to-date information?

- Do you head to the magazine rack rather than hardcover reference books?

- Did you pick out books and skim pages, or just look at covers?

- Did you buy something you didn't intend to buy, or find something you'd been looking for?

Ask a few of your very-willing experimental friends to try the same. Do you find that you're a 'typical' bookstore user having an 'average' experience, or did each of you take completely different paths? Do you think any of you fit the description of the store's target market – or did you all?

Let's apply this to our own medium. Just how do people experience the Web? How do they get to and utilize sites they find when they're browsing? There's no easy answer, given that there are so many millions of web users, and the number of people accessing the Web is growing every day. In order to best design your site to be ideally suited to as many people as possible within your target market, you've got to examine the three major elements that determine the web site experience for a user, as well as the potential problems relating to the experience. You'll probably notice that a lot of these elements overlap, and affect each other both positively and negatively, depending on the combination.

Here are the three major elements that determine the web site experience:

- The access method by which the user connects to the web

- The person using the web

- The site itself

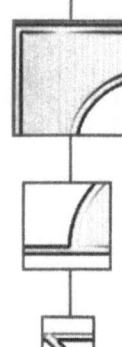

We'll take a look at all of these elements and what you and your client can do to work with them and around them.

The access method

The first element influencing a user's experience of the Web is the way in which they access it. The component of the access method that web designers have historically been most concerned with is the type of browser a person uses. While the differences among the most popular browsers have lessened (or at least become less obvious to the end-users) there can still be snags for some people out there.

This was a plus for Flash when it was introduced; suddenly (in theory) developers didn't have to worry about the browser compatibility piece of the puzzle. No matter what the browser, if it supports Flash, it can access the site.

Even with the positives inherent in a browser-independent site, there are still people out there who have absolutely no desire to download a 'new' version of a browser that may support Flash. Call it ignorance, call it stubbornness, if even a few of your site's visitors are like me, they don't like someone else telling them what to do. This is true even if (or perhaps especially because) it's 'for your own good' - which can easily be translated by some to mean, "Do this my way, or get lost!" While the percentage of people using top end graphical browsers is in the majority, it's also pretty well accepted that there will be die-hard text-browser users around for a long time.

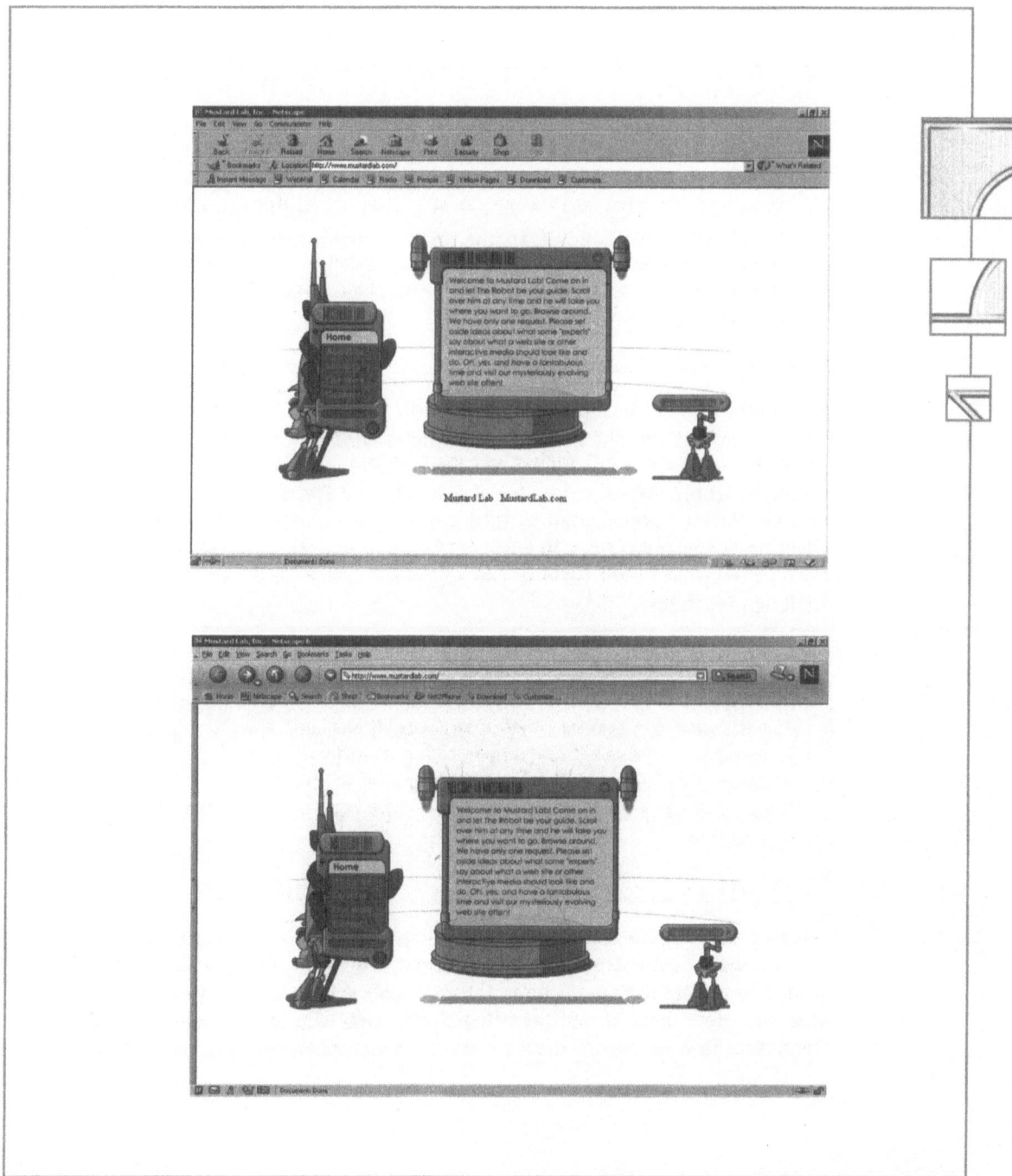

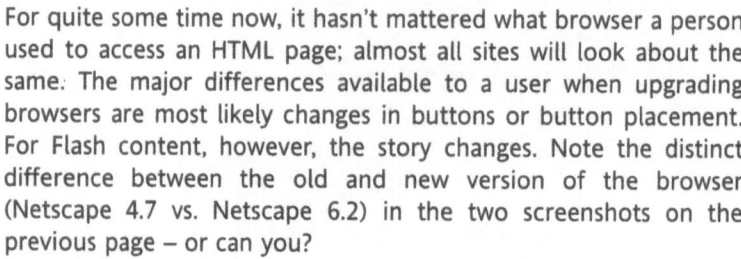

For quite some time now, it hasn't mattered what browser a person used to access an HTML page; almost all sites will look about the same. The major differences available to a user when upgrading browsers are most likely changes in buttons or button placement. For Flash content, however, the story changes. Note the distinct difference between the old and new version of the browser (Netscape 4.7 vs. Netscape 6.2) in the two screenshots on the previous page – or can you?

Even those who do download fancy new stuff may still prefer the familiar to tackling another learning curve. Even though I knew that I had to be aware of design differences for higher version browsers, for the longest time I preferred to browse with the almost-ancient Netscape 4.7 rather than the new versions. I'd grown used to how it works and displays sites. However, when designing sites I have to keep in mind that people with newer setups need to see what I want them to see within the newer version, and I've got to design for them.

Basically, knowing what browser(s) your audience uses can determine the overall navigability, usefulness, and aesthetic value of your site, as well as what kind of software you use to develop its content. They may struggle when asked to learn yet another interface on top of an interface on top of an interface.

The plus side of all this pain-in-the-neck keeping-up-with-the-browsers stuff is that *maybe*, just maybe, you can convince your audience that they won't have to worry about that any more if they're willing to hang out at your Flash sites. You don't have to tell them that this benefits you more than it does them, and how you won't have to worry about what your code is doing

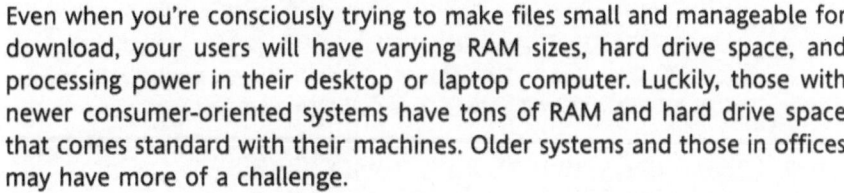

within the screen of each of their products, not to mention, each version of their products. Your competition is not only different sites, but different browsers with different snappy features that users don't want to give up. These days, browsers are full-service incorporating calendars, custom search menus, integration with other applications (and practically boil a pot of tea all by themselves).

User hardware and software limitations

Another potentially major difference between designers and a site audience is the hardware that gets them to a site. Those in the design community generally have better equipment for viewing Flash: faster computers, the latest plug-ins, larger monitors. Users interacting with Flash content may not have all the bells and whistles that designers have.

Even when you're consciously trying to make files small and manageable for download, your users will have varying RAM sizes, hard drive space, and processing power in their desktop or laptop computer. Luckily, those with newer consumer-oriented systems have tons of RAM and hard drive space that comes standard with their machines. Older systems and those in offices may have more of a challenge.

People with older equipment will probably have some serious limitations when trying to view a Flash-laden site. Even in the old days, Netscape recommended at least 8 megabytes of RAM for the old fashioned Windows 3.1, 95, and NT version of Navigator 3.0; 9 megabytes of RAM for the Macintosh version, and (gulp) 32 megabytes for the UNIX version.

I was *never* able to run Netscape Navigator 3.0 with even the 'recommended' amount of RAM with much success. While the processor speeds seem a little more reasonable (386sx for the Windows platforms, 68020 for Mac), anyone who's ever tried to run this or many other new applications on these old processors knows that they're in for some long waiting times, if they can get it to run at all.

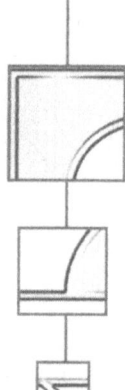

Educational facilities still might not be able to afford to replace all those text-based access terminals, or perhaps even the Mac SEs they bought 15 years ago. RAM, even at its lowest price, may be beyond budget for an office that has to upgrade multiple machines.

Plug-ins can demand a lot from an older system. Many now come bundled with browser software, so web users don't have to spend a bazillion years downloading plug-ins from creators' sites. But still, those with older computers that must use older browsers will still be bugged with prompts to 'DOWNLOAD NOW', and I've seen sites that literally go so far as to tell the user to come back when they're smart enough to have a better browser (they have obvious customer-relation problems).

The Flash Player 6 is a 400K download for PCs, and a whole megabyte for Macs – not much for a DSL connection, but old 28.8K dial-up connections still take a while, enough to be annoying for some people. You can't predict whether someone will be excited about a new plug-in requirement, or rolling their eyes at your request for them to upgrade.

Monitor size and bit depth (of monitors) play an obvious part in how a site is seen and used. Default browser-window sizes differ in both width and height, depending on the size of the screen. Even a difference of just one inch can mean a significant part of your page's content, navigational cues or design is cut off. Resizing a window may seem relatively painless, but having to do it more than once is simply a pain and a lot to ask of users to do repeatedly.

Also, most new 17-inch monitors have a default screen resolution of 800x600, when 1024x768 would be more suitable for that size screen. Many users may not be aware of this – maybe it's up to us to inform them on the home pages of our Flash sites.

Even if everyone in your audience uses the latest version of Netscape and has brand new hotshot machines, the versions on a Windows machine make some web pages look different than the versions for Macintosh. Flash helps eliminate the problems with different onscreen default font sizes for various platforms, but monitors on the two platforms show colors differently (PCs tend to show colors darker than Macs).

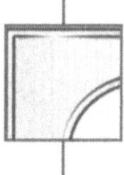

The computer platform-of-choice affects the monitor's display capability since PC video cards and Mac video cards display at different gamma levels; Mac monitors are 'brighter' than PC monitors at average settings. In other words, an image or color combination may look great on a Mac monitor, but dark, muddy, and unreadable on a PC. The color depth difference between what looks great on your screen and your user's could be significant.

Continuing with the list of potential hardware problems, you have to consider whether every user's computer will have the necessary processor speed to animate a full-screen Flash window or even a smaller piece of animated screen real estate. And if sound is integral to communicating the client's message, but the user doesn't have speakers to hear any audio in the Flash file, or chooses to keep sound turned off unless they're playing their favorite taxi-driving simulator, then the web site will be useless.

Other than the differences between the user's computer system and ours, there are other areas where we experience Flash content differently than the user. We usually have high-speed access to the Internet while the majority of Internet users don't. A key determination of a person's ability to access content is their connection speed - whether by DSL, cable modem, dial-up modem, ISDN, T1, or even faster than that.

> *According to recent bandwidth studies, 87% of users are still connecting to the Internet at speeds below 56K. A 200Kb Flash file may seem petite and graceful to us, but at 56K, especially if you're asking for more than one download per site, it can add up pretty quickly.*

Depending on the location from which a person is connecting, they may have intermittent access time at best (whether they're in an area with a bad phone service, subscribe to a too-busy ISP, or are accessing from a public facility, such as a college library). While most US ISPs now feature local calls to access their services, there are still those that may have their access time limited by long distance phone calls to their service provider. They could also be using someone else's system: the local library, a friend's computer, or one at school, and they have no control over what modem is used or how long they can stay online, and certainly aren't welcome to download plug-ins or large files.

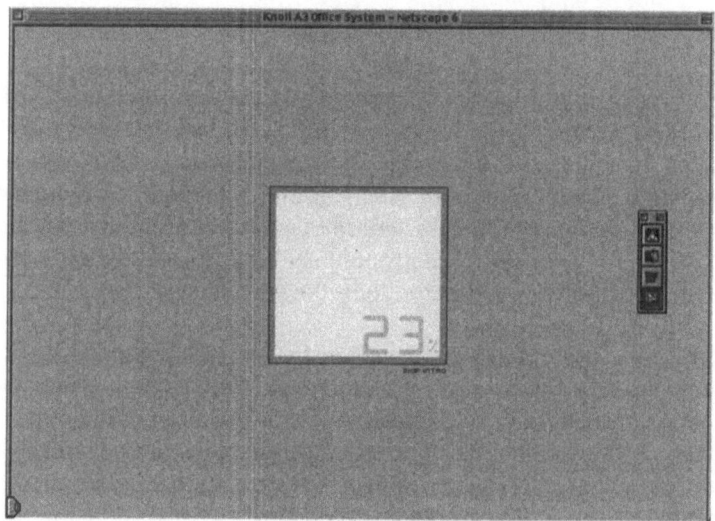

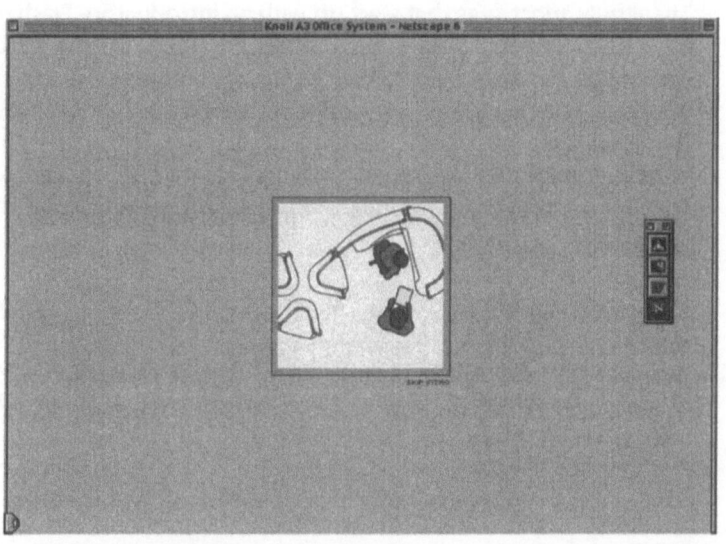

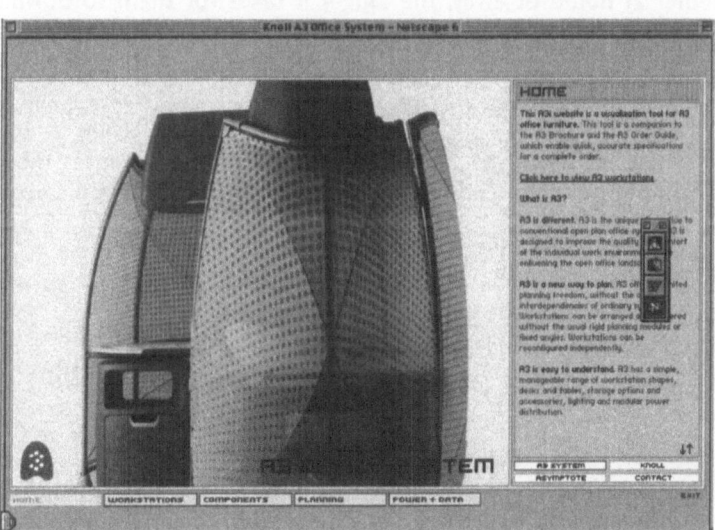

Thankfully, most sites that start off with an introductory Flash movie have also included a 'skip intro' button. I might like to watch an intro once, but after I get to the site for the first time, I'll most likely skip it on future visits. www.knoll.com sports a great example of a non-gratuitous intro movie. It shows the product featured in the site in action, and acts like an intro should: as an introduction to the product for someone who might not have any idea of what the A3 system is.

Note that the internal design is straightforward, and the content labels are clear, imperative when a Flash site takes over the browser and removes the familiar navigational buttons from the top of the screen. The designer also used HTML-like underlined text to communicate a link in the right-hand text column.

Whether at home or away, the longer it takes for them to download that 200Kb Flash animation file to their system, the less happy they will be with their visit to the site. Especially if the animation is something they could really do without in the first place. Consider the business traveler dialing in from a hotel room, paying extra phone service rates, trying to get to your client's site for important data for a make-or-break business meeting in a half hour. If they're forced to wait through a large intro Flash splash area, or wait for gratuitous files to download, do you think they'll be wanting to continue business with your client?

As designers and developers, these hardware and software limitations are rarely our own, so in just the material sense, depending on the audience for our client's site, we may be experiencing the Flash content significantly differently than the user.

The people factor

We all know that every single person is different – every person has different abilities and levels of knowledge. Some people like frames or hate them, some can tear their computer apart with one hand and put it back together blindfolded, while others are petrified that touching the DELETE key will wipe out their hard drive. In the web world, it seems that you can't please any of the people any of the time.

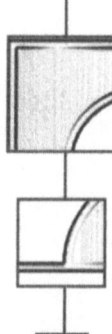

Given that we have over 500 million people online to choose from, you can see why it might be difficult to nail them down into specific demographics. This is one place where your client's experience with their target market comes in most handy, because if they don't know who the people are that they're trying to reach, then it will be that much more difficult for you to come up with Flash they'll understand and use.

For example, it's important to think about your client's audience's familiarity and comfort-level with technology if your site demands a lot from visitors, such as downloading and installing plug-ins or changing monitor bit depth. If a user doesn't know what 'point-and-click' means (yes, there are still a few of them out there), or that they have to click in a form box in order to type into it, then they'll get frustrated very easily. This doesn't mean that every site has to give people basic computing lessons, it just means that if your client is gearing their site to computer newbies, the site should be prepared to guide them through any potential rough spots - or the design should avoid potential rough spots altogether.

The language gap

Another consideration: since the Web is available in nearly every location in the world that phone lines reach, a client selling or reaching to a global market may have the need to develop multiple interfaces or even multiple sites in its target audience's native language. If you don't know Brazilian Portuguese, and Brazil is your client's main non-English-based target area, then you'll have to work (and trust) your client's ability to provide you with text that makes sense.

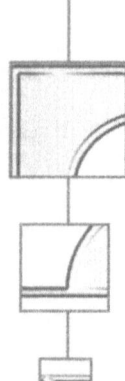

For example, if you're designing a site for a university, and all of the potential students must know a certain amount of English in order to attend your school, then you probably don't have to make translating your information into every student's native language a priority. But it is a consideration if the client intends to market to a worldwide audience, even if it's accepted that English is a pretty widely understood language. The university might consider translating introductory information explaining language requirements, topics of study, and online applications to other languages for potential students in other countries, for example. It's your job to present these alternatives to your client.

Speaking of different languages, in translating site content, proper terminology and context has to be assured. In other words, don't count on Babelfish (http://babelfish.altavista.com) to give you all the correct words for your menu items and image description translations. It's a wonderful tool, but it doesn't provide for local slang or vernacular that may validate a site and create trust amongst the site and its users.

> *Sprechen Sie Web? Você usa oFlash?* eMarketer *shows research that claims that 68.4% of all web content is published in English, with Japanese coming second at 5.9%, German at 5.8%, and all others under 4% apiece. Considering that well over half of the web population of users speaks something other than English, it seems the market at large may need to reevaluate overall usability.*

"How much?!"

The next topic we'll discuss sort of goes back to hardware, but it's really about the financial abilities of an audience, a factor that varies immensely throughout the world: Internet access doesn't come cheap in some areas of the world (including the US, UK, and other countries leading in access numbers), so you and the client have to consider the money your users have to spend.

56K modems can now be had for under $20, but it's possible some of your users spent a couple of hundred bucks on a 28.8K modem a year-and-a-half ago. If they don't spend much time online, spending more money on a modem simply doesn't make sense. They aren't as immersed in the net as those of us who thrive on it, and they're putting it off until they can justify the cost or someone buys them a new computer for their birthday.

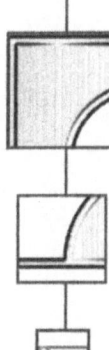

While most ISPs seem to charge around $20 a month for unlimited access, there are still those who have to dial-in long-distance to their ISP, so the *minimum* they're paying is about seven cents a minute (or $4.20 an hour) for online access. This may not sound like much, but it adds up very quickly. Since most people use the Web 10 to 20 hours a week, this can add up to a $300+ phone bill before you know it.

Other services charge less per month, but offer limited access, then throw on hefty additional charges if the user goes over the allotted time (as well as forcing them to use an altered browser sporting advertisements and limited menu choices).

Bear in mind also that outside North America, especially in Europe, the majority of phone companies charge per minute for dial-up access to ISPs. Flat rate Internet access is by no means common in Europe (except in the UK). This is bound to impact on the usage patterns of many surfers who are forced to pay per minute for their connections. If forced to stay within limits due to finances, a user will probably want to be much more 'to-the-point' in their wanderings online.

The amount of browsing time users have available may be influenced by a number of factors such as where the Web is accessed (from work, school, or from home, for example), how many other activities take priority over web browsing (family quality time, TV, studying, exercise, commuting, eating,

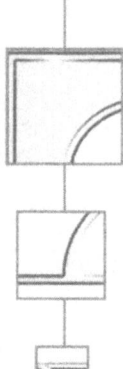

sleeping, taking the dog for a walk), and how long a person can physically sit at a computer. If someone only has web access from work, they may have the pressure of a boss looking over their shoulder, who thinks browsing is a colossal waste of time. At home, they may have a daughter who needs a bedtime story read to them. All of these factors make time on the Web of the essence. If a user wants something, they have limited time to get at it.

> *If the information, product, or service the user's trying to access is buried deep within a site, in an area that's not too intuitive to navigate, then they'll probably move on to another site that offers the same (or a similar) thing.*

Some people like to casually browse around until they find something interesting that catches their eye; others log on for a specific fact and want to find it right away. Usually the eye candy is only good for one or two visits. It's the information that keeps people, and if they can't find it, they aren't going to stay – unless they're specifically there for eye candy.

User disabilities

I mentioned the difference between usability and accessibility near the beginning of the chapter, and here's one place they're parallel. The impetus for the 'Americans with Disabilities' Act (Section 508) is a huge segment of the web audience that's often overlooked: namely people with disabilities.

This includes people with visual, hearing, cognitive or physical impairments as defined by the ADA (see focus point on next page). The Web and the Internet as a whole represents a world of information that's otherwise difficult to access. But as one person who wrote to me once said, "My friend who is blind says that trying to access information on some sites is like being blind all over again".

Legally, as defined by the Americans with Disabilities Act (ADA), examples of physical or mental impairments include, but are not limited to, such contagious and non-contagious diseases and conditions as orthopedic, visual, speech, and hearing impairments; cerebral palsy, epilepsy, muscular dystrophy, multiple sclerosis, cancer, heart disease, diabetes, mental retardation, emotional illness, specific learning disabilities, HIV disease (whether symptomatic or asymptomatic), tuberculosis, drug addiction, and alcoholism.

A person who is blind can't navigate a site that is dependent on graphics for navigational cues (unless there's proper use of ALT tags and other descriptions); a person with dyslexia may not be able to read long pages of text comfortably and perhaps with little or no comprehension; they may find graphical navigation cues much more preferable and usable than text cues.

The definition of 'disability' is far-ranging indeed, but with over 50 million people in the US alone (that's one in five, if you're curious) with a legally defined disability, it should be enough to prompt most designers to consider alternate access to their site's information.

So many people, so little control

After discussion of all the previous elements, what it comes down to is that there's only one area of the web experience you can control: your Flash creation and how it's deployed on a site. As a designer, whether you simply have a personal web page, or you're a subcontracted freelancer, or on-staff at a major business, you're ultimately responsible for how your work looks, functions, navigates, and communicates to the site's audience. While we take into account all the mish-mash of factors that affect the experience a user might have at a site, the design and successful usability of your Flash material

– and what you can do to enhance, fix, or change it – is what this whole book is about.

So, to start, what kinds of things can you control to make the most users get the best use of your site?

Your decision about **how much text and how many graphics** to put on one page, for example, determines download time no matter what the speed of access. The amount of content is important when determining how to split it up into digestible portions of information.

How the content is presented in your design is crucial to a user's experience. If the design overwhelms the content, it comes across as gratuitous, and doesn't serve the user efficiently. If design elements such as large images, distracting loud music, scrolling messages or flashing text disrupt navigation or don't serve to enhance an experience, then you're not serving your audience wisely.

The number of graphics on a page and the type of graphics you choose greatly determine the interpretation of the site's information. **Graphic descriptions**, whether via ALT tags or other image description methods or text labels on menu buttons, can play a huge part in the understanding and navigability of your site to those who are incapable of loading images, whether it's because of browser choice (for example, a text browser like Lynx) or because they can't use them (such as a person who is blind).

Generally, text descriptions don't interfere with the design of a page, and their possible assistance to those people unable or unwilling to view graphics can make a difference as to whether they get to your site's information or not. Thankfully, Flash MX's accessibility features allow us to provide brief descriptive text for Flash movies, much like an ALT tag for a GIF or JPEG, and a longer description if necessary in the Description field within the new MX Accessibility panel.

Navigational cues and how people respond to them have been the subject of many a study. While every person's perception of a site or web page can be different, there are certain logical placements of navigational cues, as well as recognizable icons (such as stop signs, and disk icons that represent a downloadable file), or logical ways of handling unique graphical iconic intimations (for example, always representing your home page with a picture of a polka-dot dog) that make for an intuitively navigational site.

If you put 'back' and 'next' arrows at the bottom on one page then keep them on the bottom of all others. Most people can quickly acclimatize to a certain cueing procedure, but they'll get flustered if you change icons, link placements or include other inconsistencies. Consistency is key. If you have text links along the top of 12 screens, but screen 13 has it on the bottom, you've just introduced an element of possible confusion and frustration.

We can't be our own beta testers

A big difference between our interaction with the Flash content we develop and the interactions of the future users of the content is that we already know how it was built. Any time that we're testing an interaction within the Flash content we're designing, we approach it from a different perspective by default. We know the expected action that will result from each interaction because we designed it. We click a button and we know what it will do. Our thought process when interacting with our own Flash content may be dramatically different from that of a user who's never been exposed to it.

The user doesn't have the luxury of knowing how the application works when they first interact with it. I may know that clicking a certain button will take me to the contact form, while the user may be thinking, "I hope this button will take me to the company's address," or, "I'm not pressing *that*!" - or even worse, may not even be aware that an element you've designed is a button at all.

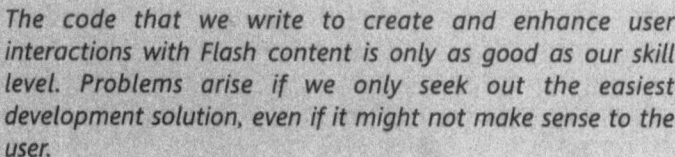

> *The code that we write to create and enhance user interactions with Flash content is only as good as our skill level. Problems arise if we only seek out the easiest development solution, even if it might not make sense to the user.*

A Flash designer who's not skilled with ActionScript may not have the abilities to implement an interface element that works the same as an equivalent element on an HTML page. This may be necessary if the client has only had HTML-based sites before, and its users are used to a certain kind of interface.

> *Before Flash MX arrived with its UI components, every developer had to create their own scroll bar, their own drop-down menu and their own radio buttons, so the potential for non-standard, unfamiliar, and frustrating interactions was immense.*

The scroll bar on one Flash site may behave completely differently from the scroll bar on another Flash site, or might even be different from similar-looking navigational tools within the same site.

From the user's perspective, the non-standard interactions that appear across Flash sites can lead to confusion and frustration, even if within our own design team the new 'improved' navigational tools seemed very cool and fun to use.

Since we're more than halfway through the chapter now, it's time to remind you again:

- You, the designer, are not the user

- The client for whom you're building the site is not the user either

Education is a two-way street

The client is the expert in his own field. As we work with our clients, we've got to be open-minded and learn as much as we can about their business. This includes researching their business and competitors; what they do, what they offer, who their customers are. Knowledge of the client's business helps us to create a design that speaks to their users.

Just as we're educating ourselves about aspects of our client's business, we should also be educating our client about aspects of ours. We need to share the importance of good usability with our clients and let them know the effects of poor usability. It's essential to educate them about the benefits of a good user experience.

Our 'audience' per se is the field of clients we pursue. Like the process of learning about a web site audience, the most crucial way to learn and be a smarter designer is to listen to them. This means surveying your proposed audience before launch, and allowing feedback from the client at regular intervals during the entire design process.

Your client as student

Just as you probably wouldn't understand the first thing about oil reservoir imaging and salt domes, oil and gas engineers aren't likely to understand how to use `loadMovie()` in ActionScript. But if they're the audience for whom we've been hired to design a site, we'll be required to at least learn something of what an oil and gas engineer expects, and how they're likely to want to interact with the site.

A client's perspective is different from the user's perspective in more ways than one. Besides being close to the project and having you at their side to help them figure out how it should be structured and used, they have their own priorities for a project. They have a message to deliver, or a service to offer. These interests may conflict with the user's needs.

If the client's not familiar with web usability concepts or even with the Web itself, they may be wide-eyed at the potential for adding music, motion, and other flashy Flash elements, just as we were when we first started playing with tags and software that could make the Web move and shake.

You may find that it becomes your role to constantly remind your client that while it's true that disco beats and light shows are all the rage, it's probably not in their best interest to have these elements featured on every page of their site unless they're a dance club or DJ talent agency.

If they're a hard sell, pick out some of their competitors' sites – ideally the successful ones – and show them why you think these competitors are successful at utilizing the web medium. Point out the necessity of finding out as much as possible about the target audience rather than relying on guesswork.

You should have a list of questions ready for your client before you even think of signing a contract. Consider how the answers you get will affect how you design Flash content. For example, how technologically advanced is the audience? Will it be necessary to create a large 'Help' area, or even to create tips on how to use the 'back' and 'next' buttons to move around? Is it necessary to teach them how to download, or simply to point them in the direction of a main site FAQ?

Ultimately, it's the client who's responsible for the content of the site. However, as a good designer and developer, you must take responsibility for the overall site experience, and neither you nor the client can judge that objectively – only the users can tell you if you've got it right.

We'll talk more about usability testing later on in the book. For now, let's see what we can learn from the client to make end-user testing less painful in the long run.

The client as teacher

Where the client can shine is in their intimate knowledge of their audience, *if* they have intimate knowledge of their target audience. There are some that will insist that they know best about their project, and what the best colors are, best typefaces, and best directives. Some clients may only be interested in saving money, skimping on usability testing, and having us just do what they say since they're paying us to do work for them.
If given free rein, their sites may be design disasters, alienating visitors and marking our portfolio for failure. Or they might be spot on – we have to be open-minded enough to consider that they might be right, or make the decision not to work for this type of client in the first place.

Other clients may be technology-wary, and simply hand you a blank check and tell you to go for it. At first this second client sounds like every developer's dream, but in either scenario, it's imperative that you get as much input from the client (annoying or passive) as you possibly can. Make them your teacher. While they won't be the best site testers, if they've been in their industry for a while, they're one of the best resources you have.

Even if they've never been on the Web, chances are high that clients are familiar with who their competitors are. They know the trade magazines that list competitors, and probably list competitor web addresses, as well. They'll know whether or not their customers are companies that stay on the edge of technology, or whether customers are non-profit organizations that depend on the generosity of others to get new equipment to access highfalutin, high-end sites.

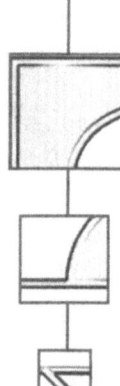

The client's business is the content, they probably know how their customers currently prefer to receive information (postcards, catalog mailings, phone calls, or other media). They hopefully have some demographic information and they know what all the insider industry terminology means and can translate that information for you.

You take what information you can from a client and organize it into digital content for users, utilizing structural and cognitive design developed through applied Information Architecture practices, which we'll look at in chapter 6.

An associate of mine likes to use the analogy of a toy store in Houston, Texas that had been run for decades by a couple of elderly ladies. The toy store had been around forever, and some of the toys seemed to have been in the store even longer than the store existed. There was no apparent organization in the store; toys were just placed in any open space the ladies could find. If customers wanted to find something in the store they had two options: browse for hours and hope that they would find what they had in mind, or ask one of the owners and she would know exactly where the toy was. The user experience in the store was made up of long-forgotten toys and dust.

For the new user of the toy store, interactions with the store were virtually hopeless unless they relied on one of the owners to find what they wanted. Luckily, the owners could find everything in their store; they organized it, and they knew how it worked.

Asking a client for usability feedback on their own content is like asking those two ladies if they have yo-yos in their own store. The content is the client's business; they will know it better than their own customers will. This doesn't discount the client's experience with your site; the client, of all people, should have no trouble interacting with the Flash content you create. If they don't know terminology, for example, or why you broke segments of content down a certain way, then that's a red flag that users will have an even more difficult time. Clients can't interact with the Flash content from the same perspective as the user, but they can offer a unique perspective that others can't.

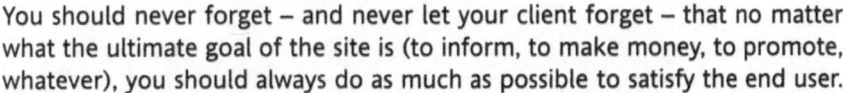

Clients don't often ask designers how to run their business. Clients want designers to build user-friendly Flash content and to design smart interface solutions, not suggest locations for warehouses or price points for new products. We should be asking clients what sort of interactions they want with their customers and tie that into the planning.

Summary

It's never too early to start talking about usability, and how important it is to the success of a project. It's prudent to bring up the subject of usability during the initial meeting with the client, especially if focus group testing will be a part of the budget proposal.

You should never forget – and never let your client forget – that no matter what the ultimate goal of the site is (to inform, to make money, to promote, whatever), you should always do as much as possible to satisfy the end user.

By bringing up usability early in the game, you can help to manage client expectations and become a representative for the typical site user. It may appear that you're working for your client, or your client's client, but ultimately, you're working on behalf of the user. Your job on the project is to make sure that the Flash content is as inviting, efficient, intuitive and memorable as possible – for the user.

If you can, get the entire team involved in making the Flash content easier to use. A great way to start off a project is with a brainstorming session on user dichotomies – we'll look at this in more detail shortly. The client can assist in finding suitable people for user testing (more on this in Chapter 12). Programmers can explore interactions that are more intuitive. Everyone on the team can contribute to the usability effort, because they're all a part of it.

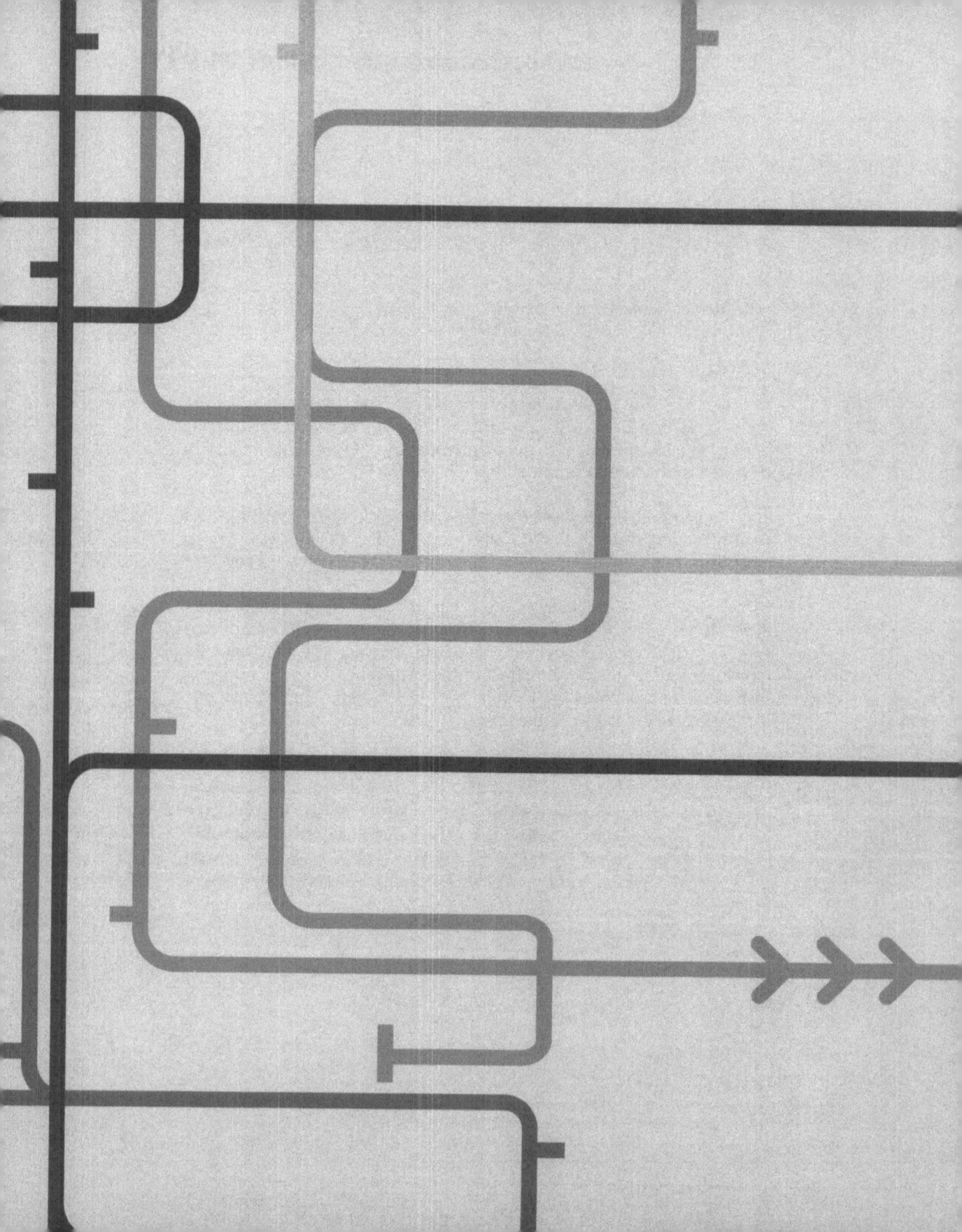

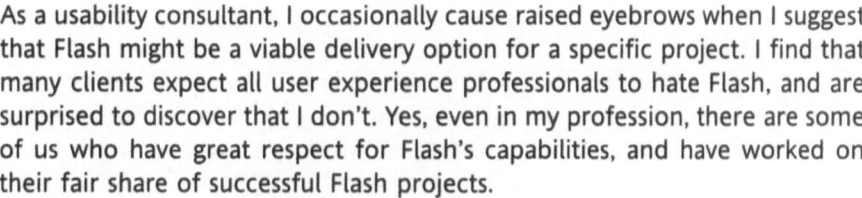

Choosing Flash

As a usability consultant, I occasionally cause raised eyebrows when I suggest that Flash might be a viable delivery option for a specific project. I find that many clients expect all user experience professionals to hate Flash, and are surprised to discover that I don't. Yes, even in my profession, there are some of us who have great respect for Flash's capabilities, and have worked on their fair share of successful Flash projects.

All the same, I frequently have to back my position up by explaining the benefits of Flash to clients. We've already seen how Flash has got itself quite a reputation for poor usability – so we need to be clear about **how** and **when** it should be used to improve the usability of a web site.

The fact is that not every web-based project can afford to be constrained by the limited capabilities of HTML. If you do need to go the extra mile, the decision to use Flash can be a very smart move. So let's take a more detailed look at those HTML limitations, and pin down what features of Flash can help to give users a better experience.

HTML vs. Flash – comparing technologies

There's far more to delivering usable web content than simply deciding which technology you prefer to use. Designers who always rely on one format to assist them in creating usable web sites may not actually be using the best one for the task at hand. That holds true for both Flash designers and web designers who work only with HTML. In any situation a good designer should evaluate the user's needs for the particular project and deliver the content in the best format to meet those needs.

In many ways, it's pretty easy to satisfy a user – just get them what they want as quickly and easily as possible. There's no reason why Flash content shouldn't offer users both speed and ease-of-use. In many cases, an effectively designed Flash site can be *more* usable than its HTML-only equivalent.

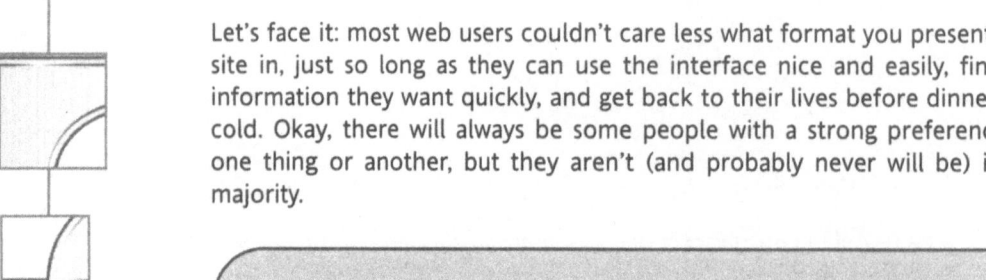

Let's face it: most web users couldn't care less what format you present your site in, just so long as they can use the interface nice and easily, find the information they want quickly, and get back to their lives before dinner gets cold. Okay, there will always be some people with a strong preference for one thing or another, but they aren't (and probably never will be) in the majority.

> *Even if we were to accept the notion that Flash was 99% bad, it doesn't follow that HTML is 99% good. Each format has its own strengths and weaknesses. For every Flash site that delivers a horrible user experience, you'll find plenty of HTML sites that are just as bad.*
>
> *Arguing that HTML, XHTML, or other W3C approved standards offer better usability just because they are open standards also misses the point. Usability is not a feature of one file format or another; it's the result of a user-centric design process. All the same, many users will have wasted far more time on badly designed Flash sites than they will have on HTML ones, so this impression may take some time to be eradicated completely.*

Each format for content delivery has its own strengths and weaknesses. Television, for example, offers an excellent user experience for watching synchronized audio and video content. You just can't beat it for that. We even accessorize our televisions with VCR and DVD players, allowing us to further enhance the experience. Even with all television's strengths, it's certainly not the best format for interactive content. Watching the television is a passive activity (hence the term couch potato). Even 'WebTV' and other 'Internet-on-TV' devices use the actual TV as little more than a monitor for a scaled-down computer.

HTML in perspective

When all's said and done, HTML really is an excellent format with which to deliver text and static images on the Web – as such, it serves the needs of most web-based development. What's more, it's easy to understand, it's easy to learn, and it's even easy to code: just about anyone can create a simple HTML web page in just a few minutes. HTML pages integrate well with the Internet: they're searchable, and they let users copy and paste text with the minimum of fuss.

On the other hand, HTML wasn't designed to create interfaces. It's really nothing more than a very simple, easy-to-understand markup language that offers designers a fast way to format their information for delivery over the Web. Most of the basic decisions about presentation are left to the particular browser application that's being used to view the page – if you've ever used a text-only browser such as Lynx, you'll really appreciate what a drastic difference that can make!

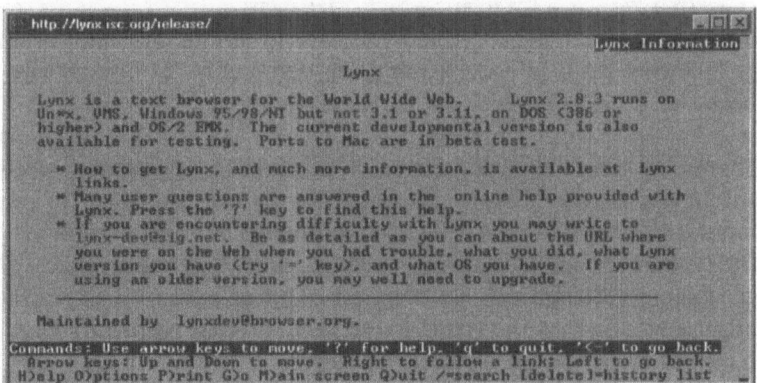

In recent years though, we've seen the growing popularity of the Web (along with the dominance of a very small number of graphics-based browsers) push HTML into taking on a number of tasks that it was never really intended to handle. Many designers are now expert at using HTML to format and

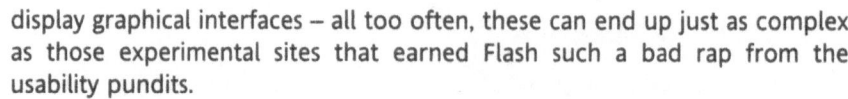

display graphical interfaces – all too often, these can end up just as complex as those experimental sites that earned Flash such a bad rap from the usability pundits.

> *One example of this is the use of <TABLE>, an HTML element that was designed to help format data into tables. Nowadays, you're far more likely to come across it being used as a kind of web-based equivalent of PostScript, enabling designers to arrange their content in ever-increasingly complex fashions.*

Responding to the user

HTML-based web pages also have a limited capacity for providing user feedback. With strict HTML, the only feedback users get is a change in the color of a link once it's been visited. That's certainly not the most responsive method for communication, and you have to turn to JavaScript or Cascading Style Sheets (CSS) in order to add the slightest bit of interactivity to your pages.

These have their own problems when it comes to deployment, since they're still relying on the built-in capabilities of the user's browser to render the interface. Some potential users may have older browsers that don't support CSS; others, overloaded with pop-up ads, may have their JavaScript capabilities switched off, disabling every bit of advanced interactivity they might encounter on the HTML-based Web. All that hard work, and a whole bunch of folks won't even know it's there!

Waiting for the server

The basic interaction model for an HTML page is essentially this:

Click —> Wait —> Load

The amount of time the HTML site **blinks** for – that is, the length of the wait between clicking on a link and seeing the corresponding page displayed – depends on several factors. Since the content has to be accessed from some remote server (which could quite literally be anywhere in the world), the delay will largely depend on the speed of the server, the amount of work it has to do, and the speed of the network connection between it and the user's machine. Someone with a high-speed connection may only need to wait for a split second, while someone else with a slow connection waits for what seems like eternity.

> *If you're trying to offer your users a really good experience, forcing them to stare at a blank browser window really isn't to be recommended. In the context of a traditional store, it would be tantamount to switching off all the lights every time your customer asked for something!*

On its own, HTML can't do much more than just provide static content to the user. If your project involves any kind of data processing (for example, a shopping cart or a database), you'll need yet another addition to handle the logic. Chances are, you'll need some sort of server-side processing functionality like CGI or PHP.

Once you start relying on the web server to process data, it's much harder to guarantee the user a seamless browsing experience. To move from one page to another, the browser has to refresh the page. If the server has to work hard, it may hold things up – more than a few fractions of a second, and the user will notice a distinct lag, if not the dreaded blank screen itself.

Even the über-usable www.amazon.com can't avoid showing users a blank screen after they've clicked on a link. Of course, you can always find the occasional exception, such as the International Herald Tribune site (www.iht.com), which uses DHTML to provide users with an impressively seamless experience while browsing through its articles.

Flash in perspective

Flash was designed with user interaction in mind, so it really excels as a medium for delivering web content that requires more complex interactivity than HTML can manage.

Nothing's left to chance when you use Flash: either it works or it doesn't. As long as users have the appropriate plug-in – and over 95% of them do – content's displayed just as it was intended to be, regardless of what web browser they're using. Simple interactivity features such as button rollovers have been a staple of Flash content since its conception – and with no need for any confusing scripts! Logic and data handling are all bundled into the movie itself, so there's no need for time-consuming round-trips to the web server every time you want to change what's being shown.

Of course, Flash content has its share of disadvantages – one big problem is that it's not text-based, so it's not possible to search for Flash content in the same way as you can with HTML. In situations where Flash cannot be best used to display certain content, it's always worth considering how it might be mixed with HTML to get the best out of both technologies. Many sites offer good examples of this approach, not least of which is Macromedia's own (www.macromedia.com).

More responsive systems

A Flash-based web page doesn't need to refresh itself every time the user interacts with it. If they click a button, the response can be immediate:

Click —> Respond

Flash allows designers to build a user experience without 'blinks'. Queries to a server can be sent and received without reloading. Screens can be updated to reflect dynamically fed information as the Flash content receives it. Even if the initial download takes a while, a Flash movie can keep users informed as to the status of the download by means of progress bars or preloaders. That's not to say they'll always be happy to sit through long, slow downloads, but it can help to ease the pain.

This responsiveness pays off. Even though many all-Flash sites are guilty of large downloads, the user's experience with the finished file is a more seamless experience. Flash doesn't constantly remind the 80% of web users without broadband connectivity how slow their connections are as they go along, instead it reminds them up front, just once.

These days Flash designers are working smarter to build more manageable download requirements by splitting a site into a number of SWF files that are loaded on demand when the user requests them. This is a good tactic to improve the initial loading time of a site, but if each section of content weighs in at over 50Kb, users on slow modem connections will quickly tire of the site. What users want access to is content, and they want it to arrive quickly, no matter if it's in one single file or a number of separate SWF files loaded into the main interface using *loadMovie* commands.

Pergo, makers of laminate flooring, make great use of Flash's responsiveness in their Flash-based 'eShowroom' (www.pergo.com/PergoDesign/US/US_Room_View/). It offers users the chance to view a sample room, and edit its interior design. With just one click, you can tweak options such as the wall color, cabinet design, and (most importantly to Pergo) the floor style in real time. All the programming logic

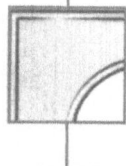

that controls what you see on the screen is built into the movie itself, so there's an instant response, and no waiting on the web server for a page reload.

In addition to customizing the look of rooms using the eShowroom, registered users can save their options onto the server for later retrieval. Registered users can even share their configuration with others, enabling the site to act as a communication tool between users in different locations.

More intuitive interactions

An important factor in the usability of web content is the intuitiveness of the interactions (which you can read more about in Chapter 7). For web pages created with just HTML and graphics, the interactions are limited to text links, form elements, and graphic links. This limitation can actually work in HTML's favor. With a limited set of possible interactions, users are better able to make decisions about the effects of interactions.

The flip side to that coin is that all interactions with HTML content have to fit within those limited options. Flash's strength is its ability to create custom interactions. Instead of just being able to click on elements of the design, Flash can allow them to respond in ways that are well beyond that of HTML-based interactions. Real-world metaphors can be more closely replicated as interactions within the Flash environment.

The Perfect Fools web site (www.perfectfools.com) shows how Flash's advanced capabilities can be used to create intuitive interaction based on a real-world metaphor. The contents of the site are presented in the form of a short book displayed on the home page. To move through the book, you simply turn the pages of the book, by dragging the bottom corner across the screen – just as if you were reading a real book.

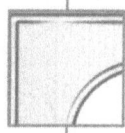
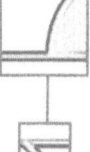

Another site that mimics real-world interaction is the Loop Labs site (www.looplabs.com), in which Flash is used as the interface for a fairly powerful music sampler. Knobs, sliders, and buttons in the Loop Labs interface function just as you'd expect their real-world counterparts to. If you have any experience of using mixers and sequencers, you should find the whole thing very intuitive.

Browser and platform-independent interactions

As any web designer will tell you, no two browsers handle HTML pages exactly the same. As soon as you use JavaScript or DHTML to add dynamic elements to an HTML page, things get even more complex. DHTML doesn't work consistently from one operating system to another, even when you're using the same browser version on each.

By contrast, Flash content being viewed on the latest Flash-enabled Mac browser should have exactly the same capabilities as the same content running on a five-year old PC system. As long as you're using the same version of the Flash plug-in, the basic features are identical. Sure, the performance on an older computer will probably be slower – but the basic functionality will be the same.

Note that some functionality – back buttons and mouse scroll-wheels for example – are still not 100% compatible with all major browsers and operating systems. For that reason, you shouldn't rely on them just yet. They're not a part of the actual Flash content, and do nothing to affect its interactivity – rather, they're external JavaScript commands that may be accessed from Flash.

Using Flash to deliver content also allows designers to focus on the interactions that they create and not the technological capabilities of the user's browser. This focus allows for shorter development times and a more stable end product.

Cost-competitive

Assuming your client wants to deploy and maintain some highly interactive content for the Web, Flash has a pretty big advantage over DHTML right away: namely, **cost**. In simple terms, Flash will usually work out less expensive.

For a start, Flash content can be cheaper to host. In addition to allowing designers to create relatively small file sizes for the amount of content that a Flash file can hold, Flash is also less taxing on the server that hosts it. Flash content plays on the client side, so your users' computers are doing most of the work when they view a Flash file. With a DHTML-based solution, the server needs to respond with information for each image needed and each HTML page viewed. Flash files can include text and imagery, not to mention sound and with the release of Flash MX, video too.

Creating a highly interactive interface in DHTML requires mastery of a number of varied technologies. Deploying a highly interactive DHTML site would require a team of designers with knowledge of HTML, CSS, JavaScript, the DOM, back-end server solutions like ASP, PHP or CGI, and cross-browser

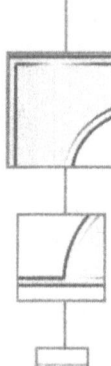

issues to support older browsers. That's a lot of knowledge needed to deploy a successful project. Let's also not forget the additional time that DHTML requires for testing across a number of different browser and platform combinations, which should be required for any Internet-based solutions.

That's not to say that mastering Flash is easy these days. While Macromedia has done its best to keep the basics of the application simple, Flash designers must still master a wide range of abilities to deploy solutions using the more advanced capabilities of Flash.

> *A client concerned with deploying user-friendly interactive content on the Web should not be surprised to find that the total cost of developing a Flash solution can be far less than deploying a DHTML solution.*

New ways to present information

As Flash expands the range of interactions available both to user and designer, new methods of presenting information via the Web become possible. Instead of displaying information such as charts and graphs in static raster images, Flash lets you present information directly in response to user actions.

The multimedia department at Spanish newspaper El Pais excels at presenting complex, technical information in easy-to-understand 'infographics'. They use Flash very effectively to illustrate all kinds of information: if you've ever struggled to make sense of soccer's infamous offside rule, then look no further than www.elpais.es/multimedia/deportes/futbol.html, where a series of simple animations illustrate how and when the ball can go out of play.

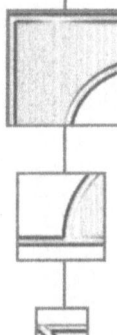

By combining animation with simple interactivity, it communicates its information effectively – and without even requiring users to understand Spanish! Even the user interface is clear and easy to use.

Other sites use Flash to help users to visualize complex sets of data. A good example of this is the community site www.communiculture.org from Future Farmers. Members of this site interact with each other by way of simple polls (which they call continuums). On signing into the site, users create an avatar to represent themselves and their position on various topics. Each continuum offers users the ability to drag their avatar to a position between the two possible answers to the question.

In the image above, the question asked is "Do you like Comic Books?" Users drag their avatars onto the continuum, and position them according to how strongly they feel about the topic. If they feel strongly that comic books are good, they put their avatar on the far left, if they hate them, it'll go on the right. If they have no strong feelings either way, they can just put in the middle.

Another thing they can do is add comments describing *why* they chose the position they did. Other users can then view these opinions by simply clicking on the avatar.

This dynamic community is an exceptional use of Flash. It lets users view the opinions of many different users and even create their own continuums. All the data is then stored in databases to keep the site growing. The way in which users interact with the site has a direct effect on the growth of the community.

This is only one example of Flash's expanded interaction capabilities. In addition to feeding and retrieving information from a database dynamically, Flash can offer much more. Many Flash-based applications are appearing on the Internet. These applications allow users to open, edit, and save information all from one interface.

TheyRule.net (also from Future Farmers) is another excellent example of how designers can use Flash's interaction capabilities to let users manipulate information on the screen. It offers the chance to explore links between the boardrooms of the 100 largest corporations in the US.

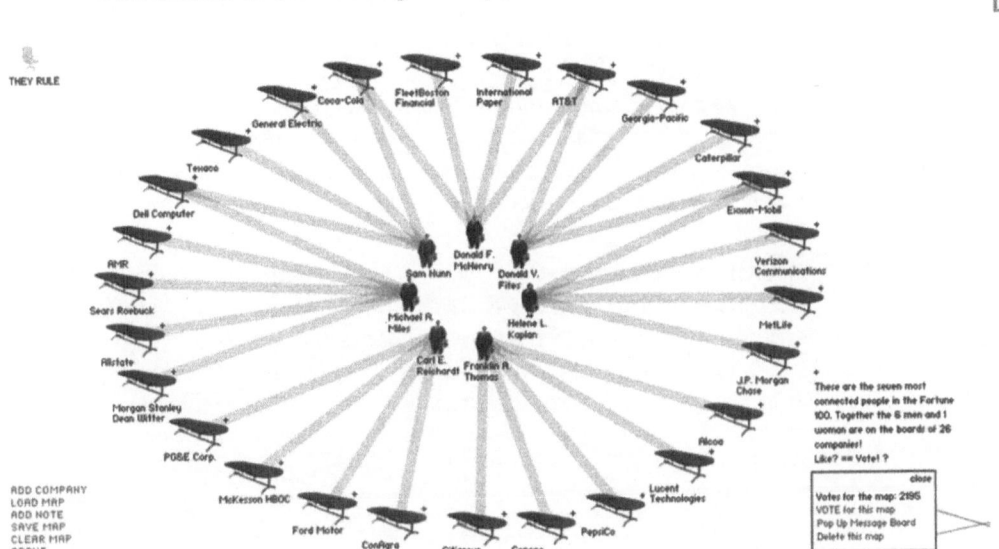

Users initiate their exploration by choosing a company from a list. From that point, they can expand the company (represented by a meeting room table) to view a list of board members. Icons depicting case-carrying figures (male or female, as appropriate) represent each member.

What's more, the girth of each figure reflects just how many other company boards they sit on – so the 'fat cats' who sit on multiple boards are represented by 'fat' icons, while less widely influential figures are represented with slimmer figures.

Each board member can be expanded to display other company boards they sit on. Gray lines between board members and the boards they sit on visually

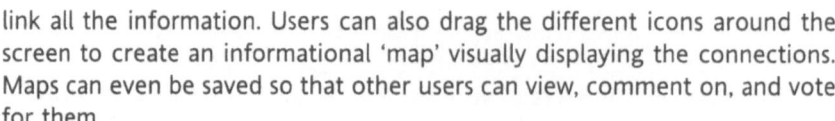

link all the information. Users can also drag the different icons around the screen to create an informational 'map' visually displaying the connections. Maps can even be saved so that other users can view, comment on, and vote for them.

> *The active involvement and decision-making offered by sites like this are excellent tools for promoting education. By interacting with data (rather than passively reading it – or having it read to you), users are more likely to engage with the topic.*
>
> *Presenting the same information in HTML and images would not provide the user with the same experience. The exploration of the data that Flash's interaction abilities offer is key to allowing users to grasp the complex nature of the information. Flash's responsiveness and connectivity are what makes it one of the most attractive web application development tools on the market.*

TheyRule.net has received many awards for its design and functionality, including the ARS Electronica 'Net Excellence' award.

Before we move on to look at best practices for Flash development, it's time to introduce a little project that we'll be developing through the course of the book.

Case Study

Future Fridges Conference web site

In order to give all this usability theory a bit more of a practical edge, we're going to take on a fictitious project, to which we can apply all the lessons we're learning. This case study will deal with the proposed web site for a conference on home fridge technology – also quite fictitious.

Of course, we're really just interested in the Flash usability issues that need to be addressed, so I'll omit some of the more technical processes.

The client, 'PDQ Events', is the company responsible for organizing this conference, and we're going to walk through each stage of the design and build processes, from the initial client brief right through to the delivery of the finished site.

This first section of the case study deals with the client brief and the designer's initial response to it.

The brief – defining the project's scope

The project's **scope** establishes the overall boundaries of the web site development. The client has provided us with the following scope:

Company Overview

The *Future Fridges Conference* is one the world's leading conferences on high-tech home fridges. The conference is three days of in-depth workshops and educational seminars on development and innovation in the home fridge industry.

PDQ Events is one of Europe's leading conference and event management companies. PDQ Events is responsible for the management of all aspects of the *Future Fridges Conference* including the conference web site.

Requirements Definition

Site Overview

The project is the development of the *Future Fridges Conference* web site. The web site will provide information on the conference, including detailed information on conference sessions and speakers.

The target audiences for the web site are potential attendees and speakers at the conference as well as the media.

Technical Overview

It is required that the web site function on all major web browsers and operating systems. It is expected that the site will be built with Macromedia Flash.

The web site will also be made available on computer kiosks within the conference environment.

All conference attendees will be issued a CD-ROM ticket, which functions like a normal CD-ROM but is the shape of a ticket. The site will be included on this CD-ROM.

It is probable that some conference attendees may have a vision or hearing impairment, thus this site must meet the accessibility guidelines defined by the 508 regulations specified by the U.S. Federal Access Board and the accessibility guidelines with priority 1 defined by the W3C/WAI.

Functional Requirements

The web site will include information on:

- The conference vision and the conference organizers and partners
- The program and seminar details including detailed session descriptions
- The conference location and venue
- Biographies of all conference speakers

The web site will contain at least one video interview with a keynote speaker, which should also be available in an audio or text format. There will also be a number of audio-only interviews with conference speakers.

Users should be able to complete a conference registration form on the web site.

Users should be able to easily print all important content on the site.

The web site will contain an interactive component that allows users to create their own session planner, which lets them plan which conference sessions they wish to attend and then print out their own custom session plan. Ideally users with Pocket PCs will also be able to download this session planner and use it on their handheld device.

The User Experience

The design of the web site will provide users with a high impact message that communicates the vision of the *Future Fridges Conference* and will incorporate clean and intuitive navigation elements to ensure that even novice Internet users will find the site easy to use. The design should reflect the innovative and professional nature of the conference.

Deliverables

The final deliverable will be a fully functional web site for the *Future Fridges Conference* web site.

Response to the brief

The first thing to consider when responding to this brief is whether the site should be developed in Flash or HTML. Although our client has already stated that they expect the site to be built in Flash, we may be in a position to influence their decision – and at this stage, it won't cost them anything to change their mind!

Before committing ourselves, it's vital for us to examine the project scope and figure out whether Flash is more likely to enhance or detract from users' experiences of the finished web site.

In this case, it looks like the client's justified. They require a site that includes audio, video and lots of interactivity, and in all these areas, Flash has the potential to offer a better user experience than HTML. Content like that can't be directly integrated into an HTML page; it would require the use of scripting languages and media players. In a Flash-based site we can have a button which, when clicked, instantly plays an audio interview with a conference speaker. This is a far more desirable experience for the user than the HTML experience of clicking a link that opens up a separate media player application.

This seamless experience that Flash can offer is particularly desirable in a CD-ROM or kiosk. In these environments users have an expectation that the interface will respond instantly; they don't expect to see blank screens as pages refresh or load in. Our client has specified that the *Future Fridges Conference* site will be available in both these environments, which further emphasizes that Flash may be the right choice for this project.

The client's request for an interactive session planner is a great example of where Flash can offer a more intuitive interactive experience than HTML. We can create a mini-application within the site that will allow users to browse intuitively through the conference sessions, easily sorting sessions by categories or times, drilling down for more detail, while building up their own itinerary. Flash enables us to build a tool that will present information in a way comparable to a calendar or event planner application. If we use HTML it ties us to a less appropriate page-and-link-style presentation of this information.

It may be possible to build something similar to a calendar in an HTML site by utilizing DHTML and server scripts. However, DHTML doesn't work consistently across different platforms and browser versions. DHTML code that works on a PC may not work on a Mac, even when using the same browser version. Once again, this is where Flash comes to the rescue – as we know, it works the same across all browsers and platforms. Our Flash site will even work the same when it's created as a standalone projector for the CD-ROM ticket.

So far then, it appears that the *Future Fridges Conference* site is ideally suited to being developed in Flash. However, there's one particular requirement specified by the client that isn't easily achieved in Flash.

Accessibility Issues

Our client requires that the site meet both US and W3C accessibility regulations. Okay, so let's develop the site using Flash MX, and rely on the Flash 6 plug-in to pass information to assistive technologies (such as screen readers) via Microsoft Active Accessibility. The trouble is, many users don't currently *have* the Flash 6 plug-in, and earlier versions didn't provide accessibility support.

The version of the Flash plug-in associated with files produced by Flash MX is called Flash 6. Macromedia retained the numbering system for the plug-in name so as to keep the detection of plug-in versions as simple as possible.

So what should be done? Do we abandon all of the advantages that Flash offers because of accessibility issues? Or do we just ignore the percentage of users who won't be able to access the site?

Clearly, neither solution is desirable. The best step is to take advantage of Flash's features while also making the site accessible. Ultimately this means building a Flash site *and* an HTML site. Let's say we propose this concept to the client – they respond by asking:

Will this cost me twice as much?

Well, it may take some extra work to produce an HTML version of the site, but if we plan for it from the start, that can be kept to a minimum. After all, the role of the HTML site is to provide the same information as the Flash site in a simple format that can be processed by screen reader software. The creative energy should go into the Flash version of the site, since the people visiting the HTML version are less likely to be concerned with design, and more with information.

The key is to try and separate the presentation from the raw information. Both sites should contain the same information – it's just that the Flash version will present it in a more interactive way. So as we design the Flash site, we'll aim to keep the information (especially text) separate so that it can be easily integrated into the HTML site as well.

Clearly there will be *some* extra work involved and hence extra cost for the client. However the client gains a lot in the process. The site becomes accessible to everyone – even users with very old web browsers – and can be logged by all search engines. What's more, the client should now be immune to criticisms of poor site accessibility; the site doesn't risk getting negative press for not providing easy access for everyone.

Other scope issues

This is a classic client scope because quite a lot of complexity is hidden within its short list of requirements.

For example, the fact that the conference registration form is only mentioned once – and then just briefly – disguises the importance of the work involved. Completing a registration form is a complex user interaction that will be critical to the site's success. If usability problems result in users giving up before they're finished, the client's conference stands to lose attendees! We therefore need to get it right, and that means first getting more information on this form from the client. If we get that information good and early in the site's development, we can carefully plan the user's interaction with this section of the site.

The statement that, "users should be able to print important content" is also worth considering. It raises the question, "Which content is important content?" The simple answer is that *all* content on the site should be printable. However, Flash can create custom print pages that may contain extra detail (or different formatting) than that displayed on screen. It's well worth considering whether this functionality could be used to enhance the user's experience.

At first glance, the scope's **Technical Overview** appears to list all the environments in which the site may be viewed: namely the Web, conference kiosks, and CD-ROM tickets. Closer inspection reveals that the client also wants Pocket PC users to be able to access a section of the site. While Flash functions the same on a Pocket PC as on the Web, the user interaction is different, with input being based on a pen not a mouse. We'll obviously need to take this into consideration when we design that particular section of the site.

These sorts of ambiguities and oversights can arise quite frequently in client briefs, simply because clients aren't typically concerned with (or interested in) spelling out the mechanics of the user interactions. For that reason, complex processes get covered in just a few words – it's left to *us* to identify and plan for these interactions, with the aim of making the user's experience as simple and pleasant as possible.

We'll come back to this project in the next chapter, once we've taken an initial look at some of the hard practicalities of choosing to use Flash.

Best practices for Flash development

As we've already established, Flash isn't designed to be a replacement for HTML; there are some things that HTML will always do better, and that's no bad thing. Both can offer a good experience to the user, but Flash has a big advantage when it comes to sophisticated interactivity – especially since it doesn't rely on users running one particular browser on one specific operating system.

But we still need to be careful! Even if we focus on the user from day one of our design process, Flash isn't necessarily the best tool for the job.

Ask yourself: do you need Flash?

Too often, Flash is used for content that really doesn't need it. Publishing Flazoom.com for the past two years has definitely taught me that. I'm sent a lot of links to Flash-powered sites; all too often, I'll check them out, only to find that they've no good reason for using Flash at all. Sometimes it seems the *only* reason a company's used Flash is so that they can say, "We have a Flash site".

In reality, having a Flash site is not like having a Boy Scout merit badge. It doesn't mean that the company's site is automatically better than the competition. If they really want a top-notch site, then they'll concentrate on delivering **good content** in a way that's **easy to use**. Amazon.com certainly didn't get where it is today by having a soundtrack and an intro-movie. It became the online giant it is by focusing on the needs of its users, delivering quickly, simply, and without fuss.

Using Flash doesn't mean that a site will get more 'hits' either. In fact, most Flash content on the Web is deployed in a way that makes it virtually impossible for most search engines to find it. What's more, an all-Flash site with no HTML-only version will decrease your audience even more.

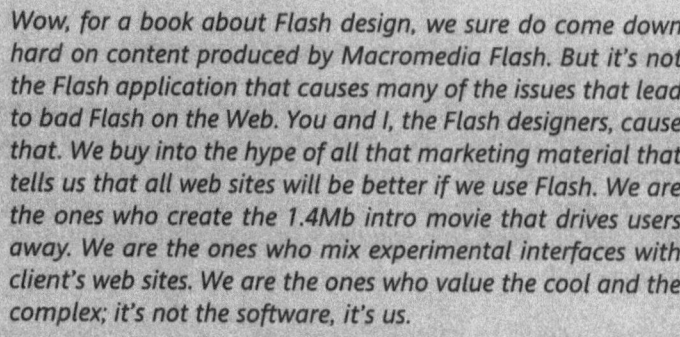

Wow, for a book about Flash design, we sure do come down hard on content produced by Macromedia Flash. But it's not the Flash application that causes many of the issues that lead to bad Flash on the Web. You and I, the Flash designers, cause that. We buy into the hype of all that marketing material that tells us that all web sites will be better if we use Flash. We are the ones who create the 1.4Mb intro movie that drives users away. We are the ones who mix experimental interfaces with client's web sites. We are the ones who value the cool and the complex; it's not the software, it's us.

All too often, Flash is used simply to make an impact, throwing slick and unexpected behavior in the user's face in an ever-increasingly desperate effort to grab their attention. But sites that are all gloss and little content don't fool users. Okay, they may be initially impressed with the shiny paint and chrome finishes, but if there's no decent content to back it up (or there *is* decent content, but they have to struggle to get at it), they probably won't bother coming back!

Flash is best applied if you're trying to provide users with a **better** way to interact with your content than HTML can offer. That may be because the content demands it – a site like theyrule.net simply *couldn't* work in HTML. Alternatively, it may be because you're meeting the specific needs of a certain type of audience. The Perfect Fools site serves as a tiny showcase for the sort of content that the company's capable of producing. Sure, they could have presented exactly the same text and images on an HTML page; but they'd have been neglecting all the visitors who came to see whether their Flash was any good.

The painful truth is that most web sites have absolutely no need for Flash content of any kind. The majority needs no more than standard HTML and maybe a few rollovers.

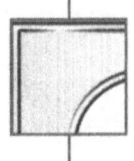

So what makes a good use of Flash on the Web? What types of content allow Flash to deliver the best possible user experience of any tool available today? How can we best evaluate a client's needs to see if Flash or another delivery option will work best for them? How can we make Flash content work well within a site's existing structure?

These questions need answers, and that's what this chapter is about. Let's try and identify when we should be using Flash to improve the usability of a web site.

Can Flash simplify the user's task?

The Web isn't filled with shining examples of good usability. Most online stores are still more complex to use than the act of walking into a physical store and buying what you need. Shopping carts lend a bit of real-world imagery to make the experience more intuitive, but the major benefit of online shopping is the convenience of being able to shop in your underwear!

Now imagine going to a physical store and having to wait in four lines, and talk to four people just to check out. On reaching the front of the first line, you find out how much the goods are going to cost. Once that's done, you have to wait in the next line, and tell the store where you want them to send your goods. At the front of the third line, you're asked for your credit card details, along with confirmation that the billing address is the same as the shipping address.

Before the store charges you for your purchase and lets you on your way; there's a fourth line to wait in. Once you reach the front, they simply summarize everything you got from the first three lines, ready for your final approval. If everything's fine, then off you go. If you've made a mistake, then tough luck – you'll have to go back to one of the first three lines to correct it.

No store is like that. No business could survive with a checkout that had four separate lines. Unless they're online, where complex tasks have to be broken down into illogical steps because of the limited abilities of HTML-based

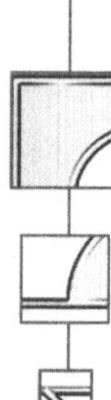

solutions. Electronic shopping isn't the only example of complex online interactions that users have to deal with to accomplish their goals. The Web is filled with them.

Flash can bypass a lot of these limitations. While HTML-based interactions need four pages to process a shopping cart order from an online store, Flash can do it in a single interface. The user has to only work with one screen – and more importantly, there's no blink!

Making a reservation for a hotel room online is often the last step in a very complex decision-making process for travelers going on a vacation. Before selecting a hotel room, travelers need to know where they're going, and when they'll need the room. The price of a hotel room is based on the number of travelers, so that information is required at the time of reservation too.

In addition to all this information that the traveler has to collect, the hotel also needs to collect together its own information to process a reservation. Hotels have to keep an up-to-date inventory status on the types of rooms and the number of rooms available at any given time. Many hotels offer a number of different types of room, each with its own occupancy limit. All of this information needs to be available for a reservation to be taken.

Traditionally, the process of reserving a hotel room online was a multi-page process that required travelers to continually go back to re-enter information when troubles arose. To finally settle on the right number of rooms, and the right type of rooms for the right number of people on the right dates an online user might be forced to redo a step over and over again. More likely, the user will change tactics and look for the reservation phone number instead of continuing with overly complex online solutions.

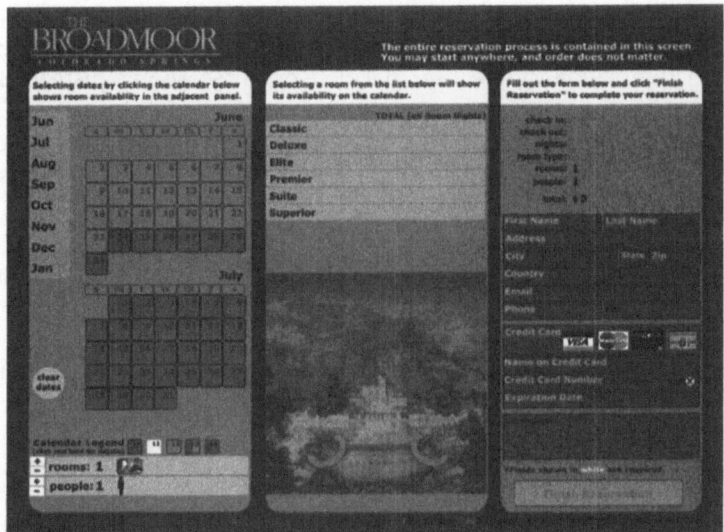

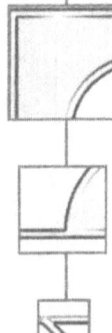

That was the issue facing a number of hotels when the designers at Webvertising started looking at Flash as a possible way to improve their online reservation service called 'iHotelier oneScreen' (www.ihotelier.com). The HTML-based form that iHotelier initially offered was four pages long and required users to frequently start again on specific tasks. The user's experience with the HTML-based forms just didn't provide the instant feedback that users needed to make the process work smoothly. Flash content, on the other hand, could provide this type of feedback by checking the user's requests against the hotel inventory as they entered the data.

The resulting Flash-based reservation form for iHotelier allows users to interact with the online system in a way that was easier than calling the reservation line. Instead of being forced to enter individual parts of the information on different pages of an HTML form, the Flash interface allows users to completely fill out the form all on the same screen. Additionally, the iHotelier Flash interface has back-end hooks into the room inventory database of the hotel. This allows the Flash interface to immediately provide feedback on what rooms are available as the user clicks on the dates they plan on staying.

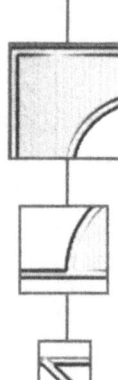

Other data is also updated immediately as the user modifies the specifics of the reservation. If the user decided on three rooms instead of two, the interface automatically updates all the onscreen data to show the results of the user's modification. The iHotelier Flash reservation interface doesn't just stop at updating information and database hooks, it also allows users to view photos of the rooms before they finalize their reservation.

The iHotelier interface also beats the HTML version by allowing users to begin the reservation process anywhere on the screen. If the user wants to enter their credit card information first, they can. The same applies to selecting the room type and dates of your visit. There's no starting place for the user, because the interface is designed to meet the user's needs. There's no step one, instead the Flash interface stands ready to assist users with whatever information they happen to have collected.

All the information that a traveler would need to book a room at the Broadmoor hotel is displayed on their computer screen (www.enteryourinformation.com/broadmoor/onescreen.cfm). The result is that users are more likely to finish the reservation process instead of calling a reservation line or moving on to another hotel. According to the iHotelier website, the Broadmoor has booked a total of $450,000 dollars in online reservations in its first 12 months. Furthermore, the resort expects to at least double that number in 2002 and is well on its way with a 100% increase in reservations in the first two weeks of 2002.

ihotelier's reservation system also offers an added usability benefit by automatically directing users with slow connection or without the Flash plug-in to the HTML version of the content. The HTML version does feature the confusion of a four-page form, but users with slow connections or no Flash plug-in are still able to complete their reservation.

All in all, the iHotelier reservation system is an excellent example of how Flash content can improve the user's experience with a complex and often confusing task. The user-focused development is evident in the site's interactions. Here the designers knew when to use Flash, and implemented it as a means to improving the user experience.

Or will Flash complicate things?

In stark contrast to the use of Flash to improve a typically complex and frustrating experience, is Sony's Connect and Create site (www.ita.sel.sony.com/ConnectandCreate/home.html). Here the designers working on the site used Flash to make the user's interaction needlessly complex and confusing, making what could have been a simple HTML form into a nightmare of usability.

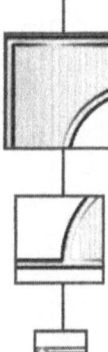

The Sony Connect and Create site has a fairly simple purpose: it lets users see how much they can save when buying a selection of Sony computer and related digital products. With such humble aspirations for a site, I have to wonder what happened? The site has collected some of the worst interactions available and bundled them together to offer little more than confusion and frustration for the user.

Let's first take a look at the main interaction, a collection of Sony products that moves and rotates in a 3D space based on the position of the mouse. This interaction is like nothing that the user has ever experienced before (bar that of other Flash sites using the same effect). There is no real-world metaphor for how this interaction works, no common experiences the user can base their interactions on. The extra mouse precision that is required to select a specific product is a serious usability issue.

That's not the only problem with the main interaction. The use of alpha channels also decreases the usability of the product. When products rotate to the 'back' of the 3D space the transparency is reduced and the product becomes smaller. This helps to keep the products in the front very visible, but unfortunately it hides selections from the user. The use of transparency also reduces the contrast on the site, making it harder for users with poor vision to use the site (not that blue and white pixel-sized fonts on a black background are going to win any legibility awards).

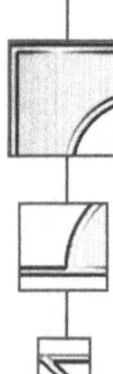

Once the user has attained the mouse precision needed to select a product, the designers behind the site put up another challenging interaction: the counter-productive drag-and-drop. For users who are controlling the cursor using a trackpad, trackball or trackpoint (the little eraser-like pointer that many IBM laptops feature), drag-and-drop interactions require more mouse control than their pointing device allows. Designers including this type of interaction need to make sure that the system is forgiving, allowing the dragged items to 'snap' into the closest logical spot when released. When a user interacting with the Sony site misses the drag-to location, even by a single pixel, the product they have selected jumps right back into the 3D space, requiring them to try again.

The scrollbars on the site also present usability hurdles. They offer little in terms of information. There is no bar that relays if the user is at the top or bottom of the content. Not that a bar is necessary, but the designers did leave room for it, and that leaves room for user confusion. If a designer is going to add something that looks like a standard interface element, they should make sure it works like one too.

A final usability issue is the lack of help in assisting the user to complete the task on this site. The first step in the process (letting the system know what type of Vaio computer the user has) is not clear. Instead of presenting the user with the two possible choices that allow them to start the interaction, the Sony site offers thirteen additional 'wrong' choices. 87% of the choices the user can make will lead to a dialog box, which really should be the first interaction the user sees.

The lengths to which this site's designers went to make these interactions more complex than necessary is amazing. Just about every interaction on the site could be easier to use, if only the designers were more interested in the user and less in showing off their Flash skills. In addition, users without the Flash plug-in or slow connections are offered no HTML version of the content. This is a great shame, as the whole site could be implemented far more intuitively as a simple HTML page, with just the bare minimum of JavaScript.

So, in this case, the decision to use Flash seems to be totally unjustified. The end result is a site that confuses and frustrates instead of offering a better experience for the user.

Does Flash add anything to the experience?

Site navigation at UMAX Corporation's US site (www.umax.com/index.jsp?worldwide=usa) shows possibly the worst use of Flash that I've ever seen from a corporate site.

The menu is a shining example of how Flash content can be misused. It's too large for the function it renders, and the animation it features has no value whatsoever. There just doesn't seem to be any good reason for its designers to have used Flash in the first place – it really makes you wonder why they thought it was necessary.

The first problem with this site is the excessively large size of the SWF file. There's no reason for the file to be anywhere near as large as this – an experienced Flash designer could create the same content in a fraction of the space.

The second issue is the side-to-side animation of the buttons. There's no point to this rather annoying motion, and it makes the buttons harder to click.

The intro animation used to 'build' the navigation also takes too long; nearly five seconds go by before all the buttons are visible. The same slow response applies to the 'Search' feature, which again takes five seconds to animate onto the screen.

The biggest usability issue with this example is that there's just no reason for it. UMAX doesn't have a large menu that needs dynamic functionality. The site structure is pretty simple, only needing six elements in the SWF navigation. HTML and images, or even HTML and CSS would deliver the same content in a more user-friendly manner and with a much faster download.

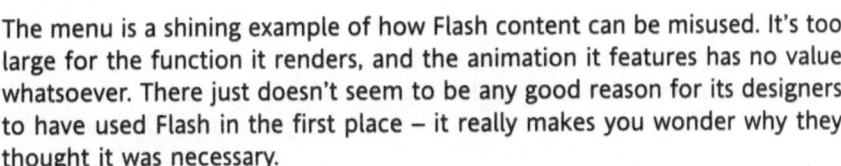

Find a useful balance of HTML and Flash

It's important to remember that HTML and Flash aren't mutually exclusive options – many of the best sites around today use a careful mix of the two.

Flash and HTML can work very well together; but as we discussed earlier, we need to consider the strengths of each format before making mistakes that harm the user experience. What sorts of content are best suited to Flash and when should HTML take on the duties?

For the most part, it's pretty simple to make the decision:

- If the content includes a great deal of text, stick with HTML. HTML allows users to easily print, scroll, copy and paste the text on the page.

- If the content needs to have dynamic, interactive elements, Flash is going to be your best choice. Flash allows real-time responses to the user's input without requiring a 'blink'.

PopeDeFlash.com is a great example of how to get the most out of both technologies at once.

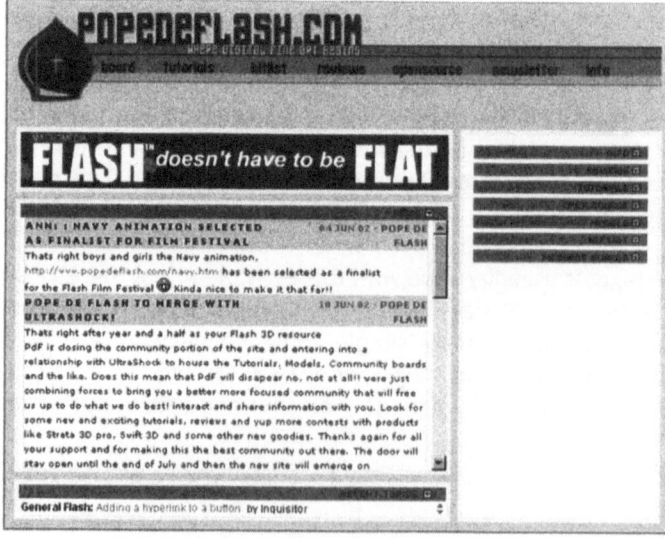

The design of Pope de Flash's site is a combination of HTML and Flash content. The page layout is created using nested HTML tables to define the basic structure in a format that web browsers can quickly display. In addition, the frequently updated 'News' section is also displayed as HTML-formatted content.

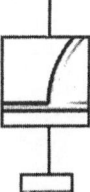

By deploying this content using HTML instead of Flash, visitors can easily control the size of the text on the page using their browser's native font-sizing controls. One other benefit to using HTML for the text content is its compatibility with search engines. The constantly updated home page content will help to make it show up higher in many popular search engine listings.

Flash is employed for the more interactive elements of the site, such as the tabbed menu on the right. Casual users may never even notice though, as it's been designed to look just like the HTML content. The right-hand menu provides users with a preview of the content they can expect to find in the rest of the site. This content is pulled from an external file and can be easily updated without the need to continually open and modify the Flash file in the Flash application.

By using Flash content to handle the dynamic elements and HTML to handle the text and page structure, PopeDeFlash.com makes great use of the respective strengths of each technology. The user is left with a very seamless experience, moving easily from one format to the other and reaping the usability benefits of both.

Tips for HTML/Flash integration

The navigation of a web site is one thing that can often be improved by means of a user-friendly Flash menu. The dynamic nature of Flash content lets designers build menus that offer more than just a set of static links, and help users find their way around the site more easily.

Navigation design is one of the most important parts of the success of a site in terms of usability. If the navigation is not easy to learn, remember, and use, then the overall performance of the site will suffer. When developing

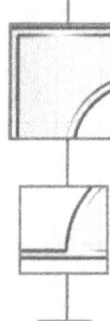

the navigation, remember that its purpose is to let the user know where they are and where they can go.

Many Flash designers create navigation systems that hide options from the user by either removing the navigation from the screen or by only showing one part of the navigation at a time. Users make decisions about navigating from the available information that's on the screen. Secondary menu elements that only appear after the user has rolled-over a design (such as pop-up or pull-down menus) can show a lot of detail about the site's structure, but without cluttering the screen unnecessarily.

Take for example the application of Flash content for menus on the main Flash MX page at Macromedia's site (www.macromedia.com).

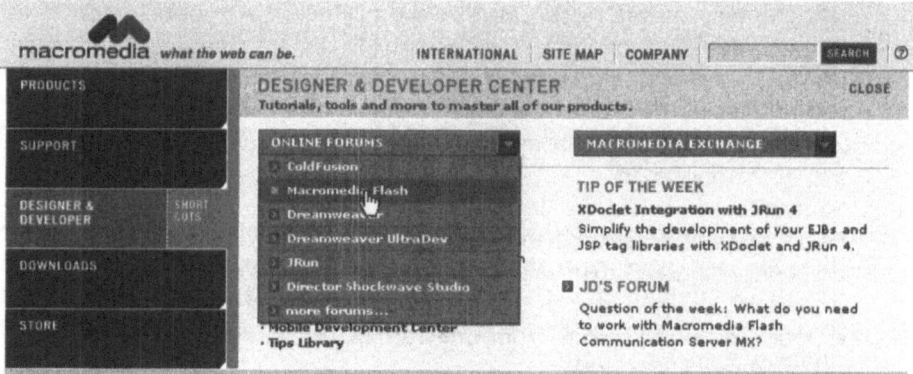

Macromedia uses HTML formatting for most of the page's structure and content. This allows the pages to load quickly and get the information to the user as fast as possible. On a slow modem connection the pages appear in a couple of seconds at the most. Obviously, the designers at Macromedia know what HTML is good for, and use this knowledge to streamline the delivery of their content for the majority of web users surfing with a modem connection.

The Flash elements on this page are used to provide further navigation to the user. On the right side of the page is an index of the information available on the site about Flash MX. Some of the sections are only a single page while others may include multiple sub-pages. All of this information is communicated to the user through the design of the menu. Sections with sub-pages have a 'toggle-arrow' to denote that the section can expand. This design convention is used in many applications and operating systems that Macromedia's users will recognize.

Navigating the menu is as easy as clicking the mouse. The animation is very quick and the visual cues in the design clearly let the user know what choice they're making when they're ready to click. Users can also expand the menu fully, so as to compare the contents of different sections. This is a major improvement over many Flash and DHTML-style menus that only let the user see the contents of one section at a time. We need to remember that users need information to make a decision. The more access to information that an interface can provide, the more likely the user will be to find the information that they're looking for.

The user-friendliness of Macromedia's Flash-based menu goes further than just the appearance of the page. The designers took great care to create a Flash menu that could be used across the entire site by separating the content of the file from the presentation. Users download the SWF file for the menu once: on subsequent pages, they need only download the text file providing the menu information being displayed. Believe it or not, the entire Flash SWF file for the menu is only 136 bytes – even the text file is bulkier, at all of 4Kb!

Macromedia could have used DHTML to provide an expandable menu with many of the same features as the Flash menu, but deploying a DHTML solution would not have been as compatible with the many varied browsers that users use to access the Macromedia web site. In addition, a DHTML solution would have created a larger file.

There are downsides to using Flash for the navigation elements of web sites. Some web navigation conventions just can't be supported via Flash-based navigation on HTML pages:

At this time, Flash content can't provide differentiated 'visited link' colors in the same manner that HTML can. Of course, these only work in HTML when the designer chooses to use text links or graphics with borders. For many web sites that rely on HTML and JavaScript to deploy image-based navigation, visited links colors aren't available to users either.

Another convention of HTML that hasn't yet been supported in Flash is the status bar metadata that web browsers provide. When a user moves their cursor over a link on an HTML page, the URL of the link is displayed in the status bar of the browser, so that users can see where the link will take them.

Summary

The decision to use Flash for content creation and delivery is one that designers need to make based on the strengths of Flash and not the allure of Flash's power. Flash content should play off of the strengths of the format, such as animation, interactivity, and compressed files. When the needs of the content lend themselves to HTML formatted pages, designers shouldn't try to force Flash onto the needs of the content.

HTML is the backbone of the Web. Its main strength is formatting text for display in the browser. For sites that require large amounts of text, there's no better solution. The limits of HTML are mainly to do with poor interactivity and server-side processing requirements. HTML just can't compete with Flash in terms of user experience when it comes to content that needs anything more than static information.

Mixing HTML and Flash content together on the same page can provide designers with an effective way to make the best of both technologies. Many designers have keyed into this technique, and the users of sites that mix the two technologies can certainly benefit when each format is used for its strengths.

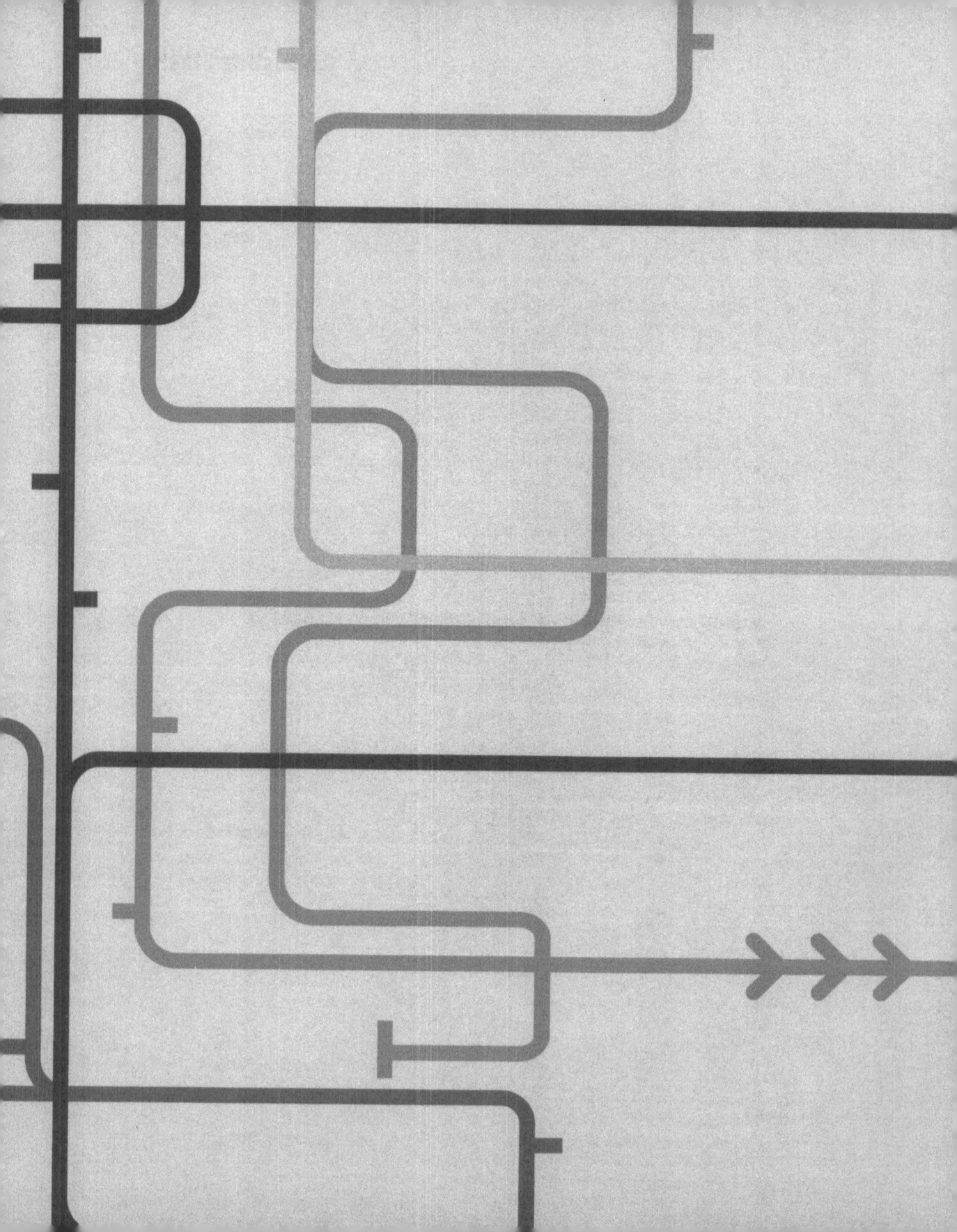

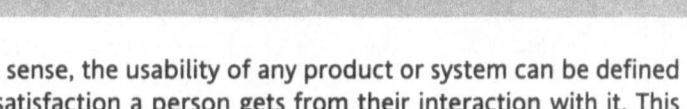

Choosing usability

In a very general sense, the usability of any product or system can be defined in terms of the satisfaction a person gets from their interaction with it. This doesn't just apply to web sites and Flash content – it applies to everything from elevator design to the cockpit of a jet airplane.

Next time you're inside an elevator (I'm guessing that not all of us have jet airplanes to examine up close), think about the design issues that make it easy to use. Notice that the buttons for different floors are arranged with the lowest numbers at the bottom and the highest numbers at the top. The reason for this is fairly obvious: floor numbering systems start from the bottom and count upward from there. By arranging the buttons to match the arrangement of floors, the interface becomes a little more intuitive than it would be otherwise.

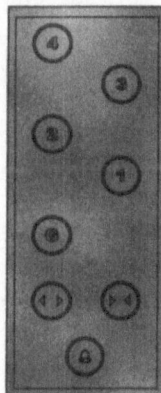

Now think about your typical interactions with an elevator. Once you get beyond the basic process of pressing buttons to call and send the elevator, there really aren't so many. Most of the time, it will run quite independently of human interaction.

The timing of the doors' opening and closing is set by the elevator itself, and it's only occasionally that it might need to be controlled by passengers. The only time you need to press a button other than a floor button is when you need to override the elevator's operation. You might need to hold the door

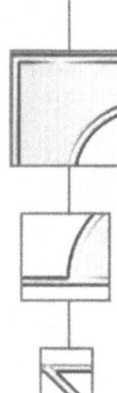

open for a co-worker or close the door faster if your boss is approaching. These features allow you a bit more control over the elevator system, and this helps you to trust the elevator.

The other buttons in the elevator are generally only used in emergencies, but it's nice to see them when you ride to your floor. They're letting you know that in the event of a broken elevator you'll be able to get help.

Good elevators also provide feedback to the user. When inside an elevator with no windows it's very difficult to tell just where in the building you are unless the elevator shares this information.

As elevator passengers ascend or descend inside, the floor feedback allows them to prepare for their destination as it nears. Really useful elevators are designed to communicate with not only the passengers they are moving, but also with their future passengers by letting people waiting in the elevator lobby know what floors the various elevators are closest to.

The same basic features of a usable interface that apply to elevators also apply to aircraft cockpits. Both interfaces need to allow for operation, status communication and additional control (just in case). Aircraft pilots require a great deal of training to make sure that they're able to use the aircraft's controls to keep the plane in the air. Elevators, on the other hand, are generally easy enough for a two-year-old to understand.

What does usability mean in practice?

The usability of many everyday objects helps people to intuitively use them. We're presented with new technologies nearly every day of our lives (a web site's interface is a new technology). The ability of people to use these technologies is what usability is. Can you **use** it?

We surround ourselves with the fruits of design, and we expect every one – be it a new PDA, a potato peeler, or a web site – to be usable. It helps us to connect with the product. But usability isn't just based on the initial perception of the user; it's a combination of several factors:

- **Is it easy to start using?** On their first exposure to a product or system, how easy is it for users to start making it do what they want? How quickly can they grasp its basic functions to accomplish simple tasks?

- **Is it memorable?** If a user has interacted with the product or system before, how much of the interface will they remember? Are the controls distinctive enough that a returning user won't have to relearn how to use them?

- **Is it intuitive?** Are all the necessary options made obvious to the user? How often do users make errors while interacting with the product or system? Are the errors they make serious? Can the user easily recover from them? Does the product or system minimize the opportunity for errors?

- **Is it efficient?** Are tasks accomplished faster once users have a greater understanding of the interface? Would an experienced user be able to use it more efficiently than during their first experience? How steep is the learning curve? Can a new user move easily to being an experienced user?

- **Are users satisfied?** Do they find the user experience to be fun? Do they return to the product or system? Do they enjoy using it?

Now, Flash designers like you and I don't get much work that requires us to think about the usability of elevator buttons or aircraft cockpits, but we do get work to develop Flash content and we do care about the usability of that Flash content. You cared enough to read this book, and this is a good place to start! So, let's take a look at each of these points in a bit more detail, and find out what usability means in practice for the Flash designer.

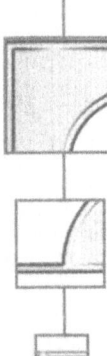

Easy

When you first expose someone to a piece of Flash content, how long does it take for them to start using it? By 'using the content', I mean actually interacting with its interface to accomplish a task – if they're sitting through a lengthy download and/or intro movie, they haven't started yet!

Get rid of as many hurdles as you can afford to

Say you build a web site that requires users' systems to meet very specific specifications – such as screen resolution, color depth, processor speed, and so on. As soon as you tell a user that they need to change screen size (or reset the color depth, download a plug-in, change their browser, install a faster processor, or whatever else) before they can use your site, you're putting a bunch of great big obstacles between them and the content – hurdles to leap before they can start to use the site. Sure, this may well make life much easier for you, but it's also going to exclude a whole lot of potential visitors who don't meet up to those requirements.

If your site has features that require very specific settings and technologies, it's best to keep those features separate from core content, and provide alternate, less technology-specific ways to access the content. The best option all round is to develop toward a user profile (more on this later in the chapter), and provide a low-tech option for users who don't meet the technology requirements of the main content.

Just a few years back, Flash content itself was a serious hurdle, as many users didn't have Flash-enabled browsers. Many sites lost valuable hits simply because they didn't provide any alternative. Nowadays the Flash plug-in has reached a level of penetration such that all but a tiny percentage of web surfers can handle Flash 5 content. All the same, plug-ins should still be counted as hurdles, and it's important to ask yourself whether the benefits of using them outweigh the associated risks. Make sure that features and options are clear.

Can users quickly understand which options and features are available? The interface design should make clear to the user what it is that they can click on, and what each click may do. Make sure that all the site's main sections are represented by easily accessible navigation links, and that content is clearly organized with appropriate labels for each section. Unlabeled buttons and hidden navigation options may seem like a really cool idea, but they're guaranteed to cause confusion, and nine times out of ten, they're just plain irritating!

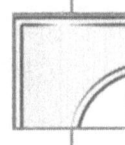

The interface should give users enough information to let them start building a mental model of how the site as a whole hangs together. Then they can start work right away, without having to stop and decipher lots of cryptic clues. You may be surprised at just how many users have trouble finding out what's clickable on a typical Flash site.

> *If part of the interface can be clicked on, then it should make its function apparent – buttons should look like buttons!*

Okay, this doesn't mean that every button in the interface needs to be beveled or have a drop shadow. But they should all be marked out clearly in some way, and not just when the mouse passes over them – they need to be obvious wherever the mouse pointer happens to be.

Ultimately, it really doesn't matter what a button looks like, just as long as the user can recognize it as a button. Fortunately for us, there are more conventions for button design than exist for virtually any other interface element on the Web. Underlines, arrows, outlines, colored text, bold text, italicized text, dropped shadows and beveled edges are all pretty standard techniques with which to scream out, "This is a button!"

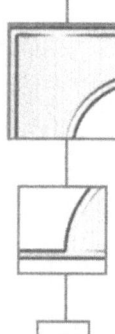

Memorable

Flash content is inherently more complex to interact with than objects like doors and books, which you simply open or read. You present users with a number of interactions for accessing and controlling the Flash content. There could be links to sections of content, buttons that activate a function within the content, or buttons that control the playing of the Flash file. For users to feel comfortable with the actions associated with different interface elements, they need to **remember** what those elements do.

A good interface will be one that helps the user to understand the system. Good interfaces build upon the experience of the user and relate the interactions available in a clear, concise way. Users should be able to return to the content and remember how to use as much of the system as possible.

Intuitive

The title of Steve Krug's popular book on usability for web designers summarizes it in terms of one simple rule:

> "Don't make me think."

Before you ask, 'me' isn't Steve; neither is it the designer, the client, nor the author of *this* book. It's **the user** every time. This is really the holy grail of any usable design: to create a working product or system that requires little or no thought from the person using it.

Okay, that's easier said than done. How can we find ways to actually make this work?

Establish a metaphor

The most potent way to teach anyone something new is to frame it in terms of something they already know and understand. When someone visits a web site, they're essentially using clicks of the mouse to represent more familiar actions: clicking on a link instead of walking from one place to another; clicking on the shopping basket icon instead of looking at what they've taken off the shelves; clicking on the Submit button instead of handing over a credit card. If you break it down into simple mechanics, the whole thing's very abstract!

That's why it's vital to establish metaphors – familiar contexts for web interactions to take place in. If users can recognize a situation (for example, "I'm in a store, with these items in my basket") then they can deduce how their actions will affect that situation ("If I leave the store without paying, then I won't get to take these items home"), and act accordingly ("I'd better pay up then!").

> *The Web itself is reliant on metaphors at just about every level. For example, the idea of a 'site' in real life implies a well-defined physical location: like a warehouse or an office. When you access a web site though, you may well be looking at content sourced from servers that are located all over the world. There's no requirement for a single location, but we call it a 'site' all the same, just as we call its URL (www.url.com) an 'address'.*

So, choose a suitable metaphor, and you can make even the most complex system seem quite straightforward. Find everyday terms in which to describe how your site works, and hook straight into your users' prior experiences: not only will this help them to learn about the available options, but it should also help them remember how the site works in future.

Choosing the right metaphor can be a fairly tricky task – it's important to achieve a balance between necessary complexity and unnecessary complication. For example, if you designed an online store, but took the 'store' analogy just a little too far, your site might end up with features

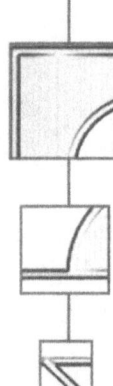

labeled 'Entrance', 'Aisle 1', 'Aisle 2', and 'Parking lot'. Familiar, but not terribly useful:

- As far as users are concerned, once they've arrived at the site, they're 'inside' the store – so there's no need for an 'Entrance' feature.

- The Web is essentially a non-linear medium, so users expect to go straight to what they want. While I may associate 'Aisle 1' with soda and chips, someone else may expect to find fruit and vegetables there. That sort of ambiguity just leads to confusion; rather than pacing up and down anonymous aisles, let your users go straight to 'Dairy', 'Bakery', or 'Frozen goods'.

- The whole point of online shopping is that you can do it from the comfort of your home, office, or favorite spot on the top of a mountain (if you have all the right equipment), so there's really not much point in having a virtual parking lot. Once a user's finished buying goods from the store, they can point their browser wherever they like – in fact they can do so at any time they like!

Metaphors can be very useful, but only when they're used sensibly: that means being unambiguous and careful not to push them too far! We'll take a closer look at the use of metaphor in the next chapter.

Make use of conventions

Of course, the average user has a little more experience behind them than a trip to the local store. A lot of 'intuitive' web controls rely on familiarity *with* the Web: most users will recognize an HTML button when they see one – sure, that's partly because it looks like a physical button (the metaphor trick again), but the main reason is that it's used **consistently** in almost every HTML page they've ever seen!

Certain metaphors are so effective that they transcend their humble origins: everyone starts to use them, and everyone gets to know what they mean. Eventually, they become design conventions in their own right.

Take for example the QuickTime interface. It doesn't take long to figure out how it works, because the main controls are designed to look just like those of a CD player. There's a slider for the volume, plus 'jump to start', 'rewind', 'play', 'fast forward', and 'jump to end' buttons.

Most media playing software uses these same symbols, because they're equally ubiquitous in the physical world of cassette players and VCRs. So, anyone who's already familiar with the standard buttons on a cassette or CD player shouldn't have too much trouble figuring out how to control a QuickTime movie – even if they've never used QuickTime before.

> *If you look under* Window > Common Libraries *in Flash MX, you can find libraries of buttons that use these control icons.*

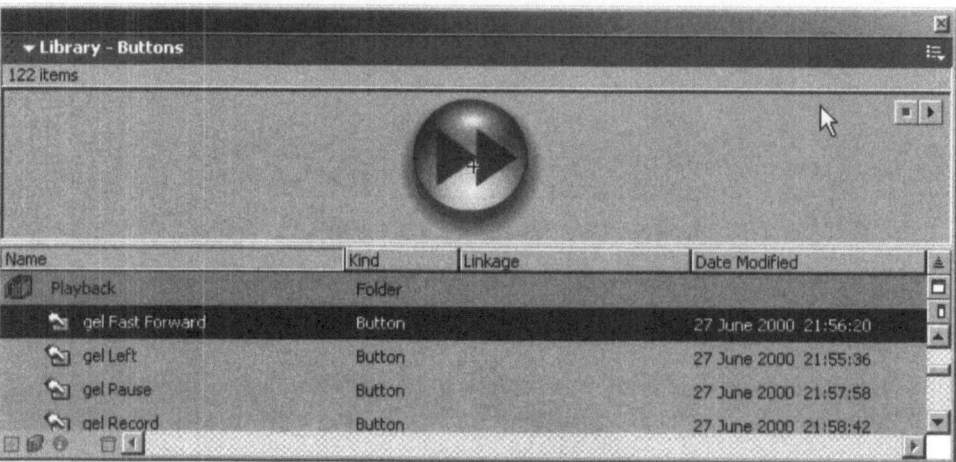

Anticipate the user

Another way to make your interface as intuitive as possible is to consider the content, features, and functions they're likely to be looking for at each stage in their experience. Essentially, you're trying to get the site to act like a personal butler, always ready with what the user asks for. That means you need to figure out what they want *before* they ask for it!

Say you're building a site that features a biography for each member of the design team. A usable site would have contact information available for each bio. If you offer up an animation, you might improve the usability by giving users a suite of controls for controlling the timeline – that's where those Flash MX libraries can come in useful!

Say your user's playing a Flash game, but they're not sure which key controls the thrusters on their star fighter. They'll want to get at the instructions good and quick, and ideally without putting their high score in jeopardy! Assuming there's a keyboard available, you can anticipate that their first action will probably be to press the 'I' key – it's 'I' for 'instructions', and that's more common sense than convention! A truly considerate designer will also realize that users probably expect the game to stop automatically at that point. It wouldn't be much of a game if you quit the instructions page to find a big 'Game Over' message plastered over the screen...

Usable interfaces also need to anticipate mistakes. Expect that users will click the wrong button, misinterpret (or just not read) something written plainly in front of them, or access features that don't actually do what they need. Mistakes are always going to happen, but **if you're** prepared for them, you can minimize the risks involved, make sure there's some kind of fix available (never underestimate the psychological power of an Undo button!) and help the user get back on track.

Ultimately, it's your job to help ensure that users don't get lost or confused while they're interacting with the content. Okay, it may not be possible to guarantee that this never happens, but by getting inside users' heads, you can significantly reduce the problems they're likely to encounter.

The first step towards doing this is to develop a user profile; that then needs to be backed up with intensive practical testing. Once we've established what we *expect* users to do, we look at what they *actually* do. We'll take a more detailed look at user profiling in the second half of this chapter; user testing will have to wait until we have something concrete to test!

Efficient

Once you've designed an easy, intuitive interface, you may think your work's done. Users can learn how to use it in no time at all, and no great mental strain is involved. Even if they do something dumb, you've already anticipated and handled it, so there's no great harm done.

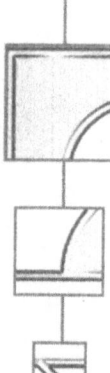

Think about a trip to a friend's house. The first time that you went to the house you probably used a map, whether visual or instructional to get there. Maybe you went online and printed out a driving map to get there, or maybe you jotted down the directions from your friend.

With subsequent trips your need for the map becomes less and less, and after time you may start taking alternate routes based on your knowledge of the area. You're looking for shortcuts to make the trip easier, and it's the same with the user's interaction with the content of a web site.

As a user's familiarity with the system grows though, there'll be less and less need for them to look and think before selecting an action. They'll start to build a mental model of the system based on how it works, rather than what it looks like. In time they'll be able to predict the outcome of any gesture in any context.

At this point, they don't really need all the super-friendly interface elements that a beginner would. In fact, they may find them quite a hindrance – nicely illustrated buttons and menus on the screen can seem really clunky if your mouse needs to take three trips across the screen and multiple clicks to achieve a simple task.

Experienced users will seek out shortcuts to allow rapid access to more powerful functions. Most desktop applications (such as Flash and Photoshop) offer familiar keyboard shortcuts for common actions. Who *doesn't* know that CTRL/CMD+X and CTRL/CMD+V will cut and paste content in most editing tools? You don't need to think about it, and you don't need to track down a couple of fiddly buttons on the toolbar every time you want to move content. You probably don't even need to look at the keyboard to find where the keys are!

The same goes for web navigation: once users know their way around a site, they won't be quite so content with the simple (and limited) navigation options you created for naïve newcomers. Ideally, they want to be able to navigate the site based on the experience they gained from using it in the past. If they have to return to the top level of content before they can access a different section, they'll just end up wasting time and probably get frustrated.

These shortcuts should be clearly displayed, so that first-time users have the same access as their more experienced counterparts, even if they choose not to use them.

Satisfying

Usability is more than just employing best practices that have worked well in the past. Usability is more than just finding a metaphor or adding shortcuts. **Usability is subjective**. Every individual who interacts with Flash content will bring his or her interpretation of how usable the content is. As Abraham Lincoln put it, "You can please some of the people some of the time, but you can't please all of the people all of the time".

When people interact with a product or system that's designed to meet their specific needs, they're likely to find the experience pleasurable. A user will get more enjoyment out of using something that they feel has been created for them. They'll be more likely to use it again, and more likely to recommend it to other people.

It's vital to keep in mind the needs of your target audience. For example, something that's geared towards children will probably have quite different design requirements than something for adults. A bicycle and a tricycle are both very similar in the sense that they provide basic transportation to their user, but their target user has very different needs. My two-year-old son, Colin, has a shiny new tricycle that suits his needs; it allows him to move about the yard without needing balance. My bicycle also allows me to move about, but my needs and skills allow the bicycle to offer features and functions that my son couldn't master.

If I were to ride my son's tricycle to the corner store for milk, it would be a long and frustrating experience. My knees and back would ache for days. My son wouldn't fare very well in the yard on my 10-speed bicycle either. Even if Colin were able to balance on my bicycle, his feet wouldn't reach the pedals. Both the bicycle and the tricycle are very satisfying to their target user, but if the user has to use the wrong product, then usability will be diminished.

What happens though, when users show up with different types of bicycles and tricycles? How do we develop content that meets the needs of the tricycle user, the 10-speed user and the BMX user? The best answer is to develop a compromise that targets the beginner and provides shortcuts to the more advanced user. Expert users won't be put off by an interface developed for a beginner if they're able to use it more efficiently.

Focus on meeting the needs of the target audience and you'll improve the overall usability of your design project (whether it's based on Flash content or otherwise). The user is more likely to enjoy the interaction experience, and is more likely to return to that experience in the future.

Usability is not for browsing

One argument that I hear from a number of Flash designers is that usability detracts from making 'cool' experiences that web surfers like to see. In some ways they're right, usability does tend to remove the fluff from Flash content and make the interactions more streamlined; but that's the point! We're developing for users who are trying to use the content that we create, and not people who are casually browsing the Web in their lunch hour, in search of something entertaining.

Walk into any retail business that uses salespeople, like an appliance store. When the salesman comes up to you and you let him know that you're 'just browsing' and have absolutely no intention of buying anything either today or in the near future, he doesn't stick around to help you browse. He's there to assist people, who are coming into the store to accomplish a task: buying an appliance. About the most that you'll get from a salesman if you say you're browsing is a polite, "Let me know if you have any questions." This is the type of attitude that we need to take with the Flash sites that we develop.

Imagine yourself as a potential customer walking into that same appliance store to buy a dishwasher. How would you feel about the business if you had to wander around the store because there was no signage or organization? Would you appreciate a salesman who first made you listen to his rendition of *What's New Pussycat* before he would help answer any questions?

> *Unless we're specifically hired to create content that entertains users who are browsing, we need to focus on users who are doing, buying, communicating. Too often, Flash designers focus on satisfying casual users, but at the expense of annoying those visitors who actually came to the site in order to accomplish a specific task.*

Let's return to our case study project, and take a look at what happens when these specific issues of usability start coming into play.

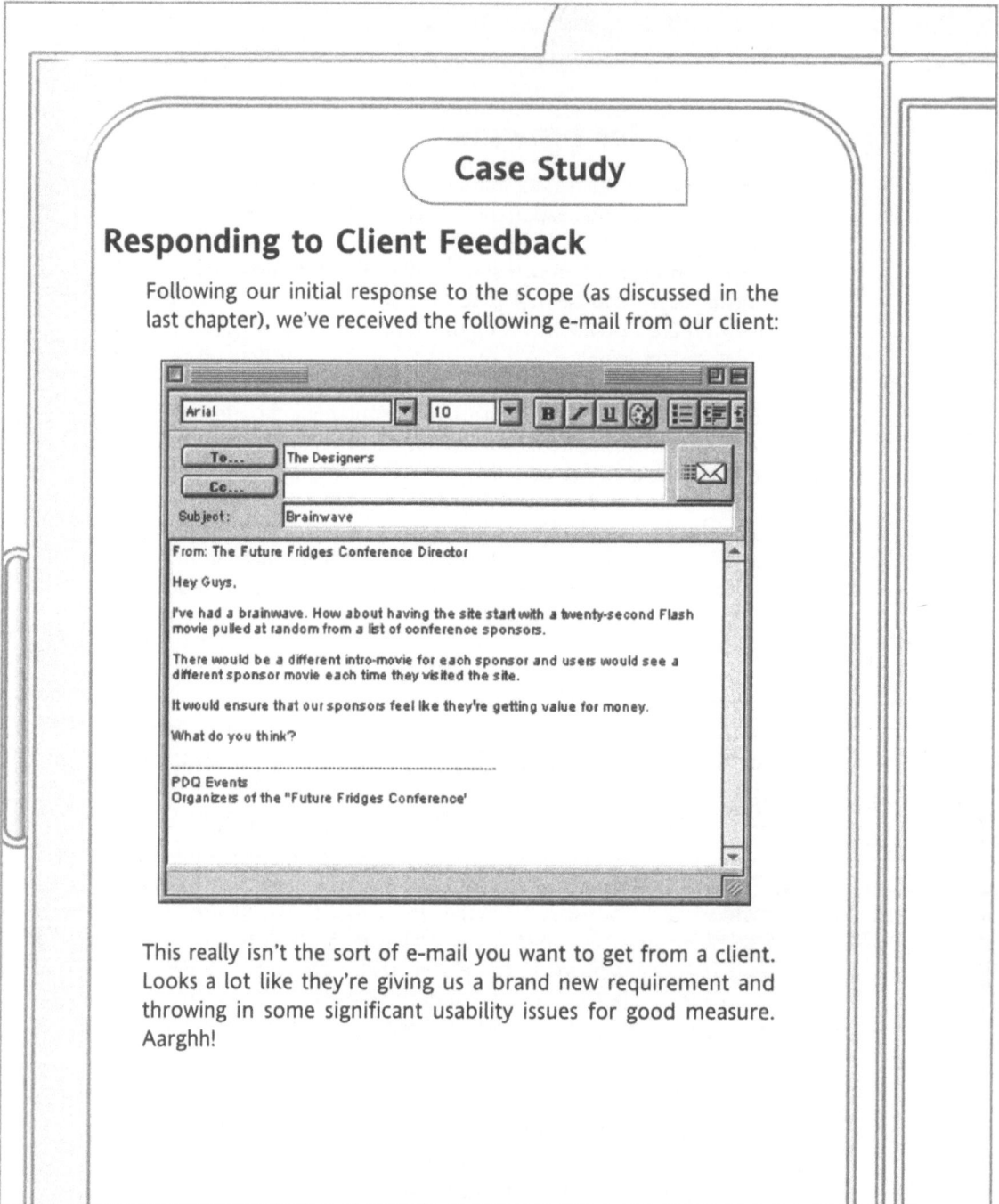

Case Study

Responding to Client Feedback

Following our initial response to the scope (as discussed in the last chapter), we've received the following e-mail from our client:

Arial   10   **B** _I_ <u>U</u>

To...   The Designers
Cc...
Subject: Brainwave

From: The Future Fridges Conference Director

Hey Guys,

I've had a brainwave. How about having the site start with a twenty-second Flash movie pulled at random from a list of conference sponsors.

There would be a different intro-movie for each sponsor and users would see a different sponsor movie each time they visited the site.

It would ensure that our sponsors feel like they're getting value for money.

What do you think?

PDQ Events
Organizers of the "Future Fridges Conference'

This really isn't the sort of e-mail you want to get from a client. Looks a lot like they're giving us a brand new requirement and throwing in some significant usability issues for good measure. Aarghh!

- Firstly, the client wants a twenty-second intro movie at the start of the site. Presumably users would see this movie before getting to the main conference information.

Chances are, they're going to visit the conference site in order to find out about the conference. So the intro movie is really just placing a **barrier** between the users and what they're trying to achieve. Twenty seconds is really quite a long time, especially when you're sitting in front of a computer. It's easily long enough for users to start wondering where else they could get the information and go to another site.

- Secondly, the intro movie isn't even going to be about the site! It will be about a sponsor, so visitors may well wonder if they've reached the right site at all. If someone arrives at a site that begins with a twenty-second animation about a fridge manufacturer, they'll probably assume that they're looking at that manufacturer's own web site. They'll ask themselves, "Whose site am I on anyway, is this really the conference web site?" So, the core intention of the site gets blurred; even when the user realizes that it *is* the conference site, they may incorrectly believe that it's the sponsor who's actually running the conference.

- Lastly, the movie is randomly displayed, so each time a user visits the site they'll think that they're on a different site. A consistent experience is critical for ensuring that a site is usable. The random intro would mean that users start the site with a different experience every time they visited.

So, how do we tell our client that this is a bad idea? The key thing to realize is that the client's aim is to please the sponsors, so we need to emphasize that adding this intro will reduce the site's usability and that won't please the sponsors. The sponsors want to be associated with a successful conference, and a less usable site will mean that fewer people will register for the conference and subsequently the conference will be less of a success.

Furthermore, users may actually get angry with the sponsor for what they would perceive as the sponsor putting their 'advertising' in the way of the site's content. Like unwanted e-mails, unwanted Flash animations typically produce resentment towards the advertiser and the user builds a negative association with the company and the site.

We would recommend to our client that there are more effective ways we can show support for the sponsors. A sponsors' section on the site could include a list of all sponsors as well as information that would be useful to users, such as details on any booths the sponsor may have at the conference and links to the sponsors' web pages. Also, the logos for major sponsors could be included within the site design.

We make these recommendations to our client who acknowledges that their number one priority is to get attendees at the conference, and so agrees to replace the sponsors' intro concept with a sponsors' section in the site.

What if the client doesn't accept our recommendation?

Sometimes it can be valuable to demonstrate the effects of usability issues to clients. If our client hadn't accepted our recommendation, we could have used the server logs for the site to demonstrate that the intro was losing the client attendees. We could track the number of users who left during the intro – that is, before they ever *reached* the main site.

For example, if one in ten visitors to the main site chose to register for the conference then you have a clear definition of how valuable each user is: every single user that leaves during the intro is losing the client potential ticket revenue.

Showing the client the daily server logs with the calculation of how many dollars worth of tickets were being lost each day would make a quite convincing argument for building a user-friendly site.

While it may be the easiest justification to demonstrate in concrete terms, it's certainly not the only one – let's explore some of the other reasons why usability's not to be sniffed at.

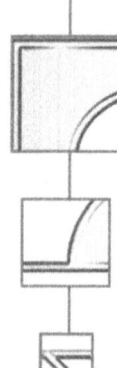

Why usability matters

Usability isn't just aimed at giving users an easier life – it wouldn't make much financial sense if that was *all* there was to it. From a commercial standpoint, that's just a means to an end: usability can be the basis for user loyalty; it can increase the user's trust in a system, brand, or product. Even more important are the detrimental effects that poor usability can have on a product, system, or brand:

- Poor usability causes a loss of communication with the user, which leads to frustration and / or abandonment of the goal

- Poor usability negatively impacts on the brand

- Poor usability causes users to explore new methods of interacting with the product or service, which leads to them 'breaking' the system

Poor usability affects communication

Flash content communicates through interaction with a user. The user makes a request of the content in the form of a menu selection or other interaction, and the Flash content answers the question through its response. If a user clicks the Locations button in a Flash site, they expect to receive information on physical locations of the company.

If the Flash content isn't clear about what types of information it offers, and how users can access it, user confusion can occur. Eventually, after enough frustration, a communication breakdown occurs. If you've seen the 'Cheese Shop' sketch from 'Monty Python's Flying Circus', then you've seen this concept taken to the extreme!

Poor usability is like a broken speaker at a fast food drive-thru. The user orders what they want from the menu, and awaits the reply from the speaker. When the resulting reply bears little resemblance to the order placed, user frustration mounts.

Some users may attempt to place their order again, and if the result is the same, they may abandon the entire transaction.

The same type of reaction occurs daily as users interact with Flash content. Poor organization, confusing menus, clunky interfaces, hyperactive animations, looping sounds, and other interactions that the user experiences can be as frustrating to a web surfer as a broken speaker at a drive-thru.

Poor usability affects the brand

The drive-thru with the broken speaker sits empty. Through experience and word of mouth, the customers of the fast food restaurant have learned to go elsewhere to get their burger and fries. Chances are, without the speaker getting fixed the restaurant will soon close down. Poor usability has affected the business. It has damaged the brand. A research study conducted by TARP Inc. (www.tarp.com), shows that customers with a positive experience will tell 5 or 6 people about their experience. People who have negative experiences tell 8 to 10 people and 10% of the unhappy users tell 20 or more people.

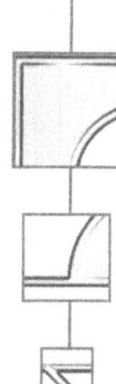

That study was done for retail businesses, where customers have to physically enter the store. It's far easier to share that bad experience online. If an online user wants to share his bad experience with everyone in his address book, it's as simple as writing a quick e-mail and clicking Send. Through the Internet, an unhappy customer can spread their opinion further and faster than ever before.

I have a friend who had an airline lose all of his suitcases on his way to speak at a conference. He shared his negative experience with the entire conference, and on his popular web site, reaching over 10,000 people in less than a week!

So, the importance of creating usable content becomes even more critical when it's online. Many products and systems on the Web rely on word of mouth to fuel growth. Good usability ensures that word of mouth will help the brand and not the opposite.

Users break the system

Poor usability does more than just interfere with communication: it encourages users to break the system. People often get frustrated when they're trying to accomplish something and no matter how hard they try they just can't seem to accomplish their goal. At a certain point some users may decide to take matters into their own hands and attempt to force the system into doing what they want. Now this doesn't mean that they'll hack into your server and start changing your files; they'll just search for a new interaction method – one that's less frustrating.

If you've ever been at the wrong end of a poorly designed phone menu system you may find yourself pressing the '0' button over and over in an attempt to get a real person on the phone. That's what I mean by breaking the system. You're not out to harm the phone system, it's just not working for you and so you look for a new method of interaction. The practice of breaking the system is the user's attempt to make something they find hard to use easier.

For example, on the Web, breaking the system may entail users entering URLs that they make up on the spur of the moment in the hope of finding pages that they're looking for. If a user can't find the contact information on a web site, they may type in www.company-name.com/contacts.html just to see if it's there.

If you have ever played with a Rubik's Cube, then you've experienced the type of frustrating usability that can lead to breaking the system. Games and puzzles all have a level of poor usability inherent in their nature. The element of mastery is part of every game from Tic-Tac-Toe to Super Mario Brothers, although that's not to say that elements of a game shouldn't be usable. Game design is a question of introducing poor usability into a controlled environment.

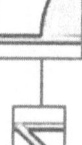

To solve the Rubik's Cube, the user needs an exceptional amount of patience and skill. With 43,252,003,274,489,856,000 possible combinations (according to the FAQ at www.rubiks.com), it could take a lifetime of twisting and turning to actually solve the puzzle. Most users don't have the patience to spend a lifetime trying to solve the puzzle, so what do they do? They look for a new interaction that they can apply to the Rubik's cube to solve the puzzle. They break outside of the approved twist and turn interaction and seek a new method.

Some of the millions of Rubik's Cube owners bought solution books; others took to a more physical interaction to achieve their goal of returning the cube to its original state. They took a screwdriver, popped a 'cubie' off and started dismantling it. Some people preferred to remove the colored stickers, but either way, the cube was broken down into easier to configure pieces and then reassembled to provide the solution. Looking smug, the user had accomplished their goal despite the usability hurdles inherent in the Rubik's Cube. The sense of accomplishment was there, however not achieved in the way that Mr. Rubik intended.

When interacting with any complex system that's not intuitive and usable, frustration mounts. Eventually the user will either seek a way to get around the hurdles that poor usability imposes, or they will simply leave, and probably never return.

The competition is just a click away...

As I mentioned before, the Internet is not a physical space. Every shoe store online is only a click away from the next shoe store. The bricks and mortar axiom, "Location, location, location", means nothing on the Internet. With prices already so low that online retailers have a hard time making ends meet, the competition focuses on delivering a usable experience.

If the site that you're working on sells anything online then usability is an essential part of every design and interactions decision made. Every part of the site should be as user-friendly as possible from the navigation to the writing of the content. Users will not feel comfortable buying anything if they don't find appropriate content relating to the object they want to buy.

With so many choices available, the user's first experience when interacting with online content will determine if they use the content again. If the user cannot accomplish his or her goal using the Flash content, they will accomplish it elsewhere. The aisles of online retail are littered with abandoned shopping carts.

The customers of the fast food restaurant were not going to go hungry at lunch because the speaker was broken! They were taking their business elsewhere. Users want to have a good experience with the Flash that they interact with. They want to feel like they're interacting with a system that cares about their needs. If attention is not paid to usability issues, the user gets the impression that the owner of the Flash site doesn't care. The end result is the user will stop communicating.

> *If we don't care about our users, we may end up with no users to care about.*

Usability is a key to success

The effects of poor usability on all aspects of the Flash content, the user's experience, and the brand provide ample justification for integrating usability principles in the design process. Just as poor usability leads to negative results from a product or system, Flash content that is developed with usability in mind offers benefits that are far-reaching:

- Benefits for business

- Benefits for your clients

- Benefits for their users

Good usability will help users achieve their goals

When a user interacts with Flash content they have a goal in mind. That goal may be to accomplish a specific task, or it could be to enjoy what the Flash content offers. Either way, the user wants their interaction with the Flash content to be simple, intuitive, and direct. The user wants to be able to accomplish their goal without frustrations.

Usable Flash content helps the user to accomplish their goal. By presenting the content in a clear, easy-to-use and understand interface, the user will be better able to make the choices needed to accomplish their goal.

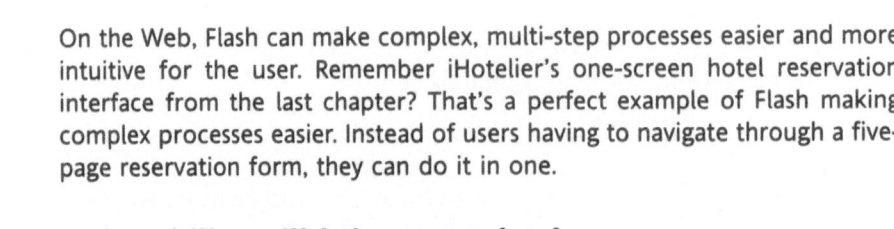

On the Web, Flash can make complex, multi-step processes easier and more intuitive for the user. Remember iHotelier's one-screen hotel reservation interface from the last chapter? That's a perfect example of Flash making complex processes easier. Instead of users having to navigate through a five-page reservation form, they can do it in one.

Good usability will bring users back

Success on the Web can mean more than just purchases made. Success is also measured in popularity, or how many individuals visit the content and how often. For sites driven by advertising revenue, attraction and retention of users are the top priorities.

If a user has problems interacting with Flash content because of usability issues, they'll be less likely to come back to that site in the future. There are so many choices on the Web that a user would rather look for a better experience than return to a bad one.

We all have a friend who expresses this desire for usability by spending fifteen minutes looking for the TV remote to change the channel when there are perfectly good buttons on the TV itself. The remote makes the TV more usable. Without the remote control can you imagine having the 100+ channels that are available today?

Perhaps a better question would be, "Would you give up your remote for 12 channels that were interesting to you?" Would you make your interactions with the TV more difficult for content of more value? Would you want to only have two small buttons on the front of the TV to navigate?

> *An intuitive, elegant interface is to Flash content what the remote is to the TV: it expands the possibilities. Users appreciate the ease in which they can interact. Once they find that sort of ease they will actively seek it out again and again. While poor usability can keep users away from the content, good usability makes them want to come back for more.*

Good usability can help to build a brand

There are web sites that have built their entire brand on being easy to use. The search engine Google built its popularity on being fast, accurate and easy to use. Amazon has always valued its users' experiences: the company's efforts to create a usable site are legendary, and the folks behind it continue striving to make their site more useful and usable by the day.

When the site was outgrowing its tabbed interface, its designers posted their potential solution and asked users for comments. While not yet a financial success, a recent study showed that one in eight online purchases are handled through Amazon.

> *Building a brand in an environment where every competitor is as accessible as you is the challenge of the Internet. Having a usable web site is the first step to building your brand online.*

Usability is such an important factor in our choice of products and services that we will pay a premium for it. For example, a cheap metal can opener costs 99¢ while the *OXO Good Grips* can opener costs $9.99. Both can openers open cans, but the *OXO Good Grips* is easier to use (see www.oxo.com for more information on the *Good Grips* can opener).

The ergonomics of the OXO can opener make using it a better experience. So users frustrated with fiddling around with a cheap can opener will pay ten times the price for one that's more usable.

> *Usability is the success vitamin for the Web. If the Flash content you develop is usable then it stands a much better chance of making an impact amongst the competition.*

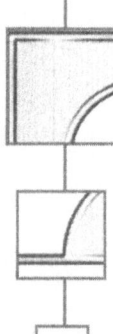

Selling usability to clients

There's a direct benefit of usability that applies directly to Flash designers who make usability an important part of their design process: it gives them an edge over those who don't.

Clients are finicky folks and, as we discuss elsewhere in this book, not always the best people to ask about the features and functions of the Flash content they're paying for. On many occasions the only factors that a client looks at when deciding between Flash designer A and Flash designer B is the proposed budgets and the portfolios of the two designers. That's not a lot of information to work from and as we know, the more informed a buyer can be, the better chance that they'll make the best decision.

Next time that you're preparing a pitch to a client make sure to include a discussion about how usability is an integral part of your design and design process. Use the examples in this chapter as talking points to bring up the issues that relate to creating usable Flash content, and why it should be a top priority for your potential client.

Share with your client that the purpose of having content on the Web is to open a new line of communication between their customers and their business. A web site with poor usability can lead to a breakdown of communications. Poor usability can lead to frustration and eventually the opportunity for any new communications will be shut down completely.

When your client's customers and potential customers visit their web site the usability of the site is the personality that the client's company has on the Web. The design is the uniform the site wears, but the user's experience with the site is the person who fills that uniform. Your client doesn't want a web site that's well dressed but with the customer service skills of bartender Moe from 'The Simpsons'. The user's experience is what affects the brand, not the design.

The Web brings with it a new paradigm of competition. Businesses are no longer competing in the same town or region; they're now competing with companies across the world. People actively seek out ways to make their lives easier, and that includes their interactions with web sites. If the client's site makes a task easier to accomplish they're more likely to find and hold onto success than one that offers no improvement to the user.

Clients who are looking to offer a service online should remember that usability *will* help improve the completion rate. When a user starts a task their natural tendency is to follow it through to the conclusion. With each hurdle that the user encounters the opportunity for frustration and eventually abandonment of the task increases. Flash content that's developed with usability as a goal will have fewer hurdles for the user. The result is that a greater number of users will be able to complete their task.

Let your clients know the benefits of good usability. Sell them on your commitment to usability and you're selling them on real benefits that clients like to see:

- Increased communication

- Increased task completion

- A better brand

These are the factors that are important in business decisions, not which Flash designer makes the best use of sound. Inform your potential clients about the importance of usability and it will be very difficult for them to justify picking an agency that doesn't care about their users.

Developing a user profile

Designers aren't like average users, but our job is to create Flash content **for** average users. Our perspective on the projects that we develop is different from the typical user, yet we're expected to create usable Flash content for those same users. Flash designers need to brush up on their ethnography and demography.

Flash designers need to begin projects by profiling the type of user who will interact with the Flash content. Flash designers need to work with their clients to research their users. We need to find dichotomies and look for metaphors that are appropriate for the target audience. Designers need to begin projects by profiling their users.

An essential ingredient in creating usable Flash content is for the designer to have a basic understanding of the end users of the content. While we as designers can't interact with the content that we develop like a user would, we can get a basic understanding of the typical user's skill level. Flash designers should first profile the targeted users for the project and the profile should be developed before any interface design starts.

> *Developing the user profile should be the first step of any project.*

By developing a profile of the Flash content's users, the Flash designer can make interaction decisions with the users in mind. The designer will then know what interface style will work best with the users. The information architect will know how to best organize the content. The storyboarder will know how to best pace the content for the profiled user.

> *The overall usability of the content will be improved if each step of the design process is guided by an understanding of the user.*

Research the users

Building the user profile starts with research. We need to find out as much as we can about who our client's customers and potential customers are. We need to research what types of interactions the users are comfortable with. We need to find out what terminology is acceptable to use with the users. We need to find out how these users currently interact with the company.

There are a number of research methods and sources for research that you can use to develop the user profile. Your client can provide you with some of the answers. They can direct you to trade shows, professional groups, and trade publications that target their customers. These events and publications provide insight into many aspects of the target user's professional life.

Your client can also be a source of information about their user, or even a direct link to the user. If possible, speak directly with the client's customers. Find out what types of services and interactions they would like to see from the project. If the client can't provide customers for research, Flash designers may find the client's sales and customer support staff excellent resources for user profiling research.

Establish dichotomies about users

The next step in building a user profile is to establish **dichotomies**. These are simple divisions to show contradictory parts or opinions: hot or cold, light or dark, you get the idea. Dichotomies help to define what type of user your content will be used by.

By establishing dichotomies about the users the Flash designer can start to think about their interface needs.

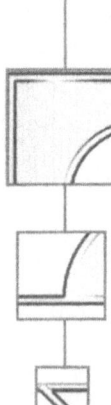

To establish dichotomies, you just need to start asking questions. Will the users who interact with this content be:

- Young or old?

- Internet newbies or experienced surfers?

- Corporate or a family audience?

- Broadband or modem?

- Men or women?

- Visually impaired or sighted?

Older users are likely to have poorer vision than a younger audience. Older users would prefer a high-contrast, easy-to-read interface, while younger users allow for more subtle design elements. Younger audiences would feel comfortable with more movement and animation than an older audience would.

Content for Internet newbies should be straightforward and require fewer decisions than content for experienced surfers. Experienced surfers will appreciate content that allows them more control. Experienced users would find a choice of launching options a part of a good user experience, while launching options may confuse newbies.

The location from where your user is visiting factors heavily into what the user expects from the content. Users interacting with content for tasks related to their job use the Internet for more task-oriented goals. Users visiting content from home may enjoy the richer experience that animation and sound can offer. The interface for a business application shouldn't have a music track, for example!

Knowing if the user visiting the site is connecting to the Internet via a broadband or modem connection seriously impacts on the entire design process. The file size of Flash content for broadband users can be ten times the acceptable download size of a modem user. Modem users will appreciate content that downloads quickly and doesn't have superficial animations, photos and / or sounds.

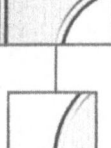

The gender of the users can be important for the user profile. A business that makes women's clothing would expect the majority of their online store's users to be female. Internet sites for sports fanatics can safely assume that the majority of their visitors will be male. Unless the content actually targets a clear majority of one sex or another it is best to design for both sexes.

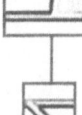

Designers should always consider users with special needs. But if we know from the start that a site is likely to have a higher than average proportion of, say, visually impaired users, we must ensure that accessibility is way up on our list of design priorities. Flash MX makes designing accessibility far easier than in previous versions of the software. We'll cover accessibility issues in Chapter 9.

Case Study

Building user profiles

The scope provided by our client contains some basic information on the types of users that will be visiting the *Future Fridges Conference* site. The target audience is described as follows:

> "...potential attendees and speakers at the conference as well as the media."

This is a useful starting point, but we'll need more detailed profiles of our users if we really want to ensure that our site meets the users' needs.

Who are our users?

Our client is the key to understanding who our users are. They'll typically have some information on who their customers are: documentation on who's buying their products or services. Orders and mailing lists can often provide valuable clues as to who and where these users might be.

Since this is the first time the *Future Fridges Conference* has been run, our client doesn't have any exact data on who'll be attending. What we have instead is a **target audience**: people who the client would *like* to be attending the conference.

Our scope identifies three key target groups:

- Potential attendees

- Speakers

- The media

Let's begin by looking at the best defined of these groups: the speakers.

Information from the client

The client can provide us with a complete list of confirmed speakers, and this will be very useful. Here's part of it:

Speaker: Dr. Steven Marr
Topic: Building a Spellchecker for Fridge Magnet Letters.
Bio: A leading magnetic robotics specialist, Dr Marr will demonstrate his amazing robotic fridge magnet letters, that use an artificial intelligence network to correct spelling mistakes.
E-mail: marr@technofridges.co.uk

Speaker: Kim Berry, M.Sc
Topic: Fridges in Antarctica
Bio: An electronic engineer for the Australian Antarctic division, Kim has pioneered the development of fridges for cold environments, where the fridge must operate when the outside environment is colder than inside the fridge.
E-mail: kb@antidivi.com.au

Speaker: Magnus Hasslemark
Topic: Audio Fridges for the Blind
Bio: Magnus' company has developed an innovative fridge that uses bar code reading technology and audio response to inform blind users exactly what's in the fridge and where.
E-mail: Hass@fridgecorp.se

This list gives us quite a few clues as to who our users are. The names and bios indicate that at least two of the speakers have a university education and all three are professionals in the high-tech fridge industry. The e-mail addresses suggest that the speakers are from the UK, Australia and Sweden respectively. Furthermore, the e-mail addresses all sound like corporate accounts, suggesting that they access the Internet from work.

So we can profile the speakers group as being professional adults with an expertise in technology, probably with tertiary education and located all around the world. They will probably access the site from a work environment, which suggests a higher speed connection to the Internet.

The most important piece of information that this list gives us is that the speakers will be from around the world. The first thing we do is to ask the client if the site will be translated into other languages. It's extremely important to establish this early in the design process, as it would affect our design process. For example, words for the same thing can have quite different lengths in different languages, which can affect the design of buttons and navigation elements.

The client decrees that the site will only be in English because the conference will be held entirely in English, but also points out that they've had early enquires from all over Europe, the US and the Middle East, implying that the site will definitely have an international audience. This further emphasizes why a usable site is so important. Our users will have different cultural backgrounds and different English language skills and thus will require a site that's very clear and intuitive.

Clues from marketing

To get more of a feel for our users, particularly the attendees, we ask the client about the marketing for the conference. We can find out a lot about our users by learning where they heard about the site.

The client plans to take out a number of full-page ads in the leading high-tech fridge trade magazine. They also plan to advertise in a number of English newspapers, a US design magazine, on a portal web site, and on an e-mail list dedicated to the fridge industry.

They've sent promotional materials about the conference to a number of media companies and universities. The promotional material sent to universities included a poster advertising a student discount, which they asked to be placed near student notice boards.

This gives us some more information on our users. Importantly, we know that some of the users may be students, who typically have slower Internet connections but a high familiarity with the Web. We buy up all of the publications that the client will be advertising in, as these will give us an insight into the background of the users. Reading through the publications that the client will advertise in gives us a feel for our users, what they're interested in, and especially what visual styles, terminology, and metaphors they would be familiar with.

> *Sometimes it's a good idea to cut out some pictures of people who represent your users and stick them near your computer to remind you that the site is being built for these people – and not for us!*

Let's have a look at a newspaper advertisement for the conference:

Future Fridges
the world's leading conference on high-tech home fridges

find out more at www.fridgecon.com

Three days of in-depth workshops and educational seminars on development and innovation in the home fridge industry

featuring
Dr Marr of Techno-fridges
and
Magnus Hasslemark
of Fridge corp

The main text used in the advertising is quite brief, just one sentence about the conference, the site URL and a list of two keynote speakers. The advertising tells us the main motivation for users visiting our site: **to find out more**. There's not a lot of hype in this advertisement: if you weren't interested in high-tech fridges you'd probably ignore it. Which means that the users that do visit the site are people who are interested in high-tech fridges and they're already thinking, "This may be relevant to me". A key role of the site must be to provide sufficient information to convince them that the conference *is* relevant to them.

There's also another very useful clue in this advertisement. The speakers are listed with their associated company. This tells us something important about how our users think. The users view the speakers and their company as interlinked pieces of information:

- Some users may know the speakers by name

- Some may not know them but will know their company

- Some may recognize the name, but only 'place it' when it's associated with the company

This will directly affect how we design the interface, as we'll need to accommodate all three types of user.

Users from the media

Our client also expects members of the media to visit the conference web site. They've sent press kits on the conference to a number of publications and television stations in the hope that they'll do a story on the conference. Our client can provide us with a complete list of the media organizations that have been sent marketing materials, so we have a clear list of this segment of the audience as we did with the speakers.

In most cases journalists will have good language skills, a fast Internet connection, and a familiarity with the Web. We can assume that journalists will be visiting the site with the aim of finding out more about the conference so they can make a decision on whether to do a story on it. We discover that the list of journalists sent marketing materials includes both print and television journalists.

This difference is important, as journalists from different media will use different criteria to decide if they do a story on the conference. Print journalists will be looking for a newsworthy announcement to write about, while the television journalists will be looking for a visual element to their story: something to *show* their viewers.

Recognizing these user motivations will help us build a site that is focused on answering the users' questions, to easily provide them with exactly what they came to the site to find.

Building a dichotomy

We're starting to build up some excellent background on our users. The next step is to work through a dichotomy with our client. Will the users who interact with this content be...

- **...children or adults?** It's expected that most users will be between twenty and sixty years old. Children are not expected to access the site.

- **...internet newbies or experienced surfers?** The users who are students or part of the media will likely be experienced Internet users. The other users will probably be people with a technical background but not necessarily a familiarity with the Web.

- **...corporate or family audience?** Mostly a corporate audience as this is a professional conference targeted at professionals.

- **...broadband or modem?** It's likely that a majority of users will access the site from a work environment, which would normally suggest a high-speed connection. However, the international nature of the audience means that we can't rely on this, as the availability of broadband varies across the globe. Furthermore our student audience will probably access the site from home modem accounts.

- **...men or women?** Our client is able to tell us that of their initial enquiries about 70% have been male and 80% of their speakers are male.

- **...informed or ignorant?** Do our users know anything about the conference or web site before visiting? The advertising provides very limited information so most users will be largely ignorant about the conference and what little information they do have is about the conference not about the site. They'll probably have no idea what the site will be like before they arrive.

- **...wealthy or not so wealthy?** Most of our users are professionals, and so the relevance and timing of the conference will be more important than cost. However, the users that are students will probably be very concerned about the affordability of the conference and getting value for money.

User profile overview

The results of our investigations let us put together an overview of who our users are. They fall into three groups:

- Speakers

- Potential attendees (some students, some professionals)

- The media

We need to build a site that works well for **low bandwidth users**, as we can't rely on our users having high-speed connections. Any high bandwidth content such as video will need to be available in a format that will work for modem users.

While our users will all have a familiarity with technology, we can't assume that all users will have a good familiarity with the Web, thus the site will need to be **clear and highly intuitive**.

Users from all three groups will be accessing the site to gain more **information** on the conference:

- Potential attendees and media will both want to determine if the conference is worth attending.

- Potential attendees will have seen advertising material that has raised their awareness of the conference and are accessing the site to find our more about the conference. The advertising has not given them enough information to make a decision on whether to attend. They'll be looking to the site to give them information on what the conference covers, who's speaking, the time, location, and cost of the conference.

- The media will want it to answer the question, "Is this of interest to my readers/viewers?"

- Conference speakers accessing the site won't be concerned with the location, cost or whether they should attend. However they may be visiting the site to find information about other speakers, sponsors, the venue layout, and session timetables.

Sample users

Using the previous information we can put together some sample users for our site. These are just fictional users that we invent to give us a feel for our users and to provide us with a mechanism to test our Information Architectures and navigation structures.

Name: **Joel**
Description: Thirty-nine-year-old male who works as a manager of research and development for a US fridge manufacturer.
Goal: Joel has seen an advertisement for the conference in the trade press and is looking for more information.

He's already confident that the conference will be relevant to him, but wants to know which companies are speaking and when the conference is being held to determine if he will attend.

Name: **Bronwyn**
Description: A twenty-four-year-old who works as a buyer for a major UK department store. Her job involves making decisions on what products the department store will stock.
Goal: Bronwyn has seen an advertisement for the conference in a UK newspaper. She's visiting the site from work to determine if the conference will give her an insight into new developments in the high-tech fridge industry. At present she's quite unsure about whether the conference is relevant to her.

Name: **Luigi**
Description: A twenty-one-year-old final-year electronic engineering student in Italy. He has recently completed a research paper that referenced the work of one of the keynote speakers.
Goal: Luigi saw a poster advertising the conference at university and is accessing the site from his home modem connection. He's extremely excited about the conference but wants to know the time, location, and cost for the conference, as these will affect his decision to attend.

Name: **Thomas**
Description: A researcher for a UK television network. He's responsible for recommending stories for a weekly half-hour technology and science program.
Goal: Thomas wants to establish if any part of the conference will be of interest to his viewers. He's especially looking to see if there will be any newsworthy

announcements, prototype product demonstrations or exciting keynote presentations.

Further along the line, we can keep these sample users in mind while putting together navigation designs and Information Architecture, asking ourselves specific questions like:

- Will this design assist or hinder Bronwyn in completing her goal?

- Can Thomas easily find the content that's relevant to him?

- Will Luigi be able to access this site quickly and easily?

Summary

Before you start designing a usable site, it's important to be clear about what goals you're trying to achieve with this nebulous 'usability' thing. Saying you want to give users a better experience is one thing, but *doing it* is quite another, and convincing your clients that it's worth a little extra time and effort is tougher still.

Figuring out whether any product or system is usable involves looking at several factors:

- Is it easy to start using?

- Is it memorable?

- Is it intuitive?

- Is it efficient?

- Are users ultimately satisfied?

For a project that's still in the planning stages, these aren't questions you can answer definitively. However, you can use them to judge how design changes are likely to influence your site's final usability. The next step is to identify and profile your expected users; then you can establish what they want from the site, and begin to practically interpret each of the five factors above.

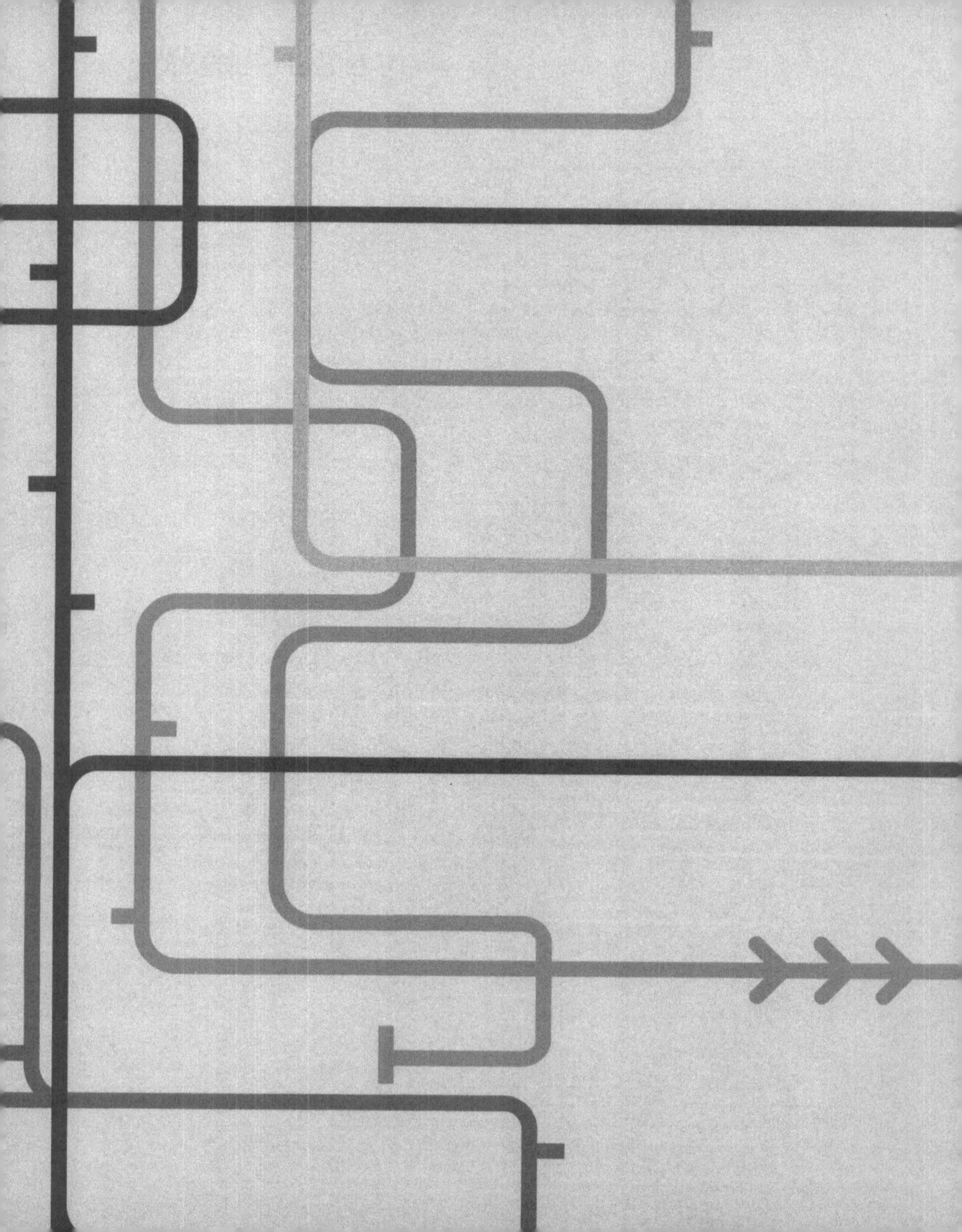

Conventions and metaphors

If there's one thing that makes users feel more comfortable with an interface than any other factor, it's a sense of **familiarity**. The effectiveness of design conventions for better usability hinges on the notion that users like to know instinctively what each interface element will do without having to test out their hunch and risk making a mistake.

Street signs are a familiar, real-world example of human interface design – they work because they're familiar, and they're familiar because they're standardized. While they may change from one country to the next, most people traveling in their own area will usually see the same range of traffic signs, streetlights, and directional signs wherever they go.

Red 'STOP' signs like the one shown above are one very common convention. Most people could probably guess what it meant even if the word 'STOP' weren't emblazoned on the sign, and even if you didn't drive a vehicle. Similarly, most people will recognize a green symbol as signifying 'GO', a silhouette of a stick figure wearing a skirt as signifying a women's restroom, and a red circle with a line through it as signifying 'forbidden'.

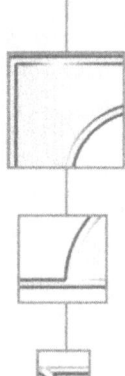

> *Of course, if the rules change, an over-reliance on the familiar may prove dangerous. I'm from the US, where cars drive on the right-hand side of the road. Before crossing a street, I normally look left to see if any cars are coming – if not, I start walking. In the UK, cars drive on the left-hand side of the street, so on my first trip to London, I was more than grateful to find 'LOOK RIGHT' painted on the ground at pedestrian crossing zones! Without that reminder, who knows what might have happened...*

So what does all this have to do with the Web and Flash usability? Simple. If your site design features elements and functionality that a user can recognize, they'll probably find it easier to use. They'll therefore have a better experience and spend more time there. If you're careless though, and misuse established conventions, you can cause confusion and mistakes – though probably not car accidents...

Lessons from history

Let's look at a few examples of how familiarity can impact on users' perceptions of a system.

Learning curve

When I worked in an office back in the days of DOS-based software, the two word processors that dominated the market and our office computers were WordStar and Microsoft Word. There was great debate over which program to standardize on.

Neither had a sexy interface, and both had tons of commands that you either memorized or referred to in the 60-pound reference manual always kept close at hand. There were strings of commands to type in order to make a word bold or underlined, and even more if you wanted something bold *and* underlined. Folks who loved WordStar would swear by it. Those that loved Word did likewise.

So, each one had its own particular advantages, but both had a *very* steep learning curve. It made perfect sense for individuals to want their favorite program to 'win' the standardization race: they'd have invested lots of time and energy in learning how to create even the simplest document. However the feature sets compared, users would root for the package they felt most comfortable using – the **most familiar** one.

Trust

The introduction of ATM machines gives us another case of familiarity winning out over design. You may recall how uncomfortable many people initially felt about using them. Never mind convenience or ease-of-use, this was something totally new, and what's more, it meant trusting our hard-earned cash to a machine. What if we deposited our paycheck and it got caught up and chewed to pieces in some hidden gear inside the machine?

People now use them without a second thought. I deposit a check and rarely worry about it getting eaten by the machine, since I've never heard of it happening in the years I've used ATMs. I still don't know how the innards of an ATM work, but now they're such a common feature, trust has grown from common experience, reputation, and familiarity.

Speaking of ATMs, here's another example of familiarity and usability clashing. All the ATMs I use have their keypads set up like this:

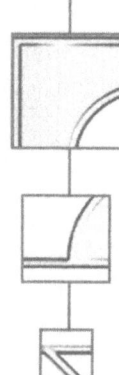

	ABC	DEF
1	2	3
GHI	JKL	MNO
4	5	6
PQRS	TUV	WXYZ
7	8	9
	0	

However, when I go to the grocery store, the debit card machine is set up like this:

	0	
PQRS	TUV	WXYZ
7	8	9
GHI	JKL	MNO
4	5	6
ABC	DEF	
1	2	3

What do you think I start to do when I'm asked for my password? That's right, I almost always start to type it in upside-down. I sometimes wonder if I'm the only person who makes this mistake – I wouldn't have thought so!

Portability

Conventions are, by their very nature, portable. Virtually anyone who's used a software application in the last few years will have experienced a graphical user interface of some sort. The success of the Macintosh operating system bred the rush to other visual operating systems such as Tandy's Deskmate, Geoworks, and of course, Microsoft Windows.

Suddenly, it became commonplace to find floppy and hard disks represented as (and accessed through) tiny images of disks, documents as sheets of paper, and directories as manila folders. We take these symbols for granted

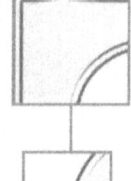

now – most people know what they mean, and what will happen if they're clicked or double-clicked upon. It doesn't matter what operating system you're using – if you're familiar with one, you won't be totally stumped when confronted with another.

Similarly, when the Web began to take off in the mid-nineties, it didn't take long for users to get used to a standard set of navigation buttons on whatever browser they happened to use.

A preference for Netscape Navigator or Microsoft Internet Explorer may well just be based on familiarity – because you've used one more than the other. The icons used on their buttons are something we quickly get used to: they're familiar representations of the actions each will perform if we click on it. Each browser gives users the option to turn off the words or the icons (or leave them both on, as shown), and navigate using whichever cues they find most helpful.

The success of these iconic interfaces stems from users' familiarity with the symbols used and the objects or actions they represent. Just as in real life, folders are used to store away files, and a trashcan is where you put things you want to throw away.

Aside from the occasional legal wrangle over copyright infringement, this standardization has been good for just about everyone. Programs on different platforms use the same (or at least very similar) commands to Save, Print, Select All, Undo, and so on.

Even a relative novice knows that most programs react to the same keyboard commands in the same way, or that clicking on the File menu will get them access to functions such as Open and Save. The Edit menu will almost always have entries for Cut, Copy, and Paste. We take it for granted – and it works.

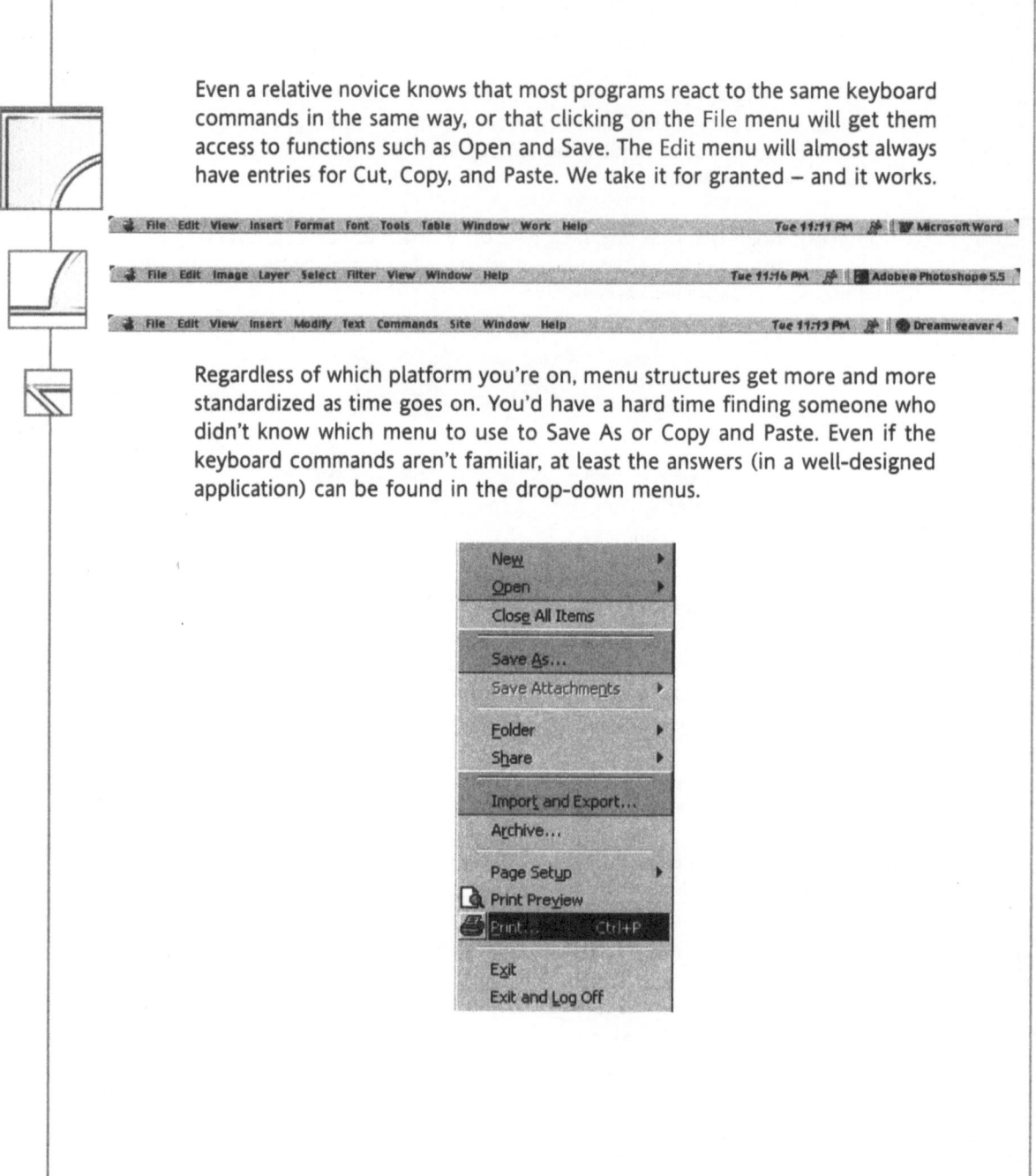

Regardless of which platform you're on, menu structures get more and more standardized as time goes on. You'd have a hard time finding someone who didn't know which menu to use to Save As or Copy and Paste. Even if the keyboard commands aren't familiar, at least the answers (in a well-designed application) can be found in the drop-down menus.

How can we make things seem familiar?

If you look back at the last example, you'll see there are two important concepts that contribute to the overall sense of familiarity:

- **Standardization** – keeping things as consistent as possible

- **Representation** – using real-world metaphors and imagery to connect with users' common experiences

Let's look at them each in more detail.

Standardization

On the Web, good navigational design weighs its success heavily on consistency. Roger Parker, author of the bestselling *Looking Good in Print* states that:

> Style reflects on the way you handle elements that come up again and again. Part of a document's style is decided from the beginning. The rest emerges as the document develops visually.

> Consistency is a matter of detail. It involves using restraint in choosing typefaces and type styles, and using the same spacing throughout your document.

Parker's book was written back in 1983, and discusses print design. However, his point stands true whether it's paper or Flash. You don't need to use the same icons or metaphors as everyone else, but you have to be consistent within the sites that you create. If users are asked to use your new navigational structure when they first come to a site, then you have to earn their trust. If an icon of a centipede takes them to one page, then the next time they click on the centipede it should take them to that same page.

Finding Conventions

We know that conventions are important, but how do we recognize them and apply conventions to our Flash design? Well, the best way to find conventions is by surfing the Web. Stop looking at the content that *you've* developed and start looking at other sites. Visit some of the most popular sites on the Web and analyze them to find which areas are similar.

- When a user visits other Flash content on the Web, do they experience any similar interactions?

- Are navigation elements on Flash pages usually located in similar areas of the design?

- How does the user interact to read text content? Do buttons look the same?

Asking yourself questions like these will help you to identify conventions that may apply to the Flash content you're designing. Of course, there are a number of conventions that we see every day in Flash content. The 'Skip intro' button is an example of a convention in Flash design.

Unfortunately the intro movie itself has become a convention of sorts on Flash sites. If a client insists on an intro movie on their site, offer the user the opportunity to skip it. Another convention is the speaker icon, used to denote audio controls.

Representation

As we've seen, other common icons include navigation arrows (for back and forward), magnifying glass (for search), a disk (for files), question mark (for help), a pen and paper (for sending feedback or signing a guest book), and so on.

These icons represent conventions in their own right, but the reason they're so successful is that they serve as a **metaphor**, representing something we know about from our everyday experience. There may be little or no learning involved on the part of a user if our design requires them to click on a familiar icon to achieve a certain task.

> *Use of metaphors and imagery in your designs can be very potent in its own right, whether or not the elements you create correspond to any established conventions.*

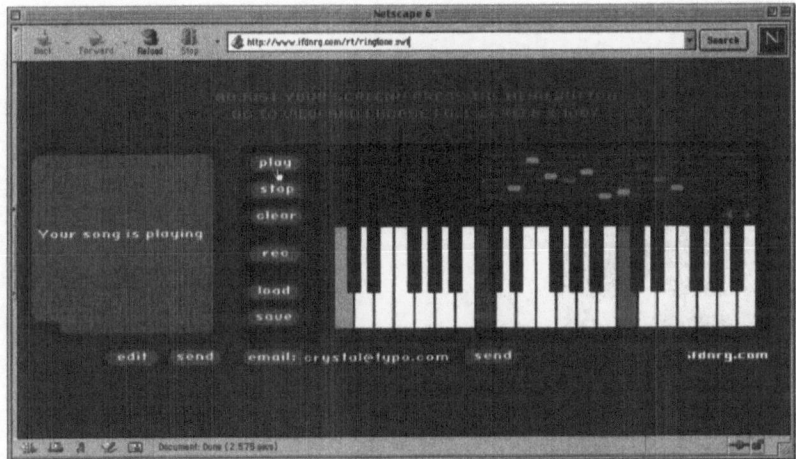

The Buildatone.com (www.ifdnrg.com/rt/ringtone.swf) experiment lets you create and download custom ring tones for your Nokia Communicator 9200 Series handset. It uses the metaphor of a piano keyboard to make the interaction as intuitive as possible.

Don't forget to offer an explanation

It's practically guaranteed that people will know what to do if faced with 'Back' and 'Forward' arrows. But what if you actually want your site to look different to everyone else's? That's fine, as long as you're willing to give explanations for your icons.

Even if you find that you're using a site's navigation via visual icons that you've grown used to, many developers include a one- or two-word explanation of the icon. If you hate the idea of soiling your icons with words, include an easily accessible "How to navigate our site" or "What our icons mean" area. Make it accessible from every page if you can.

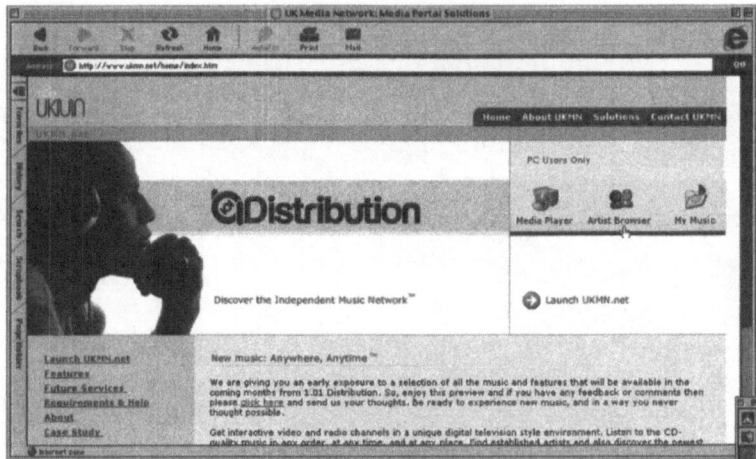

UKMN.net (www.ukmn.net) introduces its features with its own icons. By themselves, without at least this initial introduction with a couple of words to let us know what the icons mean, we'd be left in the dark.

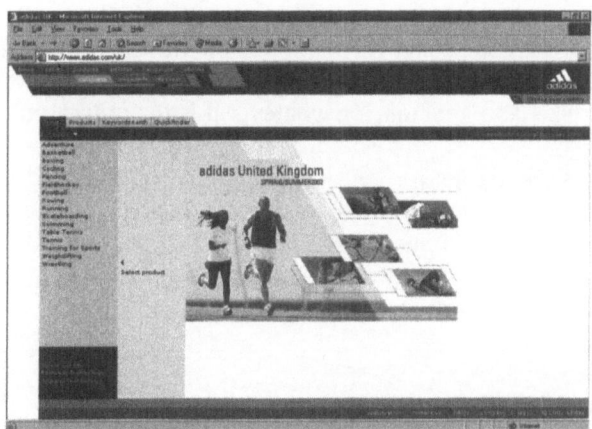
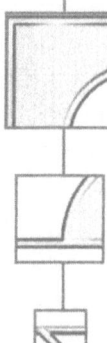

Adidas UK (www.adidas.com/uk/) uses small photos of sportsmen as icons to represent the product lines that you'll find out about if you click on them.

Will the user 'get' it?

Generally speaking, metaphor in visual design is defined as a familiar image that portrays actions or activities that work the same (or similar) to a represented real-world item. As we saw back in Chapter 4, the interface of the QuickTime Player is familiar to anyone who's used a CD player, because it uses that device as a metaphor. Buttons for 'Play', 'Fast Forward', 'Pause', and so on do just what users expect them to do, based on their prior experience with CD players and VCRs.

A computer desktop with its pieces of paper, file folders, or software that look like their tangible counterparts *are* their tangible counterparts, metaphorically speaking. We write documents, save and organize in folders, just like we do with papers and manila folders. So these items have to look like, act like, and generally *be* whatever it is they represent.

The icons you design for your client's projects don't have to be folders and disks, but the theme (or the metaphor) you decide on should be relevant to the site's message. I can make some very clever musical chickens wearing cowboy boots, but if I expect them to fly on an online banking interface, I'm in the wrong business.

> *Relevance to the market is key, because those visitors interested in the site content will more likely be familiar with the premise.*

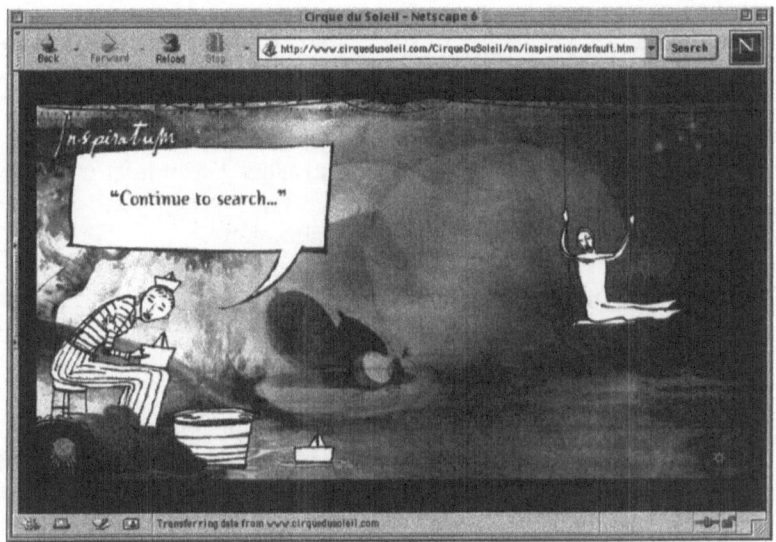

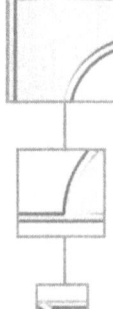

*Cirque du Soleil (*www.cirquedusoleil.com*) uses its familiar dancers and performers, as well as unique treasure-search 'intuitive' navigational schemes. Both work for this site.*

Finding your user's design

Research into possible interface and organization metaphors is an important part of a user profile. To develop an interface that's intuitive and memorable, it helps to know what interfaces and terminology the users are familiar with.

The user profile should include any types of interfaces that the user would frequently interact with. An obvious example is that a user profile for a cooking site would include a number of interfaces with which its users would most likely have experience of interacting with: ovens, stoves, microwaves, and mixers for example. The cooking site's visitors would also be

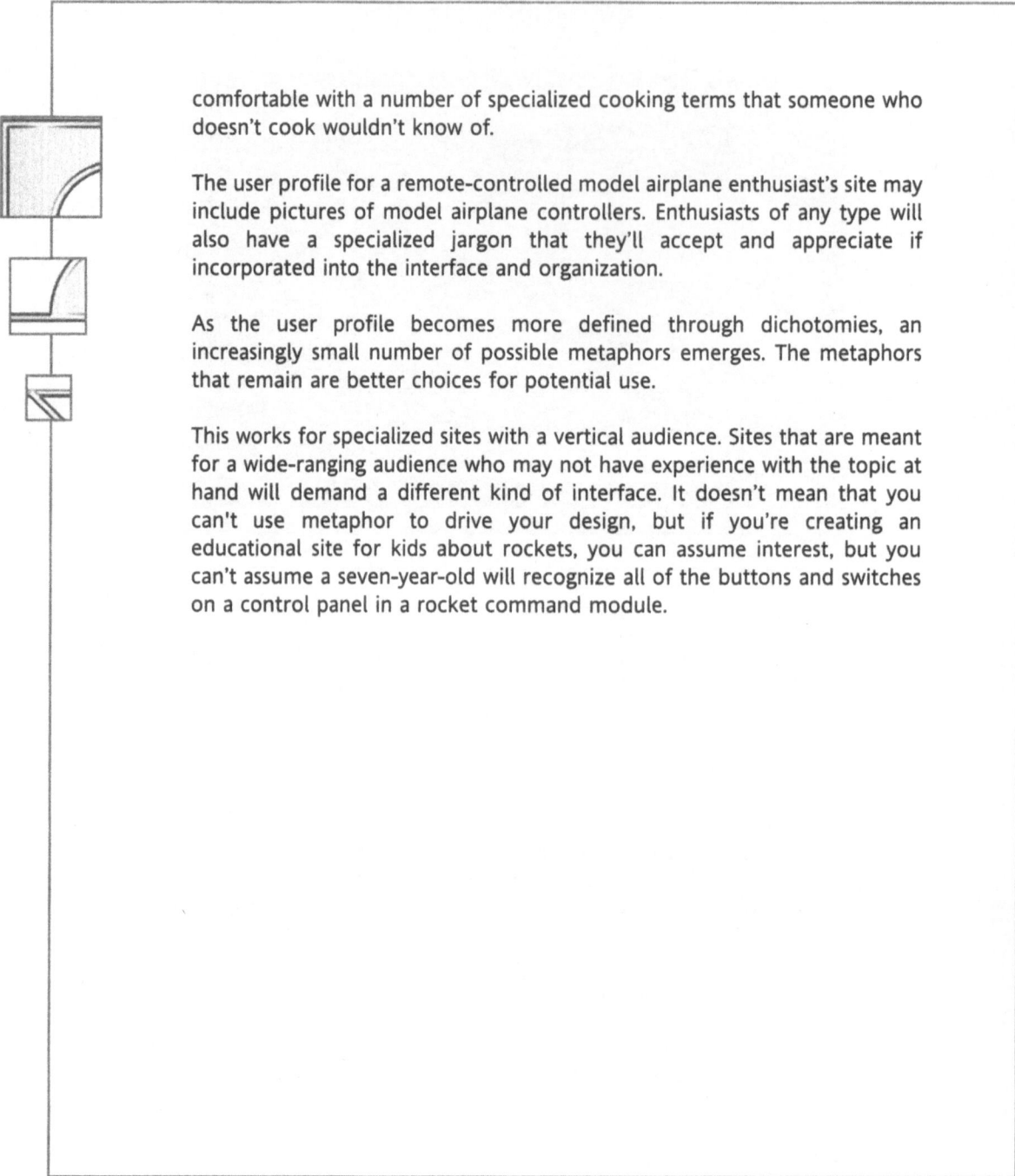

comfortable with a number of specialized cooking terms that someone who doesn't cook wouldn't know of.

The user profile for a remote-controlled model airplane enthusiast's site may include pictures of model airplane controllers. Enthusiasts of any type will also have a specialized jargon that they'll accept and appreciate if incorporated into the interface and organization.

As the user profile becomes more defined through dichotomies, an increasingly small number of possible metaphors emerges. The metaphors that remain are better choices for potential use.

This works for specialized sites with a vertical audience. Sites that are meant for a wide-ranging audience who may not have experience with the topic at hand will demand a different kind of interface. It doesn't mean that you can't use metaphor to drive your design, but if you're creating an educational site for kids about rockets, you can assume interest, but you can't assume a seven-year-old will recognize all of the buttons and switches on a control panel in a rocket command module.

Case Study

Design conventions

What design conventions can we make use of in the *Future Fridges Conference* site?

Conventions for multimedia content

The most obvious design convention that can be used on our site is the 'play, pause, stop' metaphor for video and audio content. Almost every application and site that includes video or audio content provides users with cassette player-style buttons, which let the user start, stop and pause the content. Even the buttons' icons are almost always the same: a triangle for play, square for stop and two lines for pause. This is a powerful and familiar design convention and we can make use of it.

This may seem so obvious that we think that it's impossible to build an interface for video or audio content that isn't usable. Yet it happens all the time, users often get confused if it isn't clear whether the content is loading or is paused, hence they may repeatedly press the play button when the content is still loading in. What we need to do is make sure that the user is getting feedback on what's happening so that they know if the content is loading, playing, paused or stopped.

It will also be valuable to let users know the length of the content and how much they've viewed or heard. There are two common design conventions for this. First, to use a timer display which shows the length of the content and how much has been played, for example, we'd represent that we're 23 seconds into a two-and-a-half-minute video by '0:23 / 2:30'. Or alternatively we could use a slider progress bar, which gives users a visual representation of how much of the content they've viewed as well as providing them with a tool to navigate the content.

RealJukebox has a slider progress bar to allow users to navigate audio content as well as making use of the standard button conventions.

Conventions for the session planner

The session planner component of the site is also somewhere where we can make use of some design conventions. The session planner is a relatively unusual concept, it's something users may not have seen on a web site before and so it's important that we make the interaction with the planner as familiar and intuitive as possible. We can draw on the design conventions of calendars and diaries in our interface for presenting the session content.

Using metaphors within the design process

Metaphors can be very a powerful way to communicate a lot of information very quickly and very succinctly. They can also help to focus your mind on the most effective way to tackle a problem; as such, they can be very useful to us as designers too.

I recently wrote a white paper on Flash usability for Macromedia, in which I likened the process of creating usable Flash content to arranging a vacation for someone. If you want to read the white paper in full, you can find it at www.flazoom.com/usability, but I'll go through the main points here.

The journey metaphor for creating usable Flash

The first step is to picture yourself as a travel agent. The client arrives at your agency with a big pile of cash, which is yours on condition that you put together a holiday package that takes in the sights and sounds of his local town – an ailing economy in a small mid-Western state, let's say.

Assuming you accept his offer, it's your job to gather together information on all those local sights and sounds, present them as an appealing package, and attract would-be vacationers.

Of course, if you want to preserve your professional reputation, you'll need to arrange suitable transport for the travelers who choose this package, as well as things like accommodation and insurance. Ultimately, your aim is to make each traveler's journey as smooth and comfortable as you possibly can, while ensuring they pay a visit to your client's town and spend a few bucks while they're there.

> *The clients are paying for the trip: they want users to arrive at the final destination. The designer is a travel agent whose job it is to get users going there. The user is a traveler.*

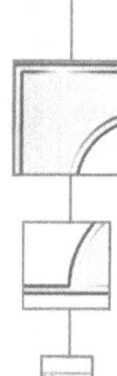

We can think of our content as being like the vacation package, marking out a roadmap, making sure there's always some way to get from A to B. There's a starting point, roads to travel along the way, and a final destination.

Our user's interaction with the content is equivalent to the traveler's *actual experience* of that journey. In real life, attractions get closed, flights get cancelled, people get ill. A bad travel agent may well just say, "Not my problem". A good one would do what they could to fix the problem – or have a contingency plan ready and waiting.

Likewise, if you think about the range of possible user interactions while you're designing a site, you can make sure there are safeguards in place before anything has a chance to go wrong. We can't control what the user (or traveler) does, but we can do our best to accommodate what they *might* do.

Using the journey metaphor

So what practical use is this? Well, we can use it to take familiar notions of 'customer satisfaction' from the real-world experience of going on vacation, and apply common sense to help us spot where things could go wrong on our Flash projects.

For a start, we can use it to help justify the issue of usability itself. It's fairly obvious that most people find a journey that runs smoothly more enjoyable than one that's fraught with problems and delays. For a good travel agent, this isn't negotiable, nor is it something that can be ignored until the last minute. The same goes for designers and usability, which ought to be an objective of any project right from the beginning, rather than something we tack on at the end.

It's a designer's responsibility to make the journey through their Flash content as enjoyable as possible, eliminating all possible delays and problems. In doing so he's making the content as usable as possible. If users give up on the journey or arrive at the destination late and frustrated, then the overall success of the project is diminished.

Meeting the client's goal

The client's goal is the end destination of the user's journey. Meeting this goal is why they hired the designer. Clients are goal-oriented. Of course, they may not seem so at first glance; but in their world, nothing gets done unless there's a specific need for it.

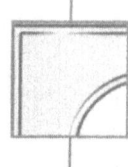

When someone hires you to work on a web design project, they're essentially asking you to help them achieve a specific practical goal. Their goal may be as broad as "give the company an online presence", or a better-defined "provide online information about the company's products and services to our users". Alternatively, it could be "collect the names and addresses of our customers for use in marketing strategies".

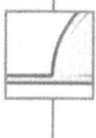

The user's goal – that is, their reason for spending time interacting with the content – is another matter entirely. As we all know, users like to do their own thing. There can be just as many reasons for a user to interact with a web site as there are different users visiting it. Some may be browsing the Web and stumble across the site at random, while others will be looking for a specific bit of information. Hopefully some will even be making a return visit, and already know what they want and how to find it.

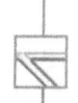

What the user wants (and how badly they want it) is ultimately going to determine just how much work they're prepared to put into using your site. If they're casual visitors, surfing at random around the Web, a long intro movie might well be enough to put them off your site. If they're after something more specific (especially if they know they can't get it anywhere else), they're more likely to persevere through any number of obscure, unfriendly interfaces.

Whatever reason the user has for interacting with the Flash content, we still have a job to do for our client: we must entice users into helping the client achieve their goal. The client's goal for the project is the destination of a

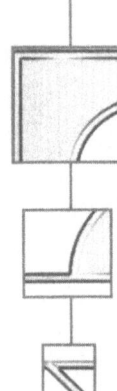

user's journey. It's the place to which we travel agents of the design world are asked to convey the user. We ultimately need to focus the varying user goals towards our client's goal for the content. To do this there are a number of factors that we should consider:

- **Determine where you're headed.** The client and the developer need to identify the primary goal for the content. The destination the client wishes the user to reach is the primary goal for the Flash content.

- **Determine what will motivate the user to take the trip.** Understanding user goals is futile without extensive research. A better strategy is to develop an offer to drive the user towards their goal.

- **Decide how the journey will be made.** The developer should decide the format for the content based on the goals. Decide whether Flash is the best format for the content.

- **Map out the trip.** Create a list of tasks the user will be required to complete to accomplish the goal or reach the destination of the journey. The developer should consider a number of different routes that the user could take.

- **Make the journey as short as possible.** Apply usability ideas to the content to make the user's tasks easier. Group similar tasks together and remove as many steps as possible.

- **Watch users make the journey.** User testing on actual end-users is a very effective method for discovering usability defects. A simple, well-prepared testing plan will suffice to provide the developers ample feedback. We discuss user testing Flash content in greater detail in Chapter 12.

So let's see how we can apply the journey metaphor to our case study. We'll have a look at our client's goals for the project.

Case Study

Client goals

The overarching goal is for the conference to be a success and hence the goal for the web site is to assist in making the conference a success. To make the conference a success, the web site needs to meet some specific goals.

Allow users to register online. The client expects that most users will register online, so if this goal isn't achieved then the conference will definitely not be a success.

Provide information on the conference. This seems like a very obvious goal for the site, but it's worth looking a little deeper into it. Why is the client providing this information? Our client wants to promote the conference to convince users to attend. But also they want to provide users with answers to any questions they might have so as to reduce the number of enquiries from potential attendees. Our client doesn't want the conference staff to spend time answering questions that could easily be answered on the web site.

Provide a session planner application. Our client wants to provide a useful service to the conference attendees to allow them to plan and print out which conference sessions they wish to attend. Why is the client providing this service? Our client will be providing attendees with something extra for their ticket price, but also plans to use this tool to track which sessions users are planning to attend. If the number of attendees at each session is known, it will help ensure that enough seating is provided so that popular sessions don't become overcrowded. Furthermore, users will be attending the conference with a custom session timetable on hand, which should reduce the number of enquiries that the conference staff have to manage.

Provide video or audio interviews with keynote speakers. This is an important client goal because it will promote the conference speakers. Users will watch or listen to the keynote speakers and be inspired to attend the conference to hear more.

So what is our content?

We can use these goals to establish what content will make up the site.

To meet the registration goal we'll need to create a registration form. Our client has identified the following as the data that the form *must* collect:

- First and last names

- E-mail address

- Street address

- Phone number

- Credit card details

The actual information on the conference that the client wishes to provide is:

- The conference vision and the conference organizers and partners

- Overview of the conference and highlights

- The conference date, location and cost

- The program and seminar details including detailed session descriptions

- The conference location and venue (including a map of the venue)

- Travel and hotel information

- Sponsors' information

- Contact information

This content is provided to us by the client in the form of a Word document.

The speaker interviews consist of one video file (MPG format) and three audio files (MP3 format).

The content for the session planner is the session and speaker details. At present this content is structured as paragraphs of text in a Word document.

It's important to realize that none of this content is in its final format. The content will need to be restructured and reformatted to be a part of our site. Furthermore we need to carefully consider how we present this content, so as to ensure that the site is easy to use and that our client's goals are met.

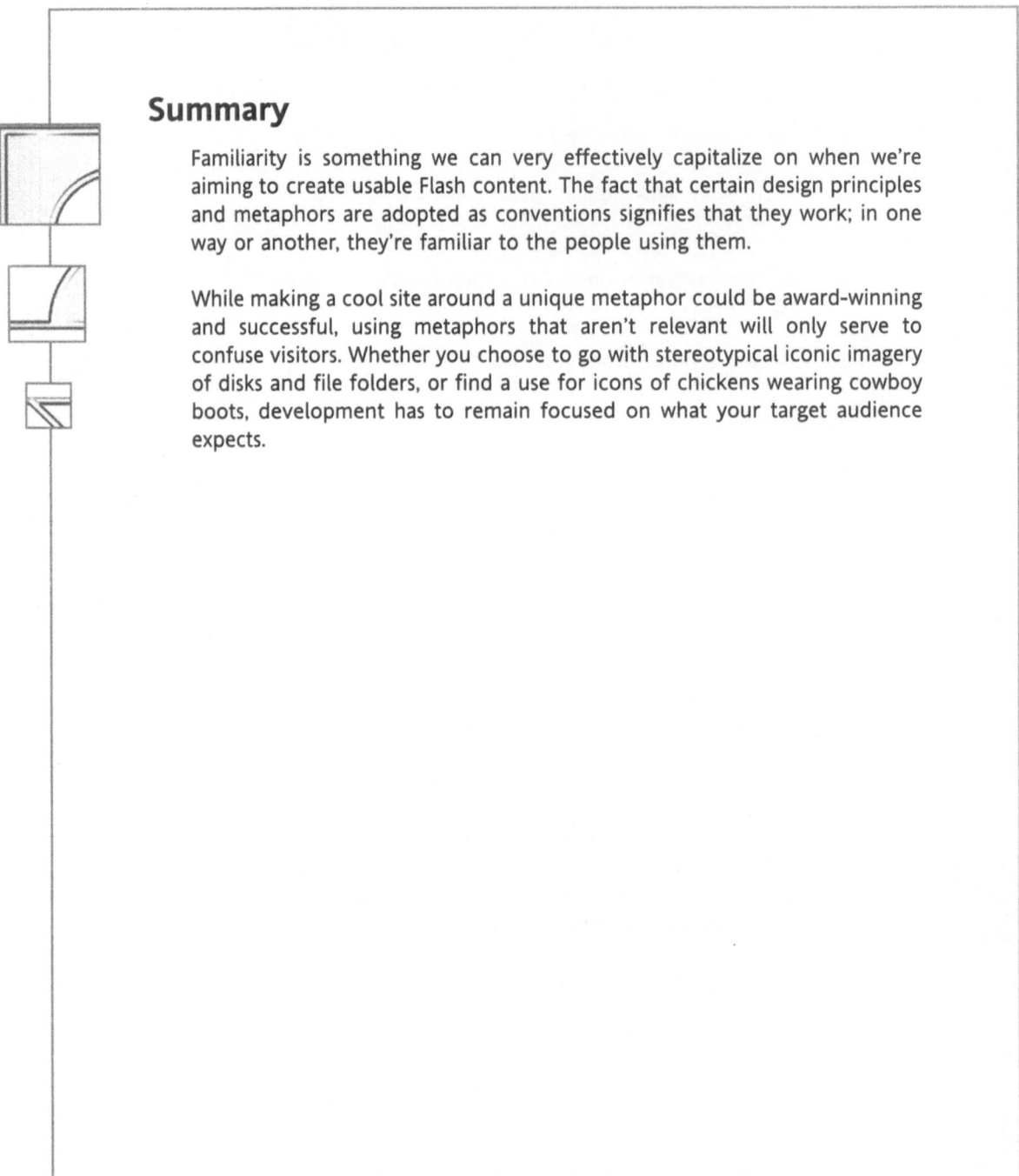

Summary

Familiarity is something we can very effectively capitalize on when we're aiming to create usable Flash content. The fact that certain design principles and metaphors are adopted as conventions signifies that they work; in one way or another, they're familiar to the people using them.

While making a cool site around a unique metaphor could be award-winning and successful, using metaphors that aren't relevant will only serve to confuse visitors. Whether you choose to go with stereotypical iconic imagery of disks and file folders, or find a use for icons of chickens wearing cowboy boots, development has to remain focused on what your target audience expects.

Conventions and metaphors 5

Conventions and metaphors

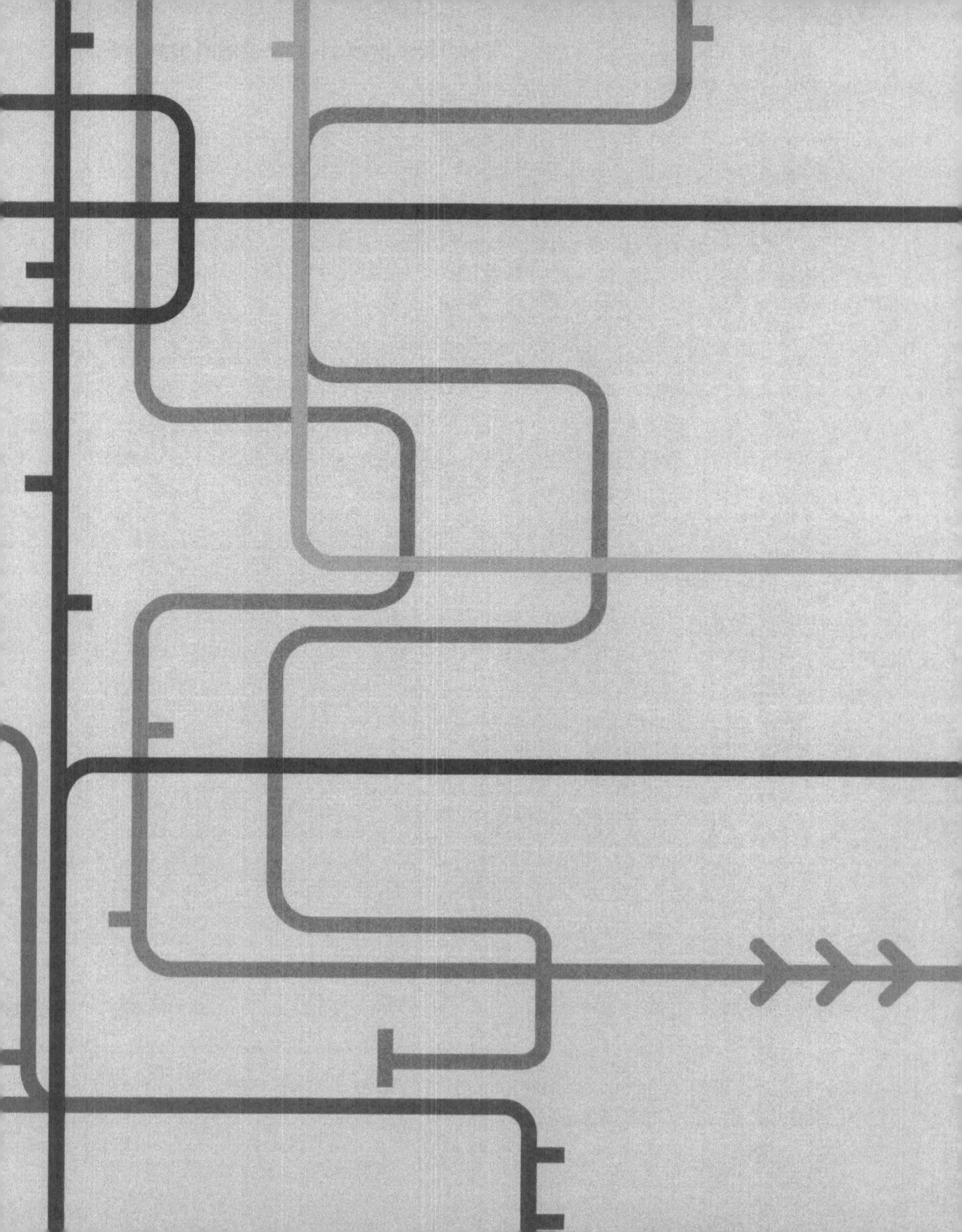

Structuring Flash

This chapter looks at a serious problem confronting most Flash sites: poor organization. HTML imposes a fairly strict hierarchy on web content, since it forces web designers to present their content in the form of discrete pages. Flash content has no such constraints, and that's one of the reasons it's so appealing to designers – it's also one of the reasons why users have such a hard time finding their way around.

We're going to consider two approaches you can take in establishing content structure:

- Information Architecture

- Storyboarding

Information hierarchies

You can get a lot of insight into an item's value by looking at its placement in a hierarchical structure. Take movie posters for example: when one person's name is more prominent than anyone else's – whether it's above the title, or in foot-high letters – it's quite natural to assume that that person played an important role in the making of the movie (and that they were probably paid a lot more than everyone else involved!) The same rule applies to the design of the interface for Flash content.

STARRING
Justin Case
Weenie Dher

IN

WILL CAALL'S

ANYTIME SOON

also appearing

Rela Tivity
Faye Lee
Conn Tentra

The most important information in the content should receive a prominent spot in the interface.

Users appreciate this, even if they don't realize it. It's one of the conventions of the Web, and of good design in general. Users may not know *that* – and to be fair, they shouldn't need to – but they *do* notice the results.

Almost by definition, prominent information will catch their senses over any other content on the page – even at an unconscious level, it takes top priority.

Your job is to make sure that what grabs them first is what you actually *want* to grab them first. You may only get one chance at convincing them that your site's worth looking around, so you really can't afford to leave it to chance.

Usability and the shopping mall

Any large shopping mall should provide you with a perfect example of how *not* to organize information for the benefit of the end user. Next time you're in a mall, take a mental note of the locations and types of all the shoe stores:

- Are all the shoe stores centrally located?

- Are sports shoes located in one part of the mall and dress shoes in another?

- How much of the mall would you have to walk through to visit all the women's shoe stores?

- Are there any two shoe stores located directly adjacent to each other?

Chances are, you'll see a pattern emerging – a pattern that you can just as easily apply to jewelry stores, clothing stores, music stores, and virtually every type of store you can find in the average mall.

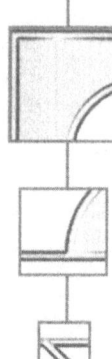

Essentially, it boils down to this: you'll almost never find two adjacent stores selling the same type of product. A couple of stores apart perhaps, or maybe five doors down the mall; but look for two that are right next to each other, and you'll probably be looking for a very long time! If you ever do come across a shopping mall that's organized by store type, consider yourself blessed - and let me know where it is!

So, if a customer wants to see a full range of the different tennis shoes available in a mall, they might just manage to wear out a pair while walking to all the different stores that sell them. You're unlikely to find a dedicated 'sports wing' where all the sporting goods stores are located. From the customer's point of view, there doesn't seem to be any organization at all...

Of course, store locations in a shopping mall are usually dictated by the owners' business interests; they don't want competitors sitting right next door, poaching their customers. For that reason, stores selling similar products are usually located as far away from each other as possible – maybe even at opposite ends of the mall.

This sort of approach can be very lucrative in a mall, especially since it entices customers to spend more time (and hopefully more money) wandering around, past stores they might otherwise not have walked by, and buying items they might otherwise not have purchased.

In terms of customer experience though, the way malls are organized could be regarded as poor usability because of its lack of consistency.

A shopping mall that was organized by type of store might be more useful to customers who are simply at the mall to pursue the purchase of one particular item. Customers would be able to spend less time shopping in the mall and would find accomplishing their tasks easier. It would be easier to compare the price of a specific product, because all the stores that sell it would be located near one another.

The implications of 'customer-centric' organization would extend beyond the interior of the mall too. The customer would be able to better plan their visit to the mall. For example, customers would know where to park their cars if they needed to shop for shoes or books. This would lead to less congestion inside the mall during peak business times.

This 'non-wander' approach also has benefits for store owners (especially those of small, non-chain stores): it may bring people to their store who wouldn't have found them had they been based in a different area of the mall.

So why split them apart? Why would little stores want to be in a mall in the first place? The mall is about convenience, not order.

According to *Shopping Center World* magazine, shoppers generally don't go to malls to buy one specific item, but to have an 'experience'. That's one reason we're seeing a trend of fewer department stores anchoring the ends of long mall hallways, but rather large 'browsing-encouraged, coffee-shop-enhanced' bookstores and multiplex movie theaters as the featured focuses of malls.

Rather than simply buying a pair of shoes, shoppers can now plan to take in a matinee, gossip over a leisurely cup of coffee and brioche, indulge in an unhurried browse among books on comfortable chairs, and perhaps even find the pair of shoes that they want at a fair price. So while one shopper may find the organization of a mall a tremendous hassle, others find it to be a good 'experience', as intended by its designers.

The Web is not a shopping mall – or is it?

There are a number of differences between the user experience of a shopping mall and that of Flash content on the Web. The main one is that a shopping mall has a geographic significance to its customers. There's one shopping mall that's closest to the customer's home. On the Web there are thousands of businesses that offer the exact same products. This

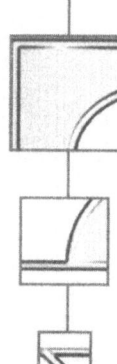

convenience allows the shopping malls to offer a more non-intuitive customer experience without damaging sales.

Once we shift our interactions to an online environment, all the geographic benefits are gone and the user's patience for bad interfaces and bad organization goes right out the door. Users don't want to have to hunt for what they need; they want content to be well organized and easy to find.

What's more, it's in our interests to make that content easy for them to find. There's no point in making someone hunt all over the site for a 'purchase this item' button – they'll probably just give up and go to another site.

Information needs to be organized

Information is useless without some kind of context, and you need organization to provide context. This may be designed to show relative importance, connections, patterns, or projections, whatever's appropriate to help users understand what it means and why they should care about what it means.

Information contained in the Flash content we build needs to be organized so that users can use it. Related information needs to be grouped together in logically named sections of content. Within those sections, further structure needs to be created for subdivisions of the information within a topic.

The way information is organized for Flash content is not that different from how someone might organize their dresser. All the socks are together in one drawer, the shorts in another, and the shirts in another. Different drawers might have further sub-categories. Socks that are appropriate for work might be separate from socks that are best worn with running shoes, but both would be located inside the same drawer.

Once organized, the drawers of the dresser get labels (these don't have to be written, labels may be the mental notes the owner of the dresser has in their head), such as 'Sock Drawer' or 'Shirt Drawer'. This ensures you'll know which drawer to open to find the article of clothing you want.

But imagine if someone wanted to borrow your clothes and your drawers weren't labeled. They'd have to open every drawer to find what they want, and perhaps even dig through everything to find the right type of whatever piece of clothing they're looking for.

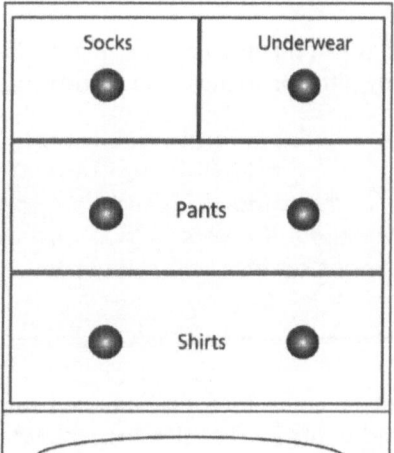

Thinking outside the socks

Organization can also help users accomplish tasks. They want to click on a button and either locate the information they want, or find an accessible menu structure to help them navigate the content. They want related content to be grouped together. Socks should be with socks, and shirts with shirts.

When users have a task to accomplish, they want to do it in a direct manner.

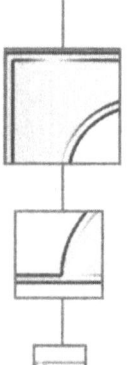

Imagine arriving in a large, unfamiliar airport where your connecting flight leaves in less than an hour. Your first action wouldn't be to wander around the airport looking at the gift shops or checking out who's in the airport bar. You'd probably sprint to the next departure gate for your destination, following signs pointing to it (assuming you already know the gate number).

If you didn't have that information, you'd start by finding it on the departures screen. If you weren't able to find the departures screen or the gate, you'd probably seek out an information booth or an airport worker.

If you had time after finding your gate, maybe then you'd wander around the airport to buy gifts for friends, and scandal sheets to read on the flight.

> *When users have a task to accomplish, they become more aware of the hurdles that get in their way and more appreciative of tools that help them accomplish the task.*

Users don't want to come to a site and find the interaction instructions, "rummage around until you find the answer". What if your airport had no signs and planes could pull into any gate they wished? You'd be doing a lot more guessing and walking and your frustration would mount.

How do we make sure that visitors to our site have instructions enough, without being bombarded with menus, help files, and arrows? How can we structure a site so that after a few clicks, a visitor might find the process intuitive and locate what they want?

There are two approaches to structure

We know that our Flash projects need structure to help the user accomplish their goals, but how do we build that structure? How do we organize information from our client to best meet the needs of the users?

There are two popular web-planning approaches that we can take to organizing the content in our Flash projects. The first approach is to create **Information Architecture**, or a topic-based structure for the information. The second approach to organization is **Storyboarding**, which is generally linear and a more progress-driven approach to organizing information.

Let's take a careful look at each one.

Information Architecture

If you've been working on the Web for more than a few months, you're probably familiar with the term **Information Architecture** (IA). At first glance, **IA** may seem to be little more than the development of a site map, but the purpose it serves is greater than just an organization of pages. For one thing, unlike a site map, good IA is developed long before any work on building a site begins.

What is IA?

Information Architecture is the organization and presentation of data to the user in a clear, consistent, and intuitive manner. The IA helps users to use the site by providing guidelines for information organization.

> *All the other parts of a web site – the interface, the design, the navigation, and the interactions are all built upon the structure provided by the Information Architecture. In many ways a good IA is the foundation of a good site.*

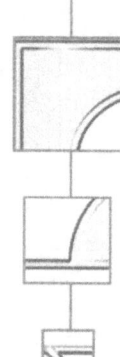

The first step in creating an effective IA is to create divisions of the information. Think how the information is going to be used: what collections of information will users want to find together in the same place? How would a user arrange the information for their own use?

Categories need to be intuitive to the user

Organizing information is an important part of making it easy to use. If the information within a Flash interface is intuitively organized with clear labels that make sense to the targeted user group, then users, in theory, will have no trouble navigating through the organizational hierarchy to find what they're looking for. If the organizational structure isn't easy to understand, then users are presented with a hurdle to leap.

The way that we organize information should be specific to the needs of the target audience:

Organizational strategy	Organizational benefits
DJs organize their CD collection by beats per minute.	This helps them to mix from one track to another without disrupting the beat.
Music stores organize their CDs by musical styles, separating hip-hop music from dance or rock. Artists within each category are arranged alphabetically.	This helps customers to browse a specific style of music, and find artists they know within the category by name.
Radio stations organize their CDs by chart placement.	The most popular songs are easiest to access.
Dwayne organizes his personal CD collection alphabetically.	He has an incredible memory for the kinds of music by each artist in his collection, so when he wants to listen to a particular style, he finds it by artist.
Crystal keeps the majority of her CDs in no particular order, but they are, at least, in one CD media shelf. Mostly.	Crystal must read every single title to find the CD she wants

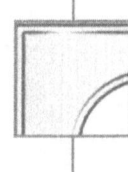

Each of these organization strategies works for the intended user, but each one certainly wouldn't work for all users. To create an organizational structure for information on a Flash site, it's critical to understand who the user is (which is why we employ user profiles as discussed in Chapter 4) and how to best organize the content for their specific needs. Will the user want content organized by beats per minute, musical style, or by chart position? Or is a random pile of CDs good enough for them?

Task-based structure

This task-based structure works well on information-based or product-based sites because people tend to want the same types of information for the same types of tasks. Next time you're in a hardware store, take time to look at how the different tools and other products are organized – it usually comes down to the types of task that customers may want tools for.

For example, all the painting products are located in the same section of the store. Paint, paintbrushes, drop cloths, and other painting-related items are grouped together so that a customer looking to stock up on the materials they need for a painting job will only need to look in one place. Other parts of the hardware store include plumbing, lawn and garden, and electrical, for example, and all of these sections are grouped by what the customer needs to do.

The same task-based structure can be used when organizing information. Consider what questions from the user are answered by the information and group it accordingly. The Flash site for a Flash design studio may include a top level IA with labels such as 'Portfolio', 'Services', and 'About Us'. These three divisions of the information answer questions for the user, they know what section to view to find the answers they need.

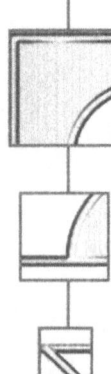

The user says:	The IA says:
"I need to know if this company can design a Flash site with a database back end."	"The 'Services' section is where you'll find a list of our services."
"My company is pretty conservative. I wonder if the designers at this company are going to be a good match for our identity"	"Our 'Portfolio' section has examples of our past design work."
"I want to work with a professional company that has been around for a few years and not some fly-by-night shop with no history."	"We've grouped information about our company in the 'About Us' section of the site."

Determining information structure

Users visiting a site looking for information on a specific product are going to expect information about that product to be grouped with other similar product data. The fact that the product is assembled in the company's plant in Kathmandu doesn't mean that the information on the product should be in the 'Global Locations' section of the site.

For example, I heard of one company who listed their web design services under 'Real Estate' because the two departments fell under the same management team. The logic of this type of structure isn't all that logical. I'm sure that you've shared my experience of visiting plenty of sites that hide their search function under a couple of layers of pages, rather than in, say, a product catalog area, where it would be most valuable.

While grouping socks with socks, and web design under 'Web Design Services' seems obvious from this angle, there are still many corporate sites basing their Information Architectures on the corporate organization chart rather than common sense. Information needs to be organized for the user's ease and not the client's.

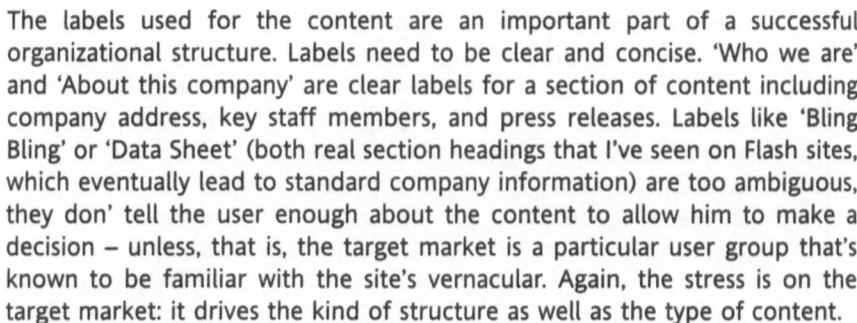

Information labels must be clear

Once we've determined the structure of the information, the next step is to think of labels for the sections. The wording of the labels is especially important, as the words we choose will be the main factor in helping users to decide where they need to go when working with the content.

The labels used for the content are an important part of a successful organizational structure. Labels need to be clear and concise. 'Who we are' and 'About this company' are clear labels for a section of content including company address, key staff members, and press releases. Labels like 'Bling Bling' or 'Data Sheet' (both real section headings that I've seen on Flash sites, which eventually lead to standard company information) are too ambiguous, they don' tell the user enough about the content to allow him to make a decision – unless, that is, the target market is a particular user group that's known to be familiar with the site's vernacular. Again, the stress is on the target market: it drives the kind of structure as well as the type of content.

The way you label the sections of your Flash content needs to be structured around the same goals. Section labels need to inform the user what they can expect when clicking on the button. They should offer an insight to the content to help the user make the best decision for their needs.

Homemade IA

Ever since I began teaching web design back in 1995, I've had a steady stream of students coming to me for advice: they want to create a web site on a particular topic (their company, family, hobby, or whatever) but often aren't clear about what they actually want it to accomplish, let alone how it should be structured.

I usually ask them to go out and buy a pack of index cards (or Post-It notes) to bring into class. They should also have a pad of paper ready, or a blackboard, or something for writing a long brainstorming list on.

continues overleaf

Here's what I have them do: First, spend some time writing down on the paper / board anything and everything imaginable that's related to the chosen topic. If working in a team, the brainstorming session should result in just one list. For example, let's say that I want to create a web site that serves women bicyclists. My brainstorming list might start out looking like this:

- women's bikes
- finding riding groups

- famous women cyclists
- health benefits of cycling
- how to buy a bike
- types of cycling
- women's cycling

- riding while pregnant
- women's cycling clothing

- tools
- routes

- bike fit
- saddles
- safety
- pedals
- commuting

- handlebars
- dealing with bike shops

- components
- books about cycling

- types of bicycles
- accessories
- road riding
- helmet hair
- mountain biking companies

- weight control

Once happy with the list (things can always be added later), the list topics are transferred to the index cards, one topic per card.

Hopefully, the classroom has lots of floor and wall space! Each student or team claims a spot and lays out their index cards on the floors or walls, tackling the puzzle of organizing their random brainstorm list into a logical, navigable, structure. Like a client, I give them a time constraint.

Teams then take turns critiquing the structure of each other's sites, playing the part of 'user' and discussing the perceived challenges and the success of the chosen architecture. Often, the fresh eyes of the 'users' come up with structural ideas that the team / student didn't even think of. The team may have placed 'Safety' in with 'Routes' under a heading of 'Riding Tips', but others thought a section headed by 'Health and Safety' would be a better umbrella for 'Safety', 'Riding while pregnant', 'Weight control', and 'Health benefits of cycling'.

continues overleaf

The cards or Post-It notes are easily rearranged, low cost, and a good way to determine if an area of your site is better suited to Storyboarding (more on this later) or IA. I find it a great way to visually conceptualize navigation and structure logic. Does one category branch out into five subcategories? Should one of those subcategories be a category in its own right? If one column of Post-It notes is 10 feet long, and all other categories only have 3 Post-Its each, it's a visual hint to consider restructuring.

While the conservative corporate board-room floor belonging to a potential client may not be the best place to start laying out a bunch of neon Post-It notes, I've always found this relatively quick practice a good jump-start to a smart architecture before getting into a project.

So why is IA a good thing?

Both designers and users can derive benefits from a solid, well-planned Information Architecture. From a designer's perspective, the IA provides a guide for the interface design, determining for example what buttons are needed on each page and at each level. This then assists in creating a design that will best serve the purpose of the site. For example, a site that has ten different top-level divisions is going to need a different type of menu design than a site with only three top-level divisions.

The IA also assists the designer by providing a clear view of the scope of a project. With the IA in hand designers will be better able to estimate the time needed to complete a project.

On the other side of the equation, the IA assists the user in building a mental model of the contents available. A logical and well-planned structure helps them make the best decision on where to click in order to locate the

information they need. That is, if content is organized consistently across an entire site, whatever users learn from interactions in one part of the site can be reapplied when they visit other parts.

The IA establishes a structure for the user to become comfortable in. If the local mall were organized into product categories, shoppers would have no problem finding the newest shoe store in the mall. Logically, it would be located with the rest of the shoe stores.

The IA gives the information within the site room to grow from within. Instead of needing to add new top-level sections onto a site, an IA provides broad enough categories for growth to happen comfortably. For information-heavy sites, the IA helps both the user and the designer keep their interactions manageable.

Just don't rely on it too much...

From a usability perspective, IAs have some fairly inherent limitations. Most importantly, they don't tell us how the user will interact with the site, just how we want them to interact with it. The user is inside a matrix of content, and their navigation through that content is left to the decisions they make based on the structure presented.

So, a good IA won't automatically fix all your problems – content still needs to be user-tested, so you can ensure things like intuitive button labeling and easily navigable structure actually work in practice.

> *Many people confuse the simple act of organizing information with the science (and art) of true Information Architecture. It's important to recognize that merely 'deciding' on a site structure doesn't mean that you've actually defined a true IA. Ultimately, it's something that takes a lot of practice, trial and error, testing, and open-mindedness to the target market's needs.*

Let's put these notions to work, and look at how we might go about defining an IA for our *Future Fridges Conference* site.

Case Study

> **Case Study**

Developing an IA for our site

So, how do we start defining an IA? Well, first we need to categorize our content; drag your mind back to Chapter 5, and you'll remember we outlined that content as follows:

- The conference vision and the conference organizers and partners

- Overview of the conference and highlights

- Video and audio interviews with keynote and featured speakers

- The conference date, location and cost

- The program and seminar details including detailed session descriptions

- The conference location and venue (including a map of the venue)

- Travel and hotel information

- Sponsors information

- Contact Information

We also considered two functional features:

- A registration form

- A session planner tool

So, which of these is our top priority? Well, we originally defined online registration support as being one of the site's primary goals – registration is a user task that every attendee will need to undertake, and the easier it is, the better it is for both the user and the client. The registration form is clearly a very important part of the site, so it must be given a good prominent place in our Information Architecture.

It's also apparent that we'll need to provide some complementary content along with the form itself (such as instructions, pricing, methods of payment, and information on refunds). So, we have our first draft category:

- The site's **Registration** category will contain the registration form along with instructions, pricing, methods of payment, and information on refunds.

What about the remaining content? Let's think about what sort of tasks will be motivating our users. In Chapter 4 we looked at user profiles, and observed that the conference advertising actually provides very little information. We therefore predicted that many users would visit the site in search of a content overview, details of time and location, as well as information on specific speakers and sessions.

This gives us a task division, split between 'looking for overview information' and 'looking for detailed session information':

- The site's **Overview** category will contain the highlights, keynote speaker information (including audio/video interviews), date, and location

- The site's **Session and Speaker Details** category will provide detailed information on the conference sessions

That leaves us with contact, sponsors, travel and hotel, vision, organizers, and partners information. We've previously agreed to include a **Sponsors** section in the site. The contact info, vision, organizers, and partners could be grouped together in an **Organizers** or **About Us** section. Finally, the hotel and travel content could be grouped together under **Travel and Hotels**.

Our 'first-cut' IA

So here's our first attempt at creating an IA for the site:

- **Registration**: containing the registration form, instructions for completing it, pricing, payment, and refund info

- **Overview**: containing the highlights, keynote speaker information (including video and audio interviews), date, and location

- **Session and Speaker Details**: containing all the detailed session and speaker descriptions

- **Sponsors**: containing sponsor details and links

- **Organizers / About Us**: containing contact info, vision, organizers, and partners

- **Travel and Hotels**: containing information on how to get to the conference and where to stay

At first glance, it seems to cover all the content quite satisfactorily. However, on closer inspection, we see that there's no suitable section for either the session planner or the venue map. What's more, the **Overview** section is *very* broad and contains quite a variety of information.

Before we make any changes, let's see what potential users think of our work so far.

Getting preliminary feedback from users

Start off by taking a blank piece of paper and drawing six boxes. Inside each one, write down the name of one of our six site sections.

We now take this piece of paper and show it to a small number of test users. At this early stage they don't need to be actual conference attendees: just anyone from the office who *isn't* involved in the site development and *doesn't* know anything about the client.

We ask these test users to think of the boxes as primary navigation buttons on our site. We want to know which box they would click on to complete specific tasks, and why they think it's likely to give them what they expect:

This is a simplified version of a process known as **paper prototyping**, which we'll use more comprehensively when we've established our second-cut IA.

Where would you click to find a venue map?
Our testers suggested that they'd either click on **Session and Speaker Details** because they assumed that session information would include information about the venues for the sessions, or **Travel and Hotels** as this may include a map of how to get to the venue.

Where would you click to register for the conference?
All testers said they would click on the **Registration** button.

Where would you click to find out about the keynote speakers?
One of our testers suggested that they'd go to **Session and Speaker Details** because it states that it has speaker details there. Another tester suggested **Overview** guessing that it would contain an overview of the speakers.

Where would you click to find information on the cost of the conference?
The typical response for this question is along these lines: "I would click on **Registration**, because I'd expect it to have introductory information about registering (such as cost and different types of registration available) before actually going through the registration process. If I didn't find it there, I would look under **Overview**, since it could be there instead."

continues overleaf

Where would you click to ask a question about the conference via e-mail?
Our testers suggested that they would click on **Organizers** because they assumed that they're the people to ask questions to and that there would be contact information provided

This very quick and simple test has illustrated some significant issues with our current IA. The registration form was easily found and our test users correctly deduced that contact details would be in the **Organizers** category. However they didn't easily find the keynote speaker information or the map, and while they guessed that the price information would be in the **Registration** section, it wasn't a terribly confident guess.

Building on the first-cut IA

It seems as though the current IA isn't going to meet the needs of our users or the goals of our client. So how can we improve things?

- Break down the **Overview** category into smaller sections.

- Move the keynote speaker information (including audio/video content) into its own section.

- Introduce a dedicated category called **Speakers**. This will provide information on the speakers, and include a section with detailed information and interviews with the keynote speakers and other featured speakers. This should help ensure that users can easily find information on the keynote speakers and hence promote the conference's 'star' speakers.

- The **Session and Speaker Details** section will now just contain session details (though it will link to the speaker information for each session), so we'll change its name to **Session Details**.

It's worth realizing that we haven't considered the issue of a home page: what are users going to see when they first arrive at the site?

What about a home page?

Typically, Flash sites have little or no content on their home pages. Designers sometimes use it as a place to put some animation or maybe a bit of marketing blurb. But let's think about this from the perspective of our users: what content do *they* expect to see first when they access the site? It's more than likely they're after an explanation of what the site is about, and possibly a summary of the most important information on the site as a whole.

For the *Future Fridges Conference* site we should include a couple of sentences describing the conference and the keynote speakers. This may be the same information that appears on the advertisement for the conference; however, we can't be sure that all users visiting the site will have seen the advertisement, so it's valuable to repeat this information. Other information we'll want to include on the home page is the date, cost, and location of the conference – this is probably the most important information our users will want.

Adding this information, particularly the cost of the conference, solves our problem of users not being sure where to look for the price information. We'll still include the prices in the registration section, as users need to be reminded of how much they'll be spending before starting the registration process.

One map or two?

Now we need to find an appropriate location for the venue map. Our test users thought that it could be under one of the **Session Details** or **Travel and Hotels** sections. Actually, this reflects two quite different perceptions of the map's role:

- When the map is associated with sessions, users expect it to indicate which room in the building they should go to for a particular presentation.

- When it's associated with travel, users expect it to help them find the conference venue. In this context, users will expect the map to show where the venue is located relative to hotels and public transport. It should also indicate where the user goes to register at the start of the conference.

We need to satisfy both of these requirements whilst also making the venue information easier to find. Easy solution: have two maps.

We can rename the **Travel and Hotels** section to **Venue, Hotels and Travel**, and make sure it contains a map showing where the venue is geographically, as well as highlighting nearby accommodation and transport options. This could also contain venue information that may encourage users to attend the conference – maybe it provides high-speed Internet terminals and a coffee bar, and is located in a historic area of the city. Every little helps!

So what about the **Session Details** section? Well, there's no reason we shouldn't include a map in there too. Of course, there's no point in featuring the same map in two different sections, but a different map serving a different role makes perfect sense – this one highlights the location of sessions *within* the venue.

*We now have two maps: one in the **Travel and Hotels** section, showing where the venue is located, and one in the **Session Details** sections, showing where the sessions are located within the venue.*

How does the session planner fit in?

Our client has asked for an interactive session planner tool to be part of the site, so conference attendees can plan and print out details of the conference sessions they wish to attend. But where does this fit into our IA?

We could be tempted to create a whole new section called '**Session Planner**' and put our tool there. But we should consider what our users are actually going to be doing with this session planner: by and large, they'll browse the session descriptions and pick out the ones they wish to attend.

Well, we already have a section dedicated to letting users browse the session details, so all we need to do is let them add sessions into their session planner while they browse. The process is basically just the same as browsing the Web and bookmarking pages you find interesting. It would be silly to have one tool for browsing the Web and a different tool for bookmarking pages!

So we'll need to add into the **Session Details** section the session planner functionality including some explanation of how to use the session planner and options to allow users to view and print their sessions.

Our 'second cut' IA

Now we have a second version of the site's Information Architecture:

- **Home Page** (displayed by default): containing a brief summary of the conference, date, location, and cost

- **Registration**: containing the registration form, instructions for completing it, pricing, payment, and refund info

- **Overview**: containing the conference highlights

- **Speakers**: speaker information (including video and audio interviews)

- **Session Details**: containing detailed session information (session descriptions to include a map showing where each session is located within the venue) and the session planner.

- **Sponsors**: containing sponsor details and links

- **Organizers**: containing contact info, vision, organizers and partners

- **Venue, Travel and Hotels**: containing information on the conference venue, how to get to the conference, and where to stay

We now need to test our IA against the sample user profiles developed in Chapter 4. We need to create a paper prototype of our updated Information Architecture.

Paper Prototyping

This simply uses eight sheets of paper to represent the eight sections of the site – one for **Home Page**, one for **Registration**, one for **Overview**, and so on.

On the **Home Page** sheet, we write in some home page text (conference summary, date, location) and draw seven boxes, labeling them for each of the other seven sections.

On each of the other pages, we write a summary of the information contained in the site section it represents. We then ask a number of test users to imagine that they're one of the sample users we devised in Chapter 4, and to think of the boxes drawn on the **Home Page** sheet as primary navigation buttons on the site. Once again, we want to know which box they would click on, and if the page they reached actually featured the information they were after. Here are the results of our testing:

Joel (R&D professional for a US fridge manufacturer)

Joel is looking for more information. He's already confident that the conference will be relevant to him, but wants to know which companies are speaking and when the conference is being held to determine if he will attend.

Our testers found the general dates for the conference on the **Home Page**. They assumed that the **Speakers** section would contain information on which companies the speakers belonged to.

continues overleaf

Bronwyn (buyer for a UK department store)

Bronwyn is visiting the site to determine if the conference will give her an insight into the new developments in the high-tech fridge industry. At present she's quite unsure about whether the conference is relevant to her.

Our testers believed that the summary on the **Home Page** and the highlights on the **Overview** page would have been enough to confirm Bronwyn's interest, but were not sure if there would have been enough information for her to make a decision. They didn't find the 'vision' for the conference as they didn't think there would be anything relevant to Bronwyn under the **Organizers** section and didn't click on it. The 'vision' may have been useful to her in making a decision on whether the conference was relevant.

Luigi (final-year electronic engineering student)

Luigi is extremely excited about the conference but wants to know if the time, location and cost of the conference, as these will affect whether he's able to attend.

Our testers easily found the summary information Luigi needed on the **Home Page**. If this wasn't detailed enough for him they would have looked under **Overview** and found more information.

continues overleaf

Thomas (researcher for a UK television network)

Thomas wants to establish if any part of the conference will be of interest to his viewers. He's especially interested to see if there will be any newsworthy announcements, prototype product demonstrations or exciting keynote presentations.

Our testers went to the **Overview** section to get a feel for the conference and assumed that the highlights would indicate what the conference organizers consider to be newsworthy items. The audio and video presentations in the **Speakers** section would have been viewed to determine whether they might grab the attention and interest of his audience.

These tests highlight the fact that some users will expect the **Speakers** section to detail which companies or organizations the speakers represent. The tests indicate that users expect the **Overview** section to provide enough information for them to make a decision on the appropriateness of the conference to their needs. The tests also show that the 'vision statement' is probably more appropriately placed in the **Overview** section.

Ultimately this testing leaves our IA basically the same, with only the 'vision statement' being moved to the **Overview** section. We'll need to inform the client that users will expect the **Overview** and **Speakers** sections to contain quite comprehensive information.

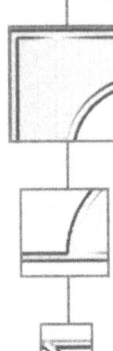

Storyboarding

If you're designing web content that has a linear structure – that is, there's a predetermined order to the content – **Storyboarding** (SB) provides a good way to plan things out. It's well suited to the development of any content that requires step-by-step navigation, such as tutorial walkthroughs and good old-fashioned 'a to b' storytelling!

Lots of Flash content involves a linear progression: the user must accomplish one task before they move on to the next. In the case of a short movie, each frame must follow the previous frame in a particular order to give the appearance of smooth animation, so Storyboarding is the logical planning tool.

Storyboarding has long been used as a planning tool for films, television, animation, multimedia presentations (such as in PowerPoint), and would probably remind most people of the panels in a comic strip. From sketches on a bar napkin to highly detailed computer drawings, storyboards represent a series of pages or sequences that the reader / viewer / user must follow in order to best understand the content.

What does Storyboarding do for us?

Storyboarding as a form of information organization serves two purposes. First, it sets out a planned path for the user to interact with the content. By mapping the information into storyboards, the designer knows what the user has been exposed to and how to best use that exposure when introducing new content.

Many game developers use Storyboarding to organize the 'How To Play' instructions for games. A sample game instruction storyboard might look like this:

1. **How to play the game**. Gives a brief explanation of the game. Shows the player's icon and covers the controls available.

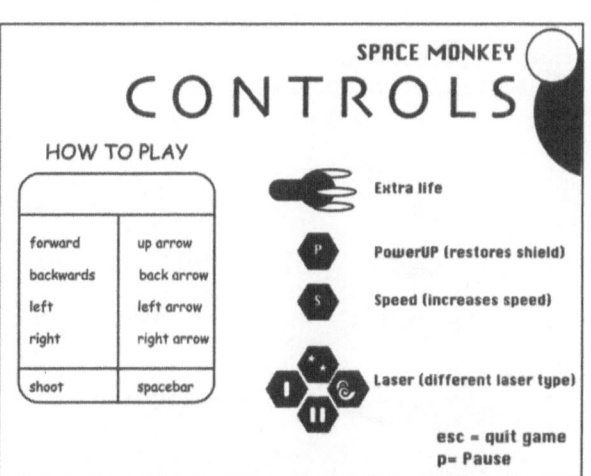

2. **What is the challenge?** Explains the challenge of the game. What is the antagonist and how to best defeat it using the player's abilities?

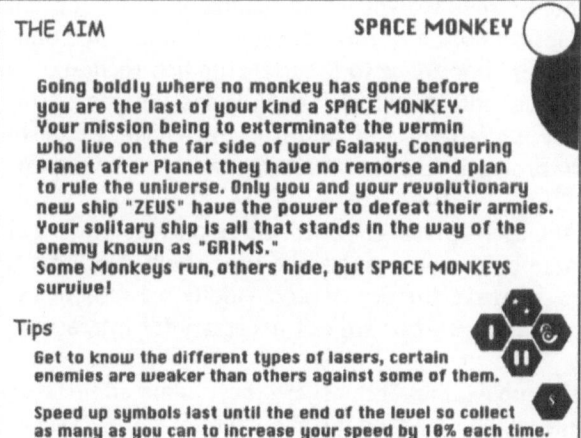

3.   **How to play really well**: This screen shows the point values for certain tasks. It would also show any special features available to the user.

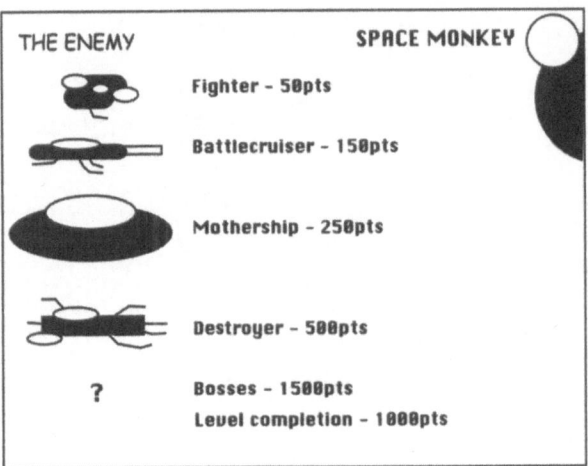

This three-screen storyboard allows the user to comprehend a fairly complex set of instructions in a short amount of time. The content is also organized by order of importance to the user. The first section of information gives the user enough information to start playing the game. The second part of the storyboard prepares the user for the challenge of the game. The third section provides details that are secondary to gameplay.

From the user's perspective, this three-part storyboard also provides content evaluated by its importance. The user could start interacting with the game having only read the first screen. Additional screens assist in preparing the user for the game, but are not necessary for interactions to begin.

Many complex interactions are best planned in storyboard format. An example would be a long questionnaire or form. Users tend to get frustrated with long forms fairly quickly, so Storyboarding the content into manageable chunks will help to keep the user involved in the process. Breaking a task into multiple steps also serves to focus the user's attention on each step. Finally, the user's progress through the multi-page form can be updated to keep the user informed on their progress.

Strengths of Storyboarding

As an organizational tool, Storyboarding offers many benefits to both designers and users of linear Flash content.

From the designer's perspective, Storyboarding offers a tighter control over the user's experience. It allows us to create Flash content that tends to flow well from one section to another. Storyboarding also lends itself to storytelling, allowing designers to plan out the user's experience with the content before the design phase begins.

> *Storyboarding is an excellent tool to evaluate the easiest method for multi-step processes. By mapping out each step of the way, the designer is able to see where potential difficulty may arise, and adjust the storyboard accordingly.*

From the user's perspective, storyboarded content usually makes them feel comfortable moving from one section to another. There's little decision-making that the user must do when interacting with a simple 'Next Page' button. It allows the user to focus on a specific task instead of many all at once.

Product demos, entertainment content, multi-step tasks and forms, animations, and presentations are the types of Flash content that will generally best benefit from Storyboarding.

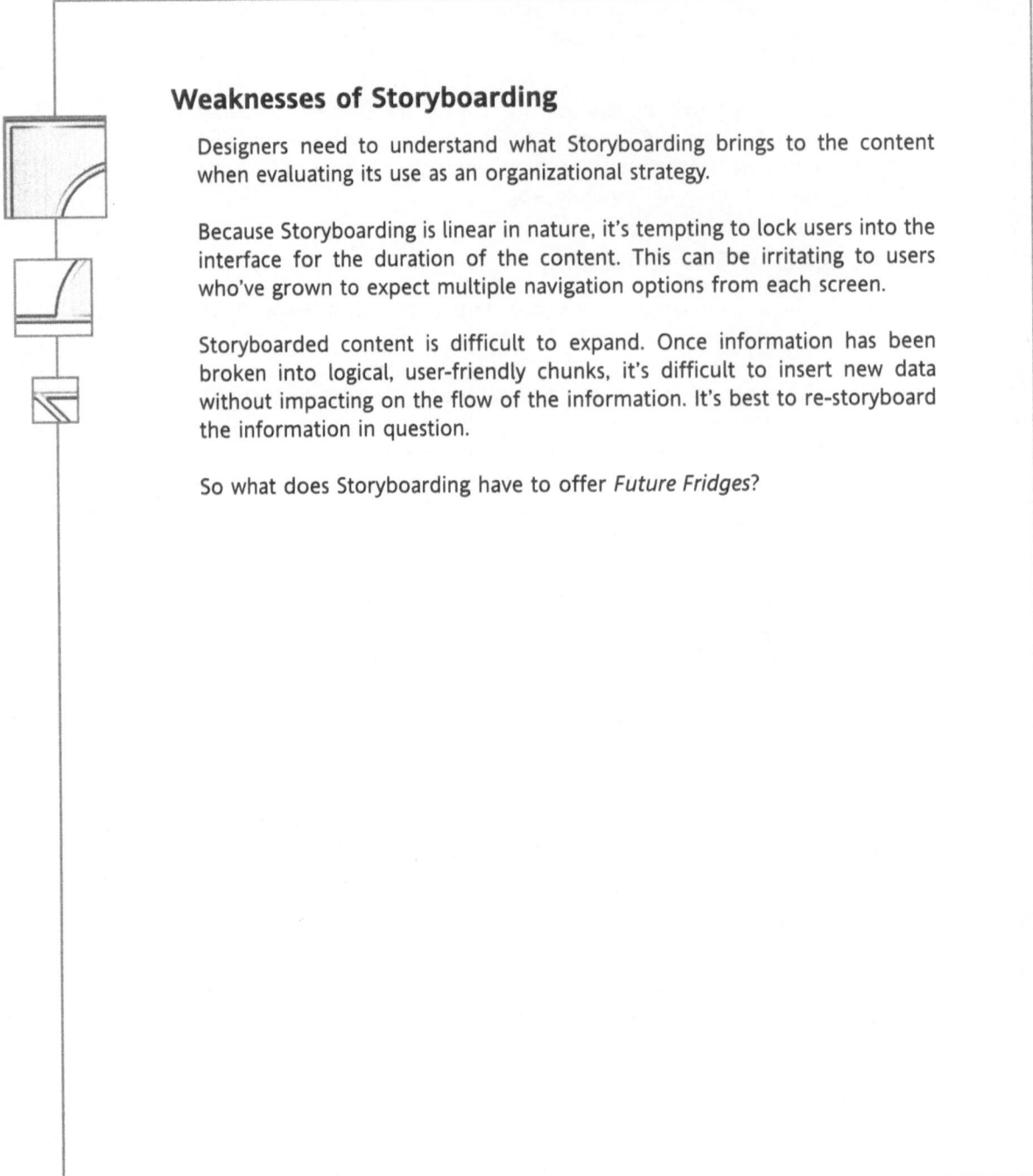

Weaknesses of Storyboarding

Designers need to understand what Storyboarding brings to the content when evaluating its use as an organizational strategy.

Because Storyboarding is linear in nature, it's tempting to lock users into the interface for the duration of the content. This can be irritating to users who've grown to expect multiple navigation options from each screen.

Storyboarded content is difficult to expand. Once information has been broken into logical, user-friendly chunks, it's difficult to insert new data without impacting on the flow of the information. It's best to re-storyboard the information in question.

So what does Storyboarding have to offer *Future Fridges*?

Case Study

Can we apply Storyboarding anywhere?

As we've learnt, Storyboarding is useful when your content presupposes that users will follow a linear progress through it. Admittedly, most of our content doesn't fit this criterion; but one section of the site will involve a strictly sequential progress – the **registration form**. So what are the steps involved here?

1. Instructions – how to register for the conference

2. Personal Information – first and last name, e-mail, address, phone

3. Credit card info – type and number

4. Confirmation – get user to confirm details are correct before sending them

5. Processing – message telling user that their request is being processed

6. Response – message indicating success (or failure) of registration

I used Flash to create the following storyboard for the registration form:

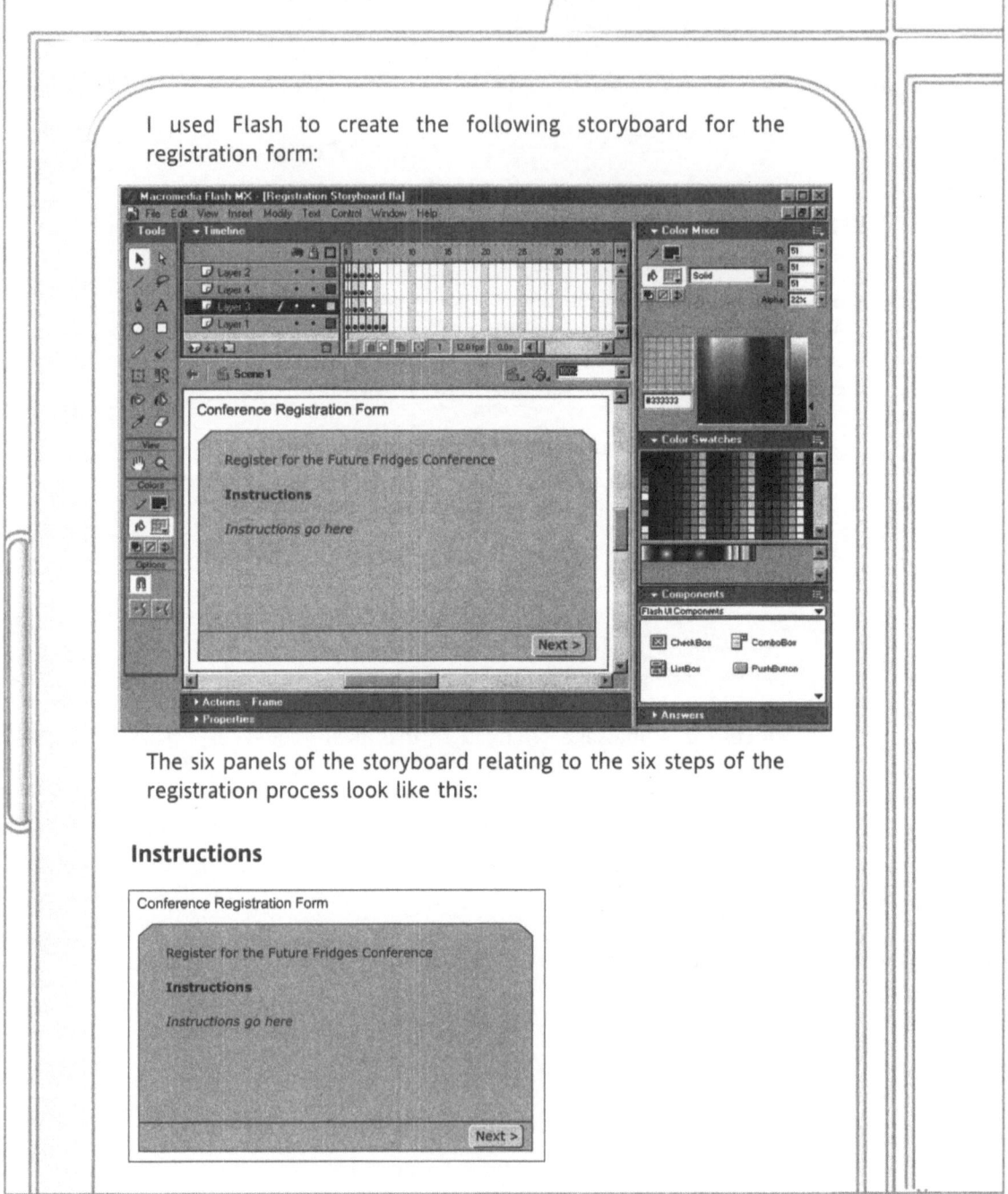

The six panels of the storyboard relating to the six steps of the registration process look like this:

Instructions

Personal Information

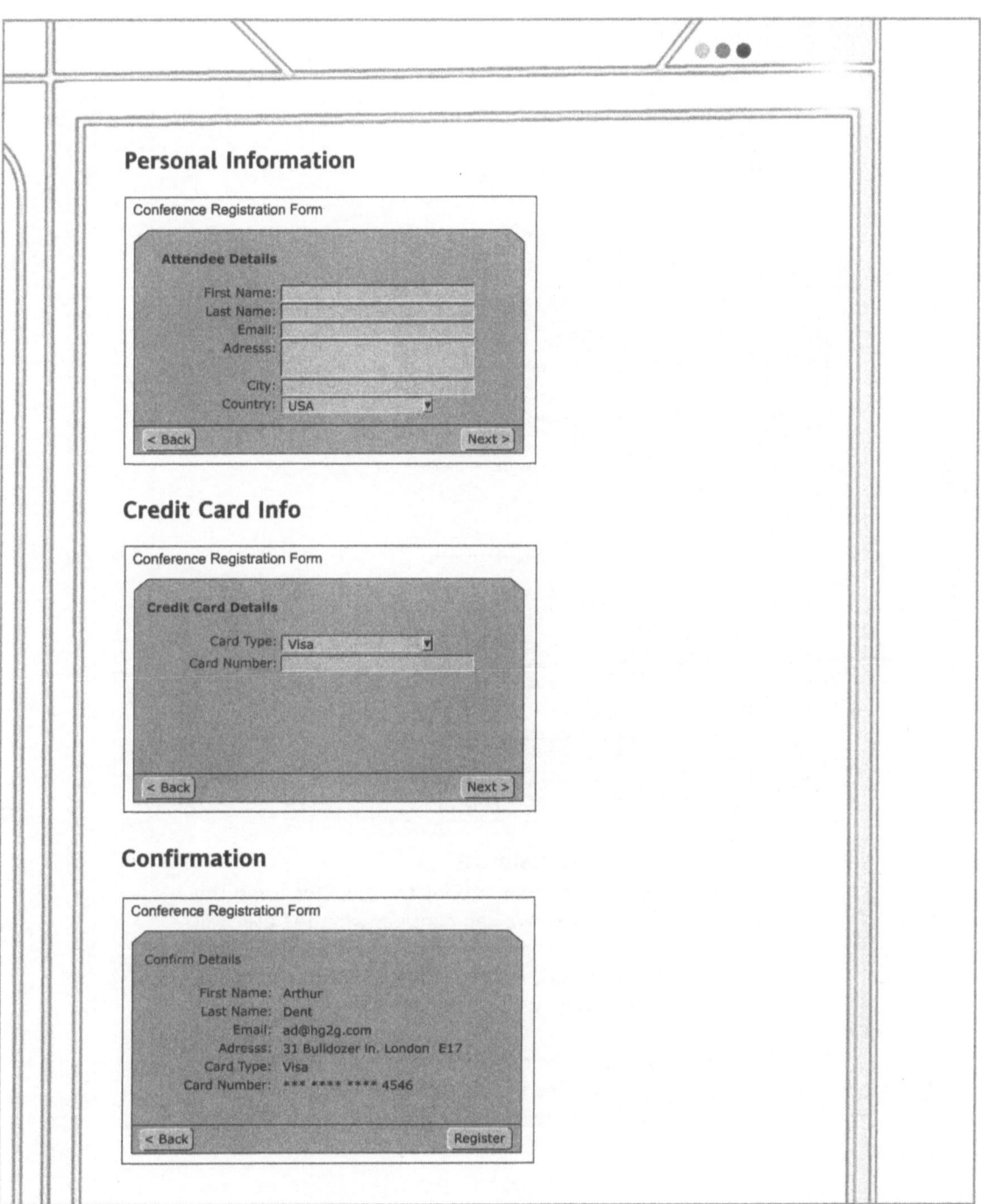

Credit Card Info

Confirmation

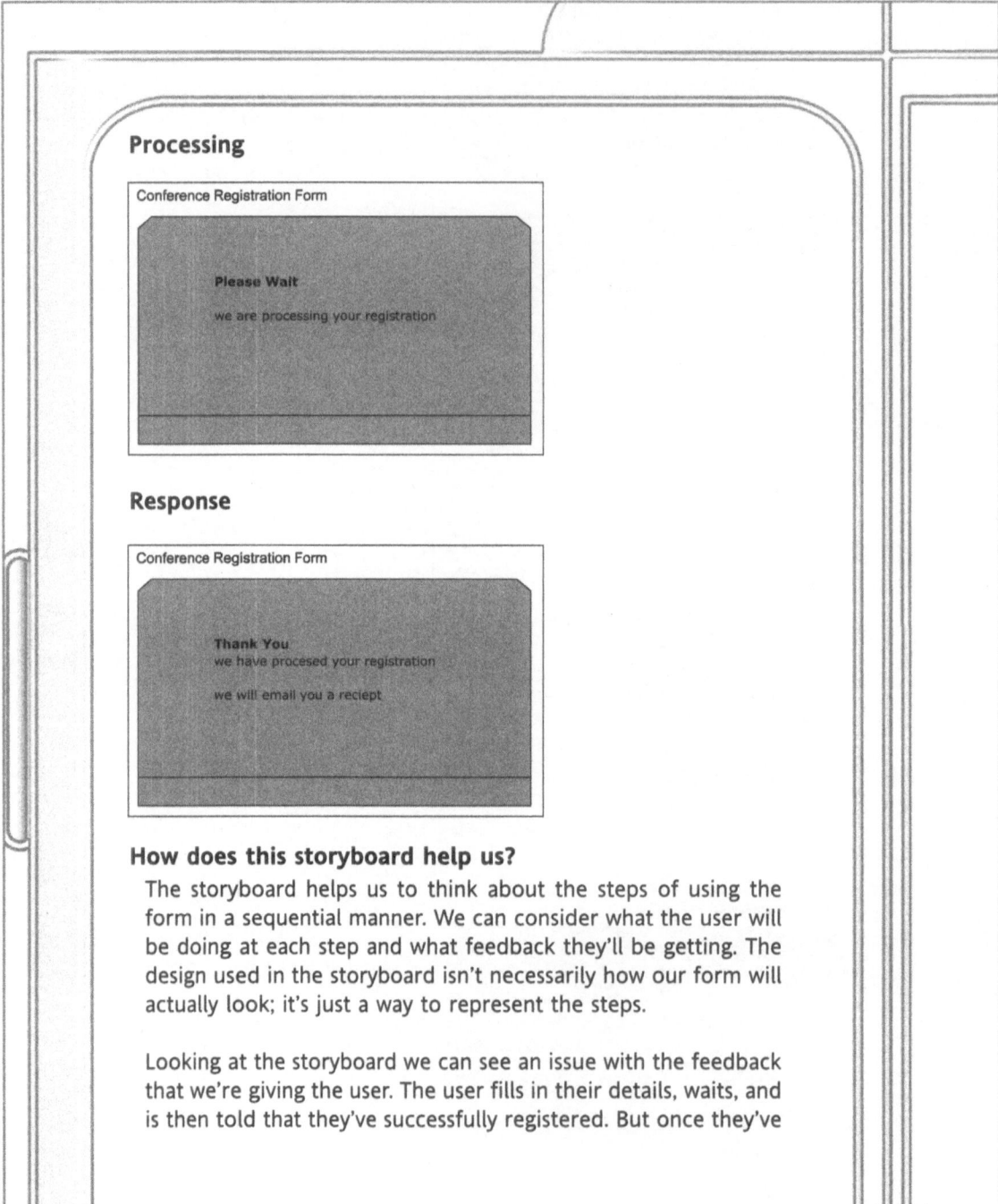

Processing

Conference Registration Form

Please Wait

we are processing your registration

Response

Conference Registration Form

Thank You
we have procesed your registration

we will email you a reciept

How does this storyboard help us?

The storyboard helps us to think about the steps of using the form in a sequential manner. We can consider what the user will be doing at each step and what feedback they'll be getting. The design used in the storyboard isn't necessarily how our form will actually look; it's just a way to represent the steps.

Looking at the storyboard we can see an issue with the feedback that we're giving the user. The user fills in their details, waits, and is then told that they've successfully registered. But once they've registered what happens then? More than likely, our users will be wondering how they'll receive their conference tickets. The problem is that we've taken their money and then left them hanging. We may be planning on sending out the conference ticket to the supplied address, but we haven't told the user that!

At this stage we have to check with our client to find out how the tickets will be sent to users. As expected, our client informs us that the tickets will be mailed out to attendees.

So we need to include information in the instructions that explains to the user that the tickets will be sent out to the mailing address supplied. For the final step we should inform users when their ticket will be sent out (e.g. next working day) and based on their address, estimate when they should receive their ticket.

Choosing how to organize your site content

Since storyboards are best suited to purely linear processes, they're rarely appropriate for entire projects. However, they can be useful when nested inside an IA, and vice versa. You might also consider presenting complementary versions of your content in parallel: an SB version for presentation and an IA version for user interaction.

Let's say you're designing course information in Flash, in which the student is hopefully going to start with the first page of Lesson One rather than the eighth page of Lesson Three. It's tempting to force them to watch the entire lesson before going on to the next one, or at least be forced to download the whole of the coursework rather than whichever class they choose. You might even show the pages full-screen, so that programs in the background won't cause distraction. The structure of this content, whether presented full-screen or not, is most suited to being planned out via storyboards.

However, since most people tend to prefer options above the will of a designer, a smart addition to the Flash content would be navigational tools or a menu to allow the student to skip to Lesson Three if they happen to be advanced or simply want to check out how much they know. These structures – the structures of the sets of lessons, as well as the navigational structure among lessons – are suited to planning out with IA techniques.

Since most Flash sites (even ones that concentrate on storytelling or courses or other linear content) feature task-based content in combination with linear content, a combination of IA and SB planning will most often be called for.

Mix the two together

Deciding whether to use an Information Architecture for information organization or a Storyboard for a particular part of your project is generally quite simple. Ask yourself a few questions about how the users are likely to use the content:

- Q: Is the content like a movie or story?
- A: If 'yes' then Storyboarding the content is applicable.

- Q: Is the content more like a database or encyclopedia?
- A: If 'yes' then an Information Architecture should be used for organization.

- Q: Is the content a portion of a larger whole?
- A: If 'yes' remember that Storyboarding is best suited to linear content.

- Q: Will users need to access specific parts of the content?
- A: If 'yes' then an Information Architecture will best organize the content for fast location of specific information.

> *Storyboarding and Information Architecture can both be part of the overall organization strategy. Many large-scale sites will benefit from a mix of the two. A shopping site is a good example of how the two strategies can work together.*

The shopping site needs an overall Information Architecture to sort the products the site carries into logical categories. This IA provides the user with the information they need to find the items they wish to purchase. If products need configuration based on options available, then Storyboarding that process will assist the user to answer the specific product-related questions.

Once the product has been selected and configured, the user moves onto the checkout portion of the interaction. As we know from experience, purchasing products on the Web usually involves a multiple page form. This checkout process would also benefit from Storyboarding to find the easiest process for the user.

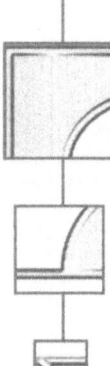

Summary

This chapter should have given you a fairly good idea about the basics of Information Architecture and Storyboarding. You should now be aware of the importance of organizing information in a logical and intuitive way. Half the battle of delivering usable Flash content is in the organization of the information making up that content.

Information Architecture is best suited to organizing the overall structure of a site as well as navigational structures within a site. Storyboarding is best used when linear progress is needed or desired from the site visitor within a specific piece of content.

However, you should also be aware that projects will often require the use of both IA and SB. The overall top-level organization of information may be adequately tackled with an IA however there may be specific processes within the overall project that will require planning with SB. Both are important and valuable techniques to the Flash designer who aspires to create really usable content.

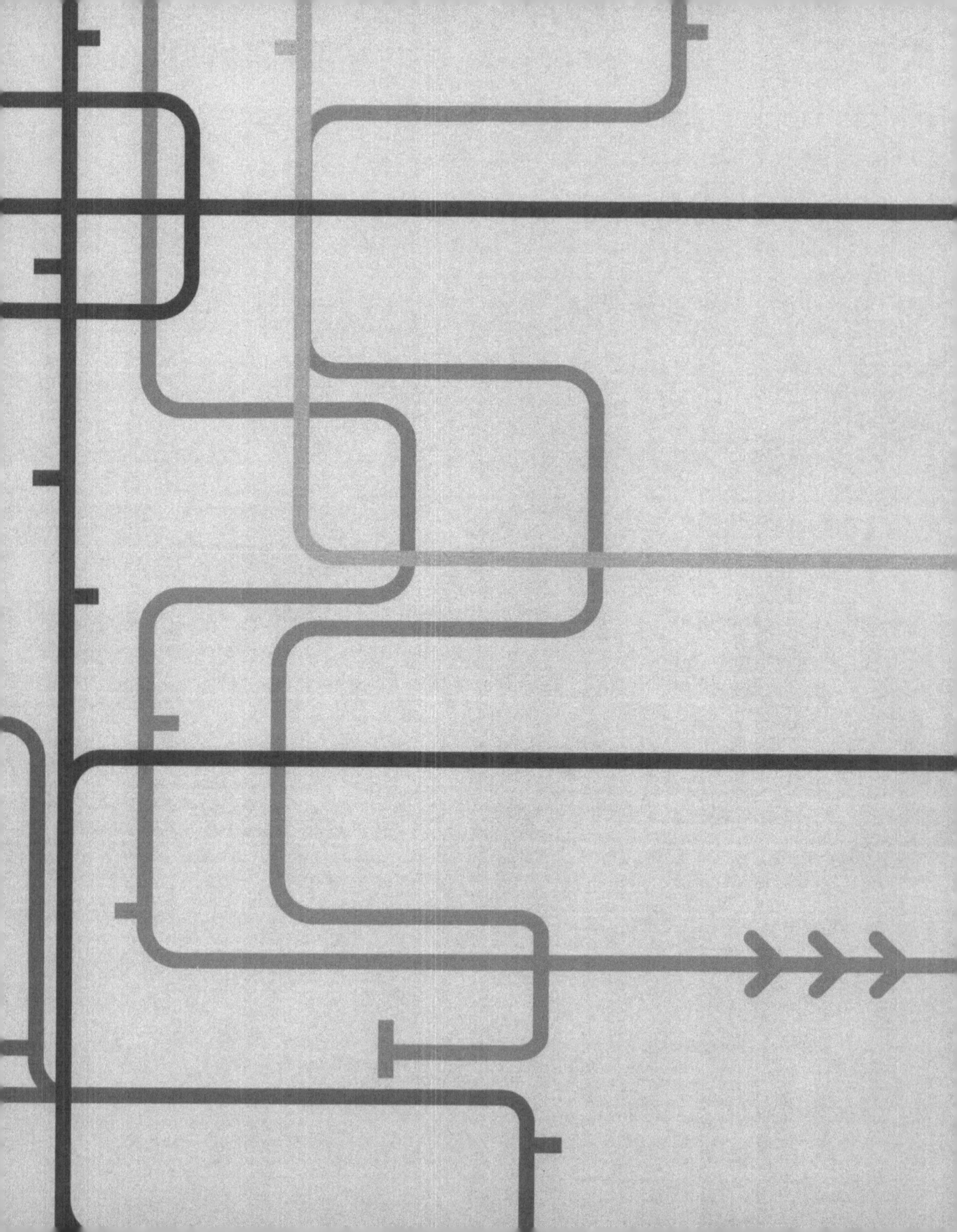

Usable interactions

One of the key factors to consider when designing a usable Flash site is this: how are users going to **interact** with the content? They have no control over the movie beyond what *we* provide them with, so the only way they have to make their presence felt is via a set of tools that we've designed to accomplish specific tasks. As such, they're limited to a narrow, well-defined set of interactions that we decide in advance.

Bundling all these interactive elements together, we build up the notion of a **user interface** (UI) for the movie. Users won't type the command `_root.content.about.gotoAndPlay('profiles')` into their browser if they want to access the **Profiles** section of your Flash site. Instead, they'll click on a button whose sole purpose it is to tell the Flash movie to jump to the section of content that's been labeled 'profiles'. This button is part of the UI along with every other button, menu, slider, or other interactive element in the movie.

In this chapter, we're going to consider what makes a good UI, and see how good interface design figures in our quest for usable Flash content.

What use is a UI?

A user interface is like a waiter in a restaurant. When the customer orders his or her food, the waiter delivers the order to the chef for preparation. The waiter then keeps the customer aware of the progress and offers to refill drinks. Once the food is ready, the waiter brings it to the customer and asks if there are any more instructions to carry back to the chef.

This is exactly what a Flash UI does, except that where the waiter acts as an interface between the customer and the kitchen, the UI acts between the user and the ActionScript commands that make the Flash content work its magic. Just as you wouldn't expect to write down your own order for the chef in a restaurant, users don't expect to have to enter any ActionScript commands to interact with our Flash content.

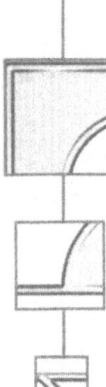

The user interface allows for communication both to and from the user – if it's unclear, hard to use, or just inconsistent at following users' commands, it'll cause nothing but frustration. Just as a bad waiter can ruin a customer's experience of a good restaurant, a poorly implemented user interface can ruin the user's experience with our splendid Flash content.

Elements of a good user interface

There's a great deal to bear in mind when designing and building a truly usable interface. Let's run through some of the most important issues.

Clarity

The interface should be **clear and unambiguous** to help make it intuitive to use and to reduce the risk of user error. If we use icons, we need to make sure that they're clearly symbolic of the actions or commands they imply. If the interface uses a metaphor, we need to run tests to ensure that the metaphor is one that users will find helpful.

Buttons need to look like buttons. That doesn't mean they should all have beveled edges and drop shadows, just that we need to provide the user with some kind of visual cues that mark out the functions of specific elements in the design.

Labels need to be clear and easy to understand. Users shouldn't have to guess at what sections contain – it should be obvious from the label on whichever button or tab they click on to get there.

Important sections of the interface need to be clear and easy to distinguish. For example, users should have no difficulty recognizing the difference between content and navigation controls.

Consistency

The user interface needs to be **consistent** in appearance and behavior. Controls of a particular type (such as navigation buttons) should look similar

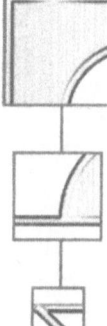

to one another, and produce similar results when pressed. This helps users with limited experience to successfully apply what they've learnt to new content – in other words, it makes the interface nice and predictable.

Established conventions are even more helpful, since users can apply things they've learnt from other sites. We need to remember that our users build their interaction expectations from every site they interact with, and not just from what we put in front of them.

Flash resource sites are full of sample scrollbars, but if every scrollbar in a UI behaves differently, users are just going to get confused. This goes the same for pulldown menus, radio buttons and other UI elements.

Flash MX offers a growing number of standardized UI components for Flash developers. By using these components in our projects we can provide users with some standardized UI elements.

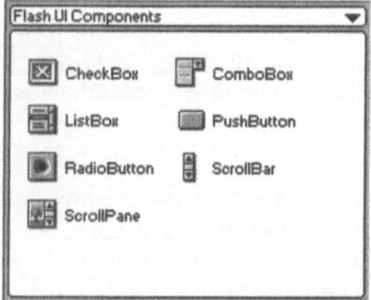

Unfortunately, all these components require the Flash 6 Plug-in, so these new features are best suited to off-line Flash content until the penetration rate of the Flash 6 Plug-in reaches sustainable numbers.

Simplicity

Complicated user interfaces are rarely thought of as 'beautiful' or 'useful'. Simplicity in the design of the user interface makes it easier for users to

interact with it. For us as designers, a simple user interface is better too, just because it's easier to build and code. More often than not, complexity just leads to confusion on both sides.

A good user interface serves to maximize the functionality of the Flash content. Buttons that move around the screen, elements of the design that respond to mouse movements, and other extraneous elements of the interface only serve to complicate the user's ability to understand what's going on.

Simplicity also means that the user interface is free of unnecessary elements. The eye candy that we add to our interfaces can be distracting to users. The human eye is attracted to movement. If the user interface contains animated elements, it can make it hard for the user to focus on the information we're presenting.

Animation, when used sparingly, can add impact to messages or deliver information in a more effective manner. It's particularly useful for communicating the fact that something's going on, when it may not otherwise be obvious. On the other hand, you should avoid making it look as if something's happening unless something *is* happening.

User control

The more control over a system you provide the user, the more trust they'll have in the system. Offer the user control over how the Flash content interacts with their needs. Allow the user to control settings like sound volume, launch window options and font sizes.

Many Flash sites on the Web respond to non-decisive mouse movements to activate elements of the user interface. Non-decisive mouse movements are made when the user doesn't actually want to perform a specific action. They may be idly dragging their mouse around the pad whilst reading a paragraph of text, deciding which navigation button to click, or even talking on the phone.

In a poorly designed interface, these non-decisive movements can cause content to move, animation to start, or mouse chasers to dart around the screen. This isn't just visually distracting, but can often be frustrating to the user, since they have no control over the extraneous movement on their screen. In a well-designed interface, the Flash content will only respond like this in response to actively performed actions, such as clicking, or clicking and dragging.

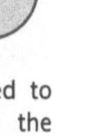

> *The user, and not the Flash content, needs to initiate actions. It should be the user who opens new pages, scrolls content and plays sounds – all by interacting actively with the user interface.*

Remember that user interactions with Flash content aren't restricted to mouse actions. Number one amongst computer entry devices is the keyboard, which lets us give far more detailed input such as commands and data. It's often a far more effective means of interaction than the mouse.

In many cases, you can harness the keyboard as an extended control for frequently performed tasks – offer users a concrete method (such as clicking on a button) and an abstract method (such as pressing a key combination).

Responsiveness

Actions performed by the user need to have clear and visible responses from the Flash content. This is known as **state visualization**. Each appearance of the user interface is known as a state. When the user clicks a button to issue a command, the user interface should respond by changing state to communicate to the user that their action has been received.

A button that doesn't provide feedback to the user may to some people appear to be broken. If you've ever pressed an elevator button that didn't light up, then you'll understand the confusion and frustration that a lack of

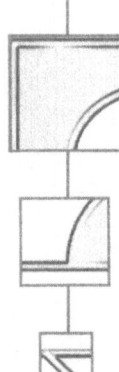

a visible reaction to a user action can encourage. The broken elevator button doesn't communicate that the elevator has received your command. All that you're left to do is hope that the button light is out of order and the elevator is on its way.

The action/reaction conversation between the UI and the user provides the reassurance that the user is in control of the Flash content.

A good UI also needs to communicate status to the user. Any time a reaction is delayed (for example, while content is being loaded from the server), the UI should let the user know what's causing the hold-up.

To some extent, we've been doing this for years, offering loading screens to tell users how much of the site has been downloaded at any given time. These screens let the user know their actions are being processed. Likewise, alert boxes that let the user know information is being passed to or from the server help to keep the user informed, making sure they don't just assume the site's crashed.

Modern operating systems use the cursor state to convey much of this information. The cursor receives more user attention than any other object on the screen – users follow the cursor with their eyes to help them navigate. In fact, it's not uncommon in usability tests to find users moving the mouse along a line of text as they read it.

Many applications use the cursor to send messages to the user. In the Flash authoring environment the cursor changes to represent the currently selected tool. For example, the Paint Bucket tool is represented by a cursor in the shape of a dripping bucket, while the Zoom tool is shown as a magnifying glass. While your operating system is busy processing a command, it probably displays an hourglass, implying that there may be a short wait.

Flash MX allows control over the display of the mouse cursor in the content you create. We should use this feature of Flash to adopt the hourglass or spinning color wheel conventions from operating systems. The cursor can also change to denote the function of different buttons. For example, the cursor can change to an icon of an envelope when the user mouses over an e-mail link.

The UI should also serve to assist the user in knowing where they are in the content. The user should be able to know their position within the content from any screen. Many solutions can be used to accomplish this. Smaller sites may have only a few pages of content, so the appropriate buttons in the interface may be highlighted to provide the user with location information. In larger sites with multi-tiered Information Architectures the use of breadcrumb navigation provides users with the necessary information they need to establish their location in the content. Breadcrumb navigation leaves a trail that the user can retrace to find their way around the site (more on this later).

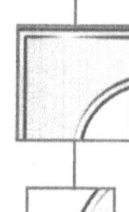

Safety

Everyone makes mistakes. How many times have you accidentally closed the wrong window on your computer or quit an application by pressing CTRL+Q when you meant to hit CTRL+A to select all? What value would *you* put on an undo feature? Mistakes are a way of life, and a good user interface will provide a safety net for users by allowing actions to be reversed.

The user interface should help the users to feel safe and in control. Many users are not confident in their computing skills; they don't trust themselves to make the right decision when faced with an unfamiliar system.

User interfaces without built-in safety features can make novice users feel frustrated and unsure of their abilities. In many cases, they'll stop interacting with content after one or two mistakes. User interfaces that encourage exploration by offering users safety features are perceived as more usable and more successful. Offering secondary verification for important commands (such as a dialog box confirming an action) will help the user to feel more comfortable using the interface.

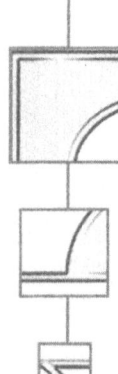

Bear in mind that more experienced users may find this frustrating. They may want to interact with the interface in a more direct manner, so it's worth offering them the option to turn off the safety features.

Aesthetics

There's nothing more striking about a good user interface than an elegant design. It's the first thing that's noticed by users and clients alike. Too often though, the aesthetics are the best thought-out part of a site's UI. Stacks of Flash sites have gorgeous designs that wouldn't look out of place in an art gallery. However, if the site you've been commissioned to design is supposed to have some kind of practical emphasis, even the best looking interface won't get you your paycheck if nobody using it can get their jobs done!

The function of graphic design within the user interface is to provide visual cues to the importance of interface elements. The navigation, content areas and branding areas all compete for the user's attention. A good design aesthetic will clearly define these areas on the screen, tying the elements together to create a seamless whole.

Flash offers another challenge to the aesthetics of the design: it's not a static medium – interactions with Flash take place over time. Users are acutely aware of anything that makes their interactions feel slow. Interstitial animations that show movement between screens can often have this effect. If you're going try the kind of impressive transitions seen on sites such as www.2advanced.com, you need to make sure they're good and fast – most users won't thank you for forcing a ten-second animation on them in response to every mouse click. Not unless it's very good, anyway.

Without navigation the user is lost

If you only get the chance to test one element of your Flash site with real users, it should always be the navigation. It's the single most important element in any user interface. A Flash site won't be user-friendly unless the navigation is user-friendly, so that should be the simplest part of the UI to master. As such, you should prioritize the creation, labeling, and design of the navigation elements over every other part of the design. That's not to say it should take a long time, just that you should concentrate on getting the navigation right first, and not let other factors compromise it without a darned good reason!

> *Navigation is more than just the buttons that run along one side of the UI. It's like the car steering wheel that drives a user's interaction with your Flash content. It's often just a matter of common sense, but it should ultimately serve to reinforce a mental model of the Information Architecture behind the site.*

Navigation elements help users to start figuring out the structure and organization of content on a site – a lot of this information comes via their labels. They can also help users to find information that they're looking for, like the department signs that hang above our heads in large stores.

If navigation options are missing, covered, or off-screen, the user won't be able to make the best decision as to which element they ought to click. Worse still, they might even get the impression that your client doesn't offer the information they were looking for, and hop off to another site!

Where am I?

As well as providing direction, the navigation system ought to let the user know where they currently are within the content. In a large store, you need only look above your head to find out which section you're in. On a Flash site, the user looks to the navigation to find out. In addition to suitable use of headings, it can be useful to highlight (and disable) the navigation element for the user's current location.

Another web convention that can easily be applied to Flash content development is the use of breadcrumb navigation, which gets its name from the fable of Hansel and Gretel, who used breadcrumbs to mark their path

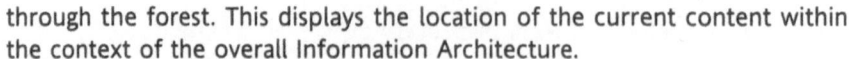

through the forest. This displays the location of the current content within the context of the overall Information Architecture.

Breadcrumb navigation reinforces the structure of your site, by making it obvious how information is grouped. By making each step of the breadcrumb trail into a navigation button, the user can quickly move back up the Information Architecture hierarchy.

Using this book as an example, the breadcrumb navigation for the section you're reading right now might look something like this:

> The Flash Usability Guide: Interacting with Flash MX > Chapter 7 – Usable Interactions >
> What use is a UI? > Without navigation the user is lost > Where am I?

Toys in the interface

Flash is an excellent application for creating online toys, and sites like 'Meet the Rabbit' (www.esu.lt/andrius/10/go1.htm) go to prove just how entertaining web content can be. However, problems can arise if we start building toys like these into the user interface. Moving buttons that the user has to 'chase' with their mouse, sliding interfaces that respond to the mouse's position, or unnecessary drag-and-drop interactions can put extra hurdles in the way of getting a job done.

Sure, if the aim of the site is to offer a fun experience, then practical ends like 'clicking on the submit button' may not be high on the user's list of priorities, nor on yours. But if the site does call for a wacky 'cursor on a spring' or similar, then it's important to think about the knock-on effect. You may want to make the buttons a little larger than normal, or build in a 'snap to' feature that helps compensate for the reduced pointer accuracy.

Building buttons

Another important interface issue related to navigation is button design. By getting this right you dramatically increase the usability of your site and ensure that users are never puzzled about how to find the information they want. It's amazing how many Flash sites out there contain really badly designed buttons – ones that are too small, inconspicuous, poorly labeled, or simply don't look like they're waiting to be clicked.

At the end of the day, that's what a button's for: clicking. It's our job to make it as easy as possible for users to find and click the buttons we build in Flash. As we've already mentioned elsewhere in the book, Flash MX gives almost unlimited scope for designing buttons. We can make buttons look and behave any way we want. But, as I hope you're beginning to realize by now, exercising that kind of design freedom isn't necessarily the best way to ensure maximum usability.

There are a few guidelines that can really help to add usability value to your button design. I'll run through a few of them here:

Apply Fitt's Law to button design

Fitt's Law is all about the way people use their mouse when interacting with a computer. It states:

> "The time to acquire a target is a function of the *distance to* and *size of* the target."

In very simple terms, this means that items close to the mouse pointer are easier to click than ones further away. Also, bigger items are easier to click. Now this may seem incredibly obvious, but it's amazing how many designers choose to ignore this simple principle.

We can use Fitt's Law to help us figure out the best place to locate important interface elements such as buttons. Imagine a full-screen Flash presentation with the user's mouse pointer inside a 20-unit radius circle around the center of the screen. Now we can determine the five best target locations; the best points on the screen to locate buttons, either individually or together in a cluster.

- The first point is the center of the screen, where the mouse is currently located.
- The other four points are in the four corners of the screen, since if you 'threw' your cursor with enough velocity, it'll inevitably land up sitting in one of them.

> *Even though the corners are the farthest points from the center of the screen, they're also the easiest to hit, since they're bordered by the screen boundaries on two sides. Each boundary acts like a trap for the mouse pointer, so the most effective trapping point is where two edges meet – in other words, in the corner.*

Bearing this in mind, it makes sense to locate navigation buttons at the edges of the screen. The screen boundaries provide an infinitely deep target – you'll never be able to move your mouse pointer past them. Ensure that the buttons are right on the edge of the screen, and we can make the most effective use of the aforementioned 'trapping'.

Fitt's Law also tells us that we should make our buttons as large as possible if we want to maximize usability. It's fairly obvious that the larger the area of a button the less chance there is of missing it when you aim to click it with your mouse pointer.

I've seen many sites with buttons no larger than a few pixels across. This not only makes it difficult for the user to *see* the button, but it makes it far harder for them to hit it first time; it may take two or three shots to get right on the button. Much more effort is required to hit a smaller button. Remember that reducing user effort is an important way to increase usability.

We have a very useful tool in Flash MX that we can use to make buttons as clickable as possible: ActionScript. We can use it to dynamically improve the target area of buttons as the mouse approaches them. Audi make use of this feature in the 'New Cars' section of their UK web site (www.audi.co.uk). Buttons on this page are pictures of the different cars in the Audi range. As you move your mouse over a button it expands to increase the clickable area and a more detailed label is displayed.

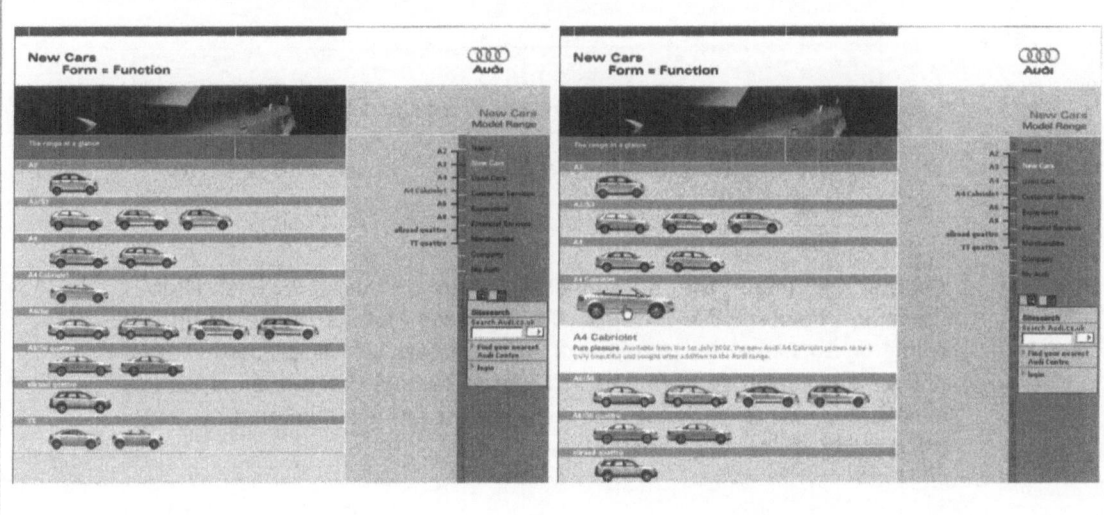

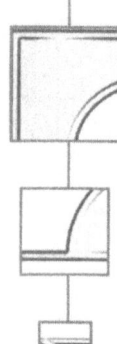

The Motion commotion

Flash MX is a **motion** design tool. Animation is what it's all about. But just because it gives us the ability to animate it doesn't mean we should use that ability willy-nilly when designing interfaces. One of the main bones of contention between Flash critics and designers is gratuitous use of animation on Flash sites. We need to carefully consider whether animation is adding value to our interface.

Animation can be a major distraction on a web site. If we do use it, we need to make sure that it doesn't distract the user from accomplishing their task. It's important not to annoy users with continuous distractions that appear to serve no useful purpose. Animation should only be used if it enhances the presentation of information and in doing so makes it easier for the user to get where they want to be in terms of completing their task.

Sometimes complex information can benefit from animation. By animating a diagram, for example, you may be able to illustrate more clearly the information that it represents. Animation can often help to make the complex simple.

> *Animation shouldn't put barriers between the user and the information they're looking for. It should only be used if it helps to convey that information.*

Another legitimate use of animation is to enhance the definition of navigation elements like buttons. We've already looked at how Audi uses animation to make the buttons on their site grow in size as the mouse pointer gets closer to them. This is a good example of using animation to enhance the user experience. The Audi site uses subtle animation to increase the usability of its navigation elements.

Sounds like a good idea

The Web has traditionally been a silent medium. So when we introduce sound we really need to be sure that it's necessary. We should also give users the option of turning off the sound. It's important to bear in mind that not all systems (especially those in corporate environments) have sound capabilities. Also, many users regard sound as a nuisance – there's nothing more irritating than a colleague at a nearby desk downloading a noisy web page.

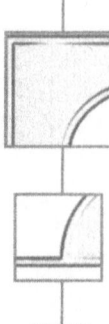

Like animation, sound should not be used in an unnecessary, gratuitous way. Sound can be a useful tool in conveying information. For example, providing a voiceover for an online presentation can add a great deal of usability value.

You must also remember that not everyone can hear. If you're aiming to produce a really usable Flash web site, then this is something you must take into account. It's essential to provide an alternative for people with hearing impairments (or those without sound capabilities on their hardware) to access the information that you're conveying through sound. We'll see more on designing for accessibility in Chapter 9.

Another important issue related to the use of sound in your interface is that it can seriously bloat your Flash files. You must experiment with the sound settings in Macromedia Flash MX to make sure that your sound files are fully optimized.

Color and contrast

A crucial factor to consider when designing an interface is the contrast between the text or other elements, and the background of the pages. The easiest way to check this is that if you can't read it, your audience won't be able to read it either. The default color scheme for most browsers is a gray background with black text, blue links, and purple visited links, but few people use this scheme any more. While it's adequate for basic reading comfort and understanding navigation, it's also pretty boring.

Although different platforms and different monitor settings can make colors appear slightly different, you can get a useful idea of a screen's readability on nearly any monitor with any graphic browser. True, PC monitors tend to show colors a little darker than Mac monitors, but if two colors contrast strongly on the Mac, they should still contrast strongly on a PC.

Color characteristics	
Hue	– The color attribute identified by color names, such as 'red' or 'yellow'
Value	– The degree of lightness or darkness of a color
Saturation	– The relative purity of a color; also referred to as **intensity**. The 'brighter' the intensity of a color, the more saturated it is. New jeans are saturated with blue; faded ones are a less saturated blue
Chromatic Hues	– All colors other than black, white, and gray
Neutral Colors	– Black, white, or gray; otherwise known as **non-chromatic hues**
Monochromatic	– Refers to a color combination based on variations of value and saturation of a single hue

The closer together two hues are, the less contrast there is between them. Even when combining colors of different hues, their respective values (darkness or lightness) will also affect the contrast between the two colors.

If you're not up for learning color theory or studying color wheels for ideal color combinations, a quick way of testing the contrast of your colors – and thus the readability of your site – is to change your monitor settings (or the image itself) to a grayscale setting. Note how even though there were a number of colors on the original, those with similar value settings (percentage of brightness) seem to fade into the background. If you want your contrast to improve, change the text or background color so that they have values that differ more.

Multi-colored backgrounds

There's not a whole lot you can do to make a multi-colored patterned background into an ideal setting for text, unless you drastically change the overall contrast and brightness of the background image. Choosing a color of text that contrasts with all of the background colors is a pretty impossible task.

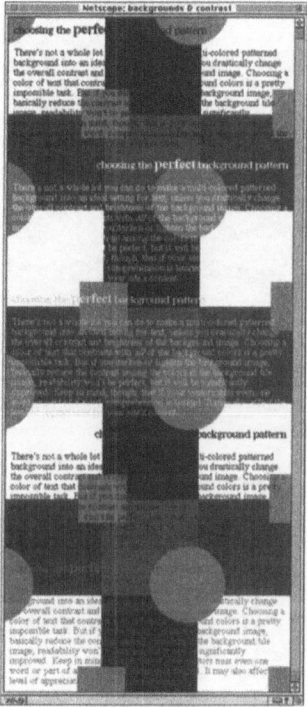

This is an example I often use to show off the difficulty of making a multi-colored background workable in a design. In color, it makes more of an impact, but even as you see it here in grayscale, it should drive home the importance of background patterns, their color value, and the contrast between background colors and the chosen type color.

If you reduce the contrast of the background colors, readability may not be perfect, but it should be significantly improved. Keep in mind, though, that if your visitors miss even one word or part of a word, you're taking a chance – it may affect the level of appreciation for your site's content.

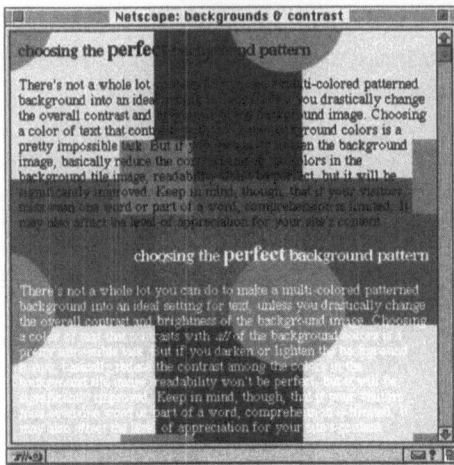 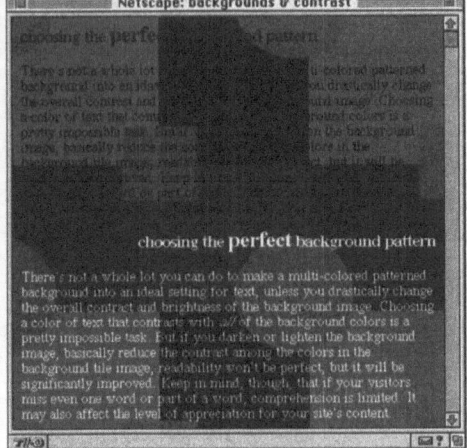

If the background is lightened or darkened, there's more of a chance that your choice of text color will contrast against it. In this case, it's obvious that the darker text contrasts best with the lighter background, and vice versa.

Picking colors

What color combinations are the most readable? It's generally accepted that the best color scheme for reading on paper is black text on a white or cream-colored background (you might have noticed that most books and magazines are printed with black text on white paper). Black text on white paper is high contrast, and high contrast is easier to read than low contrast. However, when viewing a monitor a person is staring straight at a light source, black text on a white background isn't the most comfortable to look at for long periods of time. It can help the reader if you take the contrast down *just* a touch, especially if you're asking them to read a lot of text. This could also mean using a light color rather than white in combination with black (either as a background pattern or text color). On screen, it generally seems that black and yellow make the highest readability combination.

Color blindness

Color blindness, a genetic disorder of color deficiency, affects one out of every twelve men and one in every 200 or so women. These people are unable to see the full spectrum of colors, and may have difficulty reading or viewing certain combinations of colors. A color-blind person lacks a color receptor (either red, green, and/or blue); the most common form is red-green color blindness. If a red-green color-blind person sees a red object and a green object of about equal value (or brightness), the red object will appear darker than the green one.

Colors of equivalent value can be difficult for a person with color blindness to view. One way to check for various combinations of colors that will work for most audiences, including those with color blindness, is again to test images and sites in grayscale mode.

So the key here (no matter what color or colors the person has problems with) is the fact that if the respective colors are of equal brightness, the color-blind viewer won't be able to view, for example, red text on a green background. However, if the contrast between the two colors (that is, their

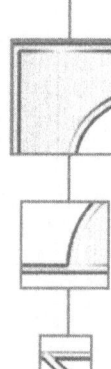

relative brightness, or color value) is great enough, then the prospects of viewing are better.

Another thing to consider is that these users will have enormous trouble if you include color-specific instructions such as:

> Click on the red dot to vote 'No', or click on the green dot to vote 'Yes'

Try adding text cues to any color-based scheme, such as labeling buttons on a navigational bar. Another option is to use shapes rather than colors as the differing aspect of each choice. For example, you can use a check mark for 'Yes', and a cross for 'No'.

As a bonus accessibility benefit, using shapes as a navigational visual cue rather than colors can assist those with some cognitive impairments. We'll look at some more tips on designing for the visually impaired in Chapter 9.

The easiest rule of thumb when it comes to color and contrast is this: if *you* can't read your web pages, others probably can't either. Variations of color hues aren't so important as variations in brightness when it comes to enhancing contrast and readability.

There are no strict rules about colors you should or shouldn't choose for your Flash creations, but before you get stuck in with any old color combination, test your images and color schemes in grayscale (and to be extra sure, in black-and-white as well) to make sure everyone sees what you want them to.

Rein in the excess

The user interface is not the place for excess. For every element of the user interface we need to ask ourselves two questions:

Does the interaction cause the user to wait? Waiting can occur both before and after the user interacts with the UI element. Buttons that move around the screen mean the user has to spend time 'catching' them with the mouse. Long interstitial animations between the user's interaction and the Flash content finishing its response also put the user in a passive state with the Flash content. We need to strive for instant click-respond interactions.

Does the user interface behave in a way that makes sense? When a user clicks a button or interacts with a user interface element, does the resulting action respond in a way that meets the user's expectations? Do the scrollbars operate the same way as other scrollbars they interact with? Do buttons act the same way as other buttons? Flash content that requires the user to double-click on a button, for example, breaks the single-click convention of the Web.

Case Study

Designing the user interface

Let's start building the user interface for our conference site. We've already identified eight primary navigation items for the site, labeled:

- Home Page

- Registration

- Overview

- Speakers

- Session Details

- Sponsors

- Organizers

- Venue, Travel and Hotels

We need to identify a user-friendly way to set out these navigation items. The most common (thus most intuitive) locations for navigation elements are either the top or the left-hand side of the interface. Let's consider these two possibilities for our site.

Primary navigation

We'll design our interface to work on a screen resolution of 800x600, which, when the browser tool bars and scrollbars are taken into consideration, leaves us with a width of 760 pixels and a height of 420 pixels. For users with a lower screen resolution of 640 x 480, we'll use Flash's ability to **scale to fit the screen** to ensure that these users aren't presented with horizontal scrollbars.

Top bar

For our initial testing we'll consider the navigation items to be rendered in the 'Verdana' font at a font height of 12 with each navigation item being separated by a space of 20 pixels. This is probably as small and close as our navigation text can be and still be clear and readable.

If we list the current navigation items in this format we find that we have a navigation list that is 745 pixels long and 19 pixels high.

| Home page | Registration | Overview | Speakers | Session Details | Sponsors | Organizers | Venue, Hotel & Travel |

This is a long navigation bar that only just fits into our interface design area. This length makes it hard for users to scan across it for the section they're interested in. However we can make a few changes that will reduce its length.

We don't really need to call the **Home** section '**Home Page**'; just the word 'Home' will do. Many web sites use this to mark a navigation link to the site's home page, so it's a convention our users will almost certainly be familiar with.

| Home | Registration | Overview | Speakers | Session Details | Sponsors | Organizers | Venue, Hotel & Travel |

We can also set out our multi-word navigation items over two lines, which will give us a shorter navigation bar.

This gives us a more readable navigation with a length of just 614 pixels and would make an acceptable top navigation bar.

Left bar

If we take the same navigation items and lay them out vertically, separated by a 20-pixel space, our navigation looks like this:

This is easy for the user to scan with their eyes, and comes in at just 246 pixels high and 134 pixels wide. The overall screen space this navigation will take up is a little greater than the top navigation, but it still easily fits into our target screen resolution.

| Home page |
| Registration |
| Overview |
| Speakers |
| Session |
| Sponsors |
| Organisers |
| Venue, Hotel & Travel |

It appears that either a top or left-hand navigation will be possible for our site. If our navigation items had used longer labels then we may have found that it was not possible to set out a top navigation that fitted in the screen area while still being an acceptable font size.

So which should we use? Before deciding we need to consider the other elements of the interface, namely the secondary navigation and the content.

Secondary navigation and content

The purpose of a secondary navigation is to allow the user to navigate the content within the different sections of the site. Each section will potentially require a secondary navigation to allow users to navigate the subsections of the content. Let's consider our site's content and what the secondary navigation elements will be.

- The **Overview** section contains details of the conference highlights. This will contain a few paragraphs of text describing the conference to entice people to attend. As it's just one chunk of information, no secondary navigation is required for this section.

- The **Speakers** section contains details on all the speakers presenting at the conference. This will need to include a secondary navigation composed of a list of all the speakers, so users can select a speaker and view their biography details.

So what about the audio and video interviews with the speakers? We could have a tertiary navigation under each speaker that lets users select a speaker's bio or interview. Alternatively we could just incorporate the interview into the description of the speaker, or we could even make our secondary navigation a choice between 'interview' or 'speaker details', with the list of speakers becoming a tertiary navigation under these categories.

How do we identify which method is best? We need to think about our users, what they'll be doing, and what information they're looking for. Most users will want to browse the list of speakers and will click on a speaker's name to find out more about the speaker.

The task the user is undertaking is 'finding out more about the speaker'. The interviews provide more information about individual speakers and therefore should be content that users find when undertaking this task. Hence a speaker's name should lead a user to an interview with that speaker, assuming one exists.

What about our test user Thomas? Back in Chapter 6, our IA testing indicated that Thomas would go to the 'speakers' section to see if there was content relevant to his television audience – he'd be especially interested in any video or audio content.

In the navigation list of speakers we'll need to make it easy for users like Thomas to know which speaker bios contain audio or video content. We'll also need to ensure that the company that the speakers work for is listed next to their names as we have previously identified this association as being important and useful to our users.

Ultimately our secondary navigation for this section will be a list of the speakers, but the list will need to clearly indicate the speaker's company and if there's any audio or video content included in the speaker's details.

The **Registration** section contains the registration form, instructions on how to complete it, pricing, payment, and refund information. The main content is the form, but we will need to ensure that the instructions, pricing, payment and refund information are always accessible while the user is filling in the form. This suggests that we won't have a secondary navigation for this section but rather a form layout that lets the user easily access relevant information while completing the form.

The **Session Details** section contains the full details for all conference sessions and incorporates the session planner tool. Effectively this section is a mini-application that will offer users a number of ways to browse through the session timetable. There isn't a secondary navigation as such, because the section content is part of an interactive navigation tool.

The **Sponsors** section contains logos, details, and links for the conference's sponsors. This is just one section of content and there is no need for a secondary navigation.

The **Organizers** section contains information about the conference organizers and their contact details. This could be broken into two sections and require a secondary navigation, however when we examine our content we realize that there are only a few paragraphs on the organizers and along with their contact information this represents only one screen of information. There's no need to force users into a second level of navigation for this section when all the content can be displayed in one screen.

Finally the **Venue, Hotel and Travel** section contains information on getting to and staying near the conference. This content clearly lends itself to a simple secondary navigation made up of these three elements.

Having taken a close look at our content we can see that the only section that has a typical secondary navigation is the **Venue, Hotel and Travel** section that has three clear sub-sections. There are also three main sections that have interactive content that require navigation elements, namely the **Speakers**, **Session Details** and **Registration** sections. In these three cases the secondary navigation will be quite large and may be difficult to integrate into standard secondary navigation structures.

Typical secondary navigation structures

Secondary navigation in web sites typically takes one of three forms:

Below the navigation

Many corporate sites use a top bar navigation and then place the second level navigation directly underneath. Is this appropriate for our site? It could be used for the **Venue, Hotel and Travel** section as shown below.

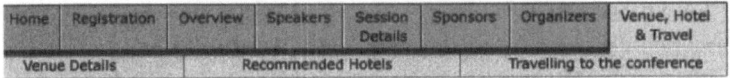

However it won't be appropriate for the other sections. For example, there's no way that we could include the names of all the speakers into this layout.

Pop-out menu

This is another popular secondary navigation method. When the user rolls over the navigation (or in some cases clicks on the primary navigation buttons) a menu of secondary options pops out. This is used in sites with top and left-hand navigation structures. Is this appropriate for our site? Again it could be used for the **Venue, Hotel and Travel** section as shown below.

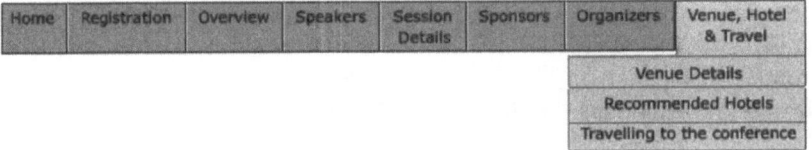

However this method also won't be appropriate for the other sections with many navigation elements. For example, the pop-out list of speakers would be huge and would obscure the site's content. The only possible solution would be to incorporate a scrollbar element into the navigation, effectively turning the navigation into a drop-down list. But drop-down lists are difficult to use and hide the navigation options, so we want to avoid that as an option.

Expanding list

Expanding lists are popular in navigation structures built with Flash. They're typically implemented using an expanding tree style structure or an expanding and collapsing menu structure. Is this appropriate for our site? It could be used for the **Venue, Hotel and Travel** section but for sections with a larger secondary navigation such as the **Speakers** section we'd need to add in a scrollbar, as shown below.

Expanding tree navigation (left) and expanding / collapsing menu navigation (right).

In both cases the navigation is expanding and collapsing to show or hide the secondary navigation. This can create quite a few usability issues; as the menu expands the primary navigation buttons below are moved down, which means that the navigation buttons don't remain in a consistent location. Especially problematic is the fact that the navigation items at the bottom of the list may be forced off the screen because of the expanding items above.

A very long secondary navigation can't easily be accommodated without needing to include a scrollbar (as shown) which forces our users into using a fiddly little scrollbar embedded into the navigation. In the example for our **Speakers** section there's limited space in the navigation, which will make it difficult to include additional information such as the speaker's company.

Recommended navigation

What we've found is that the **Speakers**, **Registration** and **Session Details** sections all contain content that isn't ideally suited to a traditional secondary navigation interface. We'll produce a more usable site by building secondary navigation interfaces suited to this content, rather than trying to force the navigation elements into a standard secondary navigation structure.

The only secondary navigation that may work in any of the previous structures would be the navigation for the **Venue, Hotel and Travel** section. However we'd not be building a consistent navigation if it only applied to one section of the site. Therefore the best option is to use either the top or left-hand primary navigation.

Draft interface layout

Having determined that we'll have a top or left-hand primary navigation and that our secondary navigation will be a part of the content area, we can now start to build up the draft layout for our site's interface.

We know that the interface will include the navigation and the content area (which will incorporate the secondary navigation when needed).

But what else needs to be a part of our interface?

- We'll need to include the name and logo of the site

- We'll also need to clearly label which section the user is currently located in

- We should include an area for a footer that can include any copyright information and a link to the HTML version of the site

Draft interface layout with top navigation

Here's a draft layout using a top navigation:

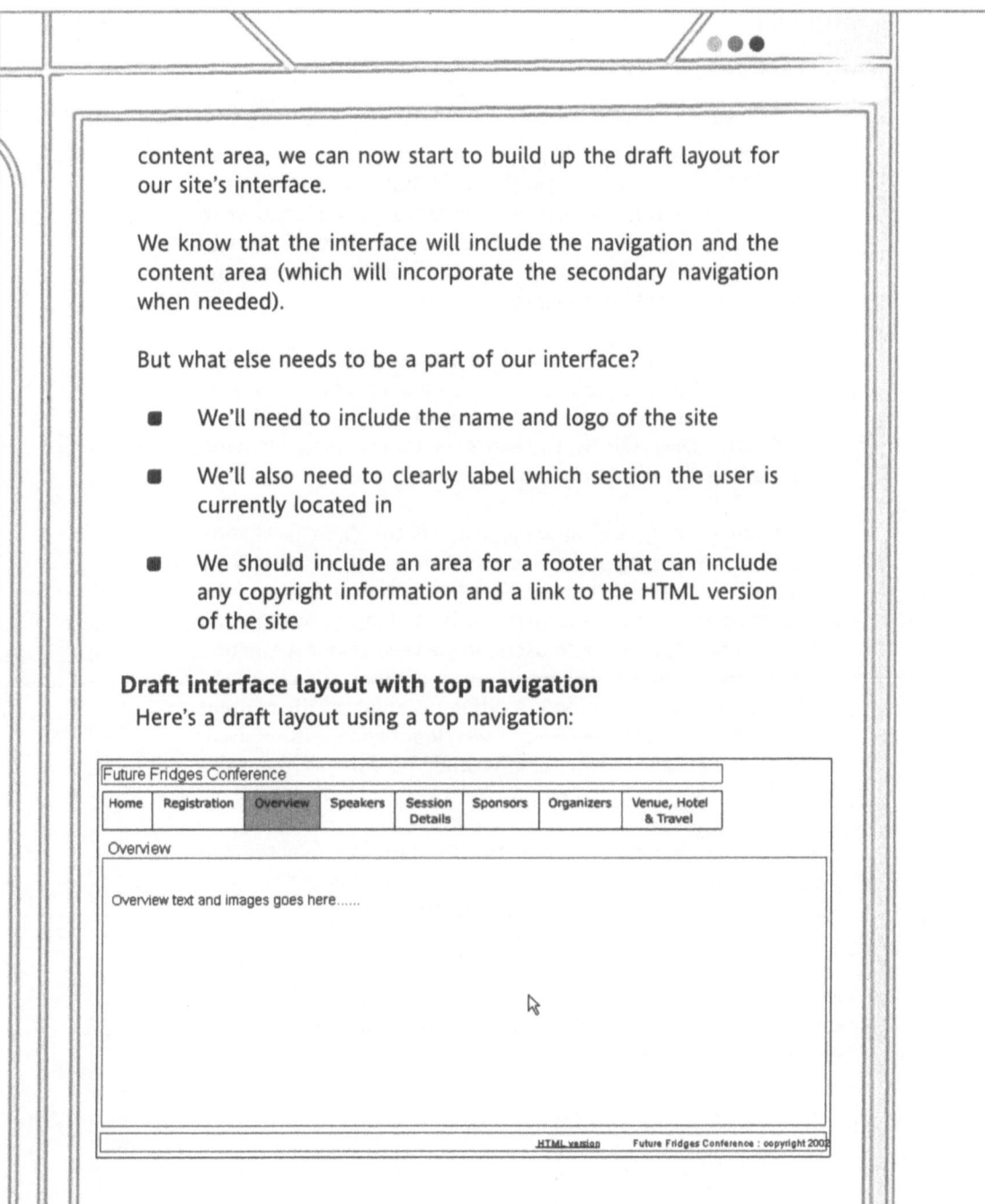

This is a **design-free** layout, we haven't yet created a look and feel for the site; all we're doing is using boxes to indicate the locations of the navigation and content areas. At this stage we're just focusing on how the interface is laid out, and not the design elements. We therefore use simple boxes to indicate the different components of the interface.

The top of the interface contains a header that includes the name of the site. This will be the same throughout the site, ensuring that our users are always aware of what site they're visiting. Effectively this is the site's main branding element, branding it as the *Future Fridges Conference* site.

Next is our primary navigation, which lists the eight navigation items, with the currently selected section highlighted. Why doesn't the navigation fill the screen? We've chosen to make the navigation only as long as it needs to be. A long navigation can sometimes be intimidating to users, so we've kept our navigation as short as it can be while still ensuring that it's clear and readable. Also the navigation is a different length to the content area, which is a visual clue to our users, identifying it as separate to the content and hence emphasizing its role as the site's navigation.

Below the navigation is the title for the currently selected site section. This ensures, along with the highlighted navigation item, that our users know exactly which section of the site they're accessing.

Next is our content area that will contain the content for all the different sections of the site as well as the secondary navigation elements when needed.

Lastly, the bottom of the interface layout contains a footer. This includes copyright information for the site, along with a link to the HTML version, so that users can switch over if they need to. For the sections of the site that require a secondary navigation we'll use the left side of the content area. For example, the layout for the **Speakers** section will be:

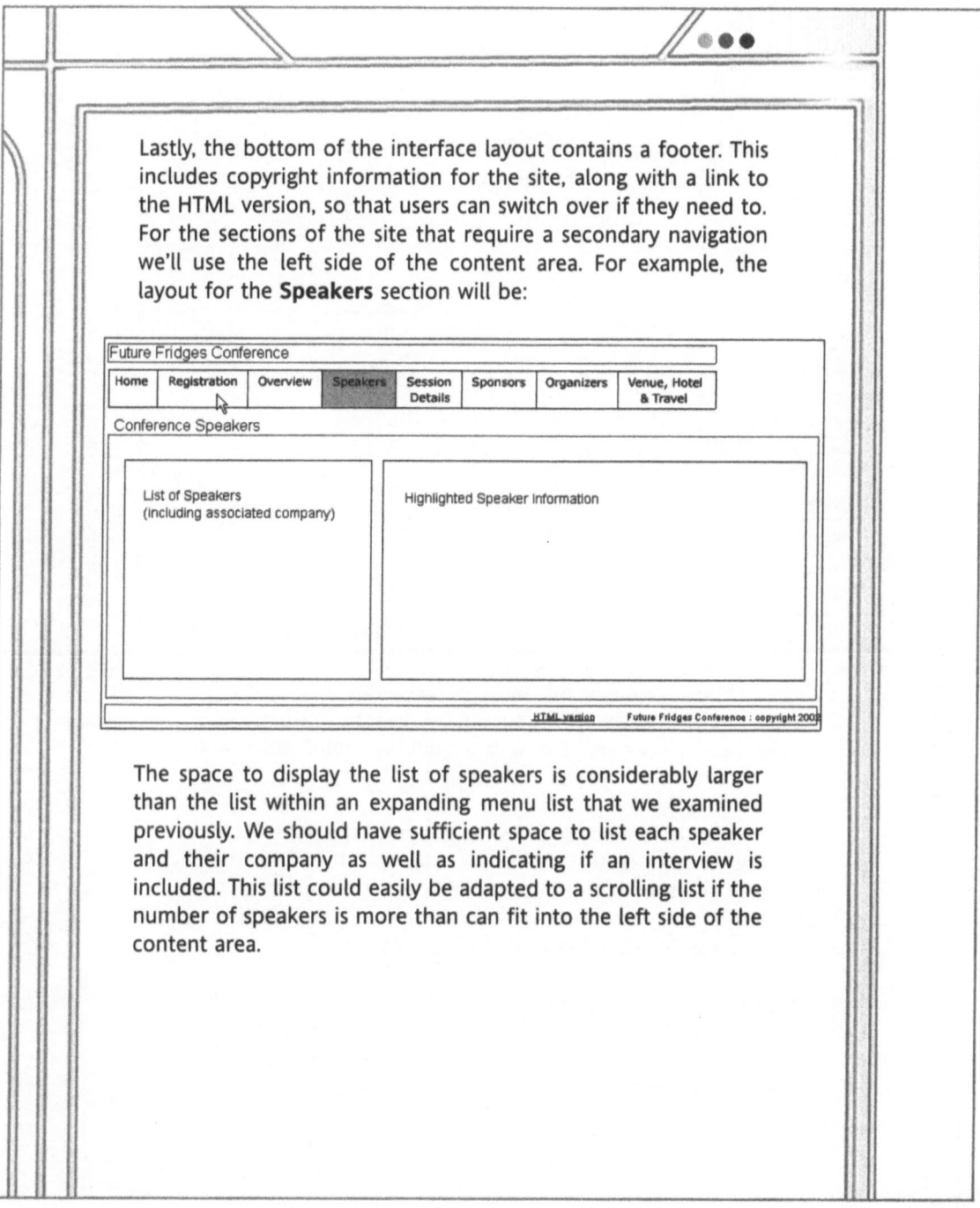

The space to display the list of speakers is considerably larger than the list within an expanding menu list that we examined previously. We should have sufficient space to list each speaker and their company as well as indicating if an interview is included. This list could easily be adapted to a scrolling list if the number of speakers is more than can fit into the left side of the content area.

Draft interface layout with left-hand navigation

Here's a draft layout for the **Speakers** section using a left-hand navigation:

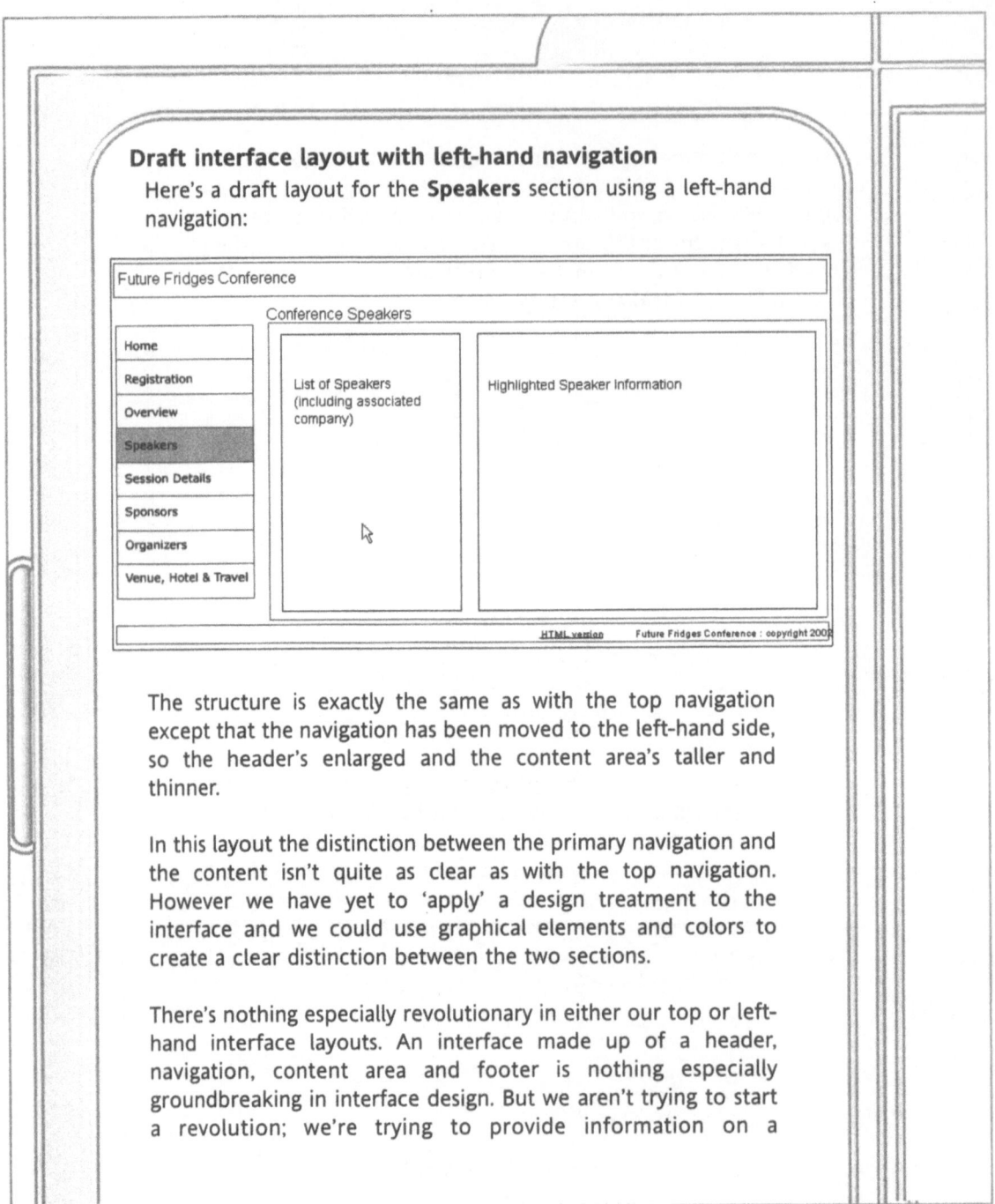

The structure is exactly the same as with the top navigation except that the navigation has been moved to the left-hand side, so the header's enlarged and the content area's taller and thinner.

In this layout the distinction between the primary navigation and the content isn't quite as clear as with the top navigation. However we have yet to 'apply' a design treatment to the interface and we could use graphical elements and colors to create a clear distinction between the two sections.

There's nothing especially revolutionary in either our top or left-hand interface layouts. An interface made up of a header, navigation, content area and footer is nothing especially groundbreaking in interface design. But we aren't trying to start a revolution; we're trying to provide information on a conference. The important thing is therefore that all these elements are clearly positioned on the screen, so as to ensure that our users can easily navigate the content. The interface layout is simple and clear and will easily lend itself to a range of different design styles.

Back to our users

We've made a step forward in our design, so it's time to get some test users in again. We have two possible layout designs and we are at an appropriate stage in the development process to make a decision on which one to work from. Of course we could make the decision ourselves or ask our client or even flip a coin, but we aren't building this site to be used by our client or ourselves; the site is for the users and so who better to make the choice.

We show a number of test users our draft interface designs. We explain that these designs don't necessarily show what the final appearance of the site will be, but they do illustrate the overall layout.

So what do we want to ask these test users? As discussed earlier in this chapter, we want to focus on some of the core elements of the site, including:

- **Clarity:** Can our testers identify which part of the interface is the navigation? Are the labels on the navigation items clear?

- **Simplicity:** Do the interfaces appear simple? Do our testers see the interface as something that would be easy to use?

- **Navigation:** Can our testers clearly identify which section of the site they are in?

Our interface should be good enough that even at this draft stage our testers can look at paper representations and identify all the key components. So we'll show our testers the draft interface layouts, and without explaining anything we'll ask them to identify:

- The name of the site

- Which section is being shown

- Where the navigation and content is located

Finally, we want to identify which navigation layout our test users prefer. We simply ask them to let us know which layout they like best. Because there's no graphic design, color scheme or anything else that might sway their choice, we can safely conclude that the preferred interface will be the one that they see as being easiest to use.

Results of the interface testing

Fortunately, all our test users were able to correctly identify navigation and content areas for both layout styles. So what about those core elements?

- **Clarity:** All users found the navigation items clear and obvious. This probably isn't too much of a surprise, as we've already tested the navigation labels when we tested our IA.

- **Simplicity:** All the test users said that the interfaces seemed simple to use. However, some suggested that the left-hand navigation layout became a little confusing when there was a secondary navigation involved, such as in the **Speakers** section.

- **Navigation:** They were all able to identify which section of the site was being represented. Interestingly, some testers commented that the highlighted button was the first thing they noticed as indicating the section they were looking at, and that this was *more* of a visual clue than the actual section title!

Overall, our users were happy with both layouts, but generally showed a preference for the top navigation style.

So our draft interface designs appear to have passed the test. Furthermore we've identified that our users will be slightly more comfortable with the top navigation layout for primary navigation, so we'll proceed using that interface layout.

Looking pretty

Taking a pretty design and making it into a usable interface is a difficult challenge. But taking a usable interface and building an attractive design for it is straightforward, enjoyable, and ensures we have a usable site at the end.

We've developed a usable interface layout, so now we can style it to reflect our client's original request for an innovative and professional design.

Pre-flight check

Before we fire up our creative juices and start designing, we need to consider if there's any usability theory we need to keep in mind while designing.

Earlier in this chapter we noted that a good design will clearly communicate to the user where they are in the site, and clearly indicate the different sections of the interface. So we should keep these points in mind while applying a design to our interface layout.

Draft design concepts

Here's our first design concept:

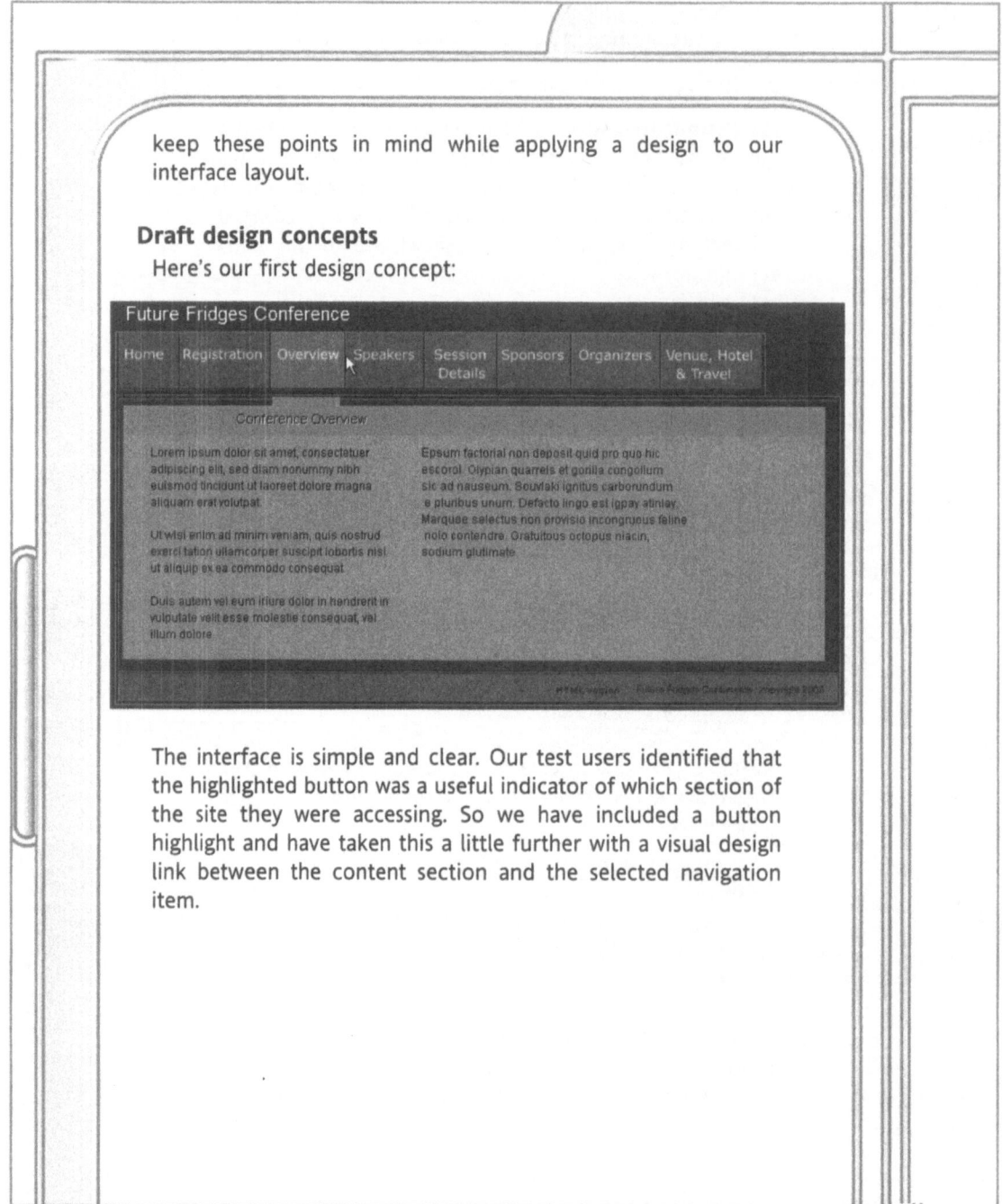

The interface is simple and clear. Our test users identified that the highlighted button was a useful indicator of which section of the site they were accessing. So we have included a button highlight and have taken this a little further with a visual design link between the content section and the selected navigation item.

Our second design concept:

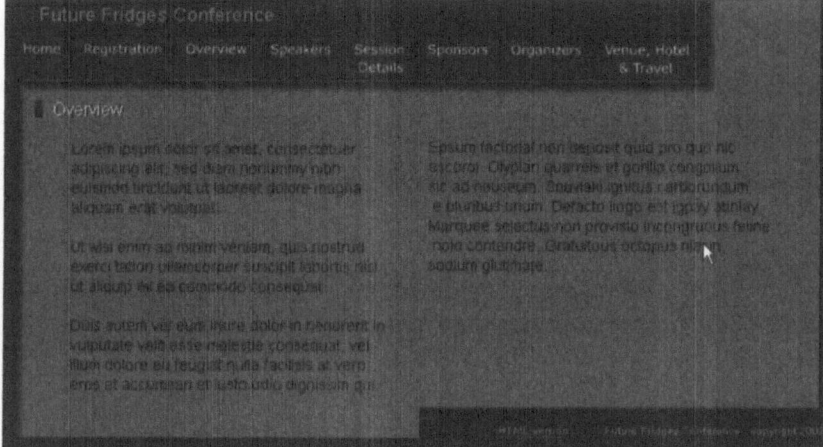

Again the interface is clear and straightforward. A slight drop shadow has been used to clearly separate the navigation from the content. In this design concept, as with the previous one, the text is presented in two columns. One of the advantages of Flash is that it offers good control of text layout, allowing us to set out our test text in a manner that makes it easy to read.

Client response to interface concepts

We show the two interface concepts to our client. At this stage it's important to emphasize to our client the usability considerations that have gone into the design so far. We focus our client's attention on the consistency of the interface and clarity of the navigation and content.

Because we're showing a static mock-up, we're able to keep the client focusing on the elements that are key to the site's usability – namely the navigation and content – instead of animation or screen transitions. Our client prefers the color scheme and design of the first (blue) concept, so it will be that concept we'll be developing into an interactive interface.

Our client's only issue with the design is actually a content issue. They would like to see more images of fridges and technology included in the site. This is actually quite easy to satisfy: we just need to obtain some appropriate imagery and include it within the site's content area.

The interactive prototype

Having successfully completed the static concept we can now move to the development of the interactive interface prototype. This will be built in Flash and will prototype the navigation interaction but won't at this stage feature any content. For now, we'll just have messages such as, "Overview content goes here", which will force us to focus on our navigation interaction. In the next stage we will incorporate the content into this interface.

All the key things we need to consider when making our interface interactive were raised at the beginning of the chapter, so let's revisit those points and look at how they apply to our site.

- There should be **consistent** behavior and performance across all aspects of the Flash content. For our interface this means that all our navigation buttons should behave the same. This should be easy to achieve because we've planned our navigation in advance. We already know how the navigation will be structured and how it should function.

- The key thing to remember here is that we don't want to distract our users, we should keep things **simple**, and only use animation when it serves a purpose. So when will we use animation, when will it serve a useful purpose? When our site is loading, we can use a progress bar animation to indicate how much content has loaded in.

We may also use a highlight or simple animation when the user rolls over the navigation elements. Users are used to navigation items highlighting when they move over them. The buttons on web browsers highlight when you roll over them. So we can give a good visual clue to our users that our navigation items are interactive by making them perform in a manor similar to a web browser's buttons.

- We should consider whether keyboard shortcuts might be useful in helping our users **control** the site. Would they need to use keyboard shortcuts? It seems unlikely they'll be repeating any tasks often enough to *learn* special keys; however, there are one or two navigation shortcuts we could implement: ALT-HOME for the home page; ALT-LEFT-ARROW for 'Back'; and ALT-RIGHT-ARROW for 'Forward'.

We should also recognize that users might use the shortcuts for cut, copy and paste if they copy text from the site. Fortunately, if we make our content text selectable, Flash will automatically support the standard keyboard shortcuts for these actions.

- Every navigation element should provide an instant **response** to the user. For our primary navigation we'll ensure the navigation items will highlight when the user moves over them and change color when selected, thus ensuring that users are getting clear feedback on their interaction with the navigation.

We'll also need to provide information to the user whenever content is being loaded. We'll do this using a progress bar animation as well as showing the percentage loaded and changing the mouse cursor. We'll also ensure that the mouse cursor appears as a hand whenever the user is over a button. Users are used to this convention on web sites and it serves to give yet another visual clue to users about which parts of the site are interactive. Luckily, Flash automatically uses a hand cursor when we use buttons, however it's worth being aware that the hand cursor is not used when `hitTest` is employed to detect mouse actions.

- We should ensure that users can **undo mistakes**. It's not a significant consideration with our navigation interface but will be critical when we look at the development of the registration form.

- Aesthetic – Our users are mostly of a corporate background and are accessing our site with specific tasks in mind. Therefore interstitial animations should be avoided, as they'll probably slow down the users' completion of their tasks. One click of a navigation button will instantly display the associated content section. Sliding, fading or any other form of transitional animation isn't appropriate for this site.

Taking all these items into consideration we put together our interactive navigation prototype:

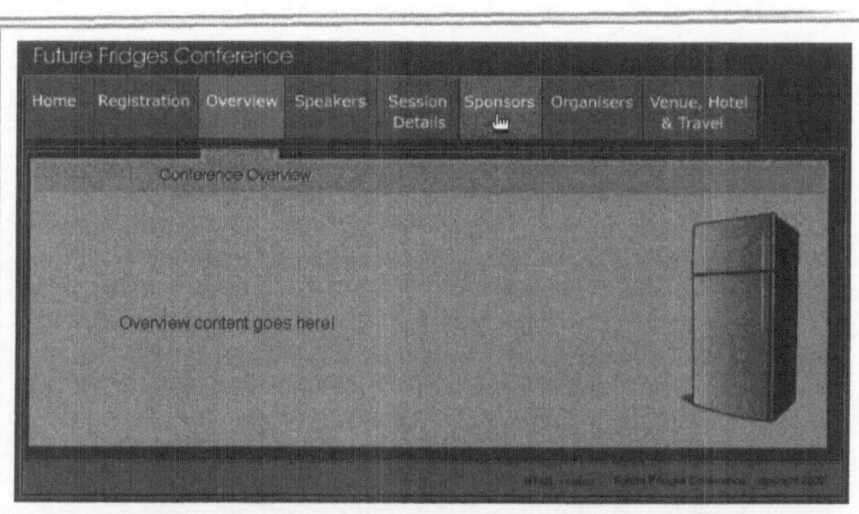

> *The button highlights and the cursor changes to a hand when we roll over the sponsors' button.*

A new request from the client

We're now able to demonstrate the interactive prototype to our client. As we would hope, they find the navigation intuitive and effective. However, after seeing the interactive prototype our client has another 'brainwave'. Our client would like a search section included in the site.

This is introducing a new navigational element at a late stage in the development of our interface and we need to proceed with caution. We *could* add a search box to the bottom left-hand corner of the site in the footer area.

However, just because we can fit it into the interface doesn't mean that we abandon all the work we put into the Information Architecture and interface layout. If we were to seriously consider adding a new navigation element at this stage, then we'd need to go back and repeat our IA and interface testing.

Before we do that though, we should consider whether the site actually *needs* a search feature.

On a site with a large amount of content, a search feature can help users to find information faster than they would navigating through the site's Information Architecture. The search function isn't a *replacement* for good Information Architecture, just an alternative way for users to find information. On a small site, a search function will only be useful if the site's Information Architecture is poorly constructed.

Let's think about what type of searching our users might wish to do. They're unlikely to search for content that's clearly accessible from the primary navigation. For example, a user looking for hotels near the conference will get information a lot faster by clicking on the **Venue, Hotels & Travel** button than they would by typing 'hotels' into a search box and scanning through the results.

So when *might* a search tool be useful to our users? The **Session Details** section will contain quite a large amount of data that a user might wish to search across. For example, a user may wish to search to see if there are any sessions on Internet-enabled fridges.

So we'll be serving the needs of our users by offering a search function in the **Session Details** mini-application. The search feature will be directly linked into the section of the site where users might want to search the content.

Summary

In this chapter, we've looked at interface design, and at a number of factors that influence how usable an interface will be. The interface is all that users have to interact with content on a Flash site, so it's a crucial element to get right.

There are seven main factors that contribute to usability in Flash interfaces:

- Clarity

- Consistency

- Simplicity

- User-controlled

- Responsiveness

- Safety

- Aesthetic

We studied the role that each one plays, and looked at broader areas such as navigation, button design, color, contrast, and sound, and their contributions to a site's user interface. Finally, we returned to the *Future Fridges Conference* site, and pulled all these issues together into a usable design for the site's interface.

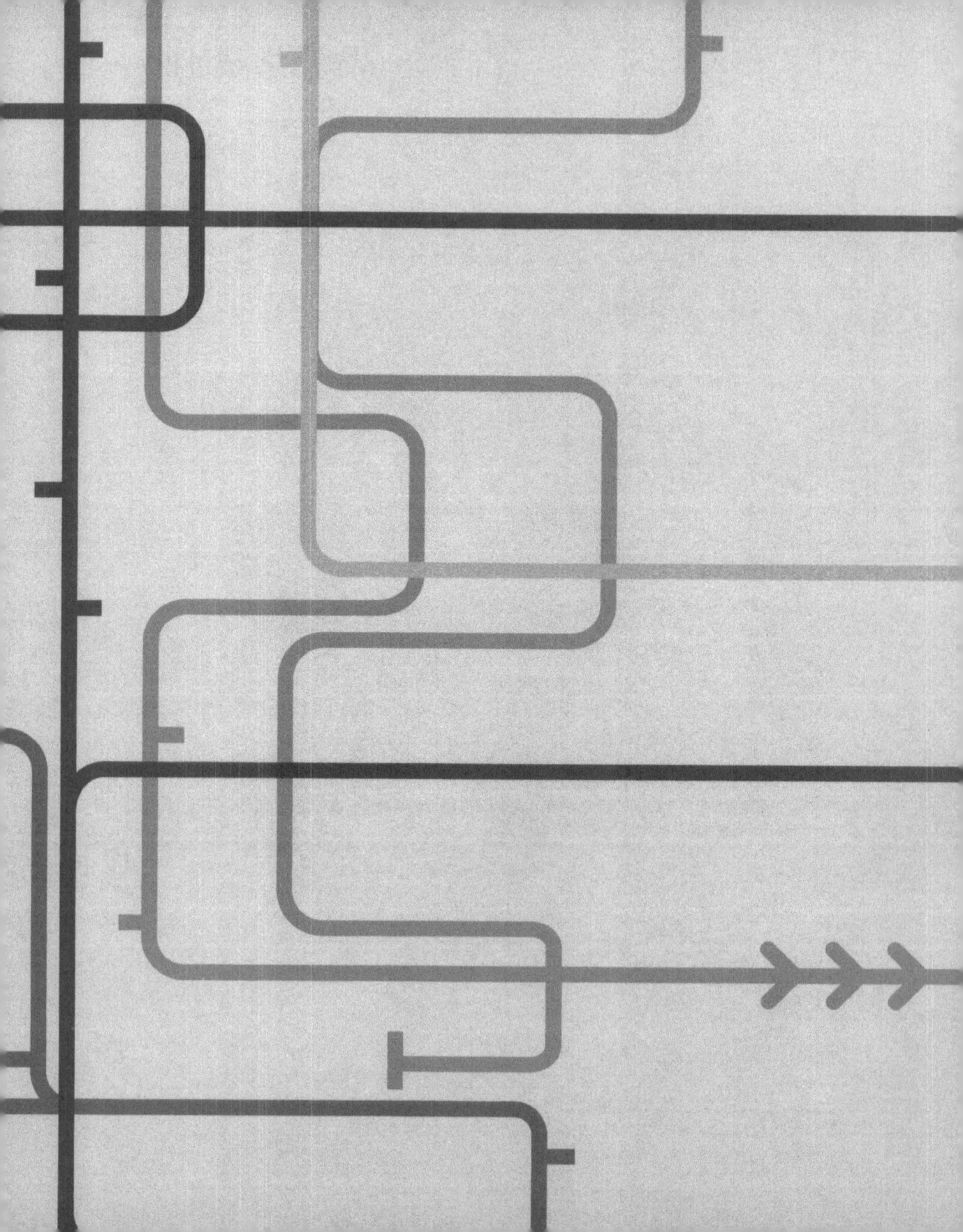

Showing users respect

For years, Flash has been held up as the answer to many web developer's prayers. In March of 2002, statistics from NPD Online (quoted at www.macromedia.com/software/player_census/flashplayer/version_penetration.html) estimated that almost 460 million Flash players were installed out there, just waiting for our creations to hit them. That means a massive 98.3 percent of *all* web users are Flash-enabled, whether they know it or not. Most users' systems are equipped to handle your Flash files; so whatever you create, your audience can embrace it with open arms. Right?

Well, ideally.

Ideally this Flash-compliant world would make your job designing and developing sites far easier. Ideally, a browser- and platform-independent site means no code tweaking to get one HTML page to look the same in multiple configurations. Ideally, there are no more hoops to jump through in order to integrate sound, motion, images, and code on the Web.

In terms of the browser wars, Flash was promoted (and widely accepted) as the safe neutral ground that developers had been waiting for. Lucky for us, most of the hype was valid – for the most part, Flash creations work and look the same in the most popular browsers worldwide, Netscape Navigator and Internet Explorer. This has resulted in less coding, fewer headaches and potentially fewer hassles.

Even though the innovations of and improvements in Microsoft and Netscape's browsers have made them very close to being equal as far as making nearly all HTML code standard, the quick spread of Flash among the developer community made all this compliance appear as too little, too late. Flash gained a lot of ground during the browser wars; the inconsistency among browsers was a boon for its growth.

Yes, Flash was truly the answer to many web designers' prayers. Flash offered what designers and developers had been asking for since browsers could first show off graphics and bold tags: tight control over the presentation of

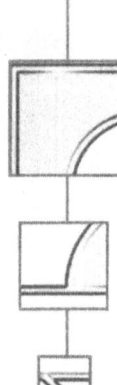

information on the Web, rather than being at the mercy of multiple browser quirks and limitations of bandwidth and platform discrepancies.

There's the rub: Flash was the answer to many *web designer's* prayers. Tighter control over presentation led to tighter control over the user's experience. This has its boons and pitfalls, supporters and adversaries; let's look at both sides.

The balance of power

Control over what the user sees isn't a new concept – after all, traditional non-interactive media have no choice but to impose presentation decisions on a helpless consumer, and who complains about non-resizable newsprint?

Unfortunately for a lot of would-be Flash designers, HTML has already given the majority of web users quite different expectations of their chosen medium. Flash started imposing itself on browsers at about at the same time that most folks were getting used to working the 'Back' button.

Now designers could build their own uniquely innovative navigation schemes (requiring a learning process for users) or didn't have to provide one at all if they didn't want to.

As with every other web technology, as soon as Flash hit the screens, there were designers who made sure that every feature was exploited: dance music pounded out of our two-inch speakers, techno-laser-light graphics bombarded our eyes, and a mouse click or rollover could result in anything from clanking, swirling text, to a gargantuan download of a movie full of more techno-laser-laden dance music and swirling text.

Flash sites appeared which took over the user's computer through pop-up windows and other tricks. Sure, a lot of these things had already been done using HTML and client scripting; but this time around it wasn't always obvious how to get rid of them.

For a while, this was fun. Sometimes, it still is.

With this new control and ability to create a seemingly endless array of interface designs comes another seemingly endless array of learning curves for users. Again, this difference of interface and navigational variety is nothing new to the world of web design.

However, Flash's more extensive abilities to customize sites without browser limitations brings with it some more issues to consider.

Visual cues

It's become fairly standard practice for HTML content to distinguish plain text from links, ads from buttons, and so on. Flash won't offer the user that type of instant visual feedback unless the designer *specifically* decides to include it.

By default, text in Flash looks smooth, as it would in a graphic. A browse through many popular Flash-based sites will find many sites offering bitmap, or pixel-fonts for text, making text sharp and crisp, but the problem is that those sharp typefaces are often set at 8 to 10 pixels in height, making the text illegible to many.

Links in Flash aren't underlined by default either. Many of the standard visual cues that a web user (whether novice or professional) uses to evaluate the structure of a web page simply aren't there in Flash because they are at the mercy of the designer.

Controlling typeface

One of the beauties of Flash is that you can use whatever typeface you like. Type and fonts aren't user-system dependent like HTML files, so users aren't required to have the same installed typefaces on their computers as you do for various fonts to appear. By default, Flash will embed font information in its SWF files, so users will see exactly what you want them to see.

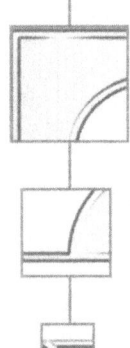

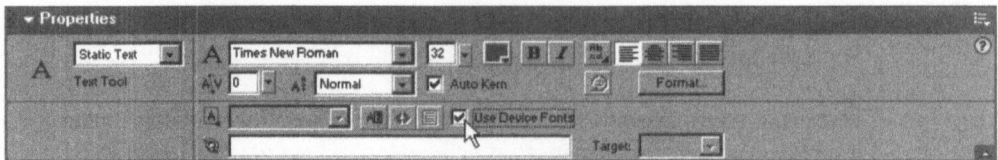

Unfortunately, this can often lead to over-indulgence on the part of less well-disciplined designers – lots of different typefaces can make a page look nothing short of chaotic. Another disadvantage to using embedded fonts is that your files will be bigger, since they have to hold so much more information. If you're particularly concerned about file sizes, you can check the Use Device Fonts option in the Property inspector, which will limit you to using standard system fonts such as Arial, Times, and Verdana.

Protecting content

From a user's perspective, one of the best things about HTML pages is that it's virtually guaranteed that you can copy and paste text and images to your heart's content. To a content provider, this is possibly one of the *worst* things about HTML. How can you base a reliable revenue stream based on content that's so inherently easy to copy?

Of course, most of the people who copy HTML content aren't setting out to make a fast buck from it. If your boss asks for a report on why you should attend a specific conference, you might well visit the conference web site, and cut and paste material from there into your report. Say you're looking for the perfect cover letter to send out with your résumé; Google can find you one in less time than it takes to open up your word processor. With the Flash 6 plug-in, selected text can even be copied and pasted using standard keyboard shortcuts. Share and share alike – that's what the Web's all about, isn't it?

Certainly, the ability to find and copy information off of the Web is one of the reasons it's so popular. The fact that so much information is freely and instantly available makes the Web an extremely powerful research tool. Most sites don't mind too much if people use some content for personal, non-commercial use. Some publish detailed usage guidelines that describe exactly when and where unlicensed reproduction is acceptable. By and large though, web users expect to be able to copy and paste material from a web page, whether or not the page owner approves of it.

Of course, expectations shouldn't be allowed to override what's legal, nor should they inspire designers to build sites simply so as to copy other peoples' content. I've always believed that one of the most important tasks a developer or designer has is to inform and educate their clients in the possibilities of protecting their own intellectual property.

The ability to lock text is a great asset to those who've struggled for years to get site visitors to respect and comply with copyright law. Owners of content-laden sites have used a multitude of tools to protect their intellectual property, converting plain text into PDF files or graphics, simply in order to stop visitors copying and pasting their content. Both formats tend to make for huge files though, so neither is really accepted as genuine 'web content' but rather as 'download' fodder.

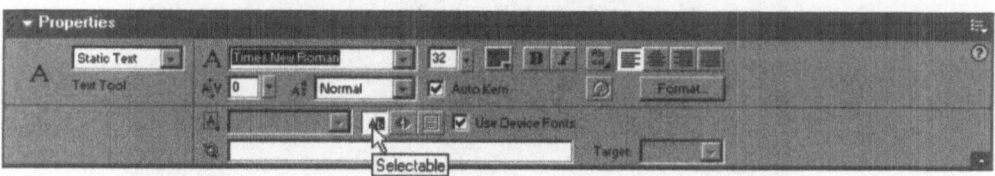

If your client wants their content to be selectable, then you have to check Selectable from the Text Options menu. By default, Flash has this box unchecked, so site visitors are not able to select, copy, or paste text from within a Flash movie. Generally speaking, text within menus and other navigational elements should never need to be selectable.

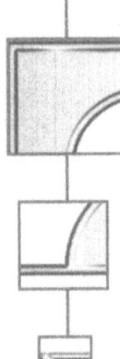

In fact, this is a perfect example of why a 'give the user what they want' credo needs to be used carefully. Users may be frustrated that they can no longer copy content, while clients sleep easier for knowing their intellectual property is more than just a couple of keystrokes away from being 'borrowed'. Some users may be frustrated at not being able to copy it for their own purposes, but the chances are that it wouldn't be there at all if they could!

The Web has become to many people what the musty set of Encyclopedia Britannica used to represent to me back when I had to write a report for fourth grade. I pulled the appropriate volume from the shelf, blew the dust off, found the topic I needed, and proceeded to copy information down in my best eight-year-old cursive. Because it's expected doesn't mean it's the right thing to do. There was no barrier to the information itself, but I'd have had serious trouble duplicating it, let alone passing my own illegible scrawls off as original content!

Let's take the Flasforward 2002 site as an example:

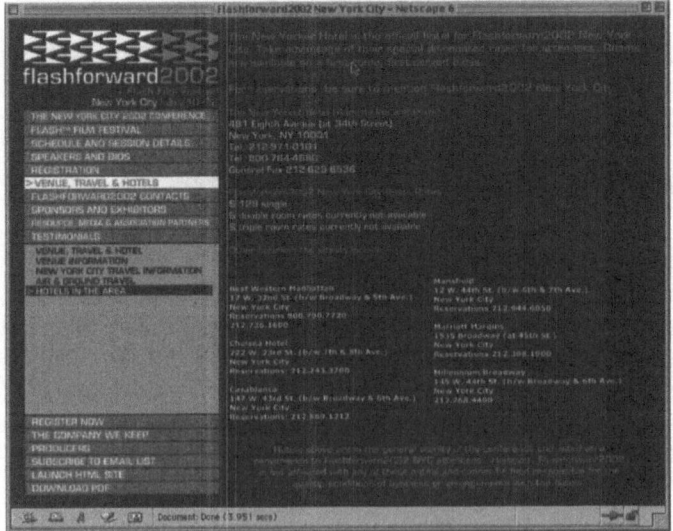

None of the text on the Flashforward2002 (www.flashforward2002.com) Flash-based site is selectable, and it's debatable as to whether selectable text is really necessary in this context. Perhaps some people would like to cut and paste hotel information to send in an e-mail to their colleagues – but it would be just as easy to send the URL so that they could access this information themselves. Result? Everyone's happy. Of course, if you were really desperate to duplicate their content, you could visit the HTML version of the same site...

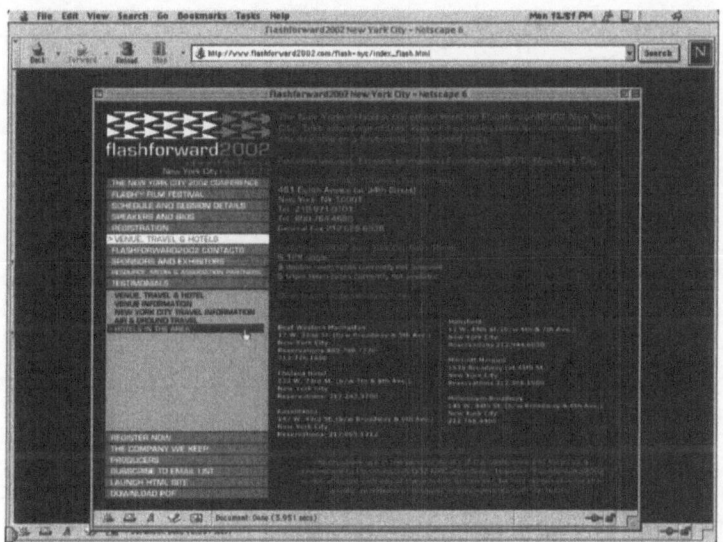

Another control issue – good or bad? Like a number of Flash-based sites, the Flashforward2002 conference site opens up a whole new window, with none of the familiar browser menus and buttons. As we discussed in Chapter 1, taking control of a browser away from the user can be disconcerting for them. However, in this case, the designers would have assumed that the target audience has enough technical know-how for this not to be a problem.

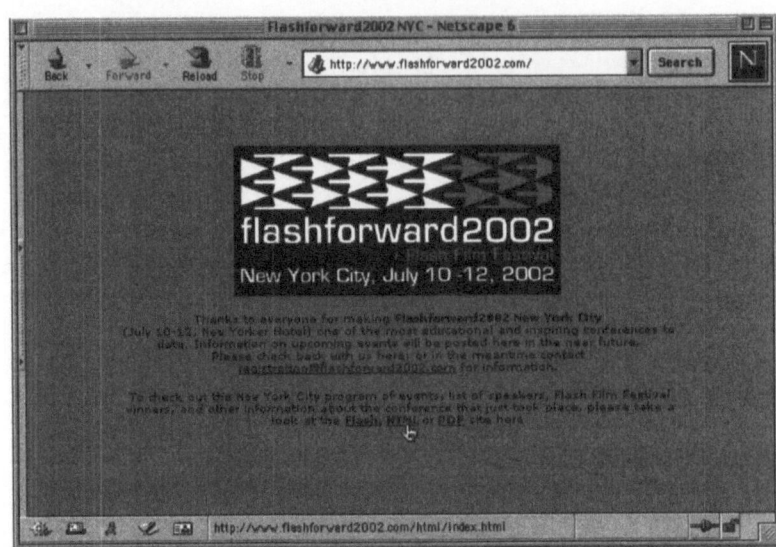

When in doubt, provide as many options as possible. Before entering any part of the Flashforward2002 site's content, users are given the choice of viewing Flash, HTML, or PDF options of the site.

The Flash content we create must show a respect for the user's choices and offer them as much control as possible – just as long as it's deemed acceptable by the client. As designers and developers, we can control as much as we want whenever we want to, and that's a lot of power. The extent to which we extend that control to users must therefore be discussed early on in the planning process. In the process, we need to respect:

- The environment our Flash content is in

- The user's expectations of the content

- The user's need for the information

- The client's requests and intellectual property rights

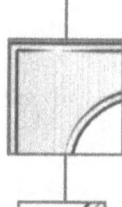

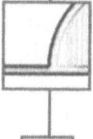

The P in PC stands for personal

These days, Flash content plays almost everywhere. Cell phones, PDAs, cars, vending machines, home entertainment systems, and everything else that Phil Torrone has in his backpack (Torrone is to Flash what Q is to James Bond, leading the way in developing Flash content for mobile gadgets and devices – check out his site at www.flashenabled.com). The experience that the user gets from interacting with content is affected by how the content interacts with the environment.

When a user interacts with Flash content on the Web, remember that they're actually using an interface within an interface within an interface. The first interface is that of the user's operating system, while the second is that of the specific browser they're using. Then comes the Flash interface that we design and develop for the content.

The Flash interface we create should respect the user's environment. If Flash content is available online, there's no telling what environment it will be played in. While Macromedia's statistics show that we may be fairly safe in assuming that the majority of our audience has some version of Flash Player on its system, we don't know whether the Flash content will be viewed via Internet Explorer or Netscape, on a computer running Windows or one running MacOS. When the rare opportunity comes along in which you do know the exact details of the environment our Flash content will be seen in, you need to take advantage of its specifics. For example, if you're developing content for a kiosk at a museum, then you should investigate the environment where the kiosk will be located (more about this in the chapter on Offline Flash).

In most cases though, we have no control over the environment, browser, sound equipment or whether it's on or off, or the input device (mouse, trackpad, or touch screen). The user, or the company that the user works for, makes all of these decisions.

We generally don't know if Flash content is being accessed from the user's home office, late in the evening. It could be accessed from a public library's computer. It could be on the computer of the office temp who's trying to look busy to keep their job who may prefer not to have a soundtrack suddenly begin blaring when the boss is walking by.

> *I'm not suggesting that a Flash soundtrack will get people fired, but there are many different factors that can make or break a site. The use of theme music or looping soundtracks on a Flash site may offer no value to a user searching for bass fishing tips, or it might be the key element to the perfect site experience when visiting a music video production site. We need to think about the impression that the site makes on the user. Generally only the president or professional wrestlers are introduced with their own theme music. Which one is your client?*

Many developers feel that music makes a site more personal. Well-selected or produced music gives the user something they can relate to, and rounds out the site experience. It's well documented that music is more memorable to the listener if they hear it once than if they were to read the same paragraph ten times.

Think of the evolution of features on a cell phone. As more and more people purchased cell phones, manufacturers started to build phones that offer the user more control. At first, cell phones only came with an on/off switch for

the ringer. After a few US judges had cell phone owners slapped with fines for interrupting their courtrooms and too many business people received glares from co-workers during business meetings when their phones rang, phones started showing up with soundless options such as blinking lights and vibration rings. These days, some cell phone companies make new ring tones available for download, sound volume settings, and multiple public 'personalities' allowing you to switch from 'traffic' setting to 'meeting' with a few commands.

Each generation of cell phone offered features to improve the usability of the phone. Today, cell phones are so advanced that even Dick Tracy's TV/radio watch seems quaint. For our Flash content to be embraced by users in the same way that mobile phones have been, we need to offer a level of control over the system, namely options that the user can implement within the client's requirements.

The first step in this process is to think of our Flash product as a guest in a user's home or office. The content that we create should be polite and courteous. We need to respect the preferences of the user's system and not attempt to take control of any of the system away from them, at least not without asking first.

Let the user take the wheel

Let's go back and revisit our analogy of Flash content being a car. In this case, we'll focus on how a driver first experiences a car.

Consider a well-respected car rental company. The rental company knows that your first impression of the car factors heavily in your opinion of the company's service. They make sure that the cars in their lot are clean and in a preference-neutral state when you get in the car. In addition to being washed and cleaned both inside and out, the rental company also makes sure that the radio is off, the seat is back from the steering wheel, and other personal preferences are left in the hands of the driver.

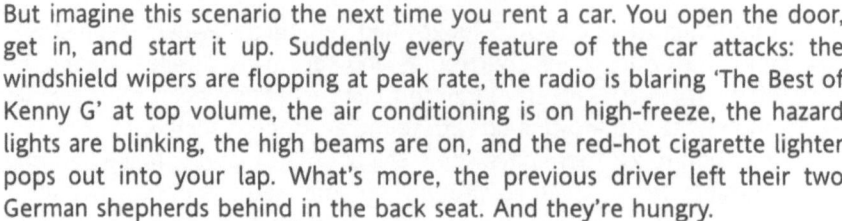

But imagine this scenario the next time you rent a car. You open the door, get in, and start it up. Suddenly every feature of the car attacks: the windshield wipers are flopping at peak rate, the radio is blaring 'The Best of Kenny G' at top volume, the air conditioning is on high-freeze, the hazard lights are blinking, the high beams are on, and the red-hot cigarette lighter pops out into your lap. What's more, the previous driver left their two German shepherds behind in the back seat. And they're hungry.

Your first interaction with that car – if you don't run away screaming – would be to locate each control, turn off the lights and the radio, and let the poor hungry dogs out. You'll probably want to set the car features to your own preferences (or at the very least, a usable state) before you drive off in it. To top things off, you'll probably never rent a car from that company again!

Now, imagine that same situation playing out every time you got in *any* car.

Making a good impression

In addition to respecting the user's preferences, we also need to be aware of the first impressions that an initial interface presents to a site visitor. Depending on the situation, based on our little car experiment, Flash content

should not open with all the lights on and sirens blaring. In most instances, the user should drive the initial interaction with Flash content.

Many Flash sites offer initial experiences that are similar to our possessed rental car. When the user first arrives on the site they are plunked into a very busy and complex interface. The interface has all of its options set to 'On'. This presents the user with a more complex interface than necessary.

Following the events of September 11th 2001, The Map Network, Inc. (then known as URHere, Inc.) published a map of New York City (www.mapnetwork.com/recognition.htm) that proved an exception to the rule of avoiding an 'everything on' approach. All optional points of information on the map are shown by default.

Some might argue that this may be too much information all at once, but even if someone has never used this site before, it seems fairly intuitive. The site also features a well-written, illustrated how-to-use area that new users can access with one click.

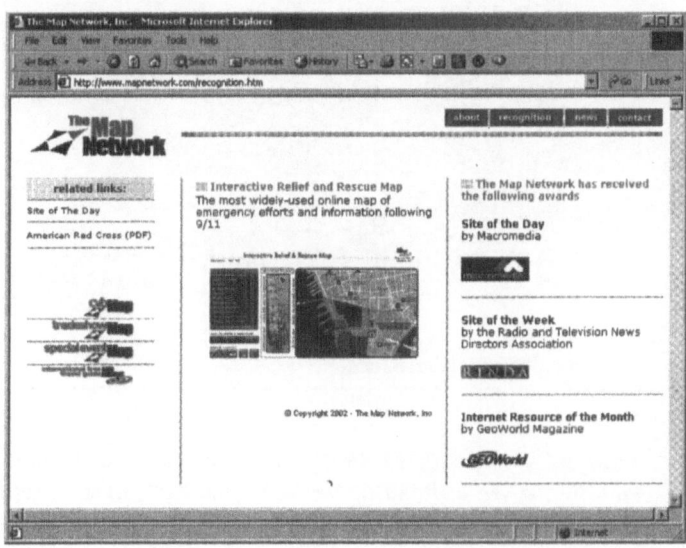

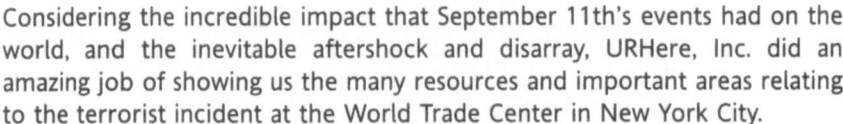

Considering the incredible impact that September 11th's events had on the world, and the inevitable aftershock and disarray, URHere, Inc. did an amazing job of showing us the many resources and important areas relating to the terrorist incident at the World Trade Center in New York City.

The site may not be a usability expert's dream, since there is so much information presented and a broad range of navigational options. Considering the great variety of site visitors' knowledge of moving around web-based maps - chances are they've used one of them (clicking on up/down arrows, using a Zoom In slider, dragging the smaller red window over the small map to show the desired view of Manhattan) - hopefully they can find what they want.

Showing the vast amount of positive resources surrounding the site was a good move for this audience. Many of us needed to see such an outpouring of goodness in light of such a chaotic time, and months of usability testing clearly wasn't an option.

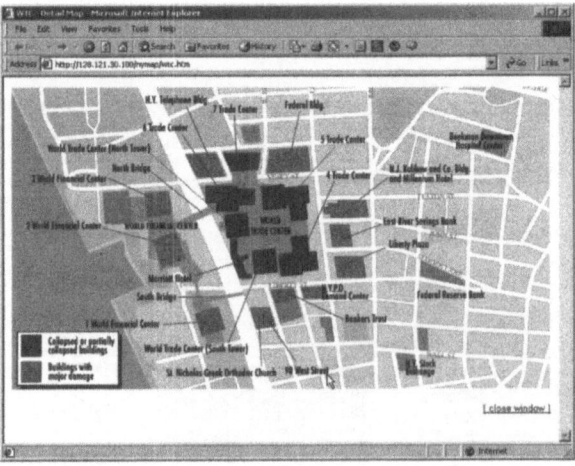

Amongst other choices, site visitors were invited to open a pop-up window to see a detail of the area damaged by the September 11 attacks. The window includes a *close window* link in the lower right.

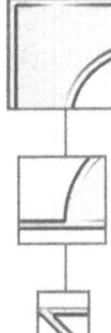

The site also included a detailed 'how to' page that's easily accessible from the main map, and opens in a separate window.

Users need to be presented with initial interfaces that they can understand easily so that they can begin their interactions. If the initial experience with Flash content is removed from the user's expectations, they'll feel much less comfortable using it.

Don't confuse the user

In addition to disruptive sounds and busy interfaces, Flash on the Web can be disruptive to the environment of the user's operating system. Flash sites that open full-screen without warning lock the user away from the operating system behind it. Sites that do this persuade most users to stay just long enough to find the close button!

For someone who's new to the Web, the opening of a full screen window can be a very jarring experience. Suddenly an interface that they're maybe just getting used to is replaced with a totally alien environment. "Oh no. Have I broken it...? "

It's important to prepare users for any potentially disorienting events, whether it's a full-screen pop-up or a brand new drum loop on their speakers – anything that may provide a jolt from the familiar setup.

People who've been using the Web for a while are more apt to be patient when faced with a new interface, navigational system, or full-screen takeover. If you're concerned with the variety of levels of technical knowledge in your audience, or of potential disappearances of customers due to confusing new features, then offer them alternatives. As mentioned before, welcome screens are a good place to offer these alternatives – users can make an upfront decision on how they wish to interact with the site and its contents.

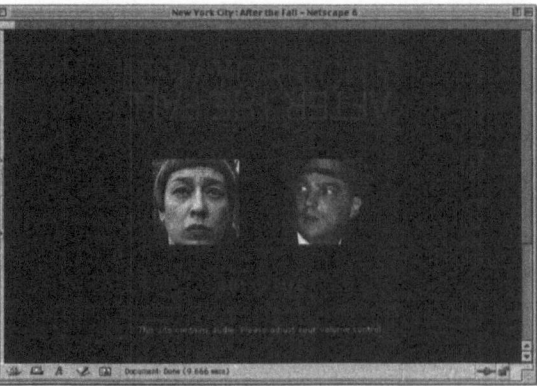

After The Fall, a pictorial site by Geoffrey Hiller (www.hillerphoto.com/nyc), warns users that the site contains audio, suggesting they check the volume control.

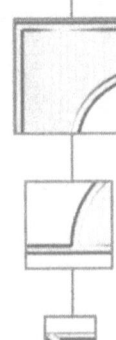

The Memphis Zoo (www.memphiszoo.org) gives us the option to check out an HTML information page rather than pulling users straight into its Flash site. It also provides download links for those who still may not have the Flash player plug-in.

As far as you can – and as far as it's appropriate to your target audience and the effect you want the site to have on them – let your users decide how they want to experience the content. For example, do they want to open a full-screen window? Chances are most people won't, but maybe a survey of your users says they do. Will the Flash content play effectively in a full-screen window on the user's computer? What kind of computers do they have? Full-screen content on slower computers really degrades the experience. Tweens slow down, and if the content is synced to an audio track, frames will be dropped if there is not enough computing power to play the animation full screen. So you would probably be pretty safe by staying away from full-screen work, especially if you don't have a very distinctly defined audience.

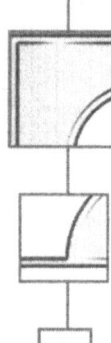

Not all sites have to look alike

One of the fears that has plagued the web design world for years is that if we all used the same standards and rely on conventions (or need to comply with accessibility requirements or suggestions from the W3C), all of our sites would end up looking identical.

In reality, conventions inspired by smart, tested design and usability principles don't actually force sites into looking the same. Think about the thousands of different web sites you have seen with the navigation system stacked in a bar on the left side of the page. Do all of those sites have the same design?

No, of course not. The convention is that the navigation is on the left. The location of this element on the page may be a familiar design choice, but isn't necessarily the same on every site. When new technologies and new interactions offer better solutions for users, then new conventions develop and are widely adopted as conventions in the future. A good designer recognizes conventions and creates new interactions and experiences that work with and may improve those conventions that work.

The eyes have it

One of my favorite features in browsers is the ability to resize a site's text if I'm unable to read it, usually because it's too small. In the same vein, making a Flash site's text a readable size is a simple solution to an oft-heard complaint about 'over-designed' sites. Sleek, small, techno-hip typefaces work for sites that target younger, better sighted viewers, and suit the audience. Giant kid-like typefaces suit kid-like sites.

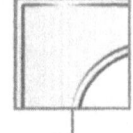

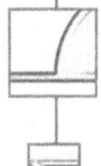

Ride Now's Flash-based site (www.otrinteractive.com/ridenow/flash/index.html) is scalable; its size is limited by the size and depth of the user's screen. On a small screen, everything is tiny...

...whereas on a big screen, the content expands to fill the available space.

If you're looking for standard navigational practices, you won't find them here. J. Otto Seibold is renowned for his kooky characters, and his Flash sites (designed, animated, and scored by Feel Good Anyway) are up to par with the reputation. BubbleSoap's interface (www.jotto.com/bubblesoap/bubblesoap.html) isn't meant to fit within any convention. Nevertheless it works, since people who are likely to visit the site are likely to be of the curious mindset to click on everything and see what happens.

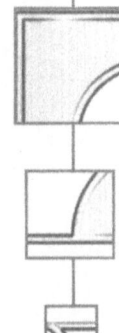

Seibold's Bubble Soap music video interface gives users the following handy usability hint: "If it's playing kind of chunky, try making your browser window smaller".

Common sense is the best remedy

In general, while conventions can be argued for and Flash features flaunted or overused, the rule of thumb is simple: use common sense. Use your audience profiles to determine what they might expect, and use your client requirements as guidelines to what you provide to the audience.

Respecting the user doesn't mean you should make your site so simple and boring that anybody can understand it – quite the contrary. Respecting the user means thinking about their range of abilities and desires, and creating an innovative design that conveys the client's message within those confines.

Let's see how this applies to our ongoing project.

Case Study

Integrating the content

Now that we've designed an interface for the *Future Fridges Conference* site, we need to start looking at how we present and deliver the content that will sit behind it.

Separation of the content and the interface

Ideally the main content of our site should be kept separate from the site's interface. This separation means we can easily update and maintain our content, as well as reformatting it for other uses, such as the HTML version of the site.

Loading the text content

We can store the text content for the site as separate text files or as data in a database and then load this content into our Flash interface. This same text content can also be used for the HTML version of the site. When we need to modify the content, we only need to change one file or database record, and both Flash and HTML versions will be updated.

The Flash interface can load data from XML documents or URL-encoded text strings (such as `var1=1&var2=2&var3=3`). If we store the text content in a database, we'll need some kind of server script to convert it into one of these formats before Flash can load it.

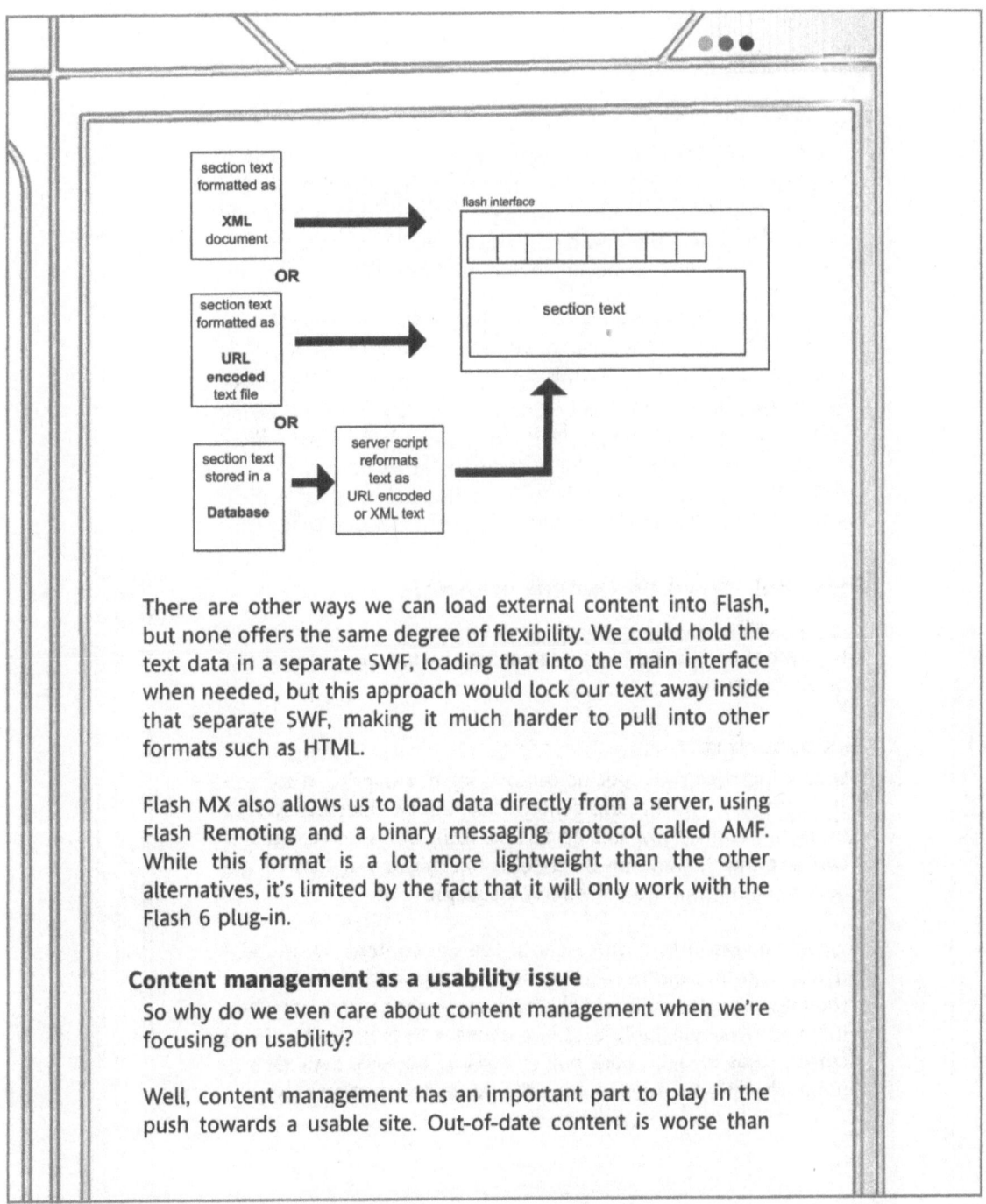

There are other ways we can load external content into Flash, but none offers the same degree of flexibility. We could hold the text data in a separate SWF, loading that into the main interface when needed, but this approach would lock our text away inside that separate SWF, making it much harder to pull into other formats such as HTML.

Flash MX also allows us to load data directly from a server, using Flash Remoting and a binary messaging protocol called AMF. While this format is a lot more lightweight than the other alternatives, it's limited by the fact that it will only work with the Flash 6 plug-in.

Content management as a usability issue

So why do we even care about content management when we're focusing on usability?

Well, content management has an important part to play in the push towards a usable site. Out-of-date content is worse than useless – you may end up misleading users if you can't keep it accurate. Just suppose our client had to change the dates of the *Future Fridges Conference*. If they couldn't update the site content to reflect the new dates, visitors would be misinformed, and the usefulness of the site would be drastically reduced.

What's more, by separating the content from the interface, we can build a site that loads large amounts of content on demand. That means the basic content loads up when the user first arrives at the site; then, if they want to watch some bandwidth-hogging video footage for example, Flash can spend a little extra time loading it up, without adding to the basic download time of the site. Likewise, we don't want to force users to wait for a 400K audio file to load until we're sure they want to listen to it.

Including text and making it usable

As we outlined earlier in the chapter, the way in which we choose to present text in our Flash movie can significantly affect the user's experience.

Selectable text

Unless the client has specific reasons for not wanting it so, you should make sure that the content text can be selected, so that users can easily copy and paste text from our site. As we saw earlier in the chapter, this is very easy to achieve: just click on the Selectable button in the Property inspector.

We've no reason to protect any of the site content, so any text fields need that button clicked. Text on our navigation buttons *shouldn't* be selectable though: the cursor changes to a bar when it hovers over selectable text, but we want to preserve the hand cursor, so as to help mark out buttons as buttons. Let's face it; nobody's likely to *want* to copy the navigation text anyway!

Readable text

Embedded fonts used for text in Flash can look very smooth and stylish. Because the fonts are embedded into the SWF, you can use whatever typeface you like. The downside is that a fancy font may make the text difficult to read, especially if there's a lot of it and the font size is small. What's more, it'll bump up the size of the SWF file. On the other hand, **device fonts** look crisp and clear at any resolution, but your choice is much more limited.

We know that users will be accessing our site to get information about the conference, so they'll want the text to be clear and easy to read. We'll therefore use device fonts for the main content text. For our navigation items and headings, where the font size will be larger and where we want precise control over the font style and layout, we'll use embedded fonts.

The **color** we choose for the text will also affect its readability. We want to choose one that provides plenty of **contrast** with the background. Since our background is pale blue, we'll need to use a dark color to produce a good contrast – let's set it to black.

Scannable text

We know that our users are mostly busy professionals who won't want to read through large volumes of text unnecessarily. We can assist them by highlighting key words in our text, making it possible for them to scan through the text for information without needing to read every word.

For example, the text in the screenshot below shows fifty-two words of text with ten key words highlighted. You only need to take a quick glance at the text to pick up on the main points. In this case, the **Overview** section is shown and the highlighted text gives glancing users the subject of the conference, the dates, and the location. If they want more detail they can read through the full text.

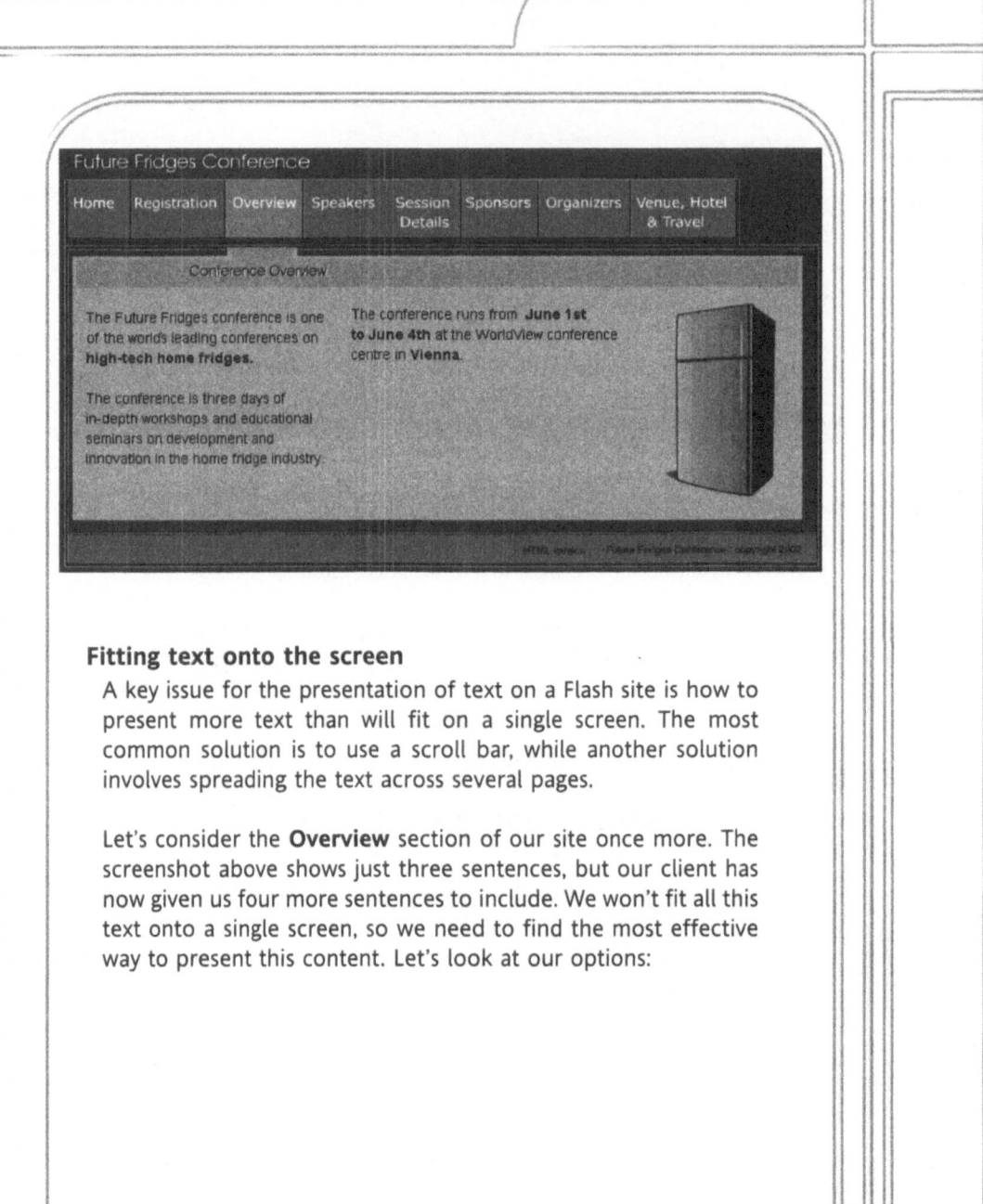

Fitting text onto the screen

A key issue for the presentation of text on a Flash site is how to present more text than will fit on a single screen. The most common solution is to use a scroll bar, while another solution involves spreading the text across several pages.

Let's consider the **Overview** section of our site once more. The screenshot above shows just three sentences, but our client has now given us four more sentences to include. We won't fit all this text onto a single screen, so we need to find the most effective way to present this content. Let's look at our options:

Using a scrollbar

Our first option is to add a **scrollbar** into the content area, as shown below.

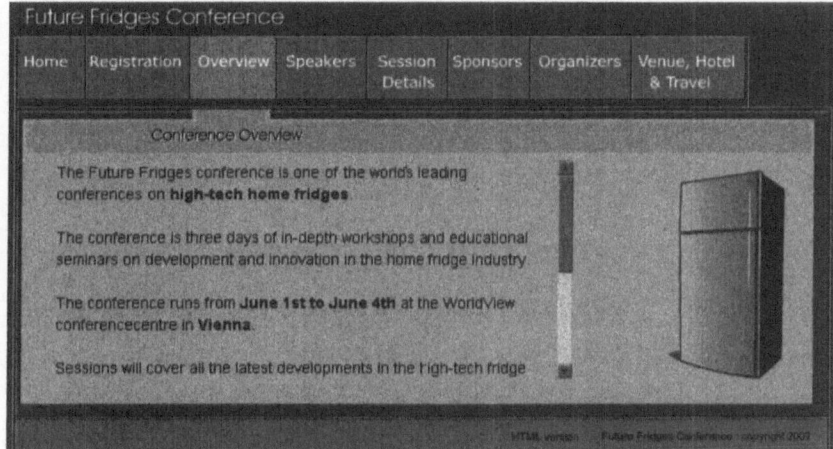

The location of the scrollbar next to the text indicates that it can to be used to scroll through the text. If this weren't clear enough, we'd need to use some other kind of graphical device to indicate an association between the scrollbar and the content – for example, a box around the text that lined up with the scrollbar.

The bar section of the scrollbar provides some feedback to the user on how long the text is and where the user is within the text. In the screenshot the user is at the top of the text and the text is about twice as long as the amount visible.

Using separate pages

The alternative is to break up the text into two (or more) pages, as illustrated below.

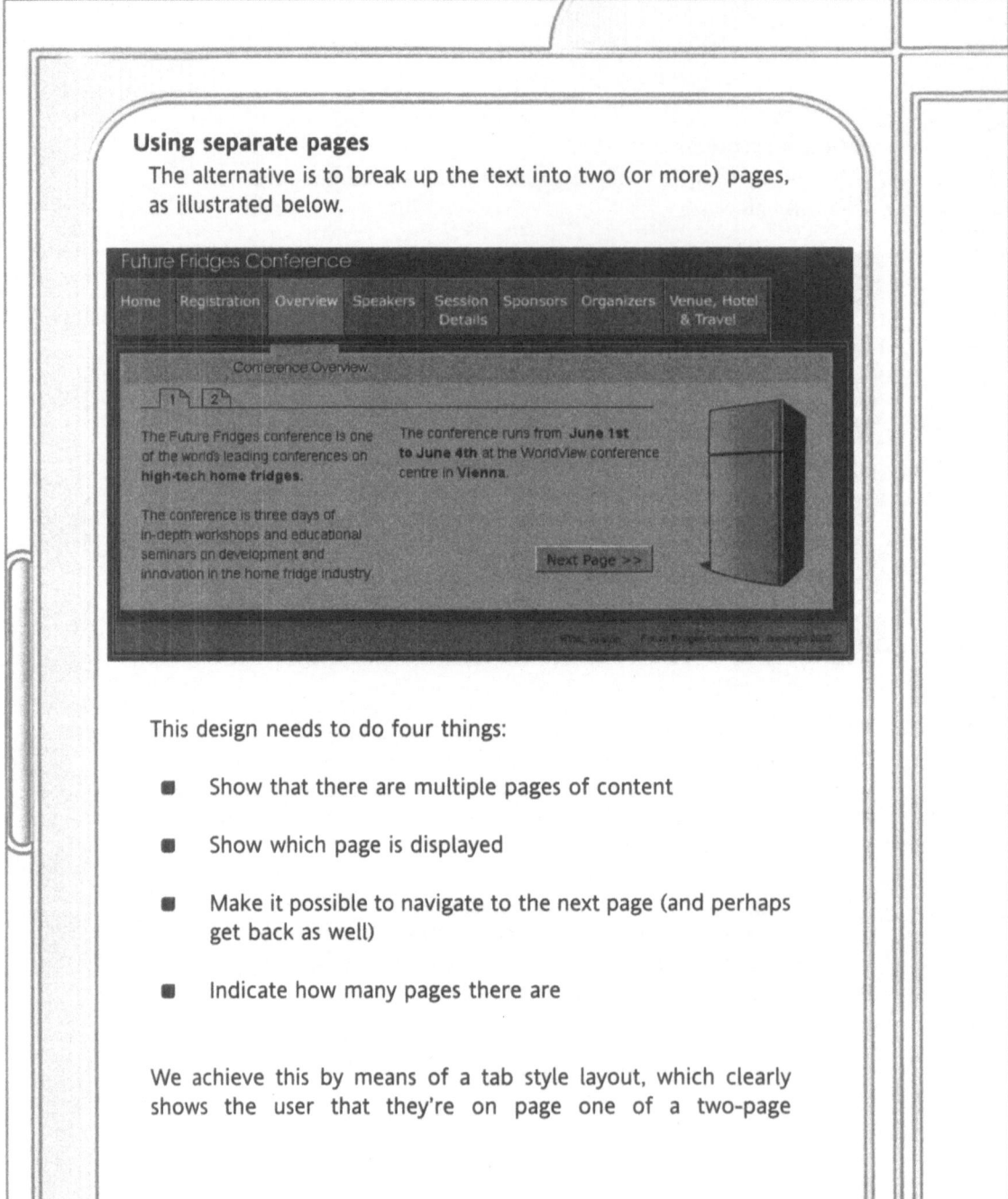

This design needs to do four things:

- Show that there are multiple pages of content

- Show which page is displayed

- Make it possible to navigate to the next page (and perhaps get back as well)

- Indicate how many pages there are

We achieve this by means of a tab style layout, which clearly shows the user that they're on page one of a two-page document. The user can either click on the relevant page tab or on the Next Page button to move to the next page.

So, should we use a scrollbar or pages to lay out our text? Both methods are clear and intuitive and let our users easily navigate the text. Either method would offer our users quick and easy access to the information. However we should consider which method would be the most consistent with the other navigation methods on our site.

As you'll see later, we'll use a scrollbar-based navigation for the list of sessions in the session planner part of the **Session Details** section of our site. So we can use the same scrollbar-based text navigation method for this section of the site.

User-friendly audio and video

Our client has decreed that the site will contain audio and video interviews with selected conference speakers. So how are we going to achieve this (especially given that Flash 6 is the only Flash plug-in that supports video) and how are we going to make it usable?

Video

We have one video interview with one of the key conference speakers, which we would like to include in the **Speakers** section of our site.

Flash MX offers excellent support for video files. Video can easily be integrated into the SWF, with powerful compression techniques helping to keep the file size relatively small. Unfortunately though, it can only be viewed via the Flash 6 plug-in – our brief is to build a site that can be viewed by users who only have the Flash 5 plug-in.

Well, providing video via the Flash 5 player really isn't an option, but we know that some of our users *will* have the latest plug-in. So ideally, what we'd like to do is to let Flash 6 users see the video proper, and give Flash 5 users a still image of the speaker along with the audio track from the interview.

At first glance it would seem that the only solution would be to build two versions of the site: one designed for users with only Flash 5, and one for users with Flash 6. Apart from that fact that it would be tedious and time-consuming to do that, it's really not necessary.

We can actually build our site in a Flash 5-compatible format and *within that movie*, detect which version of the plug-in the user has:

- If the movie detects that a user's accessing the site with a Flash 5 plug-in, it pulls in a SWF that includes a still image of the speaker and the audio track from the interview.

- If it detects that a user's got the Flash 6 plug-in, it pulls in a SWF containing the complete video file.

You may wonder if this is possible: can a Flash 5 SWF really load up a Flash 6/MX-format SWF? Yes, it can. What's more, it will work reliably on all operating systems and browser versions. The Flash 6 player will happily play a Flash 6 format SWF, even if it's been loaded up inside a Flash 5 SWF.

The code you need to detect the version is quite simple:

```
playerVersion = getVersion();
myLength = length(playerVersion);
for (i=0; i<=myLength; i++) {
  temp = substring(playerVersion, i, 1);
```

```
    if (temp eq "") {
        platform = substring(playerVersion, 1,
i-1);
        majorVersion =
substring(playerVersion, i+1, 1);
    }
}
```

This code just gets the version of the player being used – for example: WIN 6,0,21,0

It then extracts the important details (the user's operating system and the main version number of the detected Flash player) into variables platform and majorVersion.

The SWF file interview01video.swf contains the video interview exported in Flash 6 format, whereas interview01audio.swf has the audio-only version with a picture of the speaker, as exported in Flash 5 format.

We can then use the following code to load the appropriate version into a movie clip called interview:

```
if (majorVersion >=6){

interview.loadMovie("interview01video.swf ");
    } else {

interview.loadMovie("interview01audio.swf");
    }
```

This technique will also come in useful for versions of the site displayed at the conference and on the CD-ROM tickets. In these environments we can control the version of Flash that's playing the content and thus ensure that the latest version of the player is being used, with full support for our video content.

Audio interviews

The 'audio only' interviews are considerably easier to manage. Flash 5 supported MP3 compression of audio, so we don't need to do any version checking. However we can't dynamically load audio files via the Flash 5 plug-in, so we'll need to embed each audio interview in its own separate SWF. We'll then load the appropriate file into the main Flash movie and give our users a Play/Pause/Stop interface to control the playback.

The playback interface

Back in Chapter 4 we identified that we can make use of the Play, Pause, and Stop button design conventions for multi-media playback. Pressing the Play button will start the audio or video playing and the Pause button will pause the media, which will restart if you press Pause again or press Play.

But what will the Stop button do? There are actually two different implementations of this:

- On a CD player, the Stop button stops the CD from playing and resets it to the beginning of the disc. Press Play and it starts playing from the beginning again.

- On a cassette player, Stop will stop the tape from playing, but leave it at the same position. When you press the Play button, it will start playing from the location where it last stopped.

In the latter case, it effectively does the same thing as the Pause button. So a meaningful adaptation of the design convention for our situation will have the Stop button functioning as it would on a CD player, returning users to the start of the content.

We also need to include a volume control for the audio content. We know that many of our users will access the site from a work environment, so they may need to adjust the volume to avoid disturbing their colleagues.

Back in Chapter 4, we also identified that we need to ensure that our users get feedback on what's happening. That is, they need to know whether the content is loading, playing, paused or stopped. So our interface will need to show users:

- How much content has loaded in

- How long the content is

- How far they are into the content

- If the content is paused, playing or loading

Here's the interface that we develop to meet these needs:

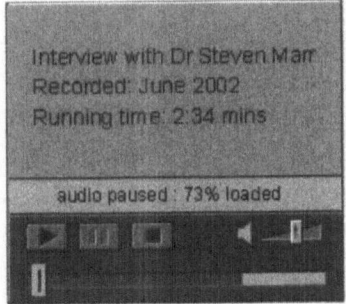

The top section of the interface shows file details, giving a simple text description of the audio that's currently playing. If we were playing a video, then the content itself would be shown here.

The second section is a space in which to display status information. In the image above, it indicates the state of the audio (paused) and the state of the download (73%). While the file's initially loading, we can use this area to display messages – for example, "Please wait... loading audio".

The bottom section contains the actual interface controls. The Play, Pause, and Stop buttons are clearly indicated; given that they're based on an extremely common design convention, they should be intuitive to use. Furthermore, we highlight the currently selected button – that's Pause in this case.

Next to the buttons is a volume control. Another design convention, the speaker symbol, is used to indicate that the sliding bar next to it can be used to change the volume. The bar itself is a triangle, alluding to the increase in volume that results from dragging the bar over to the right.

At the bottom of the interface is a progress bar. The dark section of the bar indicates how much of the total file (represented by the complete length of the bar) has been loaded. Of course, the percentage loaded is already indicated in the text display section, but it can be helpful to offer this kind of visual feedback as well.

The bar also has a slider, which can be moved to start playback at different points in the audio file. While this style of control is often used in audio playback software, it may not be familiar to all of our users. Fortunately the bar demonstrates its own functionality as the audio file plays, and the slider moves across to the right. It shouldn't take our users too long to spot the association between the slider position and the audio playback position.

We can go one step further with the usability of this interface by adding tool tips. When the user moves over the buttons or sliders a simple tool tip will display, describing the function of the associated element and thus making the role of the interface elements even clearer.

Getting the download time down

Throughout the development of our Flash site, we need to be aware of file sizes for each of the elements in our design. We need to be constantly thinking about the amount of time that our users will end up sitting around waiting for the site to download.

So far, our interface elements have all been quite small. The entire site interface (without any text or multimedia content) comes to just 7K. This is a very acceptable file size, and we've managed to keep it this small because we created a fairly simple interface.

Usability principles encourage us to design interfaces that are clear and simple. One by-product of this is that we tend to produce small, quick-loading files.

Furthermore, we've made use of symbols in our graphic design. Wherever a design element (such as a button) has been repeated, we've created a symbol and used that symbol repeatedly. This helps minimize the amount of graphical data that needs to be stored in the final Flash file.

The audio interface shown earlier in this chapter weighs in at only 1.1K. In this case, the use of simple shapes and straight lines has helped keep our file size down. If, for example, we changed all the lines on the interface to being dotted, as shown below, we make the interface look kind of furry – more importantly, the file jumps up to 8K in size.

Interview with Dr Steven Marr
Recorded: June 2002
Running time: 2:34 mins

audio paused : 73% loaded

How can we continue to keep the file size down?

We need to use vector-based graphics whenever possible. For example, the fridge graphic that we used in some of the previous screenshots is a vector graphic, and weighs in at just 400 bytes. If we included it as a JPEG or GIF file, it would add 5-6K to our file; increasing it more than twelve times over.

- 400 bytes as a vector graphic in Flash,

- 6K as a JPEG at 90% quality

- 7K as a GIF

As we've also observed, we need to be careful with the use of embedded fonts, since they can add substantially to the final size of the SWF. This doesn't mean that we shouldn't use them, just that we need to think carefully before sticking in fifteen different typefaces.

Bitmap graphics and audio are something else to look out for. The easiest way to increase the size of a SWF file is to include lots of images or sound effects. For example, if we added some background music to our site (maybe a looping moody techno track) we could increase our file size by anything from 80K to 1Mb. Again, this doesn't mean we shouldn't use bitmaps or audio, we just need to ask whether they're important enough to justify making users wait and wait for the download.

Are our users getting something that they want, something they came to the site for, by waiting for that download? The answer is probably, "No". If for some reason we did decide that it was beneficial to have background music, we'd have to accept that it wasn't especially important to our users; the most user-friendly way to include it would be to have it load in the background once the rest of the site was loaded and functional.

We should make sure that all large media elements such as our audio and video interviews are loaded **on request**. It's crucial that we ensure users aren't *forced* to download these large sections of content, but only get them if they've been specifically *requested*.

Finally, we should keep generating size reports. It's very simple to do this: just check the Generate Size Report option in the Publish Settings dialog (look in the File menu). Every time you compile the SWF, Flash will generate a text file in the same directory, reporting the sizes of each element in the SWF. This will help give us an idea of the effect each element will have on the download time.

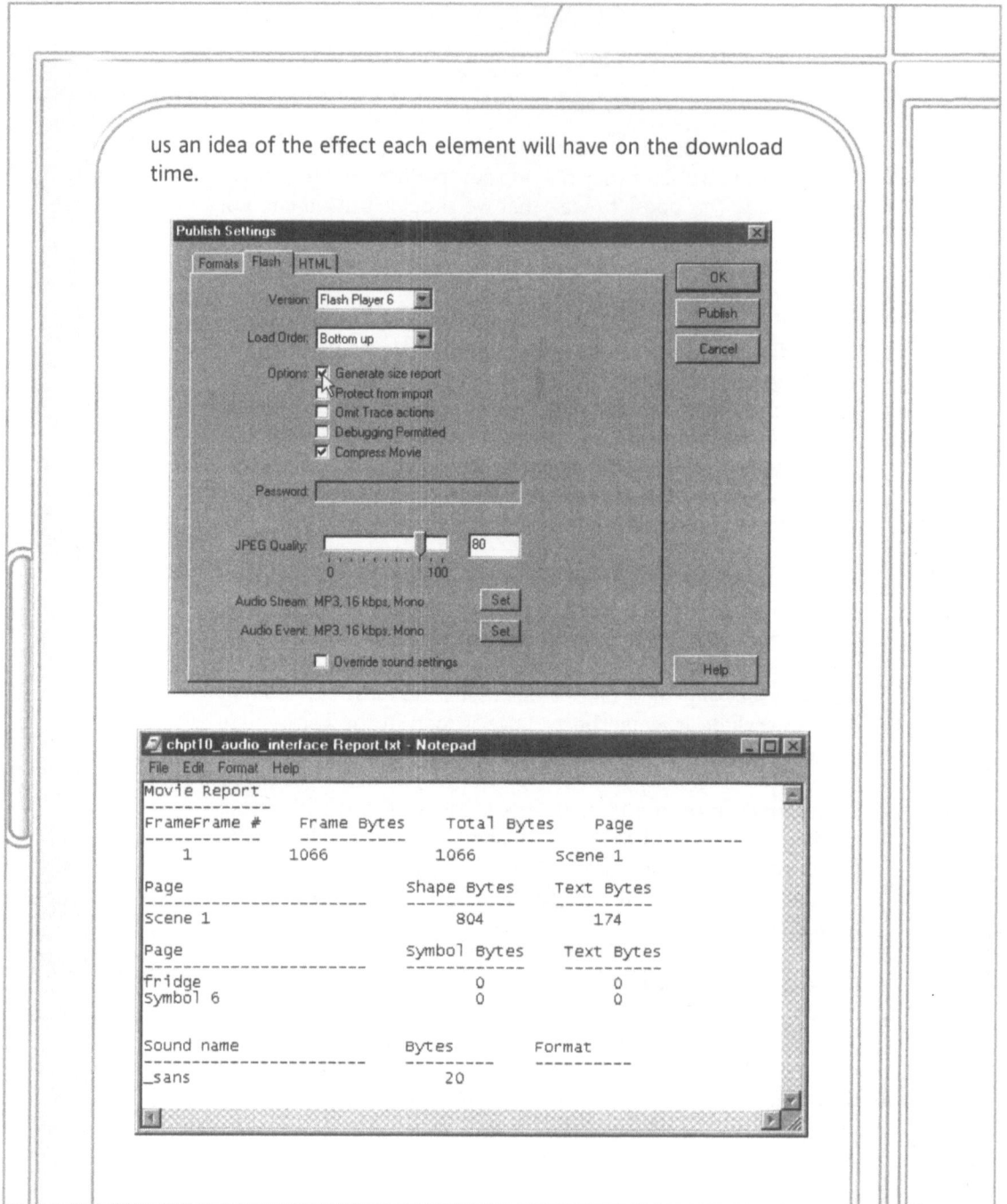

Letting users bookmark, print, and e-mail to a friend

Bookmarking

Bookmarking Flash content can be difficult, as a typical Flash site is just one HTML page. The Flash site may contain multiple sections and screens of information but if users try to bookmark a section of the site they'll actually just bookmark the main HTML page.

This isn't an ideal situation for our *Future Fridges Conference* site. We would like our users to be able to bookmark important sections, like the registration form, so they can easily return to that section. To achieve that functionality we'll need to do a little extra work.

First, we need to set up the Flash file so that the site can automatically jump to a specific section when loaded. Passing a variable to the Flash file that denotes which section to display and having some code that controls a jump to the appropriate section will achieve this.

You can pass a variable to a Flash file through the HTML in which the SWF is embedded. The HTML for our site will contain two references to the site's SWF. We just add a query string containing the variable and its value to the end of these references.

Eg: `futurefridges.swf?section=registration`

The above example creates a variable called `section`, which has the value `registration`.

We set up the Flash file for our site such that each section is located on a different frame with a frame label for each section. Then on the first frame of the Flash file we can use the following code to display the appropriate section:

```
if (_root.section != ""){
    gotoAndStop (_root.section);
}
```

This checks to see if the variable section has been set to anything, and if it has, the Flash file goes to the frame with the matching label.

Now we can get our Flash site to display any section when loaded simply by changing this reference in the HTML page. Thus we can produce unique URLs for each section of the site without needing to change the Flash file. We can either create a unique HTML page for each section with the only difference being the section reference. Or we could use a server script (e.g. PHP, ASP, CFM), which is passed a section reference and creates the appropriate HTML.

The important thing is that we have only one version of the site SWF, but we can have different, special 'bookmarkable' URLs that will jump directly to the different sections of the site.

Now we need to add a button into our site that lets users bookmark the different sections. As we noted above, if users just bookmark the page using the browser's 'Add to Favorites' or 'Bookmark' option they will just bookmark the current HTML page. However, what we want is for them to bookmark our special 'bookmarkable' URL associated with the current section.

What we do is create a button in each section labeled something like 'Bookmark this Section', which when pressed opens a new browser window displaying the page to bookmark. For Internet Explorer users we can actually launch the favorites window with the URL filled in. The following JavaScript will launch the favorites window with the URL www.mysite.com/myurl.html ready to be bookmarked:

```
<script LANGUAGE="Javascript">
<!-// Hide codeif ((navigator.appName ==
➡"Microsoft Internet Explorer") &&
➡(parseInt(navigator.appVersion) >= 4))
{
    window.external.AddFavorite("http://
➡www.mysite.com/myurl.html");
}
 // end hide ->
</script>
```

E-mail to a friend

A very useful option to offer users is the ability to e-mail to a friend a link to the current section of the site. The existence of an 'e-mail to a friend' option will motivate users to share the site with their friends and colleagues and in our case will increase awareness of the conference. It's also important that we encourage our users to use our e-mail to a friend option rather than copying and pasting the URL from the browsers window. As we noted above, the URL displayed in the browser will be the URL for the current HTML page and not necessarily a direct link to the current section.

We want our users to send to their friend the unique URLs for each section that we created for bookmarking.

So clicking on the 'e-mail to a friend' button will open a window in the Flash site asking the user to enter at least their name and their friend's e-mail. We'll then send this data, along with the special URL for the current section to a server script that mails this off to the friend's e-mail address. Scripts for sending an e-mail are freely and widely available for all server scripting languages, just look for a script that sends data from a form (like Matt's Perl script at www.scriptarchive.com/formmail.html).

Printing

Our client specified in our scope that users should be able to easily print all important content on the site. However if we try to print the site's content using either the browser's print button or the Flash menu print option we find that not all the content gets printed. Most notably the complete text within a scrollable text box doesn't get printed.

The solution is to make use of Flash's ability to create your own print pages. Flash allows us to create completely different pages for printing by creating movie clips that aren't displayed on screen but can be sent to the printer using the `print()` command. This is a real bonus for usability, as we can ensure that the content sent to a printer is formatted so that it will be clear and readable when printed. There are some key differences between print and the screen, most notably the layout is reversed (i.e. printed pages are long and narrow, while the screen is short and wide). Also we know that most users will be printing on white paper, so we can ensure that our printer version is formatted to work with a white background.

So we'll add a print button to our site. This button will use the Flash `print()` command to send to the user's printer the 'printer version' movie clip of the current section.

However, we need to explain what's happening to our users. They'll expect that clicking the print button will print exactly what they see, that's how print buttons normally work. Because we are doing something unexpected we need to use a message box to explain to our users what we're doing and give them a chance to opt out if this isn't what they want.

The screenshot below shows the message box for our print function. This box is displayed when the user clicks the Print this section button. If the user clicks OK then the printer friendly content for the section is sent to the printer.

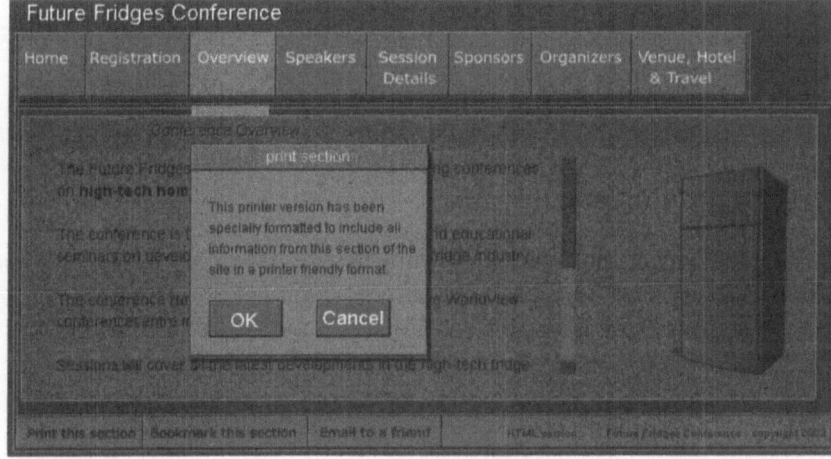

Note that we've also dulled out the content when the message box is displayed. This is achieved by putting a semi-transparent rectangular graphic over the main content and is done to direct the user's attention to the message box.

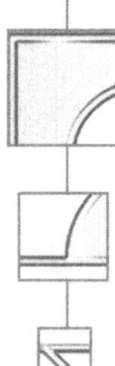

Summary

In this chapter we've attempted to show the importance of respecting our users when designing for usability. Flash gives us a great deal of control over how content is displayed and structured and we can use that control to optimize usability by showing a little respect towards our users.

It's important to make the users feel that they're in control of what's happening on their computer. For example, we've learnt that opening up a full-screen Flash movie in front of a user's browser window may cause frustration and confusion, unless you keep the user informed about what's happening (e.g. how they can close the full-screen movie).

We should never confuse our users with unfamiliar methods of navigation or interface components. We can avoid confusion by providing enough help and information to the user that enables them to interact with our Flash content easily and efficiently.

What it all boils down to is common sense. As long as we keep thinking about how users will feel when we present our Flash content to them, we should be able to create a usable system that doesn't confuse or frustrate them.

Showing users respect   8

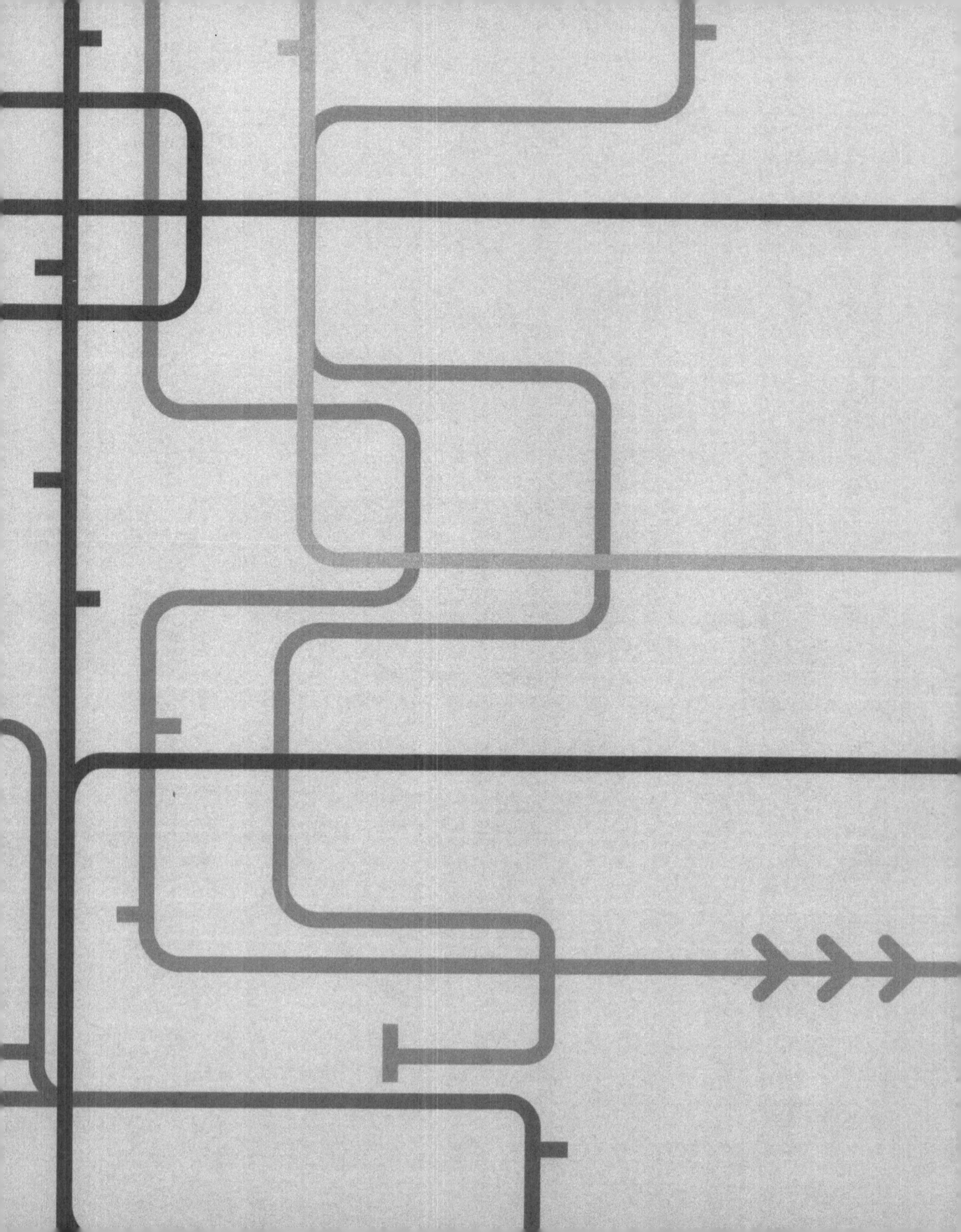

Think Accessibility

What is accessibility?

The term 'accessibility' refers to making services and information available for people with disabilities. With regards to Macromedia Flash MX content, accessibility means making the same web content available for all users.

To create Flash content that works for people with disabilities, designers and developers must understand the different ways that people interact with web content. A blind person using assistive technology to listen to a page will interact with Flash content in a manner very different from a sighted user with a mouse. The interface needs to be carefully designed and tested to ensure a good experience for both users. The goal of accessibility is to create content that not only works, but works well for users with disabilities. This is where the goals of accessibility and usability overlap. Just as users without disabilities want and expect sites that are easy to use, so too do users with disabilities.

Accessible Flash content has to work at two levels. First, the content should meet accepted accessibility standards such as the **Section 508** standards or the **Web Content Accessibility Guidelines** (described later in this chapter). It's important to note, however, that these accessibility guidelines were written either with HTML in mind or to cover the broadest possible range of applications. They don't reflect the techniques of Flash designers or the complexities of Flash content.

> *The most significant step in creating accessible Flash content is identifying and providing text equivalents for all elements and information in the feature.*

Since the release of Flash MX and the Flash 6 player, screen readers such as **Window-Eyes** from GW Micro and **JAWS** from Freedom Scientific have been able to access text and text equivalents in Flash.

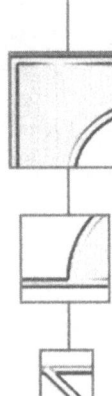

The second level is ensuring that the Flash content makes sense to the user. Just as with other environments, coherent organization, consistent navigation, and clear content are central to accessible Flash content. Understanding the needs of the users and the usage behaviors of people with disabilities is a critical step in developing usable content.

This chapter takes a closer look at accessibility, usability, and Flash MX. The first of the chapter's two sections provides a more complete definition of accessibility in terms of the range of disabilities commonly found among web users, the assistive technologies used, and the policies governing web accessibility. The second section walks through the process of making Flash content accessible. This section examines three cases:

- A blind user of Window-Eyes

- A user with a mobility impairment using a mouth-stick

- A deaf user

For each case, this section identifies the obstacles faced by the user and offers techniques to remedy these issues.

Defining disabilities

A 1997 report by the US Census Bureau categorizes 19.6% of the United States population as having some sort of disability. This percentage is generally considered to be consistent with worldwide statistics. Within the broader category of disability are the following specific types:

- visual impairments

- hearing impairments

- mobility impairments

- cognitive impairments

This list is deceptively short, as each of these categories includes a more extensive range of issues.

Under the category of **visual impairments**, there are individuals with low vision, color blindness, and blindness. The tools and techniques addressing issues for people who are color-blind are very different from those that address issues for those who are blind.

For users with color deficits, the designer needs to pay attention to cues provided with color and make sure that there is sufficient contrast in foreground and background color combinations to make text readable. For people who are blind, the designer must consider software compatibility issues in addition to design issues. Blind computer users often use software known as a screen reader to read the contents of the screen out loud. The Flash designer needs to ensure that the visual information and controls presented to the sighted user are also available to the screen reader. At the same time, this information needs to be presented in a manner that makes it easy for the user to understand the content.

Mobility impairments include a wide range of disabilities such as quadriplegia, cerebral palsy, severe arthritis, repetitive stress disorder, or even a broken wrist. Many people with mobility impairments will rely on the keyboard, a modified keyboard, a joystick, or foot pedals rather than a mouse to navigate Flash content. It's therefore crucial that accessible Flash content allows users to access all buttons and controls using navigation methods other than the mouse.

Even more complex is the category of **cognitive impairments**. This group includes people with seizure disorders, as well as people with learning disabilities and those with developmental disabilities. Building sites that are accessible to people with cognitive disabilities can be a complex task as the obstacles to comprehension often lie in the content as well as in the Flash design. More than any other tool, however, Flash provides a unique set of features that allow the designer to present information in a variety of forms simultaneously.

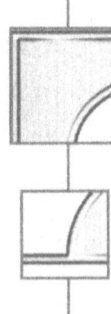

The combination of text, video, audio, animation, and interactivity that Flash allows offers users with cognitive disabilities the opportunity to engage with content in ways not possible with text alone.

Assistive technologies

Users with disabilities frequently rely on hardware and software to aid them in accessing web content. These tools, known as **assistive technologies**, range from screen readers to mouth-sticks and screen magnifiers. Just as designers routinely consider how designs are affected by implementation across platforms and browsers, it's likewise important to evaluate how the designs work with a variety of assistive technologies.

Blind computer users frequently use screen readers to read the contents of the screen out loud. Two common screen readers, already mentioned above, are JAWS and Window-Eyes. Screen readers enable users to hear, rather than read, the contents of a Flash movie; however, a screen reader can only read text, not images or animations. To address this obstacle, designers can add a name and description for visual elements of a Flash movie to help explain the contents and significance to a screen reader user.

Users with impaired mobility may rely on the keyboard instead of the mouse to navigate Flash content. Using only TAB and ENTER on the keyboard, it's possible to negotiate a page without using a mouse. Many users of the Internet have this capability and are simply unaware of it. In Microsoft Internet Explorer, pressing TAB moves the focus of the Flash movie among all available controls on a page. Pressing ENTER activates the control, much like clicking a mouse. In some cases, users may employ a tool to press the keys on the keyboard. These tools, such as head pointers or mouth pointers, may be as simple as a stick held in the user's mouth or mounted on a head strap.

Many of the same challenges for users with mobility impairments apply equally to blind users, because most blind users do not employ a mouse. If you can't see the cursor, the mouse is of little value. This is one of the reasons the screen reader is such a common criterion for evaluating Flash content for accessibility. The screen reader provides a concrete environment for designers to evaluate access to visual content as well as access to content via the keyboard.

Accessibility standards

Accessibility policies vary from country to country, but many countries, including the United States, Australia, Canada, the European Union, and Japan have adopted policies based on standards developed by the World Wide Web Consortium (W3C). In 1997, the W3C began investigating accessibility issues that might be encountered by people with disabilities on the new emerging World Wide Web. This group led to the formation of the Web Accessibility Initiative (WAI). The WAI consists of several efforts to improve the accessibility of the Web. Perhaps the most widely used document is the Web Content Accessibility Guidelines (WCAG).

For each of the fourteen guidelines that constitute the WCAG 1.0, there are a series of checkpoints rated as Priority 1, Priority 2, or Priority 3:

- Priority 1 checkpoints are the actions designers *must* take to make a site accessible

- Priority 2 checkpoints are the actions designers *should* take to make a site accessible

- Priority 3 checkpoints are the actions a designer *might* take to improve the accessibility of a site

The Priority 1 checkpoints of the WCAG serve as the basis of accessibility standards in almost every country where a formal policy has been adopted.

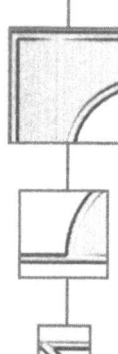

The exceptions are Canada and the United Kingdom, where web site designers for the national governments are required to follow the Priority 1 and Priority 2 checkpoints of the WCAG.

In the United States, the law governing web accessibility is commonly referred to as Section 508. The Section 508 amendment to the U.S. Rehabilitation Act prohibits federal agencies from buying, developing, maintaining, or using electronic and information technology that's inaccessible to people with disabilities. This amendment mandates standards for accessibility; moreover, it gives members of the public and government employees with disabilities the right to sue agencies in federal court and file administrative complaints for noncompliance.

As of June 21, 2002, all federal Web sites are expected to comply with the standards mandated under Section 508. These standards are based on the Priority 1 checkpoints of the WCAG, with one Priority 3 checkpoint thrown in for good measure.

The difference between Section 508 and the WCAG is subtle but important. Section 508 was intended to define when a problem was **severe enough to serve as the basis of a lawsuit**. The WCAG defines a **set of goals** for accessible design. Consequently, the Section 508 standards were designed to be more easily evaluated.

This has made the Section 508 standards a popular basis for accessibility policies at the state, local, and institutional level. Designers and developers in these settings are often under no federal mandate to follow the Section 508 standards. Instead, their local accessibility policy may require use of these standards. This distinction can be confusing but important. The consequences for non-compliance may vary significantly from place to place.

Flash and accessibility standards

Use of Flash content is allowed under both W3C guidelines and Section 508 standards, if not expressly defined. In both cases, Flash content is included within the broad category of 'plug-ins'. Guideline 11.1 of the WCAG reads, "Use W3C technologies when they are available and appropriate for a task and use the latest versions when supported."

The caveat here is that designers should be thoughtful about their choice to use Flash rather than HTML or XML. Section 508 standards are more specific with regards to the use of plug-ins. According to Section 508, all plug-in content is its own piece of software. Consequently, each piece of Flash content has to meet the same standards used for applications. These guidelines are similar to the Web content guidelines except that they don't assume that HTML is the underlying structure.

> *The Section 508 application standards can be found at*
> www.section508.gov/index.cfm?FuseAction=Content&ID=12
> *To learn more about the Section 508 standards, visit*
> www.section508.gov *or*
> www.macromedia.com/macromedia/accessibility.

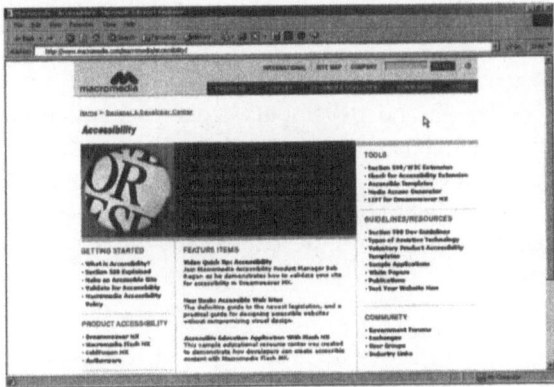

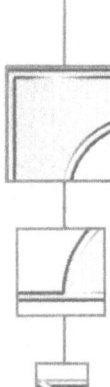

While Section 508 and the WCAG allow for the use of Flash, neither sufficiently addresses the most common problems that degrade the usability of Flash content with assistive technologies. In order to make content that's truly accessible using Flash, it's necessary to examine the user experience in more detail, as we will do later in this chapter.

Flash MX accessibility overview

This section provides a brief overview of the improvements made to the Flash Player and the Flash MX authoring tool. A more detailed discussion of accessibility issues and techniques for accessible design is included in the second half of this chapter.

Flash Player 6

Flash Player 6 has integrated support for Microsoft Active Accessibility (MSAA). MSAA serves as a bridge between Flash Player 6 and assistive technologies such as the Window-Eyes screen reader. By default, Flash Player 6 recognizes text symbols, movie clips, and button symbols, even if the content was created in Flash MX. Text elements and buttons in Flash movies created in Flash 4 and Flash 5 are thus available to screen readers, without modification. This means that the majority of Flash content available today will be significantly more accessible using Flash Player 6. This doesn't necessarily mean, however, that the content designers create will meet desirable standards for usability.

Flash MX

To help designers and developers create accessible Flash content, a new Accessibility panel has been added to Flash MX. The Accessibility panel allows text equivalents to be specified for elements of Flash movies and provides control over how assistive technologies handle these elements. The Accessibility panel allows designers and developers to specify a brief descriptive text equivalent in the Name field. A longer text equivalent, if needed, can be placed in the Description field. MSAA then passes this information on to the assistive technologies.

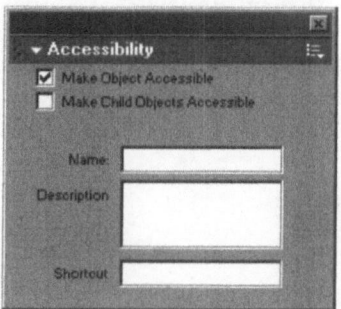

The Accessibility panel includes two options at the top: Make Object Accessible and Make Child Objects Accessible. It's not always necessary or helpful to make all elements of a movie accessible. Take the example below. The animation shows an electric car engine running. When the Play button is pressed, the car becomes transparent, illustrating how power is transferred between the engine and battery:

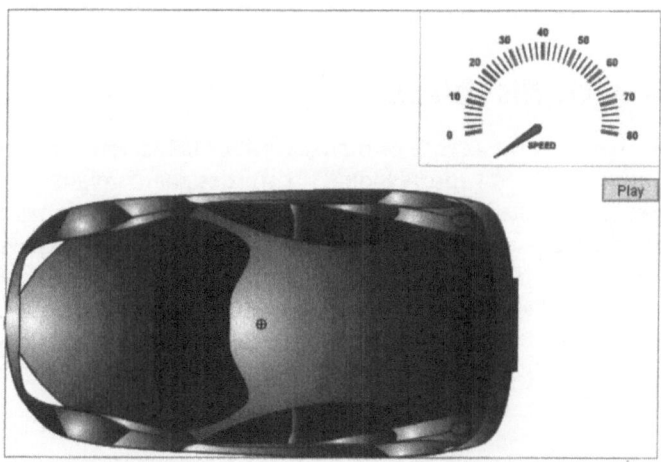

Since the relationships displayed here are inherently visual, it wouldn't be helpful to provide names for the parts of the engine. Instead, the designer may provide a single text equivalent for the entire animation that describes what's being displayed. In the Accessibility panel, the designer or developer deselects all elements on the stage. The Make Object Accessible option should be available and selected. The Make Child Objects Accessible option is deselected, and a description for the animation is displayed.

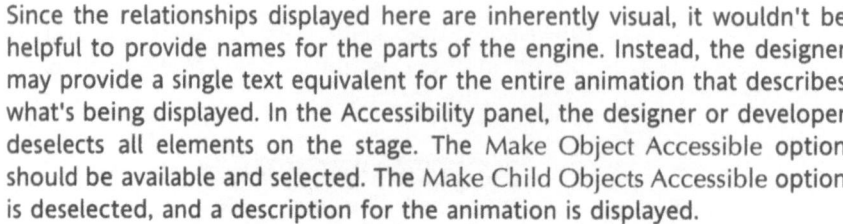

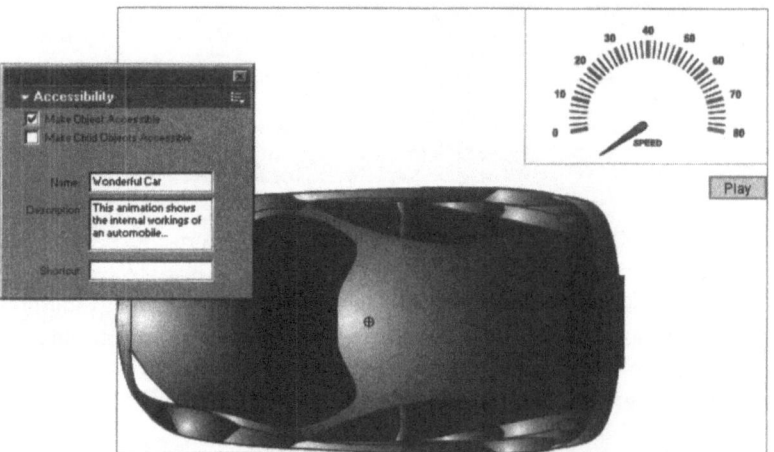

Users with disabilities

Now that we have a sense of the basics, let's take a look at some of the more common problems professional Flash designers might encounter when working to create accessible Flash content. This section looks at the cases of three different users of Flash content: a blind user, a user with a mobility impairment, and a deaf user. For each case, we'll examine some of the most common challenges for the user, as well as design techniques that may be used to address these issues.

Case 1 – Ann

Ann Ullman is a blind woman working at the National Science Pool researching consumer applications of superconductive materials. Known as 'Absolute Zero' around the lab, she's quite proficient at using her Window-Eyes screen reader from GW Micro. She uses her computer much of the day to research articles and to write up lab results.

Ann recently started working with Flash content. After visiting a number of Flash sites recommended by the grad students in her lab, she describes her experiences as frustrating. She mentions that it often takes her several passes through to get a sense of what a site is all about. She commonly encounters this problem when she works with simple HTML pages, but working with Flash seems to exacerbate the difficulty.

On some occasions, Flash movies cause her screen reader to continually refresh. This is especially frustrating since it causes Window-Eyes to constantly repeat the phrase, "Loading page...Load done." Ann also mentions that sometimes the Flash content just doesn't make any sense. There are buttons mixed in with paragraphs and headings. "It sounds like someone took the web page and put it in a blender," she reports.

Exposing structure

When a sighted user first encounters a Flash screen, their eyes will normally scan immediately through the visual elements. They'll read the text, process the images, and identify the buttons. Experienced designers know how this process works for most users and take advantage of it. Important elements are organized into rows and columns, usually starting at the top left. Color is used to group elements and also to distinguish them. Visual cues are used to identify the relationships among items and, ideally, what can be done with them.

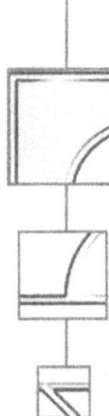

For a blind user, none of this visual design is apparent. They're limited only to the text that's read to them. That doesn't mean there aren't ways to convey the same information as the visual design, but they are necessarily different. While the designer relies on the sighted user to scan the screen and quickly assess its meaning and how they can interact with it, it's imperative to use accessible text to orient the blind user to both structure and function.

Flash MX provides a simple way to do this. It's possible to attach a text equivalent to an entire Flash movie that briefly describes the design of the movie and its major elements. The description should introduce and explain both the purpose of the screen and its layout.

In the example below, a simple registration form has been created in Macromedia Flash MX. This form includes seven form fields and a Submit button:

It's possible to add or modify the accessible name and description for the entire movie by going to the `_root` timeline, and deselecting all options.

The Accessibility window should change to indicate that only the name and the description can be modified:

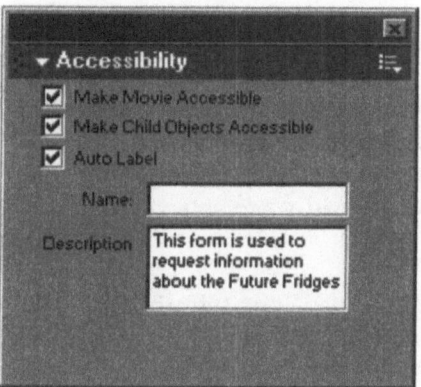
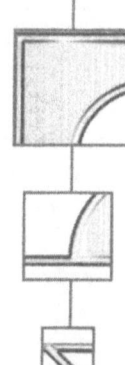

In this case, the designer might enter the following as a description for the form: "This form is used to request information about the Future Fridges conference via mail."

An alternate method is to attach a description to a movie clip in the upper left corner of the screen. This clip can be small, but it must contain some art; empty movie clips, even those with accessibility properties, are not accessible using screen readers. If the clip is placed in the far upper left-hand corner, its description will be read first whenever the screen is loaded. This allows more control over when the text might be read. For instance, a different announcement could be read every time there's a significant change to the Flash screen. This method is also more reliable since Window-Eyes tends not to read the description field the first time through.

Navigation – naming buttons

Users can be impatient, a fact that's true of the blind as well as the sighted. Sighted users, however, have the advantage that their eyes can scan the

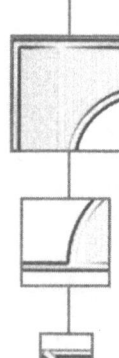

page, only coming to rest on the parts that interest them. Blind users must often rely on the TAB key to scan through the contents of a page.

One trick that Ann has always used when navigating HTML pages is to listen to the links on the pages by themselves. With most screen readers, it's possible for a user to extract a list of links from the page, enabling her to jump to a specific section without listening to the entire page first. Window-Eyes, however, doesn't support the links list in Flash. To get around this problem, Ann simply jumps between buttons and other controls by pressing TAB. This action allows her to ascertain quickly which controls are available on the page.

TAB advances the focus box from button to button on the current Flash screen. When the screen reader comes to a button, it reads the label for that button. By default, Flash will automatically assign a label as the text within the button. If there's more than one text symbol within the button, the one closest to the upper left will be read as the label. Any other text on the screen is ignored, just as it would be in HTML. This includes text in the Over state of the button.

The designer can specify the label for the button using the Name and Description fields in the Accessibility panel. If a name is specified, the screen reader will not read the child objects of the button.

A basic rule of HTML is to avoid using 'click here' as link text. The same is true in Flash. The purpose of the button should be clearly based on the label alone. To allow Ann to move quickly through the list of available links and find what she's looking for, the labels should be short but sufficiently descriptive. In cases where the user might encounter a button only once, or if it's too complicated to explain in a few words, a description can be used. With usability in mind, the designer or developer must try to optimize both the coherence of the descriptions and the speed with which the user can find what she's looking for.

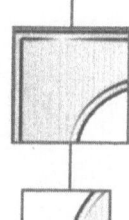

Similarly, it's important to provide full descriptions of input text to avoid ambiguity. You don't want users confusing a 'shipping address' with a 'billing address'. Unfortunately, the UI components currently included with Flash MX are not accessible, so you may be limited to using input text or checkboxes when a combo box might be more desirable. Alternatively, you could code your own accessible version of a combo box. Keep in mind that building accessible components requires that the MSAA information be directly included.

Coping with change

One of the chief challenges of describing the structure of a Flash screen is that the screen often changes. After all, designers use Flash because they want to make their web sites more dynamic.

When a user interacts with a Flash Movie using Window-Eyes, each screen change is announced by the sequence of phrases, "Loading page", and, "Load done." This message is spoken whether the screen is changed by a keyframe (in the `_root` timeline or even within a movie clip), by the `loadMovie()` method or, as you might expect, by loading another page by using `getURL` or a similar method.

These phrases may seem misleading – in many of these cases a new page hasn't loaded – but they're used because there needs to be a consistent method of alerting the screen reader user to the fact that the screen has changed. Unfortunately, in a Flash movie that makes use of a lot of symbols or ActionScript, the user can be bombarded by a steady stream of "Loading page ...Load done" announcements that signify nothing.

For example, imagine an animated logo in a movie clip. The logo is intended to draw the user's attention, but not to distract her from the task at hand. The default behavior of the blind user's screen reader, however, is to announce each keyframe of the animation, creating more of a distraction than an enhancement.

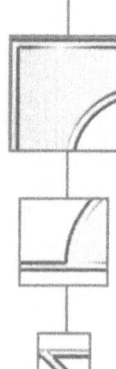

One solution to this difficulty is to make the object accessible by checking the first box in the Accessibility control panel but leaving the second box unchecked, thereby rendering its child object inaccessible. Now the user can hear a brief description of the animated logo without having to endure a steady stream of "Loading page ... Load done":

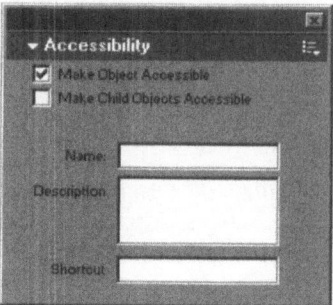

When it comes to loading external SWF files into the current movie, it may be desirable to leave the Make Child Objects Accessible option selected. A common way to allow users to download content on demand is to use the loadMovie() method of a movie clip to replace its current contents with the contents of another SWF file.

This can be a powerful way to reduce or control the amount of time a user spends waiting for downloads, but it's important to be careful about the accessibility settings. If the SWF being loaded contains buttons or movie clips that must be accessible, then the movie clip into which it's loaded must have the Make Child Objects Accessible option selected, otherwise the screen reader will not be alerted to the accessible content of the newly loaded SWF.

Revealing state

As Ann encounters new screens, it will become necessary to orient her. Remember, the same design goals apply to sighted users and to blind users: it's the medium that changes. The designer needs to answer the same basic questions of navigation and orientation for both groups: "Where am I now?", "What can I do?", and "Where can I go from here?"

For sighted users, Flash designers often make use of the Over state of buttons to indicate where a button might take the user. A simple change of picture or text indicates both that a graphic is clickable and gives a hint of what it might do. For someone using a screen reader, however, these Over states are invisible. Not only can they not see them, but if they're using Window-Eyes, the screen reader does not alert Flash that the button has been selected.

Toggles create a similar challenge for accessible design. Any two (or more) state buttons must indicate to the user both what the current state is, and what's likely to happen when the button is activated. This is true whether the user is sighted or not, but it's easy to overlook or take for granted the visual cues that the sighted user relies on to indicate both where he is and where he might be headed. Consider the following example:

Page: 1 | 2	Page: 1 | 2
This is the text for page one. We have two screens worth of text to display.	This is the text for page two. Because there is so much text, we spread it across two screens.

For the sighted user, it's clear that clicking on the number 2 will take her to page 2. Once there, the visual feedback changes to indicate that she's now on page 2, and that she can click on the Page 1 button to return to the first page. The visual clues make it clear what the current state is and what will happen if the button is activated.

It's easy to see that the default screen reader behavior could be confusing. On page 1, the screen reader reads, "Page 1. Button 2," which may be clear

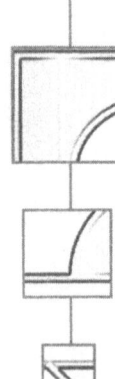

enough. On page 2, however, it reads, "Page. Button 1. 2." Worse, if the blind user uses Tab to jump straight to the buttons, she'll only hear "Button 2" on page 1 and "Button 1" on page 2, which is very confusing.

The solution is to embellish the accessible text to make it clear to the user where she currently is and where the button will take her. A simple approach to solving the problem on the second screen ("Page. Button 1. 2") would be to combine the text "Page" and "2" into one movie clip with one description, so it would be read "Page 2." This movie clip tells the blind user that she's currently on page 2. The button with the description, "Button 1", should be clear without any changes.

A more sophisticated option would be to make a movie clip of the entire collection of page numbers and buttons and use ActionScript to change the accessible text dynamically. This can be achieved through the undocumented _accprops property of a movie clip.

Although ActionScript can't read the current accessibility settings, it's possible to modify them by creating an _accprops object for the movie clip and then modifying its properties. Here's some sample code that would change the accessible name of an existing movie clip:

```
myMovieClip._accprops = new Object();
myMovieClip._accprops.name = "dynamic content"
```

The _accprops object has six properties that can be modified. Three are strings: name, description and shortcut. Three are Booleans: silent (equivalent to Make Object Accessible deselected), forceSimple (Make Child Objects Accessible deselected) and noAutoLabeling.

Speaking and tab order

Ann describes how, in some cases, the Flash content sounds incoherent, as if it's been put in a blender. This happens when Flash handles the reading order of its content in a fundamentally different manner than designers

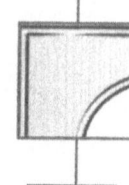

expect. In HTML, the reading order of the page is based on the order in which the contents appear in the HTML document itself. In Flash content, there's no underlying code on which to base the reading order. In situations where the default reading order or the default tab order isn't necessarily the logical order, a `tabindex` may be specified. This procedure will be covered in greater detail in the next section on keyboard accessibility.

Case 2 – Michael

Michael Hoffman is a quadriplegic who works as a tech support specialist at Internet Appliances. He helps customers install software and updates in the latest model of the iFridge. Since Michael has limited use of his hands and feet, he employs a stick held in his mouth to navigate around the keyboard. Using the mouth-stick, Michael presses the buttons on his computer keyboard to navigate a page.

Michael has been using Macromedia Flash for a while, and he can usually access Flash content, but he has encountered a couple of areas of difficulty. First, Michael notes that it's frustrating for him when TAB won't bring him to all of the items on the screen that are obviously buttons. Second, Michael frequently finds that once he uses TAB to get into a piece of Flash content that's combined with HTML, he can't use TAB to get out. This can be especially frustrating since it often requires him to use significantly more key presses to get where he wants to go.

Tab order

There is some overlap between the needs of a blind user and those of a user with a mobility impairment. Both are limited to using a keyboard or keyboard-equivalent for input. In most cases the user can use TAB and SHIFT-TAB to move a focus box from button to button. Pressing ENTER or RETURN is equivalent to clicking the mouse button.

A problem arises because a necessary part of the default behavior of Flash is a default sequence of buttons. Flash has no way of knowing what the buttons signify or what would be a sensible order in which to read them, so it has to guess. The results are not always predictable.

The default tab order can be roughly estimated based on the following formula:

```
Tab Weight = 2y + (x/3)
```

where x and y are the coordinates of the object. The button with the lowest tab weight will be first in the order. The next lowest is second, and so on. The illustration below shows the reading order moving down as it moves across the page:

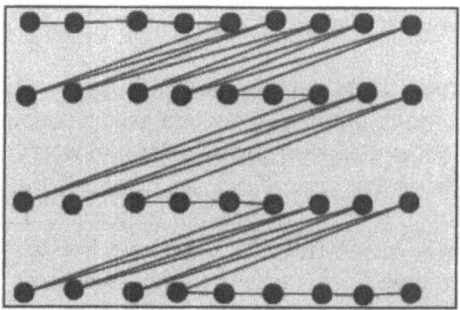

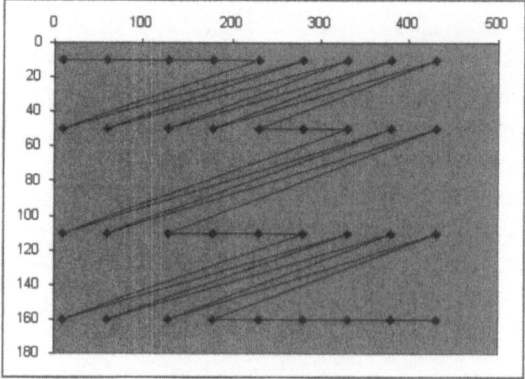

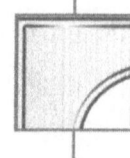

A sighted user like Michael may be willing to live with the default tab order, because he can see the focus box highlighting the current button. Even if the sequence doesn't make complete sense, he can tell from the visual design how the buttons are grouped. In the case of Ann, however, who's blind, she has no visual feedback, and she's likely to be confused if the left navigation is intermingled with the top navigation.

Fortunately, Flash MX offers a way around this problem. The default tab order can be modified programmatically. Each button has a `tabindex` property that controls where the button will appear in the tab sequence.

Modifying the tab order is relatively easy, but it's important to remember that once the `tabindex` property has been set for one instance of a button, it must be set for every instance on the stage, or the results may be haphazard. For a sighted user without a screen reader like Michael, instances without a `tabindex` won't appear in the tab order at all and will be impossible to access. For Ann, a user of Window-Eyes, the tab order would revert to the default order.

Keyboard shortcuts

Another way to increase the usability of a Flash movie for Michael is to add keyboard shortcuts so that he can quickly navigate around the screen. Keys may be enabled using ActionScript. The following is one method of enabling a keyboard shortcut. In this case, the combination of CTRL+1 (CMD+1 on the Mac) will execute the function `activateButton1`.

This example uses listeners, but the same result could be reached using an `enterFrame onClipEvent` to continuously check the last key pressed:

```
// sample ActionScript for capturing keystrokes
//(frame script)
myListener = new Object();
myListener.onKeyUp = function() {
  // Key.CONTROL is either one of the control keys on
```

```
// Windows or either of the COMMAND keys on the Mac
// ASCII 49 is the '1' key
if (Key.isDown(Key.CONTROL) and (Key.getAscii() ==
➥49)) {
    activateButton1();
}
};
Key.addListener(myListener);
```

Because many keys and key combinations may already be in use by system software and assistive technology, it's recommended that keyboard shortcuts be limited to modifier keys like CONTROL and ALT and the number keys.

When establishing shortcuts, it's important to include that information in the Accessibility panel. The shortcuts will then be exposed to MSAA, which ensures that screen readers will interpret them properly.

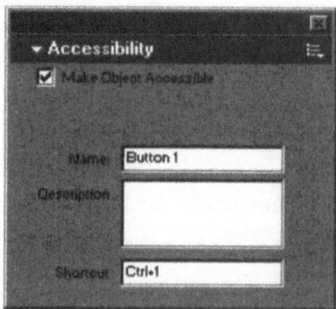

Hybrid pages

Pages that mix Flash and HTML content can pose another problem to keyboard users like Michael. While it is possible to use TAB to navigate from HTML into Flash content in most browsers, it's not possible to use TAB to navigate from the Flash content back into HTML. This means that if there are any HTML links that appear on the page after the Flash content, the keyboard user may not be able to access them.

There is a workaround to this problem, developed by John Norgaard, and described on his web site at www.sonokids.com/tabnew.html. Using a combination of ActionScript and JavaScript, John's Flash movie detects when the user has used TAB to navigate past the last button in Flash. It then messages a JavaScript function, which changes the focus to the next HTML link. Unfortunately, John's code works only in Internet Explorer. (But remember, in Ann's case, Internet Explorer is currently the only browser that works with Window-Eyes).

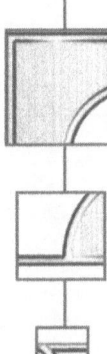

Case 3 – Delores

Delores Benedict is a deaf woman who teaches refrigerator economics at MIT. She frequently creates Flash learning objects to help her students understand the complex modeling that's invariably associated with global refrigerator econometrics. She recently joined the faculty at MIT from the London School of Economics.

Delores is looking forward to the *Future Fridges Conference*. She'll be presenting a paper entitled, 'The Impact of Fridgeless Households in Postmodern England'. When registering for the conference, Delores was frustrated because the conference web site's video segments were not captioned. The site includes a number of interviews with keynote speakers, and Dolores was hoping to review these sessions in preparation for her own talk.

Adding captions or subtitles to a Flash movie provides access to audio content for people who are deaf or hard of hearing. Outstanding examples of captioned Flash movies such as 'In His Own Words' on the PBS American Experience Marcus Garvey site serve as exemplary illustrations of how captions may be employed in Flash. With the recently added support for video within Flash MX, the need for captions in online multimedia is significantly greater than it was in previous versions. At the same time, the improved support for XML in Flash MX allows designers new and easier ways of providing captions.

Captions are the display of spoken dialogue as printed words on the screen. Captions are specifically designed for deaf and hard-of-hearing viewers and are used to display dialogue and identify speakers, on- and off-screen sound effects, music, and laughter. Subtitles, on the other hand, translate only the program's dialog or narration into a different language. Designed for a hearing audience, they don't contain sound-effect cues or other useful information normally found in captions.

> *Some Flash movies don't require captions. A navigation bar that has no audio components or one that plays a small sound when the mouse is passed over the buttons has no need for captions. A movie containing an audio recording of a historic speech or a video of a sales presentation would require captions.*

A children's game that instructs the user to "click on the button that sounds like an elephant", could use captions to ensure that the audible content is available to all users, irrespective of their ability to hear sounds. In general, if a sound is important to the message or necessary for the operation of a Flash movie, captions should be provided.

Delivering captions and subtitles

There are at least four methods for adding captions to a Macromedia Flash movie:

- Captions may simply be placed on the stage by hand

- Captions may be added to Flash content that's played in QuickTime or Real

- Video content that's already been captioned may be imported into the Flash file

- Flash may import caption data from a separately created XML file

Adding captions manually

The easiest method for providing a text alternative to audible content in a Flash movie is simply to add the text on the timeline. An advantage of this method is that the designer has a fine degree of control over the placement, appearance, and even movement of the text. The disadvantages are that it's laborious to synchronize the appearance of text on the timeline with longer sound files and that 'effect' caption writing is a skill that is honed through practice and hard work.

The typical Flash designer isn't trained as a captioner in the same way that the average caption writer isn't trained in Flash design. This method involves the Flash designer with captioning at a level that's potentially beyond his or her ability and interest.

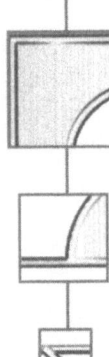

Macromedia Flash in Real and QT

If the destination of the Flash content is the QuickTime player or RealPlayer, captions can be added using the caption formats associated with each player: QTtext or RealText. The caption file used is a text file that can be composed in any text editor or by using MAGpie, a free application from the National Center for Accessible Media (NCAM) at WGBH for creating captions for online media (http://ncam.wgbh.org/webaccess/magpie). The synchronization is accomplished either by adding the text track in QuickTime or by using SMIL (synchronized multimedia integration language).

Import captioned QT movie

If the part of a Flash movie that needs captions is a video or an audio file, the new capabilities of Flash MX simplify the process. By importing a previously captioned QuickTime movie, captions can be displayed as part of the overall presentation. A disadvantage to this method is that the QuickTime caption text won't scale well when displayed in the Flash player. When the caption text is displayed in QuickTime, QuickTime renders it as text, allowing the movie to be shown full screen with no loss in caption clarity.

Displaying captioned video in the Flash Player is limited to Flash 6. Advantages of this method are that the caption file doesn't need to be created by the Flash designer but is a task that can be outsourced, and designers familiar with ActionScript can create controls that allow users to turn the captions on and off as long as the video and the captions are imported as separate elements.

Caption data from an XML file

Significant improvements in XML parsing in Flash Player 6 allow another technique to be used to include captions in a Flash movie. **Captioner**, a tool created by Jason Smith of the American Association for the Advancement of

Science, available at the Macromedia Accessibility Resource Center, can be used to integrate XML caption data.

Parsing and displaying XML caption data

1. The first step is to create a caption file. This XML file can be composed in a text editor, but MAGpie Version 2.01's (http://ncam.wgbh.org/webaccess/magpie) XML format used for saving caption projects was the model for the Captioner tool. MAGpie has two application windows: the player where the media is played, and the captioning grid where captions are typed and timed. MAGpie is capable of captioning media that plays in QuickTime and RealPlayer, including MOV, WAV, and SWF files. When encoding digital video (DV) directly to Sorenson Squeeze or using a media type that doesn't play in QuickTime or Real, it's necessary to encode a temporary version to be used in MAGpie for captioning.

    Once the media has been captioned and timed and the MAGpie project saved, the MAGpie project file can be used with the Flash Captioner tool. Additional information about how to use MAGpie is available at NCAM's Rich Media Accessibility web site (http://ncam.wgbh.org/richmedia).

    It's important to note that MAGpie uses HTML font sizes, but when the caption data is imported into Flash, Flash interprets the font size as points. Therefore, the font size references of the MAGpie file should be changed; for example, every `font size="3"` in the MAGpie file should be changed to `font size="16"` before being used in Flash.

    Moreover, there's information in the MAGpie XML file that's not needed by the Captioner tool. Additional tools for reducing the MAGpie XML file to the bare minimum are available at the Rich Media Accessibility Web site above. Finally, before using the MAGpie XML file

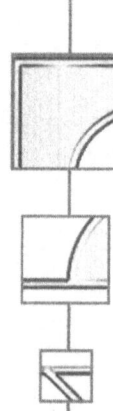

with Captioner, it's necessary to change the extension from `.magpie` to `.xml`.

2. With the XML file in hand, we are ready to use the Captioner. Once the Captioner extension is installed using the Macromedia Extension Manager, it can be located in Common Libraries under the Window menu in Flash MX. Drag the item named Captioner onto the stage.

3. When the Captioner element on the stage is clicked, the Property inspector displays its parameter settings. The parameters should be set to the following:

Method	1
Splash Text	This can be changed or deleted
Debug	0
StreamName	should be modified to match the file name of the XML caption file. It's important to make sure that the XML caption file is in the same directory as the published SWF file.
DefaultLanguage	en is the default

4. When the SWF file is published, captions will be displayed. The Captioner tool includes a button that allows the user to turn captions on and off.

5. A final step to consider when adding captions in Flash MX is ensuring that the captions will be hidden from screen reader users. If the captions aren't hidden, then the screen reader will refresh its view of the content with every new caption, resulting in "Loading page ... Load done" being voiced repeatedly in Window-Eyes. To hide the captions, select the caption area and deselect Make Object Accessible in the Accessibility panel.

While this process simplifies the creation of captions, it can limit design options. Moving the caption area around so captions are displayed in an area of the screen that helps to indicate who's speaking or where a sound originates is difficult, because the text of the captions is only visible upon playback.

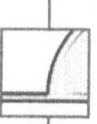

This method does have several advantages, including scalable display of text, the ability to outsource caption writing, and the potential to provide captions and subtitles for multiple languages that are displayed based on browser language preference settings. Another advantage is that because the captions are drawn dynamically from the XML caption file, any errors in the caption text can be corrected without modifying the FLA.

Case Study

Accessibility and our site

We've previously decided to develop a companion HTML version of our site to ensure that the site meets the section 508 regulations. However that isn't the only step we can take to ensure the accessibility of our site. It's quite possible that some users with disabilities will prefer to access the Flash site and there are a number of things we can do to assist these users.

As our site's being built for the Flash 5 plug-in we can't make use of the Flash MX accessibility features outlined in this chapter. Yet we can still make some improvements to the accessibility of our Flash content.

Our site contains a video interview and a number of audio interviews. This content may not be very accessible for users with any form of a hearing problem. Clearly we can improve things by including captions with our interviews. We could either use the XML captioning method discussed in this chapter, or alternatively we could provide a full transcript of the audio interviews, which would mean that users wouldn't need to wait for the audio to download but could just read the transcript.

Validation and Testing for Accessibility

As with any project, testing is important to ensure that the Flash feature functions correctly for all users, including those with disabilities. There are no products currently available that perform automated checking of Flash content, but we expect to see such products in the near future.

Testing Keyboard Access

The easiest form of testing is for keyboard accessibility. While testing, the mouse should be put out of reach. Testing the tab order within Flash content can be done with either Flash Player or within the browser, but to ensure that strategies for using TAB to navigate through the Flash object in a web page are effective, it's necessary to test in the browser. It's also important to keep in mind that screen readers like Window-Eyes modify the keyboard behavior. To be completely confident in the keyboard accessibility test, ascertain the movie's keyboard functionality both with and without a screen reader.

Testing Captions

Testing captions is also easy in that no special equipment is required and testers do not need to learn a new way of interacting with the computer. It may be difficult, however, in that captions need to be well written to convey all audible information clearly. For captions – particularly if the captions were not authored by a trained captioner – mute the speakers and watch the captions to make sure that the content is understood. It's recommended that a person not already familiar with the content be asked to perform this test. If possible, testing with a person who depends on captions regularly will provide the most accurate and thorough assessment of the quality of the captions.

Testing with Screen Readers

Testing with screen readers and screen magnifiers is the most difficult, because of the specialized and expensive tools that are unfamiliar to most testers.

> *A screen reader is a sophisticated piece of software with a steep learning curve. It's necessary to find someone familiar with screen readers, preferably a regular user, to conduct your final testing.*

Screen readers that currently support Flash are Window-Eyes 4.2 ($600 - $800 depending on operating system) from GW Micro (www.gwmicro.com) and JAWS 4.5 ($900-$1200, depending on operating system) from Freedom Scientific (www.freedomscientific.com). A demo version is available for each of these products that functions for a short period of time (around 30 minutes) before requiring a restart.

Freedom Scientific also offers Connect Outloud ($249), which is based on the JAWS product, but rather than serving as a screen reader for all functions of a computer it is limited to use within Internet Explorer. Currently, only Windows screen readers (there are few non-Windows screen readers) are capable of reading Flash.

Learning how to use a screen reader at a rudimentary level is recommended for QA testers and Flash designers, if only for a first level of testing. A designer working to ensure that the tab order is correct for screen reader users can perform a test and continue with the task, rather than waiting for a report from a tester. With a basic knowledge of screen readers, other simple tests can be performed, such as ensuring that labels are associated with controls in forms, verifying that all elements have appropriate equivalent information, and identifying elements that cause the screen reader to repeat information continuously.

When performing testing with a screen reader, the monitor should be off or covered. Begin by using TAB to move through the Flash content, listening to the spoken output. Consider whether the structure of the content is apparent. After what's likely to be several passes through the tab order, let the screen reader read the entire feature. Again, listen for the content of the feature, including the reading order, as well as the structure to ensure that each is clear.

As with testing captions, regular users of screen readers will provide the most thorough and accurate feedback. Conducting user testing with individuals with this expertise will provide great insight and will ultimately lead to the best possible finished product.

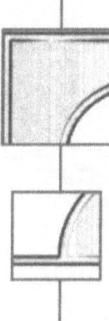

Summary

Hopefully this chapter has given you an insight into the accessibility features in Flash MX. Accessibility is an important issue that all designers must consider. Contrary to what many people may assume, Flash content can be just as accessible as HTML content. As long as we're all aware of the accessibility capabilities of the Flash authoring environment there's no reason why *all* content created in Flash shouldn't be available to *all* web users. When considering how to make our Flash content as usable as possible there's no way we can ignore accessibility issues – accessibility and usability go hand in hand.

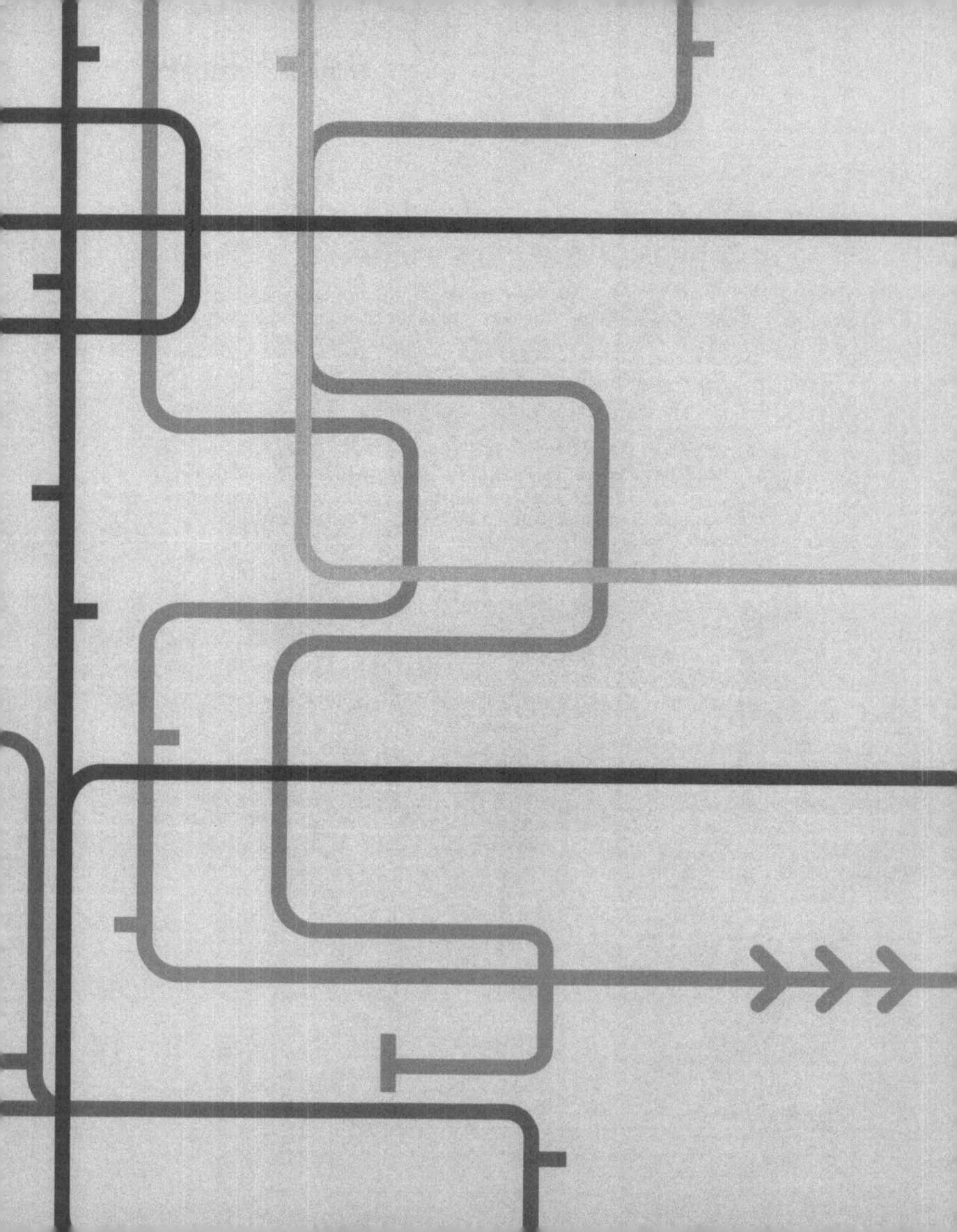

First impressions

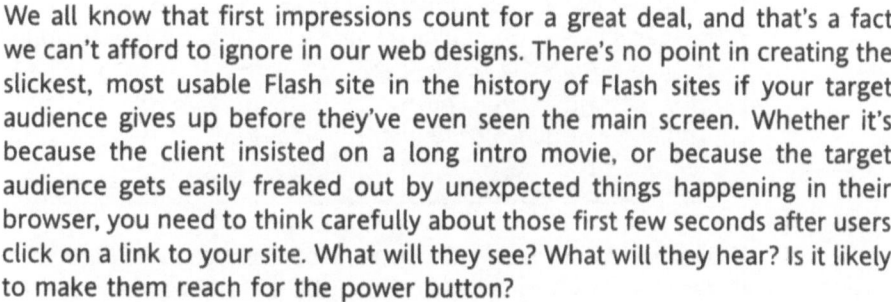

We all know that first impressions count for a great deal, and that's a fact we can't afford to ignore in our web designs. There's no point in creating the slickest, most usable Flash site in the history of Flash sites if your target audience gives up before they've even seen the main screen. Whether it's because the client insisted on a long intro movie, or because the target audience gets easily freaked out by unexpected things happening in their browser, you need to think carefully about those first few seconds after users click on a link to your site. What will they see? What will they hear? Is it likely to make them reach for the power button?

In the main part of this chapter, we're going to look at a number of design conventions that can be used to help keep users on side long enough for them to absorb the sheer quality of your work on the site.

Smoothing the jolt into Flash

One of the great myths that anti-Flash 'experts' seem to take great delight in propagating is the notion that, almost by definition, Flash interfaces confuse people. Yes, just imagine an innocent user surfing the Web, clicking from one HTML page to another, to another, and so on. It's all nice, simple text and pictures, with links underlined and shown in blue, and only the occasional pop-up to interrupt the steady ebb and flow of information.

All at once, they come across some Flash content, which starts *doing things of its own accord!* Obviously, at this point their brain melts, and someone has to unplug the computer and call the emergency services.

Not a pretty picture. Not a terribly accurate one either, and I doubt even the sternest Flash critic would suggest that might happen for real. But it does illustrate a perception amongst the design and development community that 'them out there' (and that could be most of our potential users) will simply freak out as soon as the Flash plug-in is invoked.

As you've probably already realized, it's not quite that simple. Certainly, Flash-based web content has been known to cause much wailing and gnashing of teeth to the uninitiated; but we've already established that it's usually something you can put down to shoddy design rather than something that's inherent to Flash.

> *The key message here is this: if someone doesn't know what to do when they encounter a Flash movie on the Web, it's not because they don't understand Flash – it's because they don't understand the movie. Expecting users to 'get' Flash is like expecting a VCR owner to have a diploma in applied electronic engineering: simply unrealistic.*

The initial, often overwhelming rush of Flash content onto the Web was understandable. It was cool stuff, and still is. But it was very different to what had gone before. People who knew the Web as a quiet place of scrolling text and images (with just the occasional rash of animated GIFs to spoil the view) suddenly found their computers taken over by speaker-pounding, dizzying, techno-psychedelic stage shows. To many of *us* it was a technological marvel – to many of *them*, it was unexpected, alien, and downright alarming.

Some of this can be put down to taste, but a far more important factor is familiarity. Flash isn't HTML, and it comes with none of the strict conventions and familiar certainties that many people normally expect of web content. The best way to make the jump as painless as possible is to keep the learning curve nice and shallow – you're ultimately aiming for a seamless transition between familiar HTML and foreign Flash content.

Working from extreme feedback

It can be crushing to get letters from users saying they hate your site, that they despise the browser-replacement super-animation that you spent weeks making, and that they think your new and innovative navigational system is the most confusing thing they've ever attempted to use.

But remember that these extreme reactions can help us focus on improvements. Even the most dramatic of user reactions can teach us – if we're willing to listen. Knowing what our users want (and moreover what they *don't* want) is hugely important in achieving the goal of making a usable site.

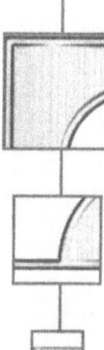

Tell users your site contains Flash

One oft-used 'solution' to this Flash clash is simply to *tell* users that a site contains Flash content. Well-intentioned as it may be, this isn't usually much help. Sure, it may ease the jolt of the unexpected for someone who already knows what Flash is. If they *don't* though, you may as well tell them it's made using blue cheese, so hold on tight. Say you knew someone who'd never driven a motorcycle, and told them all about your new Ducati with its air-cooled twin cylinder engine. They still wouldn't know what to do with it, and you certainly wouldn't expect them to be able to take it for a spin.

So we basically have to separate the 'users don't know our content's Flash-based' issue from 'users don't know how to interact with our content', and treat them as distinct from one another.

Add a short tutorial

Say you're going to tell your audience that your site is Flash-based. You know that they're web-smart, though not technologically adventurous, so a short tutorial of sorts may be a good solution. Help files are always a good idea, no matter what the audience's technical level of knowledge is, since your

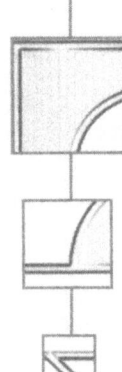

content arrangement and navigational schemes are likely to be different from other sites.

The Road to Perdition site (www.roadtoperdition.com/) tells visitors that the site requires Flash Player 6 before entering. If they don't have a Flash Player, they're invited to download it. Upon clicking ENTER HERE, visitors are routed through a detection script to make sure they are able to go further, just in case they didn't know whether they had Flash or not.

Here's a better solution from the same site: instead of asking a user whether they have a Flash Player or not, the copy reads, "Can't view this page? CLICK HERE to download Flash Player 6". On a site with such a wide range of technical knowledge in its target market, it's more intuitive to present the user with the clear result of not having Flash Player ("can't view it?" or "nothing happening?") rather than asking them something they may not know about, or where to look for it (the software). The question's more likely to make sense to people in the target audience, so they're more likely to give a useful response.

The extent of help given, and the blatancy of its availability, is up to you. A one- or two-liner added to an introductory page may be sufficient:

> This site was created in Flash MX, and requires that you have the appropriate Flash plug-in. If you are on a dial-up connection, initial load time may be close to two minutes. If you prefer, here's our faster, plainer HTML site.

A solution I favor for sites whose majority target audience is non-technical is to present Flash content in a non-Flash way. Most state, "Flash Player version n is necessary to view this site", or will ask the user, "Do you have Flash Player 6?" Those users might have *heard* of Flash (since they might well see the word on the Web every day), but when they're told to go *look* for it on their system, they're lost.

A better approach is to ask a user something you know that they can answer, such as, "Is anything showing up here?", or state, "If nothing is showing up here, here's what you do". You can then proceed to give suitable, practical instructions. Give guidance with links and as much help as you can provide, such as:

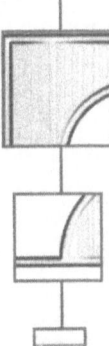

> If not, click here to download Flash Player *n*, and follow its installation instructions. If you need help installing the Player, www.macromedia.com gives great step-by-step troubleshooting instructions. Then come back to this page, which you should bookmark before you go.

Some sites have full-on 'how to use this site' tutorials, walking the user through each part of the site. Others have extensive site maps or virtual tours, while others still have a simple explanation of what a user might find in each area of the site, and what to click or do to get there.

The IMAX Space Station site (www. imax.com/spacestation) wants to make sure its visitors have all their technological bases covered. Within the Film Mission area, you're greeted with a Film Synopsis that states:

> This tour requires that you have a frame-capable and Java capable browser such as Netscape 3.0 or greater. The Virtual Tour can be CPU intensive. Please close all non-essential applications on your computer. The Virtual Tour relies on Java to allow the user to view the orbiter and payload. Please make sure your browser has both Java and JavaScript enabled in the Preference section.

But none of this information is about 'how to use Flash'. That's where the seamlessness comes in. Whether a site has Flash or not, if people can't get to the content and figure out how to move around in it in order to find more content that they want, there's a problem. If they can't get out of the site when they want to leave, there's a problem. They don't know what to do with it, no matter what authoring tool it's made with. It's your role and responsibility to give them what they want in a format they can manage, or with instructions they can follow without having to go back to school.

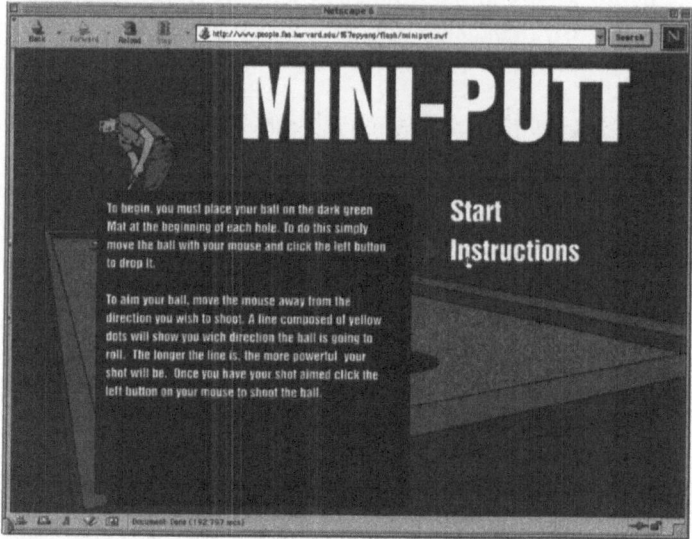

On entering the Mini-Putt site (www.people.fas.harvard.edu/ %7epyang/flash/miniputt.swf), users are given a link to 'Instructions'. These don't tell the user how to use Flash, but teach them how to play the game. After all, that's what they're there for!

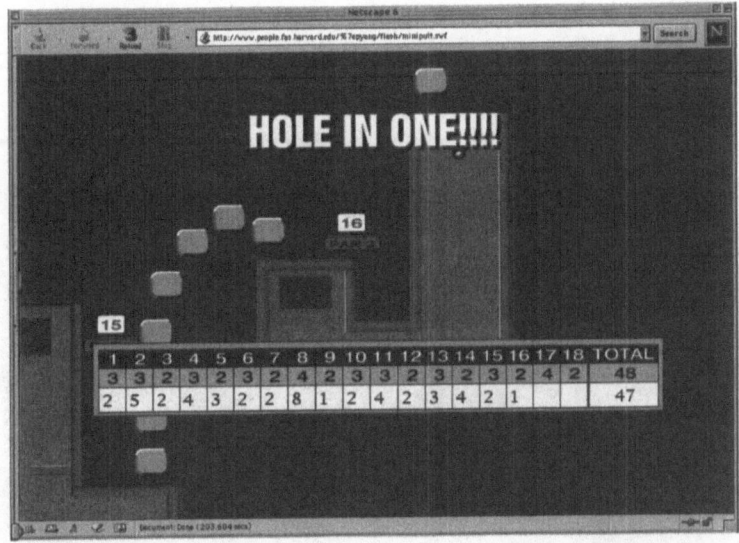

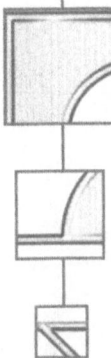

This screenshot from Mini Putt shows the feedback a user gets after each hole is played. It also proves that I got a hole in one.

Don't use Flash if there's no need

Another solution is to present a mix of Flash and HTML, using Flash to deliver content only when it's specifically needed or has advantages over HTML. The Wheaton College site (www.wheatoncollege.edu) is a nice example of Flash-where-appropriate design in action.

Most of the site presents information about the college in HTML, with a feature presentation made available as a choice for visiting users. Those who want to go on to see the Flash-based content are given a bit of advice on what they need before they get into that area, and are told that they should turn on their speakers – a warning that the area of the site they will be entering contains sound. This is a great way to give a heads-up so people can turn on their speakers if they're off, or turn them off and put on headphones if they think the sound will bug other people in their surroundings.

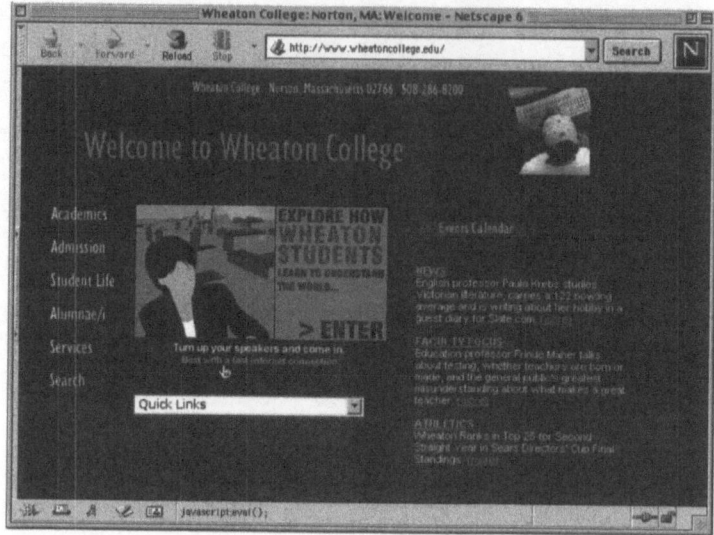

Wheaton College's Flash content is well introduced and well labeled on its site (www.wheatoncollege.edu/). "Turn up your speakers and come in", it says, along with advising, "Best with a fast Internet connection". A student in a high-school library who is considering Wheaton could plug their headphones into the computer, and avoid disturbing other students when listening to the Wheaton Interactive Exhibit.

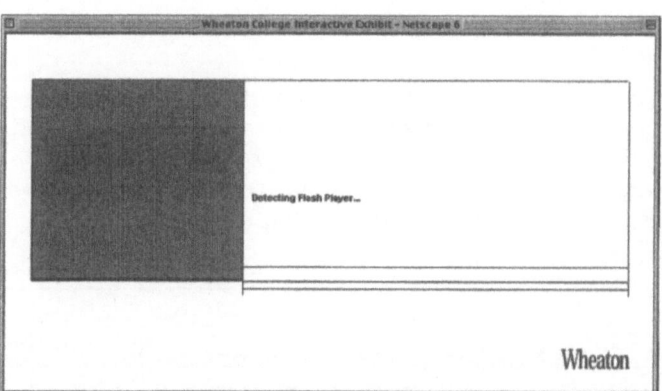

If you click on Enter, a new window pops up, and a search begins to verify that the user does, in fact, have the appropriate Flash player installed. The designer could have skipped telling us what was going on, but any time there's a pause in screen action like this, it's always best to give a hint to the user to give them the perception that everything is moving along the way it's supposed to.

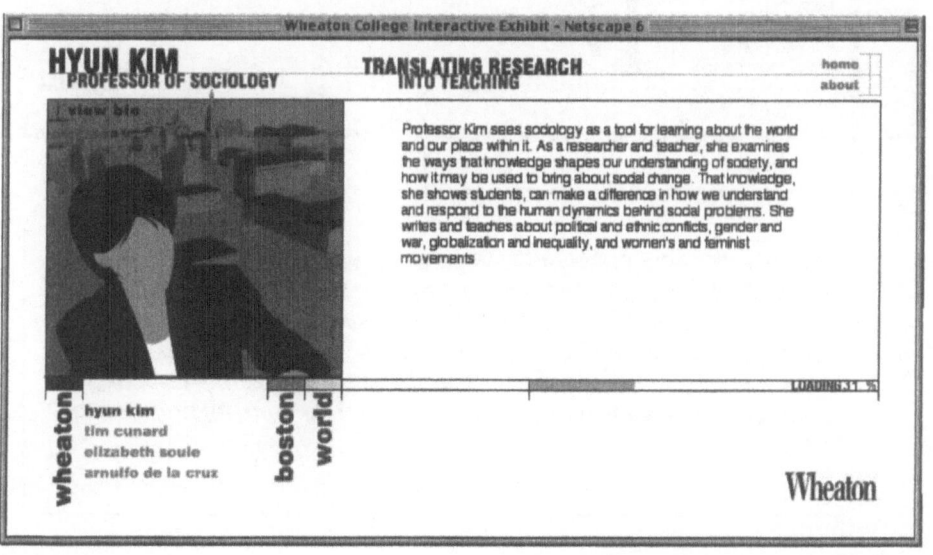

All along the way, the Wheaton College Interactive Exhibit provides "loading" percentage feedback so the user knows something is going on and that the loading is progressing. While the site is loading information, the text box gives the visitor complementary and introductory information about the topic coming up.

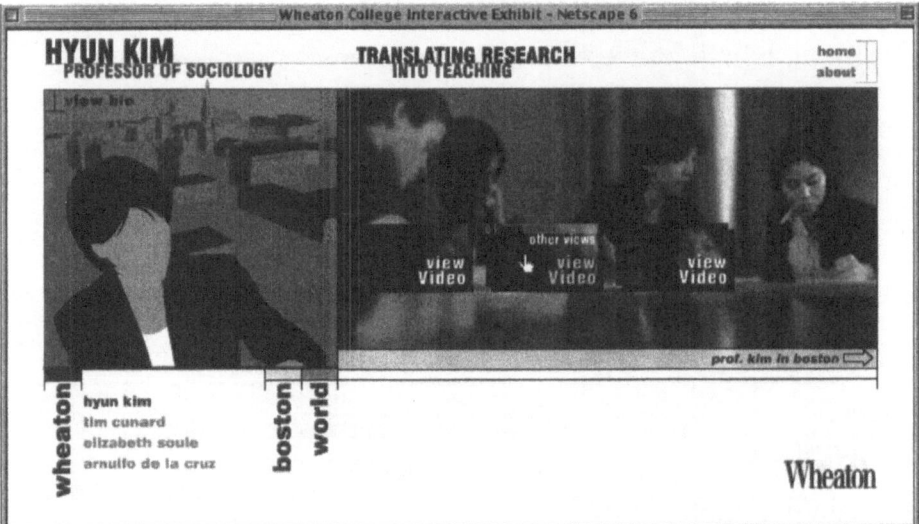

When site users are presented with video options, a mouse-over reveals the length of the movie. Some people may not wait for a half-hour movie of video shot for the Exhibit, but breaking it down into small, less-than-a-minute clips may be worth the download. Users may be more apt to look at more of the clips within the site if they can get snippets at a time, and the site meets a goal of disseminating more information to its audience.

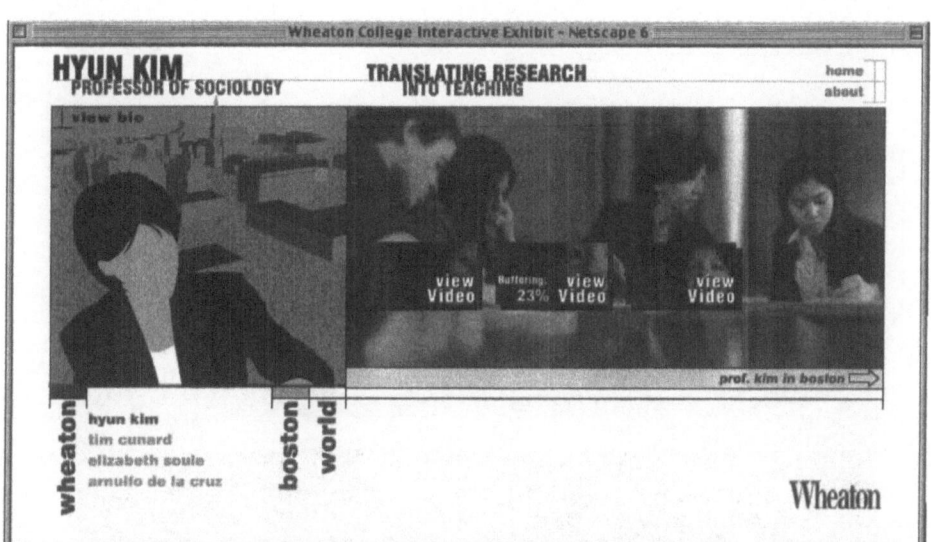

Again, the designer provides feedback after the user makes a choice by clicking. If you don't provide visual or textual feedback to a user, they might presume nothing is happening, and back out of the site.

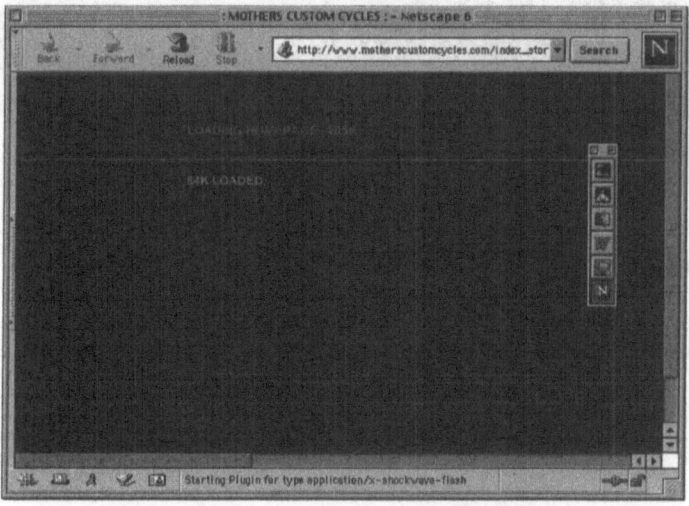

After entering in the URL to Mother's Custom Cycles (www.motherscustomcycles.com), designed and developed by Breckenridge Communications (www.breckcomm.com) a site visitor is brought right into its Flash-dominated site. Feedback while the site is loading, however, helps a user know that they're in the right place and aren't doing anything wrong.

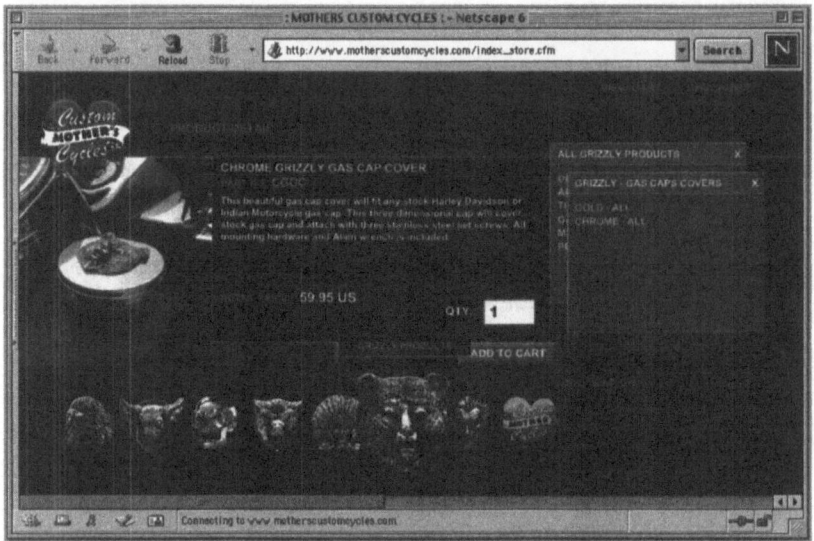

Once loaded, the Mother's Custom Cycle site boasts an innovative navigational structure. Choosing Grizzly Products pops up a mini-window of choices; click on one of those choices and another mini-window pops up. Most people should be familiar with the 'X' as a close-window feature.

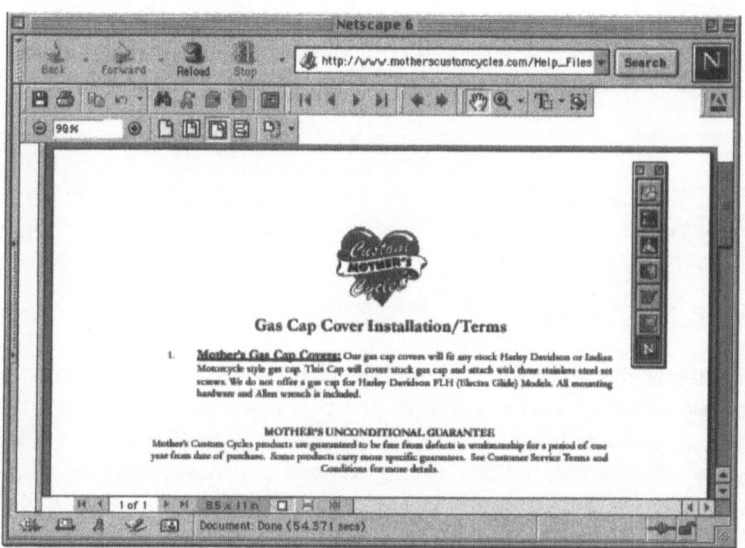

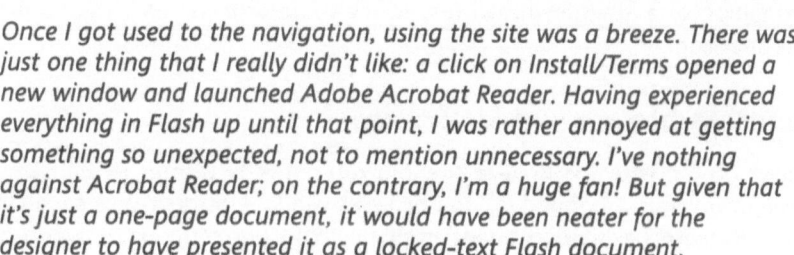

Once I got used to the navigation, using the site was a breeze. There was just one thing that I really didn't like: a click on Install/Terms opened a new window and launched Adobe Acrobat Reader. Having experienced everything in Flash up until that point, I was rather annoyed at getting something so unexpected, not to mention unnecessary. I've nothing against Acrobat Reader; on the contrary, I'm a huge fan! But given that it's just a one-page document, it would have been neater for the designer to have presented it as a locked-text Flash document.

Offering choices and feedback

Over and over we've warned against the deployment of full-on Flash-based (or otherwise developed) sites that take over a user's computer without their permission. There are few things more jarring whilst clicking along happily than when the screen suddenly goes dark, browser buttons and menus disappear, L... O... A... D... I... N... G......   L... O... A... D... I... N... G......   L... O...

A... D... I... N... G...... spells itself out over and over in the middle of your screen, and nothing else seems to be happening.

> *If a user's lucky enough never to have had this happen to them before, it's a pretty scary experience. If they have seen it before, it's downright maddening.*

Fortunately, many designers (even before Flash came along) learned to offer site visitors a choice as to whether or not they wanted a computer takeover. Often, an introductory page will list various versions of the site: Flash, HTML, text, or other combinations. Giving users the power of choice goes a long way in keeping a visitor coming back.

Giving some heads-up about what to expect when entering is a good idea, too, whether it be a browser takeover, sound clips, processor-intensive graphics, or a long download (especially valuable if the user's got a dial-up connection).

Choosing browser window size

Back on the Wheaton College site, did you notice how after we hit ENTER and the new window popped up, the browser window lost its resize capabilities? The Wheaton exhibition opens itself up to fit perfectly in the width of an 800x600 screen. It doesn't go all the way to the bottom, so windows behind the top browser window can still be seen, if they extend below the top browser window.

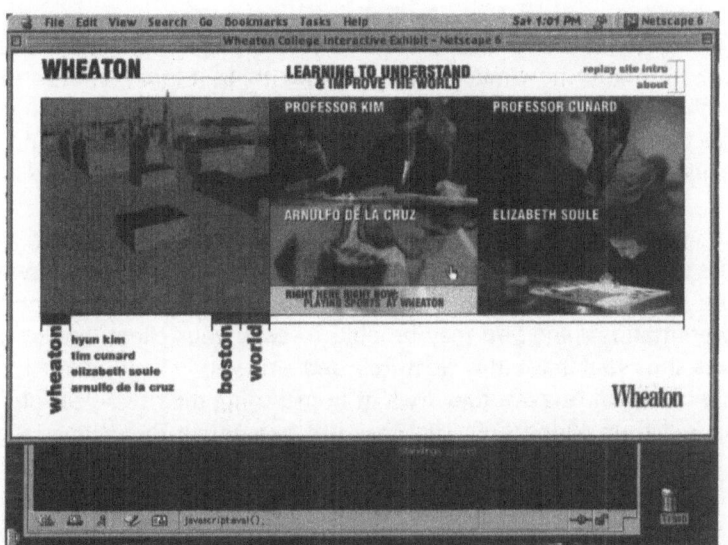
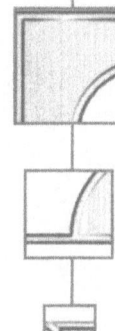

The Wheaton College Interactive Exhibition window pops up over the launch window, and fills the width of an 800 x 600 screen. While this allows the designer some control by making the window as wide as they'd like, it also allows access to windows behind this one, even if it can't be resized. Lesson: if you insist on making a window pop up to the size you want to suit your design, at least be polite about it.

We've already determined that if an audience is technologically educated or experienced, even a jarring, whirling, clog-hopping, full-screen Flash site is manageable, or at least they'll know how to get rid of it and go on to a site that they like better.

The most argued-over and complained-about 'feature' of this control we have over Flash presentation is taking over a user's screen, especially with fill-up-the-monitor presentations. Many believe that while it's great we have this flexibility of power, we should never yield to it. Taking over a browser is

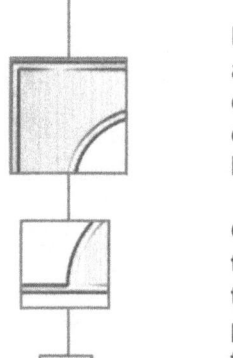

like walking into a stranger's house and rearranging their furniture. Chances are, no matter how much nicer you may think it looks, and no matter how enthusiastically you point out Feng Shui enhancements, the stranger may still call the police, who will then call the local paddy wagon, and have you hauled away.

Of course, even if your client insists on a full-screen presentation, it's unlikely the police will have to get involved, but your site may lose a few visitors all the same. Be patient and explain the concerns you have about full-screen presentations, and you may be able to sway your client. Maybe pick out a few sites that have this 'feature', and ask your client to make their way around them. Suggest they try it at home, using their two-year-old computer via a dial-up connection. That may just be enough to convince them.

> *Full-screen takeovers aren't recommended. Full-browser takeovers are more acceptable, since at the very least, they can be closed. Pop-ups, pop-ins, and pop-overs are fine, as long as users have an option to move or remove them from the screen, and as long as they enhance – rather than get in the way of – the meat of the site.*

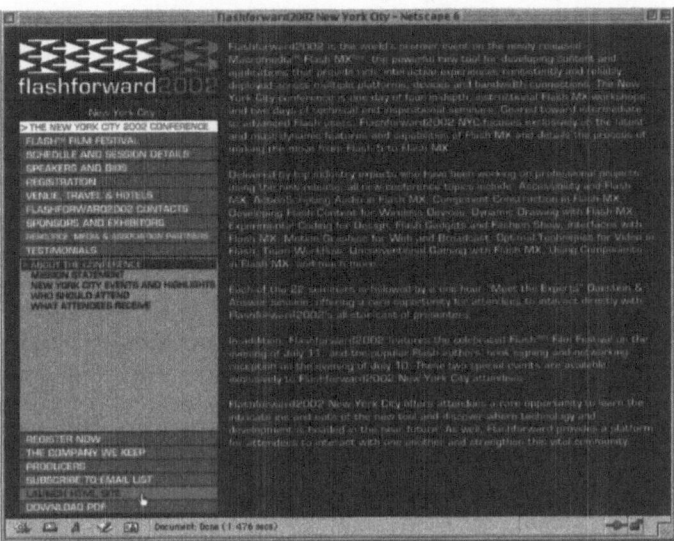

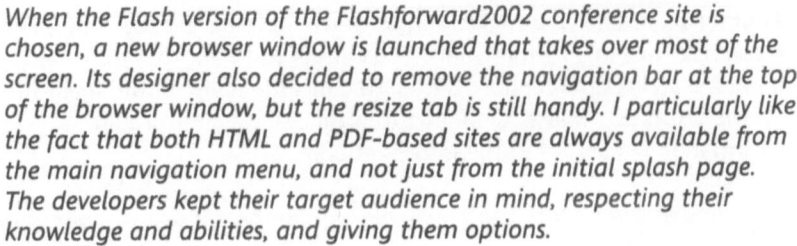

When the Flash version of the Flashforward2002 conference site is chosen, a new browser window is launched that takes over most of the screen. Its designer also decided to remove the navigation bar at the top of the browser window, but the resize tab is still handy. I particularly like the fact that both HTML and PDF-based sites are always available from the main navigation menu, and not just from the initial splash page. The developers kept their target audience in mind, respecting their knowledge and abilities, and giving them options.

Skip Intro

This can probably lay claim to being one of the very first conventions to get established in Flash web design. The logic's simple enough: if you have a great long intro movie for your site, give users a button they can press to skip to the main part of the site.

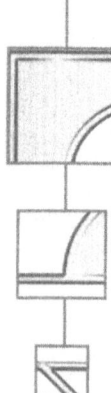

Skip Intro is popular because it's an almost immediate way for a site user to regain control of content access. I tend to watch introductory movies at least once, on the first visit to a site, but generally take advantage of Skip Intro after that. You can see it on loads of Flash-heavy sites; in fact it's become so ubiquitous as to be recognized as a noun in its own right. It's also a feature that's widely come to be expected.

It's also popular because of the fact that users, even relative novices, have grown to recognize it and its function immediately. While we could probably come up with a spunkier-sounding name for its function, Skip Intro will be around for a while to come.

So when *wouldn't* you want to use Skip Intro? Well, if accessing the content of your site *requires* the watching of an introductory message, or perhaps you change your intro movie on a regular basis, perhaps you don't *want* people to be able to skip it. Ask yourself though, "Am I sure there's no other option? Are my users likely to thank me for imposing it on them?" I'd personally favor user choice almost every time.

Another bit of advice is to avoid intro movie looping. Let the intro play once. If you have any inkling that your site's visitors will want to watch it again, give them a 'Play Again' function. Better still, include a link in the main site back to the intro for those who might want to watch it again, or refer to information presented in the introduction.

Let's look at some more useful conventions in the context of our continuing example.

Case Study

Forms and applications

One of the biggest challenges in web design is finding a way to make it quick and painless to get users to part with personal information. HTML forms are traditionally considered one of the most awkward elements to use effectively, and are the source of many a bad user experience.

One of Flash's big advantages over HTML is that it can build intelligent forms, making the information gathering process easier all round. Flash can help users fill in their details, and help us not to lose them or their data along the way!

Let's have a look at how we're going to approach a registration form for the *Future Fridges Conference* site.

The registration form

A standard paper form will consist of some instructions and lots of colored boxes that need to be filled in. Paper forms are often complex and intimidating, typically including numbered sections and instructions such as:

> ...if you answered yes to q41 do not answer q42-45.

They don't offer any way to check the validity of the data entered, so if you miss a field or make a mistake, you probably won't find out until the form is processed.

HTML forms really aren't that much of an improvement over paper forms. They can provide feedback on missing or invalid data, but this is limited to response pages or JavaScript pop-up messages at best. For example, if the user misses a required section the form may be redisplayed with the required section highlighted.

Furthermore, HTML forms are typically spread across multiple pages, so you can't see the whole form at the start. You don't know what data will be required and can't easily estimate how long the form will take to complete.

Flash allows us to address many of these issues. We can build single-screen forms, where all the input fields are displayed or can at least be easily browsed using a tabbed interface. We can make the form intelligent, so that only the relevant sections of the form are displayed. For example, if the user indicates that their shipping address is the same as their billing address, then we can hide the shipping address section of the form. We can also give instant feedback if the user enters invalid data or doesn't fill out a required section.

So what do we need to consider for our registration form? We need to ensure that:

- Only relevant sections of the form are displayed

- The complete form can be browsed

- The user is given feedback if they enter invalid data

- Instructions for filling in the registration form are clearly displayed

Back in Chapter 6 our storyboarding process helped us identify the need to ensure that once a user has filled in the form, they're given clear feedback on *what's happening now* (for example, the form is being processed) and what will happen afterwards (for example, the tickets will be mailed out).

Furthermore, when we defined our user interface in Chapter 7, we identified the need to ensure that information on pricing, payment, and refunds is always accessible while the form is being filled in.

Let's take a look at a layout for our form.

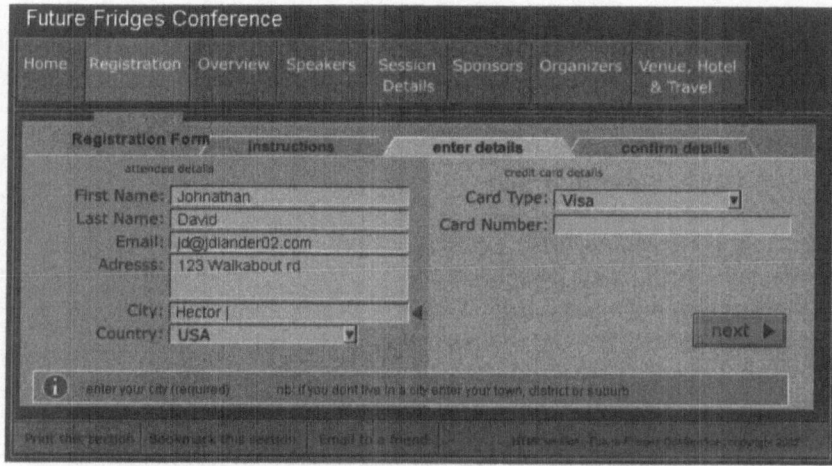

Note that we've divided it into three sections, which the user can navigate between by means of a tabbed interface or by using the next button:

- The instructions section outlines the steps involved in the registration process as well as the pricing, payment and refund information.

- The enter details section is the heart of the form, with the input boxes for the user's details.

- The confirm details section lets the user recheck the information they entered before the data is sent for processing.

Many of the elements we use here (particularly in the enter details section) have been specially designed to make our form easier to use:

The buttons look like buttons and the input boxes look like input boxes. This may seem like an obvious statement, but it's important that our user doesn't get confused about the purpose of the different elements of the form. In Flash it would be quite easy to make the input boxes look flat, similar to the colored boxes of a paper form. However, that wouldn't be consistent with other input boxes that the user's encountered on the Web, so it could be a source of confusion.

The currently selected form element is highlighted. A small triangle has been used to indicate which form element is currently selected. In the image above, the city input box is shown as being filled in. This is a subtle visual clue, which serves to remind our user where they're up to in the form. If they're interrupted during the process of filling in the form, this will guide them back to where they were.

There is an 'extra information' box. At the bottom of the form is a box that's used to provide extra information about the currently selected form element. This lets us offer the user extra hints or advice, relating directly to what they're currently doing. The information shown in the screenshot informs the user that the current selection is a required field, and explains that the user should either enter the name of a town, a district, or a suburb.

Not everyone lives in a city, yet almost all online forms require you to enter your city! Many non-city-dwellers usually just take a guess as to what to include in this field. But why make them guess when we can use the dynamic nature of Flash to explain it to them?

We can also use this box for the e-mail field, to explain *why* we want the user's e-mail address. They may not realize that it's so we can e-mail them an invoice and update them on any changes to the conference program. Making this information available may help alleviate the concerns of those users who don't like revealing their e-mail address. Similarly, for the credit card field, we could refer to the encryption methods used in handling transactions.

The tabs correspond to stages in the process. The tabbed navigation makes it easy for the user to navigate back and forth through the sections of the form. It also serves another important purpose: showing the user what stage comes next.

Users like to know what will happen next, especially if the next step could involve charging their credit card! In this case, the tabbed interface clearly shows that the next step will allow the user to confirm their details.

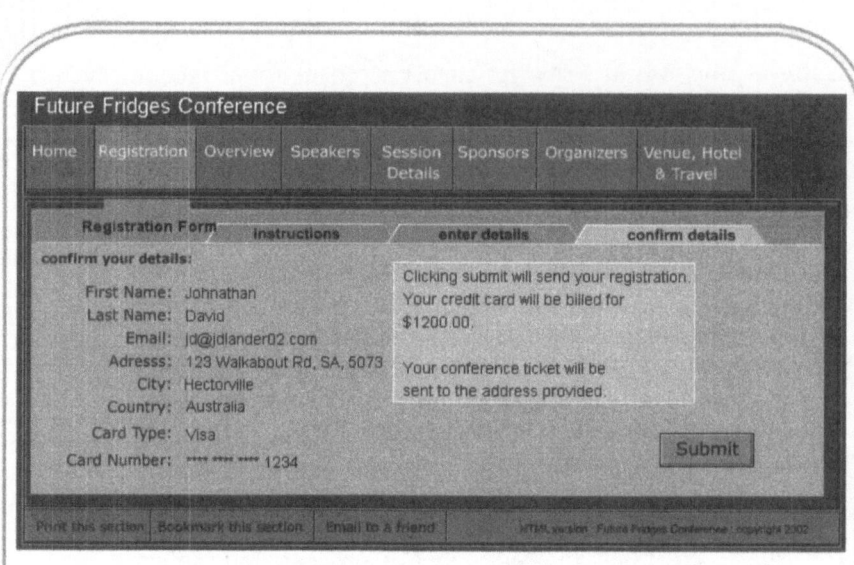

In the confirm details section of the form, the user can confirm that the information they've entered is correct, and press a single button to submit that information. As we identified in our storyboarding section, it's important to make sure they know exactly what will happen when they submit their details. So, possibly the single most important part of this section is the box letting them know what happens next – yes, it's a recurring theme!

In this case, the user is clearly informed that clicking on Submit will result in their credit card being billed for $1200 and tickets being sent out to their stated address.

Once the user has clicked that button, the form will follow the stages we outlined in our storyboard:

■ First, the form area displays a message indicating that the information is being processed, along with an estimate of how long this will take – for example, "Your details are being processed, please be patient. This may take up to two minutes".

Once the information has been processed, a message is displayed indicating if the transaction was successful or not.

- If the transaction isn't successful, the message will explain why not, and provide contact details for someone associated with the conference ticketing, just in case the user wishes to query the result.

- If the transaction is successful, the message will explain that a receipt is now going to be e-mailed to the stated e-mail address, and give an estimate of when the user can expect the tickets to arrive.

Now let's take a look at the **Session Details** section of the site.

Session details and the session planner

This section will contain all the information on the conference sessions, including a map showing where each session is located within the venue. It also incorporates functionality that helps users plan and print out a list of the conference sessions they wish to attend. We also identified the need to include a search feature in this section, so that users can search for sessions on topics that interest them.

We can treat this section of the site as a mini-application, which allows users to browse and search the session details, mark out which sessions they want to attend, and create their own session timetable to print out and carry around at the conference.

Constructing a mini-application

So how do we begin to construct this mini-application, and how do we produce an intuitive navigation system for such a complex interaction? Well, let's start by thinking about what our users will actually do. They'll typically follow a clear sequence of steps:

1. First, they'll either browse or search to find specific sessions that they want to attend.

How do they browse? Well, they look through a list of session titles organized in some kind of meaningful structure, such as 'sorted by time', 'sorted by topic', or 'sorted by speaker'. Note that these structures all relate to decisions that our user might usefully wish to make – for example, find out what sessions are on at 3pm Friday, when Dr Marr will be speaking, or when there are sessions on Internet-enabled fridges. In theory, we could sort sessions by title, but users aren't likely to know the titles of sessions in advance, so they're unlikely to find such an option useful.

2. Once they find a session of interest, they'll read through the accompanying details and maybe view a map of where the session is located.

3. If they're interested in the session they'll want to **mark it** for inclusion in their personal session plan.

4. They'll then repeat the first three steps until they've looked at all the sessions of interest to them.

5. Finally, they'll view their completed session plan and print it out.

Clearly, we need to ensure that browse-and-search functionality is easily accessible when users first visit the **Session Details** section of the site. They also need to be able to mark up sessions for inclusion in their personal session plans while viewing the session details. Finally, we need to make sure that users can move easily from session browsing to viewing and printing their session plans.

Browsing the session details

The screenshot below shows the default view of our **Session Details** section. By default, we should display the information we believe most users will want to access first, thus minimizing the number of clicks they have to make.

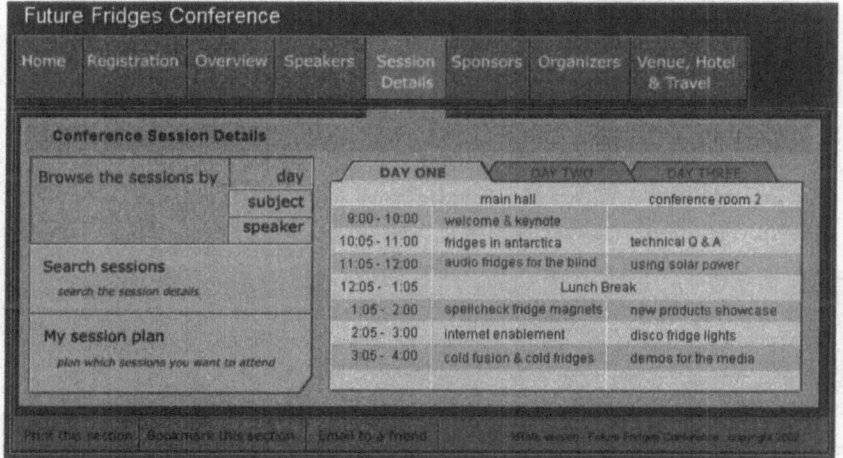

In this case, we've assumed that users will want to start by browsing the sessions by day. Our final site testing will show whether this is the case, and it can easily be changed if they reveal, for example, that most users actually prefer to browse by speaker.

Users can easily tab between the three days of the conference and can click on the title of a conference session to see more details in a pop-up as shown below.

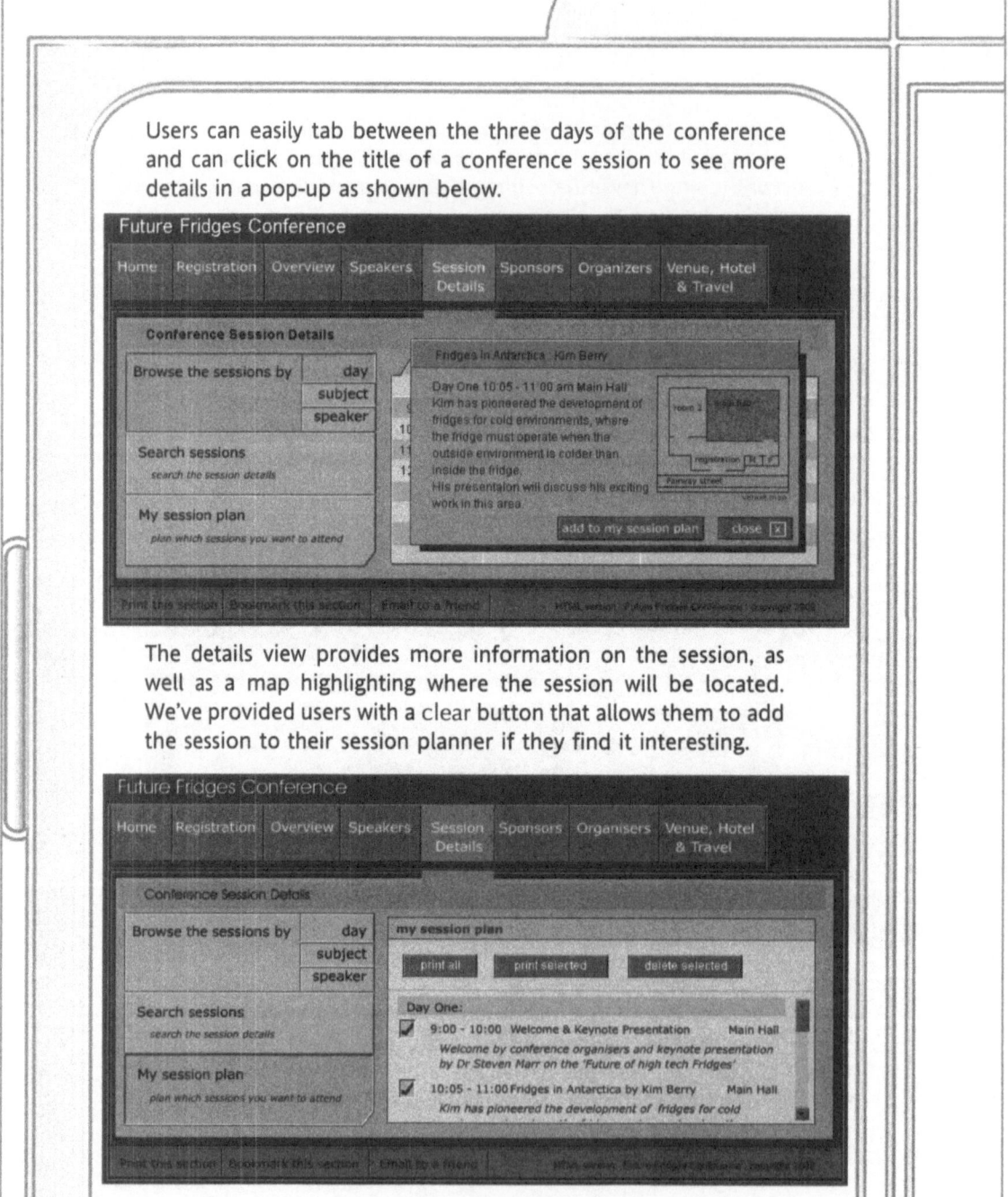

The details view provides more information on the session, as well as a map highlighting where the session will be located. We've provided users with a clear button that allows them to add the session to their session planner if they find it interesting.

Furthermore, we provide them with the option to print specific sessions from their plan, and also to remove sessions from the plan. This is achieved by including a check box next to each session description. The marked check box indicates that a session has been selected, and our users can then use the print selected button to print out just those sessions.

It's important that our users have a way to remove items from their session plan. The delete selected button allows our users to remove from their session plan any items that they selected using the check boxes. Whenever you build any kind of 'delete' function, it's essential to have it prompt the user for confirmation before removing any data. So, when a user clicks the delete selected button, a message box is displayed explaining the implications of the action and giving them the opportunity to cancel it.

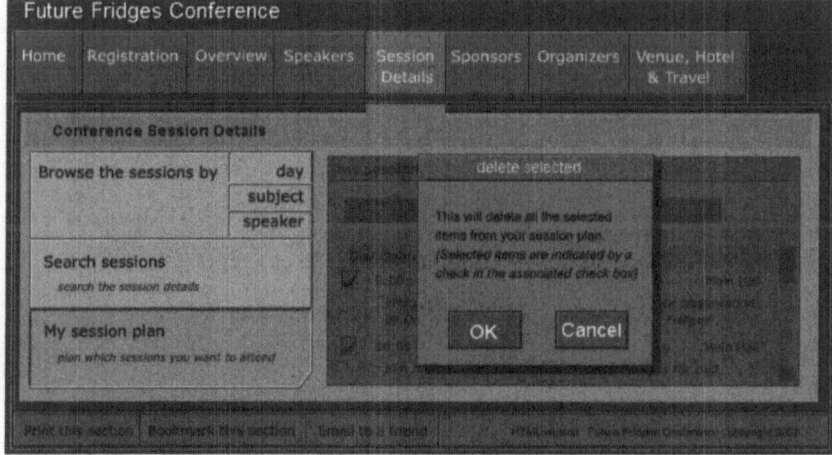

Of all the interactions in our session details mini-application, this session selection is probably the least intuitive. Using check boxes to select items from a list is a reasonably common interface interaction, but they're not nearly so commonplace as the buttons, text boxes, tabs, and scrollbars that make up the other interactions on our site. It will therefore be important for our final site testing to gather user feedback on this aspect of the tool, to identify whether it's as intuitive and user-friendly as possible.

Searching the session details

Our users can easily switch to the search function by clicking on the Search sessions navigation button.

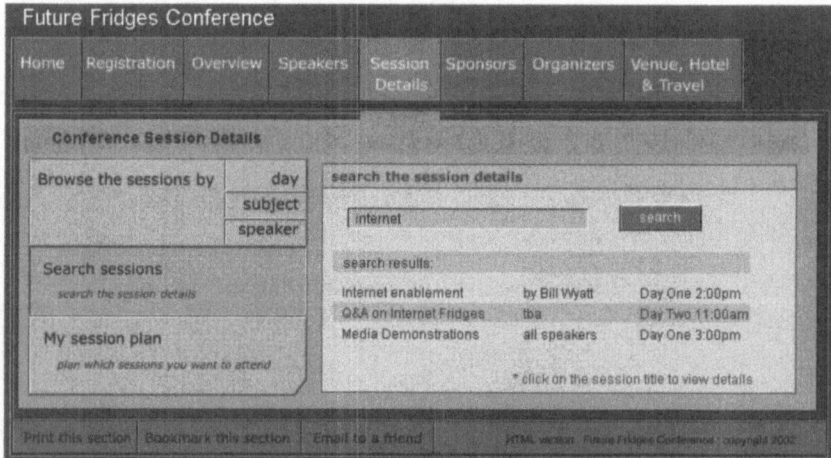

The search function is intentionally kept simple, with just an input box and a search button. Why so simple? Well, our site contains a relatively simple set of data: just the details for thirty-two sessions, so the number of results from a search will typically be small. So as to ensure that users have the maximum chance of a positive result, our search function looks at *all* of the session details.

If our users wanted to search across a large selection of complex data then we'd provide them with a far more advanced search tool, allowing them to refine each data set they wanted to search across.

This stripped-down search tool also simplifies a user's interaction with this section of the site. They don't have to think about search parameters or ordering options, they just type in a word and click search.

My session plan

The My session plan page uses a scrolling list to display details for any sessions that the user has added to their session plan. Users can simply click the print all button to print out their session plan.

Summary

Experienced developers seem to agree that a balance of HTML and Flash elements is ideal for deployment of Flash files. Good integration between familiar browser environments and cool new Flash-formulated site content gives users the benefit of something they know, with the features for which Flash is embraced: fast-loading files; smaller, higher quality graphics files; smoother presentation, and more control (for the designer) over presentation.

In the *Future Fridges* study, we worked out how the registration form, session details, and session planner elements would operate. We included a lot of interface elements and text content in a fairly small area, but tried to ensure that they still offered a nice, easy-to-follow navigation interface. Most users should be able to use both form and mini-application with no need for explicit instructions or prior experience.

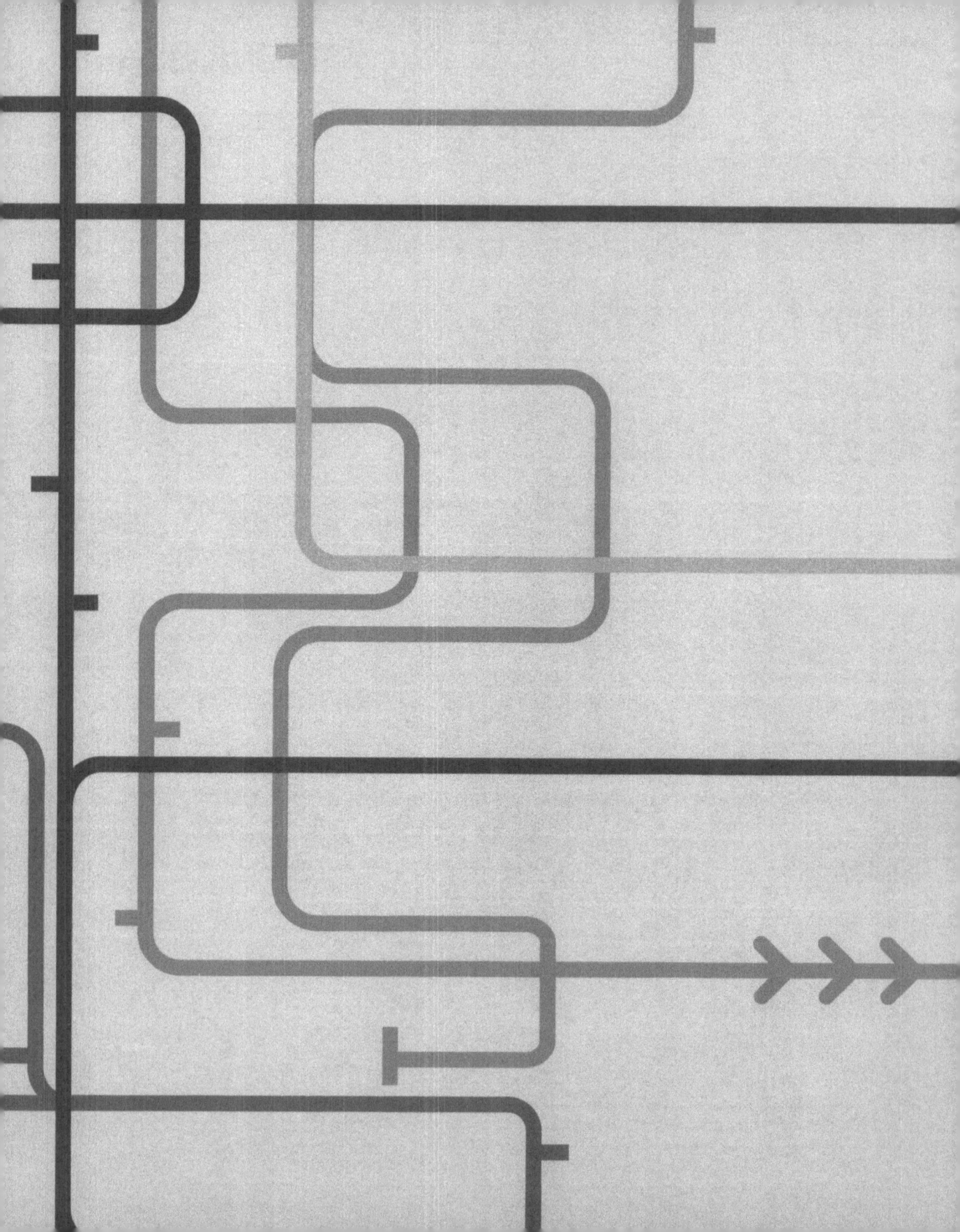

Offline Flash

Throughout this book we've been covering usability issues with Flash content for specific browser-based delivery. Many of the issues we discussed stem from the fact that Flash content – whether it's on the Internet or a corporate network – is viewed within a web browser. Once the Flash content we create steps outside of a browser-dependent delivery system, we can start exploring new interactions that no longer need to meet the expectations of a web-based user.

This isn't to say that good usability for online Flash content shouldn't apply to offline Flash content. For most interaction issues, the guidelines listed in this book will give your project the same usability benefits both online and off. But once Flash content is able to interact with the user outside of the browser, new opportunities become available.

Many of the Flash projects I've worked on in the past few years have been specifically targeted for offline delivery. Whether you're working on CD-ROM-based product catalogs, touch-screen kiosks, or promotional materials, user-focused development is still an important part of creating a genuinely user-friendly experience.

Before you redeploy all your Flash projects as downloadable projector files though, there are some fairly substantial issues of usability for offline content that you should be aware of. In this chapter, I'm going to look at the three main platforms for offline Flash delivery:

- CD-ROMs

- Kiosks

- PDAs

For each one, we'll look at the extra constraints they put on your Flash content, and offer tips on how best to deploy that content.

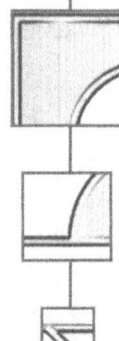

Flash on CD-ROMs

CD-ROMs are the second most frequently used medium on which to deliver Flash content after the Web. Let's look at the main reasons for this:

- Many of Flash's rich media capabilities tend to be prohibitive on the Web, simply on grounds of the **large file sizes** involved. With up to 700MB of storage space per disc, this isn't an issue with CD-ROMs. Each one holds the equivalent of 39 hours' worth of 56K Internet downloads. If you want to incorporate lots of audio and video into your Flash content, it's a useful medium to consider.

- Flash's **cross-platform compatibility** makes it a natural tool for CD-ROM development. As long as you publish both Mac and PC projector files, users with either platform will be able to view and interact with your Flash content. What's more, by exporting the actual content in the form of SWF files, each of those projectors just needs to provide an interface – the rest of your content can be loaded up directly from the SWFs.

- Flash content can scale to meet the **physical dimensions** of the user's monitor. Flash content need only be developed to match the aspect ratio of the intended user's computer if the CD-ROM Flash content is launched full-screen. By designing to a 4:3 aspect ratio, designers can create content that will target a wide range of display sizes; Flash will automatically scale all the content to fit the available screen.

- Whenever Macromedia announces a new version of the Flash player plug-in, there's always initial excitement from the Flash design community about all the **latest features**. Of course, in reality it usually takes another six to nine months before enough web users install the plug-in for clients to view the new features as ripe for exploitation. Deploying content via CD-ROM means there's no need to accommodate users who don't have the latest plug-in. The projector created by Flash MX allows for virtually all the new MX features to be deployed right from the CD.

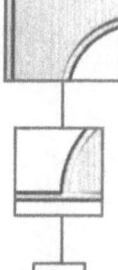

- Perhaps the most important feature of using CD-ROMs to deliver Flash content is the **freedom** CD-based content gives the user. Web-based Flash content relies on the user being connected to the Internet, whereas a CD-ROM lets them access it whenever and wherever they want.

- Users tend to have **less rigid expectations** of CD-ROM content than they do to what's encountered on the Web. This lets us explore Flash's potential somewhat more freely, giving us the opportunity to build a richer user experience.

From our perspective as Flash designers, the freedom to ignore things like low-bandwidth connections, the browser user interface, and physical connection to the Internet are all excellent reasons to apply Flash to CD-ROM based content. However, the decision to publish your content on CD-ROM isn't something you can take without making some compromises:

- When you publish content onto the Web, it's fairly easy to **make updates, corrections, usability enhancements, and other minor changes**: you just have to upload the new files to a central server. Once it's been burned onto a few thousand CD-ROMs though, you relinquish that control. It's out of your hands, and the best you can do to update it is to put out a new CD. This can be fairly expensive, what with duplication and labeling costs. You therefore need to devote more time to testing and quality assurance. Usability must be an integral part of the entire development for CD-ROM based Flash content.

- You **lose the familiarity that the user has with Web content**. When interacting with Flash on the Web you can build your interactions based on the user's expectations for online content. Users perceive CD-ROM content as being more 'application-like' in nature. Less

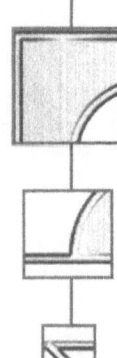

familiar expectations for CD-ROM content may require a 'help' section to cover basic functionality.

- Web-based Flash content can be **customized for optimal deployment** on the user's computer, using JavaScript to make their browser pass on system information (such as available screen resolution, color depth and cookie information) to the Flash content. This isn't an option if your content is delivered via a projector on CD-ROM. Projector files are essentially closed environments, so the only option you have is whether or not to run full-screen.

- Web-based Flash content offers more **connectivity options** than content deployed via a projector. If you're using a projector, database interactivity must be simulated using static data sources such as XML or text files. There's no server back end to a CD-ROM that can apply the logic needed by Flash for many of its advanced connectivity features. In addition, projector files on the Mac will crash when connections to remote data sources are attempted.

- Flash content delivered via CD-ROM will be treated **more like an application** in its own right than content delivered via the Web. You may therefore need to extend your usability concerns to include trouble-shooting support and help content.

Usability tips for Flash on CD-ROM

Now let's consider a few practical tips for producing Flash content to be deployed on CD-ROM.

Creating a projector file

Flash content in the form of SWF files requires the user to have a version of the Flash player available on their system. When deploying Flash content on a CD-ROM it's best to use projector files to bundle the Flash player and the SWF content into one easy-to-manage file.

Projector files are composed of two parts. The first half of the file is the Flash player, the instructions that the computer needs to play Flash content. The specific capabilities of an individual Flash projector file are dependent on the version of Flash that we use to create the projector.

> *Using Flash 4 to create a projector would allow the Flash content to access only Flash 4's features. Using Flash MX to build the projector will offer Flash MX's features.*

The second part of a projector file is the SWF content that will be played. The final size of the projector file will depend on the amount of data needed for the SWF portion of the projector.

Projector files are essentially platform-specific applications. Simply put that means that a Mac projector will not run on a PC and a PC projector will not run on a Mac. CD-ROMs targeting the widest number of users should offer both Mac and PC versions of the projector content.

Creating projector files with Flash is a fairly easy process. Just open the publish settings from within Flash and add both Windows and Mac projector files to the list of output options. You can also use the standalone Flash player to create projector files by accessing the 'Create Projector' option from the File menu.

Auto-run feature

One of the great features of CD-ROM development is the ability to deploy CDs that automatically start to play when the user inserts the CD in the computer. From a user-experience perspective, the auto-run feature certainly smoothes out the initial interactions that the user has with the CD.

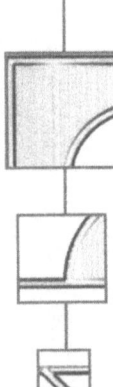

Not all computers have the ability to detect and play auto-run CDs though. Many users will have disabled the ability to recognize auto-run-enabled CDs turned off. Because of this, it's still important that designers deliver easy to understand instructions for launching the projector with the CD.

Creating a PC auto-run CD-ROM:

Creating an auto-run projector file on a PC is actually one of the few areas that the PC wins on the usability front. Designers need nothing more complex than a simple text editor to write the file needed to enable this feature.

To enable the auto-run feature for Windows based PCs, we need to include an INF file in the root directory of the CD-ROM. Open any text-editor (Notepad on the PC or SimpleText on the Mac will do) and create a text file named Autorun.inf.

The Autorun.inf file needs only two lines of text to successfully enable the auto-run feature:

```
[Autorun]
open=projectorfile.exe
```

The value of the open variable is the name of the projector file that you wish to launch. If your file is called futurefridges2002.exe the file contents should look like this:

```
[Autorun]
open=futurefridges2002.exe
```

An optional third line can be added to the Autorun.inf file to specify an icon for the CD-ROM:

```
icon=iconfile.ico
```

The value of the 'icon' variable is the name of the icon file on the root directory of the CD-ROM.

> *For information on creating Windows icon files, I recommend the free online icon generator at Favicon (www.favicon.com).*
>
> *For more information on creating auto-run applications, see the Microsoft technote: "Creating an AutoRun-Enabled Application"*
>
> (http://msdn.microsoft.com/library/default.asp?url=/library /en-us/shellcc/platform/shell/programmersguide/shell_basics/ shell_basics_extending/autorun/autoplay_works.asp).

Creating a Macintosh auto-run CD-ROM

Enabling the auto-run (called autoplay) feature on Macintosh-formatted CDs is more complex than just editing a few lines of text in a text editor. The software you use to burn the CD will handle the specifics of identifying the file to launch on the Mac. This means that designers wanting to deploy autoplay-enabled content for the Mac must burn the master copy of the CD *on* a Mac.

The expectations of Mac users should also be taken into account when developing Flash content on CD-ROMs. A few years ago, autoplay was exploited by one of the few Mac viruses, which used the feature to propagate itself. So while the majority of PC users still use the auto-run feature, the practice is not as popular on the Mac – for good reason!

Most Mac CD-ROMs actually do little more than open a window with an icon ready for the user to double-click. Mac CD creation software allows designers to customize the view of the CDs content window when the CD is inserted. Window size, placement and icon organization can all be set at the time of burning.

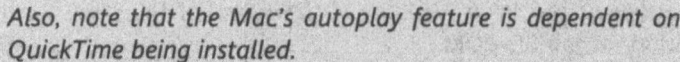

Also, note that the Mac's autoplay feature is dependent on QuickTime being installed.

The process for identifying a file for autoplay is handled during the burning phase of the CD-ROM development, and access to the autoplay option will vary according to the CD burning software you're using. Most Mac users use Roxio Toast as their software of choice for burning CDs. For detailed instructions, see the manuals that came with your software.

Flash designers creating CD-ROM-based content should always make the effort to publish both Mac and PC projector files. Remember that it's your job to deliver content that meets the **users' needs** – not to demand that the user meets your own. The time and effort it takes to build an extra version of the projector is so negligible that there really isn't any reason not to!

Exiting

Flash content deployed from a projector on a CD-ROM should always include an 'Exit' or 'Quit' button on all screens. This is even more important for Flash content that's played full-screen. Many novice users don't have the experience to quit the Flash content without a button on the screen specifically telling them how to do so.

This is actually quite easy to do in Flash once you know how, by using the fscommand action to communicate directly with the host program – whether it's in a browser or as a projector – using JavaScript. You can simply attach the fscommand call to a button, or use a callback to dynamically attach it as I've done here. The movie clip that I'm addressing has the instance name exitBut, and this code is then placed on the root:

```
exitBut.onRelease = function() {
    fscommand("quit");
};
```

Full-screen toggle

When you create Flash content that plays full-screen, remember that you're essentially taking away the user's access to the rest of their computer. As long as Flash is hogging the screen, they can't see the windows and folders located behind it. So, in addition to an 'Exit' button, you should also offer them a 'Maximize/Restore' button, giving them a way to return Flash to the confines of its own window.

Maximizing and Restoring Flash content is similarly done with `fscommand`. As above, I've used a callback structure to attach the code to my two movieclips called `maximizeBut` and `restoreBut`.

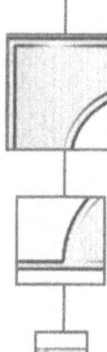

```
maximizeBut.onRelease = function() {
    fscommand("fullscreen", true);
};
restoreBut.onRelease = function() {
    fscommand("fullscreen", false);
};
```

It would be a simple enough task to set this button up as a toggle so that when the window's maximized the button will restore it, and when the window's normal the button will maximize it. That way it would mimic the behavior of the normal maximize button on a Windows machine.

CD burning issues

In addition to a good usable interface, auto-run features, exit buttons and screen toggle buttons, there's another usability issue related to CD-ROM production: how to burn the master CD that you send off for duplication.

One of the main problems encountered – one which causes many a CD-ROM to fail whilst being burned – is the **buffer underrun** error. This happens when the CD data being pulled off your hard drive gets interrupted or slowed. Once the CD burner runs out of data, its laser has nothing to write onto the disc. Unfortunately, it can't just stop and wait for more, and you're left with a shiny coaster: a CD that's useless.

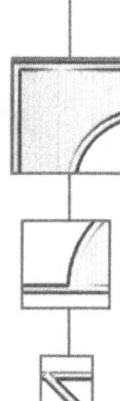

To prevent this happening and create a master disc that can provide the best data source for duplication, you can try these steps before starting to burn:

- **Burn at a slower speed.** Many CD burners can write at speeds up to forty-eight times the playback speed. While this can be very convenient for making fast copies of CDs, the result is data that is not so well formatted on the disc. When preparing a master CD-ROM for the duplication house, burn at 1x to 8x speed for the best data integrity. In addition to providing protection against buffer underrun, the resulting disc will play better on computers.

- **Turn off non-essential software.** Software that taxes your processor (such as screen savers, chat programs, and MP3 players) can cause buffer underrun errors by slowing the data transfer rate.

- **Disable the auto-run / autoplay preference for your OS.** This may also cause interference with the CD burner's activity.

- **Optimize your master files.** Defragment the hard drive (or external drive) on which your project files are stored. This collects data into contiguous segments on the drive, making less work for the data transfer, and preventing buffer underruns.

- **Use high-quality CD-ROMs for mastering.** CD-R discs can cost as little as a few pennies a piece, but be warned: you get what you pay for. CD-R discs that use aluminum or plastics do not offer the data integrity that those with a gold writing layer offer. When making the master copy of a CD for the duplication house, it's best to use the highest quality disc that you can find. Experiment with different brands to find the best discs for your recorder and consult with your duplication house to find the best master CD-R to use.

Flash on kiosks

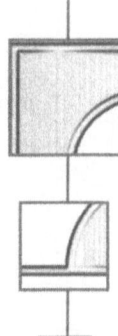

Kiosk development is a relatively quiet area of Flash development, mainly due to the fact that most kiosk-based projects are not intended for viewing on the Internet. Kiosk development can certainly benefit from the use of Flash for creating interfaces, and when usability principles are applied, the resulting kiosk can offer a really geat experience.

One of the most important features for kiosk development is security of the software used to create the interface. Not security as in 'keeping the data safe', but quite literally to stop users accessing the OS behind the interface layer. Our clients are not going to want a kiosk that needs constant attention because some crafty swine's figured out how to shut the whole thing down!

In fact, Flash is exceptionally good at protecting the OS layer in kiosk deployment, through the use of full-screen mode and keystroke capturing. By simply including the following Actionscript:

```
fscommand("trapallkeys", "true");
```

you can lock the Flash presentation on the screen and protect the system from malicious users.

This command tells Flash to capture all special character key presses, and pass them over to pre-written handling code, rather than allowing them to perform their normal functions. By adding this line to the first frame of your kiosk-based Flash content, you can prevent users from exiting the Flash content (either by accident or maliciously).

So, how does the client exit?

Of course, once this preference is set, the Flash content becomes very difficult to quit – especially on a touch-screen kiosk. It's essential to provide your client with a hidden exit option, allowing them to access the operating system whenever they need to perform maintenance. You should design this exit option so that it's complex enough to prevent unintentional use, but easy enough for your client to remember it.

> *When I worked on a touch screen kiosk for a children's store we implemented a touch-pattern exit option for the client. The client's system administrator had to touch all four corners of the screen in a certain order to access the exit function. For kiosks with keyboards, you can use a certain string of letters to exit the Flash content.*

The usability issues of kiosks are quite different from that of web-deployed Flash content. Their interfaces must be obvious and easy-to-use, since users will have no preconceived expectations of how the kiosk operates. The actual design of the kiosk also features highly in its overall usability.

Let's consider some important usability guidelines for Flash based kiosk development:

- **Kiosks are for transient users.** Kiosks are usually located in well-traveled areas and are designed for multiple users. Generally users will interact with a kiosk briefly and repeat interactions are unlikely, therefore interface retention is almost impossible. Kiosk interfaces need to be obvious, as the majority of users will be interacting with the content for the first time. This is one example of Flash content that runs in a non-personal setting. Flash designers creating kiosk systems can fully control the specifications of the environment that the Flash content runs.

- **Content should be full screen.** The interface should make full use of the available screen real estate. Menu bars, status bars and scroll bars only serve to clutter the interface and confuse the user.

- **Disable the cursor.** Unless the kiosk provides a mouse, trackball, or trackpad there is no need for the cursor to appear on the screen. The cursor will distract the user from the content of the screen. In Flash this can be accomplished by including the `mouse.hide();` command in the first frame of the Flash content.

- **Interfaces should be high in contrast.** Kiosks are deployed in a wide variety of settings. The ambient light can cause glares on the screen and low light conditions may make the screen difficult to see. To assist users in focusing on the screen, instead of glare or fingerprints left by previous users, design using light backgrounds and high contrast colors. Backgrounds should have subtle patterns to help the users focus on the interface and not the reflections on the screen. Type on the screen should be large and high in contrast too. Large, black, sans-serif typefaces on a white or light colored background will improve legibility.

- **Buttons need to be large, clear, and isolated.** Interacting with a kiosk is generally not done in the most ideal of situations. Frequently users will need to juggle items they are carrying (such as bags, briefcases or children) to use the kiosk. The standard input on a kiosk is the user's finger, which in the circumstances may be less than precise. To assist users in interacting with the kiosk, create large and well-separated buttons that act to prevent errors by non-precise touching. A good test for buttons is to try interacting with the content using your elbow or knuckles.

  Button size is also important due to the angle of viewing. A very tall user will perceive the screen layout differently from a short user due to the light from the screen being bent by the glass of the kiosk. Test your kiosk from varying heights to make sure that the angle of viewing is consistent with the button targets.

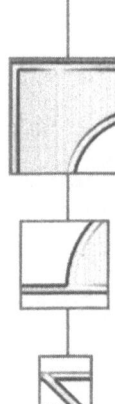

Make sure that buttons are clearly labeled and logically placed. The user should not have to think about the function of a button; that should be clear from its label.

For kiosks using touch-screen interfaces it's important to remember that there's no mouse-over state for buttons. The interaction on a touch-screen interface interprets only 'clicks' from the user's touch.

- **OS-like interface elements should be avoided.** Standard OS interface elements like close boxes, scroll bars and multiple windows do not translate well to kiosk interfaces. These elements are unlikely to be recognized by non-computer literate users and therefore are non-intuitive. In addition, certain interactions that we take for granted from a user with a mouse are not possible on touch-screen interfaces. Users cannot click and drag, nor click and release outside. Each touch is a click.

- **Provide feedback for all actions.** When a user clicks a button, let them know that their action has been registered. If your kiosk will include sound, provide a sound for button clicks. If the user's action requires processing, display a progress bar or clock icon to let the user know the status of their action.

- **Provide navigation at all levels.** Navigation within the kiosk's content should be easy to access and clear to the user. Allow user control over the information they interact with at all levels. Kiosk interfaces should always include a button to return the interface to its default state. The interface should also provide clear direction as to the actions the user can take. Descriptions of content will assist users in making the best decisions about their interactions.

- **Provide appropriate languages.** Kiosks located in areas frequented by users from different countries or speaking different languages should have multiple language options to improve the usability.

Make a key feature of the interface the ability to switch languages from any point in the user's interaction with the content.

- **Provide instructions for use.** Again, kiosk content should be obvious, yet some features of the kiosk system may require extra instruction for the user to interact with. The best solution is to provide clear instructions for all the interactivity required of the user. Remember that users interacting with a kiosk may not have experience with computers, so the clearer and easier to use you can make the interface the better the usability.

- **Make applications fast.** Slow responses to interactions invite the user to walk away from the kiosk. Create interactions that fire quickly to keep the user's attention. Optimize the environment to make sure the Flash plays as fast as possible, lower screen resolution, faster frames per second settings and faster processors can help Flash content be more responsive. In addition, a fast responding system is less likely to invite vandalism.

- **Use sound if possible.** Audio feedback will assist users in interacting with the content. Use sound to verbalize the requests of the user. This will assist users who may not be able to read the on-screen instructions. Be aware of the environment in which the kiosk is deployed. Sound in a busy hotel lobby may be hard to hear if the ambient noise is too loud. Also, positioning multiple kiosks next to each other will confuse the user as to which kiosk they should be listening to.

- **Refresh the content based on user inactivity.** When users interact with kiosks they may stay for a few seconds or a few minutes. When users leave a kiosk it's unlikely that they'll return the Flash content to its default state. Flash designers should create time-sensitive loops that refresh the Flash content to its default state after a period of inactivity.

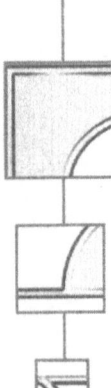

These refresh loops should offer the user the ability to continue their interaction by pressing a button on the screen if the pre-determined time elapses. The timeframe for these loops should be directly related to the sensitivity of the information on the screen.

Once the refresh loop reaches its time limit an alert box should appear asking the user if they require more time. This alert box should also have its own refresh loop in case the user has left the kiosk and is unable to answer.

For example, if a kiosk is used to enter personal information a short loop will assist in clearing the personal information if the user has to leave the kiosk before they are finished. In addition, if the kiosk is used in a high traffic area, refresh loops will also serve to prompt the user to complete their interaction faster.

- **Kiosks should be both environmentally and informationally sensitive.** Kiosks should be designed for comfortable interactions. The screen should be positioned for comfortable reading and touching. If a chair is provided, make sure that it's not fixed to the floor, which would make the kiosk difficult to use for people in wheelchairs.

  The overall kiosk design should also suit the environment. Photos and descriptions of the kiosk's function can help to get users to interact with the kiosk. In addition the kiosk should be sturdy to prevent it from damage and to provide a sense of security to the user. Users may be hesitant to interact with a kiosk if it feels as though they could tip it over.

  If the purpose of the kiosk is to collect personal information, make sure that the design of the kiosk provides privacy to the user. No one wants to enter their personal data when prying eyes can see.

- **Create an 'attraction animation'.** When a user is not using the kiosk create an animation (including some catchy music) to attract the attention of other potential users. Think of the attraction animation as a screen saver that advertises the features and functions of the kiosk. The use of sound can also help to attract users. The attraction animation should begin after a period of inactivity and should be easy to exit.

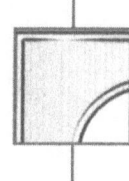

- **Testing kiosk systems.** If we've done a good job with this book you should be aware by now that user testing is an integral part of any Flash design process. A thorough testing of the system should be carried out before displaying it to the general public. If testing with user subjects, then make sure that a fair proportion of them have little or no previous experience of interactive systems. These users are more likely to pose unexpected problems for the system and will therefore provide a more thorough test. If possible, include elderly and disabled users in the testing.

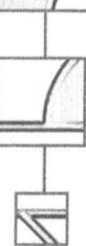

Flash on PDAs

PDA-based Flash – that is, Flash content that's designed to be viewed on a Personal Digital Assistant rather than on a desktop monitor – is a new and exciting area of Flash design. Right now, only PDAs running the Windows Pocket PC platform can play Flash content, but this is rapidly changing: new PDAs are being released that will support Flash in the near future.

> *It's also important to note that the Pocket PC player is generally one version behind the standard web browser plug-in in terms of features. At the time of writing, the Flash 5 plug-in for pocket PC had only just been released.*

Currently, Flash content on a Pocket PC PDA must be embedded in an HTML page, which plays in the Pocket PC Internet Explorer. There's no standalone

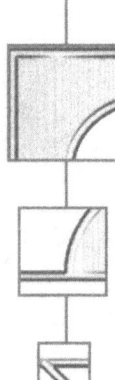

player, so the `fscommands` aren't available. In addition, different Pocket PC devices have different processors, and this means that the Flash content may not play at the same frame rate across all devices.

The ability to develop Flash content that plays on Pocket PCs is a fantastic extension of the abilities of Macromedia Flash. This opens an entirely new computer platform for Flash designers to create content for. In addition, it's relatively easy to move content designed for the Pocket PC to the Web.

From a usability perspective PDA Flash development is very similar to designing content for a touch-screen. Many of the same interaction limitations that are placed on interfaces for touch-screen kiosks apply also to PDAs. A PDA screen is essentially a touch-screen, but the user generally uses their stylus (a plastic-tipped pen) and not a finger for interaction.

Here are a few usability guidelines for Flash content playing on a Pocket PC PDA:

- **PDAs are more personal and less powerful than computers.** PDAs are generally used more for reference and short tasks than for desktop application-like tools. Content developed for a PDA should focus on short tasks that can be accomplished quickly by the user, rather than complex tasks that take a great deal of time. For proof of this, look no further than the lack of success that the electronic book concept has had. PDAs are simply not designed for long periods of interaction.

  Additionally, PDAs rarely have multiple users. They are personal in nature and the user interface development process should reflect this. Create easy-to-understand interfaces that communicate on a one-on-one level.

- **Screen size is limited.** The screen size of current Pocket PC devices is limited to just a few hundred pixels in either dimension. The standard size for Flash deployment is 240 by 240 pixels, reflecting the dimensions of the browser's active region. Some designers use

240x263 pixels, assuming that the browser's address bar will be hidden – note that this is not the case for most users.

- **Interfaces should be high in contrast.** PDAs are designed to be used anywhere, and they have a variety of screen types and color depths. When designing the interface for PDA content, subtle colors and detail can be lost on users in less than optimal viewing conditions. The interface should be high in contrast to work in both low-light settings or on less-than-ideal screens.

- **Typography on the small screen.** Whichever typeface you choose for the interface of your Flash content, it needs to be clear and crisp. Many Pocket PC Flash designers use special 'pixel fonts' that are designed to remain crisp at specific sizes. Type on the screen should be large and high in contrast too. Large, black, sans-serif typefaces on a white or light-colored background will improve legibility.

- **Avoid needless animation.** Pocket PCs are nowhere near as powerful as desktop or laptop computers. Their processor abilities are very limited and any interactivity that taxes the processor (such as animations and alpha tweens) will noticeably degrade the performance. Go easy on the processor-intensive interactivity and focus more on quick interactivity.

- **Buttons need to be large, clear and isolated.** Because PDAs are designed to be small and portable, interfaces that require any great precision are rarely successful. The standard input on a PDA is a stylus or the user's finger, which is rarely precise. To assist users in interacting with PDA content, create large and well-separated buttons that act to prevent errors by non-precise touching. Make sure the buttons are clearly labeled and logically placed. The user shouldn't have to think about the function of a button – that should be clear from its label.

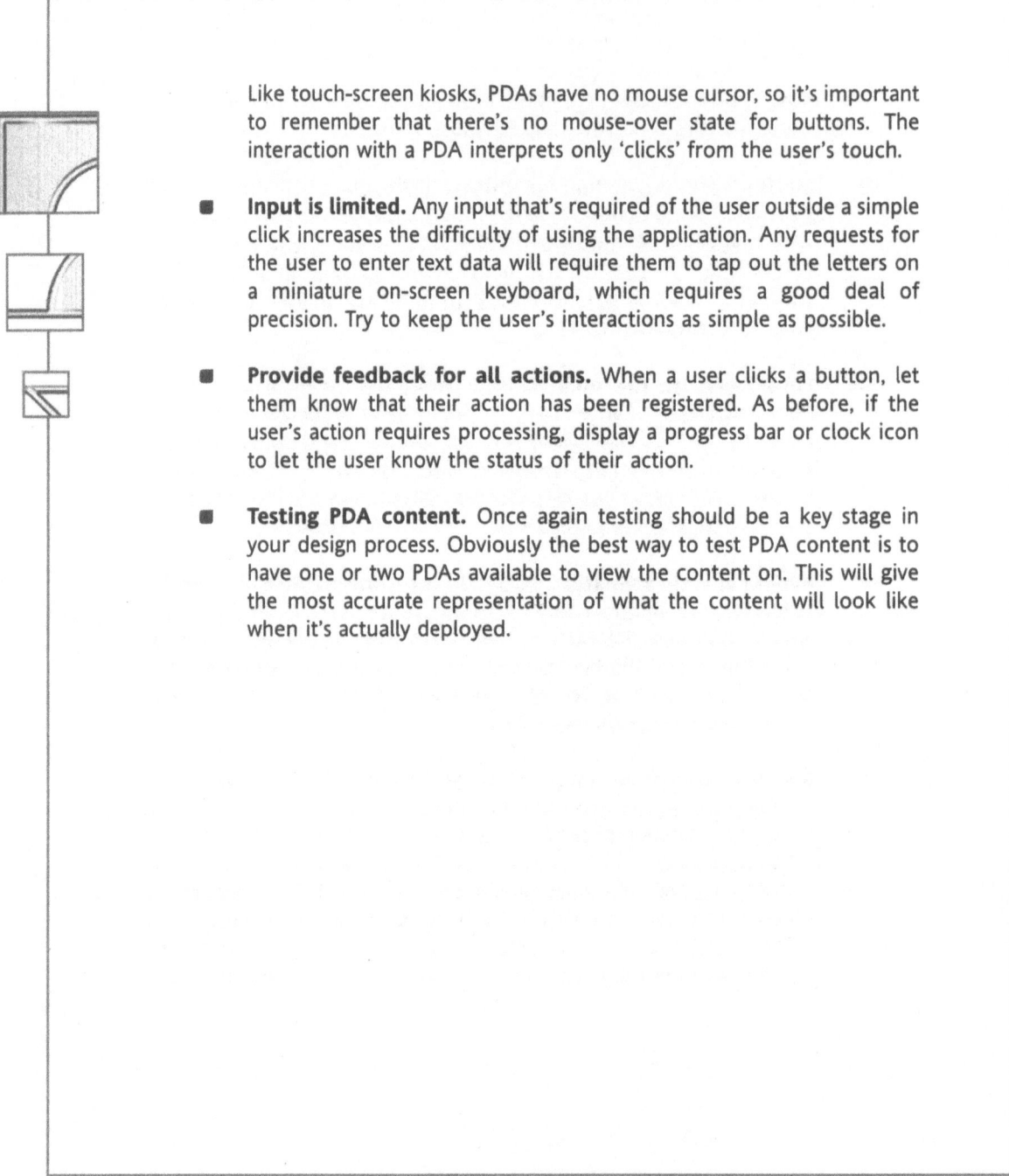

Like touch-screen kiosks, PDAs have no mouse cursor, so it's important to remember that there's no mouse-over state for buttons. The interaction with a PDA interprets only 'clicks' from the user's touch.

- **Input is limited.** Any input that's required of the user outside a simple click increases the difficulty of using the application. Any requests for the user to enter text data will require them to tap out the letters on a miniature on-screen keyboard, which requires a good deal of precision. Try to keep the user's interactions as simple as possible.

- **Provide feedback for all actions.** When a user clicks a button, let them know that their action has been registered. As before, if the user's action requires processing, display a progress bar or clock icon to let the user know the status of their action.

- **Testing PDA content.** Once again testing should be a key stage in your design process. Obviously the best way to test PDA content is to have one or two PDAs available to view the content on. This will give the most accurate representation of what the content will look like when it's actually deployed.

Case Study

Offline Flash

The *Future Fridges Conference* site isn't just going to be viewed on the Web. Our client has asked for the site to also be included on the CD-ROM tickets for the conference, as well as being displayed on kiosk terminals in the conference environment. Furthermore the session details section of the site will be available for download for Pocket PC users.

Our site on CD-ROM

We'll need to produce a modified version of the site for use on the CD-ROM tickets.

How is the CD-ROM version of the site different to the web version?

As was outlined in this chapter we'll need to add some extra interface elements to our site. We need to add a 'Quit' (exit) button that lets users exit the CD-ROM content as well as 'Minimize' (restore) and 'Maximize' buttons to allow our users to switch between full screen and a window. These are easily created using `fscommand` as outlined earlier in the chapter.

Because this is a CD-ROM, we can make use of the latest version (6.0) of the Flash player to create our projector file. This means that our users will be able to view the video interview in the speaker's section of the site. The code we used in creating the speakers section is designed to detect which version of the Flash player is being used and if the users have the Flash 6 player they'll see the video content. Hence we don't actually need to change anything about how our site works to ensure that it makes full use of the latest Flash player.

Considering the context of our content

We need to consider if users accessing the site from a CD-ROM ticket will have any different requirements to our web users. Specifically we need to consider if any of the site's content needs to change for this different context, such as content that connects to a web server or database.

The **Registration** section of the site connects to a web server to send the user's registration details. This functionality won't work if users are accessing the CD-ROM version of the site while they're offline. However, if our users are accessing the site from a CD-ROM ticket then we can be confident that they've bought a ticket and no longer need to register.

Consequently the registration form isn't required for the CD-ROM version of the site. In fact, including it on the CD-ROM could confuse users, who might wonder if they have to re-register. So our CD-ROM version of the site won't include a registration form. The **Registration** section of the site will still remain because we should include the refund information on the CD-ROM ticket since it's still relevant.

Testing before production

We'll produce Mac and PC versions of the site's projector file and will use the auto-run methods outlined in this chapter to make the site's content display as soon as the CD is loaded. We'll need to carefully test the CD-ROM on all operating systems before production of the CD-ROM tickets. This is especially important because this is a CD-ROM ticket; if it doesn't work correctly then our ticket holders may wonder if their ticket is valid.

Furthermore we should ensure that assistance information is printed on the CD-ROM that clearly outlines what information the CD contains, what to do if it doesn't auto-start, as well as a contact phone number and e-mail address for assistance.

Kiosks at the conference

In the original requirements specification for the site our client requested that the web site be made available on computer kiosks within the conference environment.

The term 'kiosk' is often used by clients to refer to a range of different things. It could mean a touch screen display booth where the users interact with just the touch screen, it could be a touch screen with a keyboard, or it could be a normal PC with a keyboard and mouse. So it's important to establish exactly what type of kiosk our client is referring to, as well as establishing the environment in which the kiosk will be located.

For the *Future Fridges Conference* the kiosks will just be standard PCs with a mouse and keyboard, set up on stands near the conference entrance. Our client wants the site to run within the browser, not full screen, so users can use the same computer as an access point to check their e-mail and browse the Web. Our client has also specified that kiosk computers won't have printers attached.

Effectively the site will just be the default home page on a number of free Internet access computers. This simplifies our kiosk development significantly, as we don't need to worry about disabling the cursor, having large clear buttons or running full screen. However there is one important tip mentioned in this chapter that's still very much appropriate, we need to consider transient users. On any day of the conference we may have hundreds of attendees using the same computer to access information about the conference.

Because of this we need to consider the appropriateness of our session planner application given the different context. Users won't be able to print out their session plans and a session plan saved by one user may then be modified by the next. The reality is that most users will be using the site in this context to quickly see what sessions are on and make a quick decision on what they're going to attend. They may also use it as way to look up more information on a particular speaker.

But users are unlikely to want to plan and save which sessions they wish to attend and so the session planner functionality is not of value in this context and will be removed from the kiosk version of the site. Furthermore, as the kiosks will be located within the conference environment, the registration form is also inappropriate and as with the CD-ROM version of the site, will be removed.

As the kiosk computers are being used to browse the Web we should ensure that we make it easy for our users to get back to the conference home page. The browsers' default home pages will be set to the conference site and they may also be customized to have a special toolbar button that clearly links to the conference site.

(Information on creating a custom Internet Explorer toolbar can be found at http://msdn.microsoft.com/workshop/browser/ext/tutorials/button.asp)

A session planner for Pocket PCs

One of the nice features of Flash is that it can scale to any size.
However a site that's usable at one resolution may not be usable
when viewed at a lower resolution. The screenshot below shows
the **Session Details** section of our site as viewed at 240 x 240 -
the basic resolution of a Pocket PC.

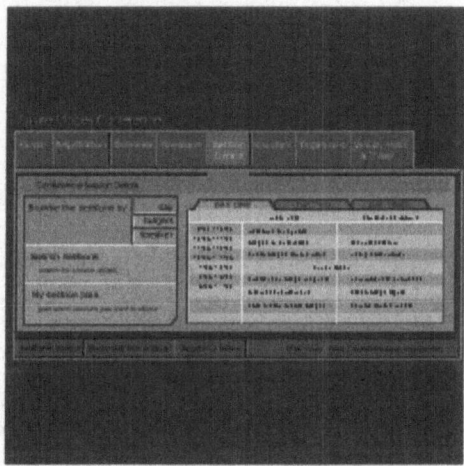

Clearly the site isn't useable at this resolution. The text is
unreadable and the buttons are tiny.

So, to provide a Pocket PC-friendly version of our session planner
tool we'll need to restructure our content to work at this lower
resolution.

The first step is to remove all interface elements that aren't
required. As we're providing only the **Session Details** section of
the site, we can remove the main navigation elements.

Our intention is that users will use the Pocket PC version of the session planner to produce their own portable offline session plan, thus the Internet relevant navigation elements such as the links to the HTML version and Email to a friend can also be removed.

We're left with the secondary navigation to browse, search and plan the sessions and the associated content. On our site we've used a wide layout for this navigation and content, which reflects the *letterbox* shape of computer screens. However, the display area for a pocket PC is small and square, which requires a different layout for the interface.

How do we ensure that our buttons remain large enough to tap on and our text large enough to read? The key here is to think about how much information can be displayed on the screen and still remain usable. If the content starts to become unreadable or unusable then it needs to be spread across multiple screens.

The solution for our session details tool is to break the navigation menu and the content into two separate pages or screens. The navigation is displayed first then the user taps on the menu item that they wish to select (for example, Browse Sessions by day). The navigation slides away to the top of the screen and the user can browse the conference details by day as they could on the original site, tapping a session title for more details. If the user wishes to return to the main menu they just need to tap on the menu tab at the top of the screen.

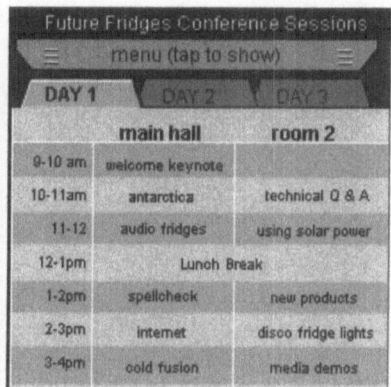

The restructuring of the session details content in this way is actually quite simple. The graphical elements need to be resized slightly and the menu needs to be enclosed in a movie clip that can be shown and hidden; overall the adaptation is reasonably minor. The only significant modification is to the text boxes. As outlined earlier in the chapter, we need to ensure that the typography is legible at this low resolution and so we use crisp, black, sans-serif typefaces for all the text.

To work with the reduced screen space we also need to reduce the title descriptions for the conference sessions. This is a case where we have to balance two usability constraints, namely readability and clear descriptions. To keep the original full session titles would've required either unreadably small type or a more complex navigation, so we've opted to remove some detail from session titles, leaving just a keyword or words. When our users tap on the session titles the details will be displayed in a pop-up box (as with the standard version of the site) and this will include the full session title and description.

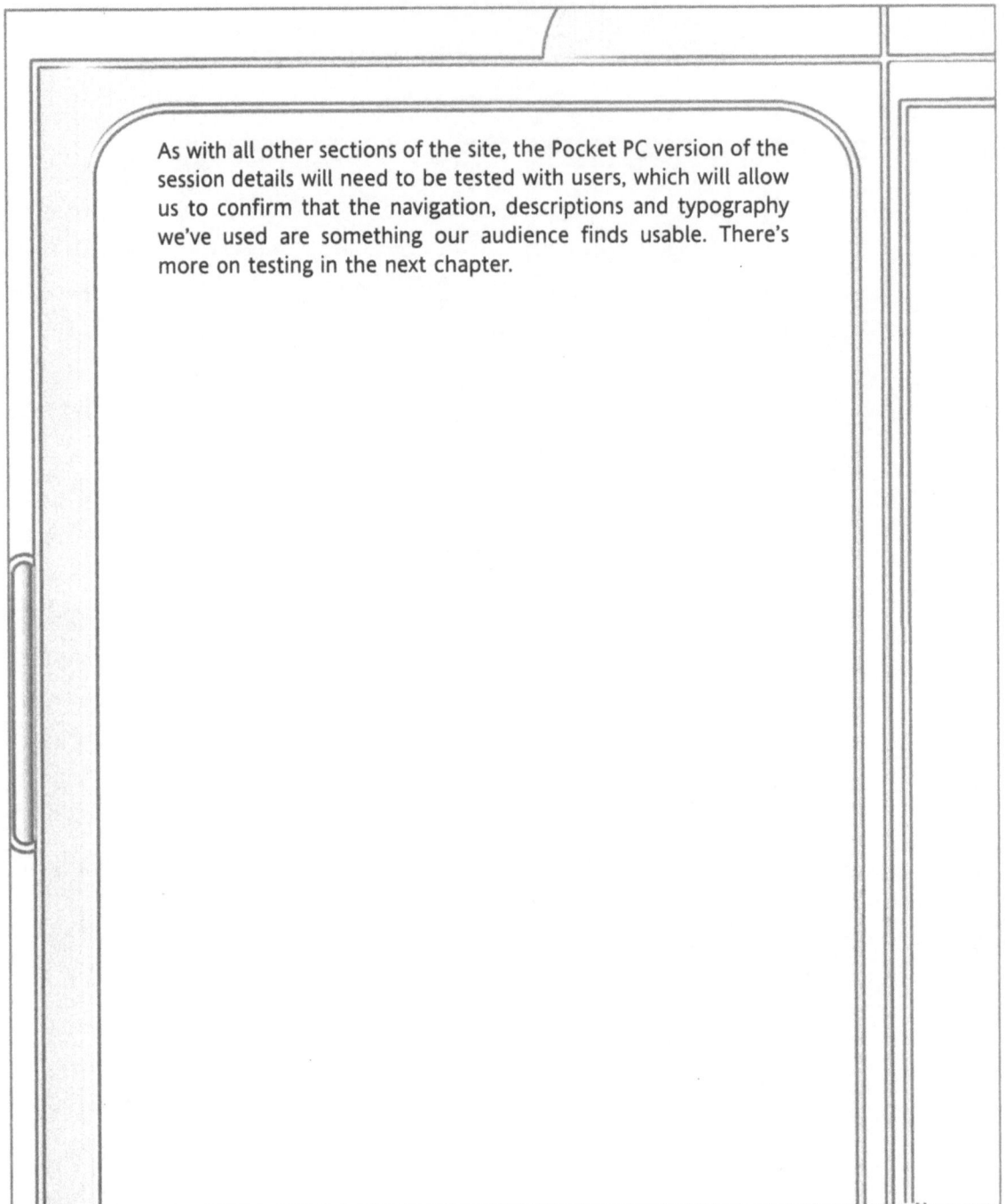

As with all other sections of the site, the Pocket PC version of the session details will need to be tested with users, which will allow us to confirm that the navigation, descriptions and typography we've used are something our audience finds usable. There's more on testing in the next chapter.

Summary

This chapter has taught you that while most of the usability principles you've learned earlier in the book are transferable to offline Flash content, there are a number of more specific guidelines that need to be followed to ensure good usability across these different platforms.

This is a rapidly growing area of Flash design and we should all be aware that usability issues are just as important off the Web as on it. Once you've got used to designing for usability in your online projects it should become second nature to apply that good practice to work you do on different platforms.

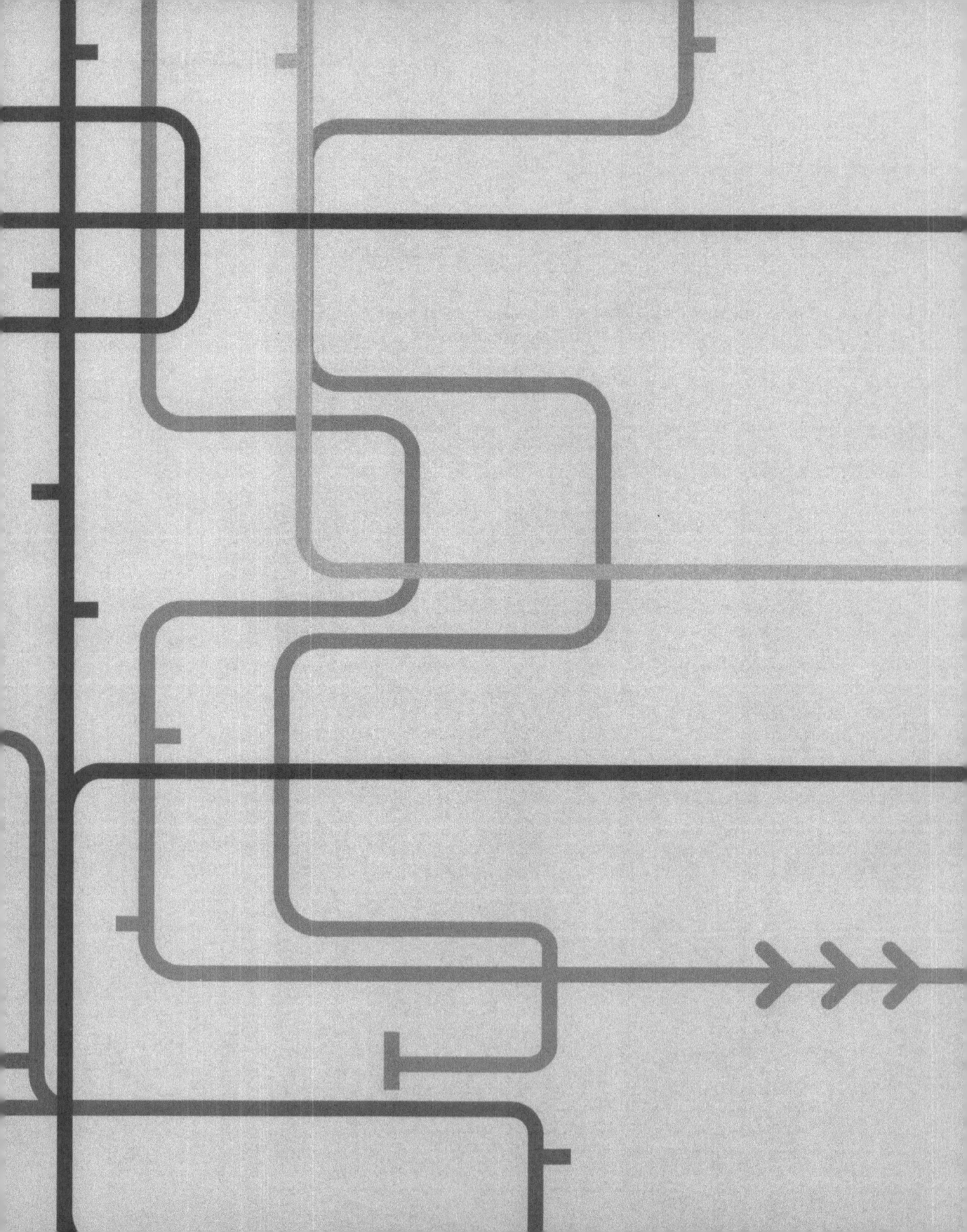

User testing

Throughout this book, we've been talking about **users** and **user testing** as the bedrock of all things truly usable. I don't know about you, but a great many designers will take all that business about user testing with a very large pinch of salt. They know their market inside out – they're constantly talking to potential users, and there's nothing you can't tell them about what that person wants. If you push them for an answer, they'll tell you user testing's just a pointless luxury – a waste of time and money.

In actual fact, a good knowledge of your target market is something that often makes user testing even more useful than it would be otherwise. Being so close to your users, you may take certain things for granted, and overlook important issues. User testing casts *new* and *objective* eyes on your project; the results either confirm that your design and structure work, or tell you that they need improvement.

While the users may have significant vested interest in the site's subject matter, they've never been to the site before (or this version of the site), and can give feedback that others, especially you and your client, can't really have an objective view about since you've been so close to it for so long. You know, for example, that a non-stereotypical icon takes people to a site map, because you put it there. But if no one ever clicks on that icon, or notices that it's there, then there's a usability problem that needs to be considered and solved.

User testing, done properly, will help you to find the areas in which you need to improve, and give hints about how you can improve the interactions you design. Users will often give practical ideas on how to improve navigation and content presentation either indirectly or simply by saying "I can't get that information, I wish it were over there!"

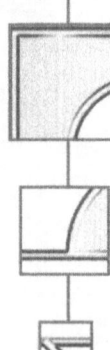

Practical approaches to user testing

There are all kinds of methods for user testing, ranging from 'Hey Joe come check this out' to a full-blown professional approach, employing dedicated facilities and a permanent staff of specialists.

The first time I ever participated in a usability study, I found myself in a very elaborate user testing facility. I wasn't told what software I'd be testing, so I didn't even know if I'd have the faintest idea how to use what they presented to me, just that I should plan to be there for up to four hours.

Once the test started, I was put all alone in a room with a one-way mirror on the wall. A number of video cameras recorded my face, my hand movements, and the screen. My keystrokes were also being recorded, along with the number of mouse clicks I made.

The software appeared – it was a word processing program with which I had some very limited experience, but it wasn't a program I used regularly. The man running the test would occasionally tell me what to do through a loudspeaker. He would describe a task, such as, "Start a new document and create a simple graphic, then save it to disk".

I was then given a second program, and asked to perform the same tasks.

I'd been instructed to talk out loud while attempting each task, describing what I was doing, why I was doing it, and what seemed confusing or easy to me. I was to say whatever came to mind, whether specific observation, or just a stream of consciousness. I was to voice opinions and criticisms out loud. After each hands-on session, I completed a written evaluation, ranking various elements of the software on a scale of one to ten.

I was well paid for my trouble, but never discovered what I was testing the products for, or how the two were being compared. I don't know whether or not the testing was funded by one of the companies behind the software. I never even found out why I'd been asked to take part, except that I'd responded to an ad and my profile somehow fitted the testers' requirements. The testers wanted me to be as oblivious and as objective as possible.

Was I a typical user of this product? Maybe. Was I someone who fit the profile of someone that they wanted to convert to their product? I don't know. Was their test successful? Well, it didn't make *me* want to purchase either product, but perhaps they made changes to one or both applications that made both of them better, deduced from the collection of data they received from the number of people that they tested. If it was a competitor's test, they could see what theirs had that others didn't and vice versa. Bugs in either application could have surfaced, confusing menu items clarified, and icons made more applicable.

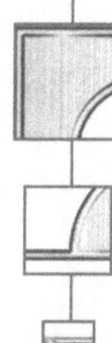

Was the test fair? Well, I was left in the dark, almost literally. It could be argued that it was unfair because I already knew the scenarios when faced with the second application, so I might already have formulated a plan to accomplish the task faster or more efficiently, or known what to look for because I knew what questions were going to be asked of me later. My eyes might have scanned to a place where I expected something to be, because it was there in the other application (this is referred to in usability testing lingo as **practice effect**, or the inevitability of a user gaining knowledge of the procedure and applying it to the next test product).

Perhaps the whole test was off because I wasn't used to the placement of the keyboard or comfortable in the chair, or self-conscious about so many cameras pointing at me. No matter how scientific a test can be, it all comes down to the fact that it's a human being doing it. Which, of course, is the whole point.

Designing a test

Of course, not all of us can afford to employ professional usability firms. Fortunately, as the designer and developer of a site, you're in a good position to come up with your own tests. Even if you hire other people, your

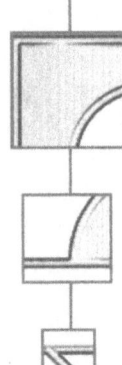

experience will be invaluable in helping them to produce scenarios, write questions, and figure out what the test goals are in the first place.

So what *do* you want to find out? Before signing off a project to your client, you want it to be as tight as possible. Do you want to identify problems or potential problems, compare your site with other sites, or confirm that you've met the goals that you set out to meet?

If you want to identify problems in your site, whether it's design, coding bugs, or even aesthetic appearance, this is often referred to as **diagnostic testing** or **diagnostic usability testing**. You find out what works, and what doesn't, and continue to work with what works, and fix what isn't working. This seems to be the goal of most testing, at least as far as designers go.

Comparative testing is just what it sounds like: either comparing the site that you've designed with one or more competitors' sites, or comparing one of your own designs with another, to help choose which one works best and which one to launch.

When the site is finished or near finished, **verification testing** is often done to see if the site has met the goals of the project. This testing is to corroborate whether or not you've been implementing all the results of the previous tests to make the site better.

Types of test

You'll find many different trademarked names and consultancy-branded terms for different types of usability test. Ultimately though, you just want to know which approach is most likely to help you improve your site. Here are a few of the more popular ones.

- The **coaching method** involves direct interaction between the tester and the site designer. The expert 'coach', or the one familiar with the site, answers questions the testers might have, and coaches them along in their use of the site. This is most often used with novices, and the goal is to find out what sort of direction they might need in relating to a site.

- **Focus groups** generally entail a group of about five to ten people, who work with a moderator to go through the testing. The group discusses their opinions and experiences with a site. Generally the moderator is an objective professional who guides the discussion. Typically focus groups are held in rooms with one-way mirrors, allowing the site designers a view into the session.

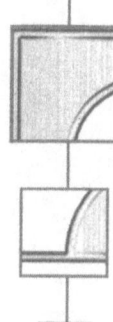

- **Thinking aloud** is like the test that I participated in, mentioned at the beginning of this chapter. The user is encouraged to think out loud, explaining movements and voicing concerns and opinions.

- **Performance measurement** is a quantitative testing method, used to obtain data about how test participants executed various tasks. For example, the test may have five or more users try to access a certain area of a site, and time how long it took them to get there and count how many clicks it took to find. It can be used to test sites against one another, or to test the usability benchmarks of one client site. This is one of the more formal testing methods, and is often used in conjunction with interviews and questionnaires.

- **Question-asking** is much like the thinking aloud test, but the persons giving the test ask direct questions about the site. It's believed that this helps the user verbalize their thoughts more thoroughly.

- **Co-discovery learning** (or **constructive interaction**) involves letting two test users try out a site together, and letting them try to solve problems by helping each other. It's a thinking aloud method, and it's based on the notion that people will express problems and solutions more directly when they're trying to work together towards a common goal.

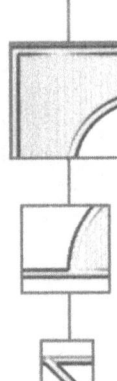

Retrospective questionnaires and interviews can also be useful. While the answers you get may be less definitive and results less subjective, it's often helpful to have post-testing questionnaires and interviews with test users. This method is also used for those in remote testing; volunteers in remote areas could answer questions about the site (as simple as a one question poll or a more complex five-page multiple choice questionnaire) and mail them in by a deadline date.

Types of result

There are quite a few other formal ways of testing users. However, there are a limited number of results categories, all of which are beneficial to site development for differing reasons.

- **Behavior** results are just what their name suggests: results of watching or recording a person's interaction and behavior with a site. Watching people's behavior will give you hints on what parts of a site are frustrating to navigate, or fun to use, or that never get found because the users' behavior is to avoid that particular link.

- **Opinion** is what the person thinks of the site from their experiences with it. Finding out what people think about a site, their gut reactions, even simple things like, "I really like the color!" can prove very helpful in development.

- **Subjective** results are those that are influenced by feelings or temperament. For example, if you're asked to judge a site that you created, it's impossible for you to be completely objective, since you have invested time (and possibly emotion) into its creation. Subjective results can be interesting, but since the person may have something invested, their opinion may be biased.

- **Objective** results are those not affected by outside emotional influences, and therefore less biased and most likely more helpful to the developer.

- **Qualitative** results are those that can't be measured against one another, since they're based on the tester's quality of experience.

- **Quantitative** results are those that can be counted and measured against one another, such as how much time it took for five people to get to the same area of a site from the home page.

Your role as designer

Possibly the most important mindset to have when going into usability testing is that you'll never please all of the users all of the time, and you'll never, ever, make your site perfect. Managing your own and your client's expectations is crucial. You will find out definitive, constructive information, but you'll never get everything right. Keeping that in mind makes multiple testing a little easier to handle, and allows you to maintain boundaries with clients when they make demands for an absolutely flawless site.

There are various levels of user testing, anything from informal, "Hey, how do you like this?" inquiries to days of intensive questioning, retests, data collection and evaluation, and reworking of the site. And then, doing it all over again. Your role in all of this, whether you're doing it all by yourself, with an in-house testing team, or with a consultant, is to be there as the site expert, helping to come up with questions, figuring out the best way to test, and of course, creating solutions with the results in hand.

Whether you decide to go with formal or informal user testing, it's very important that you and your team stay objective, and remain as detached from the users as possible:

- Avoid leading users by defending your design decisions

- Let them work at their own pace while you observe and take notes

- Listen to what they're saying and watch what they're doing

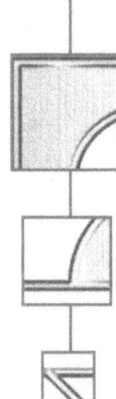

- If they make a mistake, don't jump in and tell them what to do, unless that's the kind of testing that you're doing (see **coaching method** above).

- If they don't know where to find something, don't tell them where to go.

- Whatever you do, don't criticize their abilities or actions.

- If you're extremely sensitive to criticism, let someone else sit with the users.

Where do you find users?

If you already have an established site or user mailing list, put out the word that you're looking for people to test your site. Ask your client for a list of people who have contacted them about the site, and ask them to participate.

Ask your client for a random selection of five or so employees: one from marketing, one from sales, one from content, one new employee, one veteran, for example. This will help you to get a relatively balanced insider's view of the site.

Setting up scenarios

Before you start testing, decide on a few scenarios that you want your testers to explore. For example, if your client's site is an online product catalog, ask your testers to register on the site, purchase a pair of shoes (or whatever it is the client sells), and check up on their order. Ask them to contact customer service, make an exchange, or use a discount code that was e-mailed to them.

Cost factors

How much it will cost you to incorporate user testing into your process depends on the kind of user testing you decide to do. It depends on how many people you intend to test, how formal you need the testing to be, and how many times you plan to do the testing.

You'll notice that many of the costs associated are indirect costs based on time spent testing. Only you know how much you and others in your team get paid and how it might break down on a per-hour basis, or how much it costs to hire a firm in your area. It will also cost the client waiting time for the site, planning time for the preparation, and time to implement changes. Some direct costs include:

- **Recruitment:** This may be from duplicating flyers that you hand out to people at a trade show, from purchasing classified advertisements, or from making long distance phone calls. If your firm or the testing facility you're hiring maintains a database of interested parties over the years, then this cost may be lessened by using resources you already have in the database.

- **Lab space, equipment, and testing experts:** If your firm doesn't have an in-house testing facility and you're considering more formal user testing, it will cost you to rent an appropriate space, computers and videotaping equipment, if you don't provide your own. Of course, if you need to hire experts to help out, you'll be paying their fee.

- **Participants:** Unless you're doing really informal testing with your friends or co-workers who walk by your cubicle on their way to the vending machine, you'll want to budget for either cash or gifts for your test participants. I've seen user tests paid for in pizza, while others pay quite high hourly stipends. If you're happy to identify your company to participants, branded freebies (mugs, mouse mats, coasters and the like) might make a nice bonus gift. However, while these may seem 'free', somewhere down the line someone has paid for them, so make sure they're included in the budget.

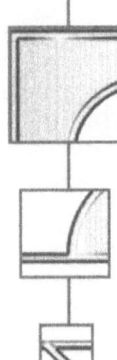

Testing, testing, one, two, three...

It's often wise to run usability tests at several points in a project's lifespan, rather than waiting until the end and testing the whole thing once. A few one-hour tests at various stages are usually more valuable than one big fifteen-hour test when you're all done.

One of the more obvious reasons to do tests along the way is that you can fix problems as you go, and probably prevent a good many snags by paying attention to what users really want and like. Having feedback to act on during the process can be a real boon for us as designers, whether or not it's complimentary: negative feedback gives us something to learn from, while positive feedback can encourage and inspire.

Testing things yourself

Before you get into testing your site (whether formally or informally), it's worth having a go for yourself. This may seem fairly pointless in light of what I've been saying above, but it'll save you a lot of time and money – not to mention embarrassment – if you can resolve some of the more common site problems *before* you run it past your testers.

Test the uploaded site

One common problem that affects both usability and navigability on your site is that of missing pages. Everything may work fine on your own machine, but over on the remote server, you find that half your links don't work – the pages aren't where they're supposed to be. The most likely explanation for this is that there's a difference in structure between one version and the other. Make sure all of your files are in the same relative position as they are on the drive on which you built the site.

Other browsers

Even though Flash isn't browser-dependent and should look the same on either Netscape Navigator or Microsoft Internet Explorer, if you're creating a site that's HTML-based and Flash-enhanced, you'll want to make sure that it looks the same (or as much the same as possible) in each browser.

Other platforms

Keep in mind that sometimes things don't always look the same on different computer platforms. For example, graphics often show up darker on a Windows monitor. You may want to alter your images' brightness or contrast so that they're more easily viewed on various platforms. Keyboard commands are usually different on Macs and PCs, so if you require specific keyboard commands or ask users to choose something from a menu, be sure you specify for both platforms.

Check contrast

It's important to keep text and links readable on the background. This is a very easy thing to check, and it's very logical to figure out what's wrong and what has to be done. If you can't read the text, the people coming to your site won't be able to, either. The most important key to readability is contrast. If your type color is light, make your background dark, and vice versa. If you use background tiles that have both light and dark colors in it, neither light nor dark text will read very easily over it. Make sure your tiles are either overall light or dark – the opposite of whatever color text you're using.

Modem it

As someone who lives in the middle of a rural state, I can attest that there are a lot of sites out there, even the low-K Flash ones, that can take a long time to appear on my computer. Most people still dial up, and even with the fastest modem, the Web is a slow place to visit. Buy yourself a modem (they

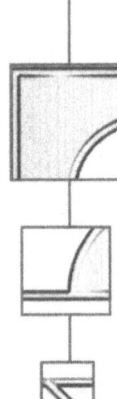

are cheap and probably tax deductible for you; check with your accountant), and test all of your sites via dial-up.

Navigational options

How many navigational options do you give users to navigate your site? Whether or not your site is Flash-based, a navigation bar on the page, or access to a site map or other overall navigation, will help to guarantee access to those parts of the site people want to get to.

Do you continue to provide navigation tools throughout the site? If someone has wandered into the depths of your content, can they find their way back using the options you've provided? Do users have access to the browser's Back button, and if so, does it suck them right out of your site, or get them back where you want them to go?

Window size

Do people have to widen their browser window to get a full look at your site? If you ask them to widen it one time, do they have to widen it again when they hit another page? Don't make your visitors have to resize windows to get all of the information. Widening a browser window a little isn't much work, but a user shouldn't have to keep doing it for every page they visit.

Browser control

How much do you control your user's window? Do they lose all sense of being on the Web, and can only get to your information? Nowadays, most designers agree that full-screen Flash presentations, and those that take over too many navigational elements of a browser, are not desirable.

Avoid gratuitousness

There's no doubt that your cool Flash animations are, well, cool. These creations can enhance a page, a site, and a user's experience. But if the person visiting your site has to take a half hour to download something that serves no informational or entertainment value, then everyone's time is wasted. If the site's purpose is to show off your or your client's Flash skills (such as in a portfolio site), then it makes sense to load up the site with cool stuff. But consider giving users opt-out options, or letting them know that a part of a site contains a large file. You'd much rather impress than annoy your visitors, if you want them to return.

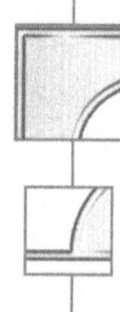

Contact us

Make a point of giving people an obvious method to contact you *especially* since you're trying to make the point of getting people to give you feedback as they go through the site. Whether you provide e-mail, phone, street address, and so forth, make it easy to get in touch with you. And respond when appropriate.

Consistency

Are your links and icons consistent? Use the same link names and icons for an area throughout your site. For example, if you use a compass icon on one page to give people the option to view your site map, use the same icon for the same purpose on other pages.

When you provide links to the areas on your site, be sure to maintain both consistent labeling of the links, and the same order in which the links appear in each case. Changing the name of a link, say, from 'Catalog' to 'Our stuff' or 'Products', is confusing. Changing the order of links around forces your visitor to re-read the menu bar to make sure they're clicking on the right one.

Besides using the same icons, don't forget consistent placement of your navigational structure: If you've decided to put your menu bar on the bottom of pages, make sure it stays at the bottom of pages so people don't have to work to find it.

Now let's take a look at how all this user testing theory relates to our case study.

> ## Case Study

Final testing

Having completed our site, it's now time to put it through the final user testing before the site goes live. As we've tested the site throughout its development it's unlikely that we'll encounter any significant usability issues at this stage. However we may encounter minor issues that we can address to increase the overall usability of the site.

Testing the navigation

We'll ask our test users questions to identify if the navigation is clear, simple to use, and clearly indicates location. As we did when we first looked at the navigation we want to test the clarity, simplicity and location.

But surely we user-tested this back when we developed the draft navigation structure, so why do we need to test it again? Well, since then we've integrated the site's content and applied a design style to the navigation. We need to make sure that neither of these has compromised the ease of use of our navigation.

Clarity: Can our test users clearly identify which part of the interface is the navigation? Are the labels on the navigation items easily readable?

Simplicity: Does the navigation appear simple and easy to use?

Location: Can our test users clearly identify which section of the site they're in?

Results of the navigation testing

Our primary navigation performs well in the testing: test users find the primary navigation clear and easy to use. The text on the navigation buttons is easy to read and all users report that they can clearly identify which section of the sit they're accessing. A few users comment that they find the highlighted navigation item and the graphic design link between the navigation item and the content especially useful in indicating which section of the site they're accessing.

The secondary navigation doesn't do quite so well in the testing. While the navigation is found to be mostly easy to use and intuitive, users did identify one readability issue and a number of functionality issues.

Readability issue

A few users commented that the text on the print section, bookmark section, and e-mail to a friend navigation buttons was a little difficult to read. While the text was at an acceptable size, they felt it showed insufficient contrast with the background.

None of the users reported the text as being impossible to read, but this still needs to be treated as an important issue since it may affect the site's accessibility. A user with poor eyesight may find the text impossible to read. Luckily the solution to this issue is quite straightforward: we simply modify the color of the text to create a greater contrast with the background.

Functionality issues

The usability of the two functional elements of the site, the **session details** and the **registration form**, is critical to the success of the site and ultimately the conference. Our test user feedback on the **Registration** section was extremely positive. Our users found the form very easy to use and found the extra information box in the form especially useful in clarifying the purpose of the form's input fields.

The **Session Details** section didn't fare quite as well. On the whole, users found it useful and easy to use, however three recurring issues were identified.

- Users who accessed the my session plan section before selecting any sessions for their plan were confused by the empty plan.

- Some users reported that they didn't initially realize that they could click on titles in the session list to access relevant details.

- We observed that users who wanted to delete an item from their session plan had a difficult time. All sessions are selected by default, so users who wanted to delete just one item from their plan had to go through and deselect all but one of the items before they could delete it.

The first two can be seen as 'not enough information' issues. What may be intuitive for one user isn't necessarily intuitive for another. We just haven't provided sufficient information to guide all users through using our site's interface.

To solve the first issue, we just need to include a message on the blank session plan, telling users how they can add items to it.

For the second, we need to give users a suitable indication that they can click on the session details. The simplest way would be to include a line of text such as, "click on a session title to view the details of that session" next to the lists of conference sessions.

The third item is a real functionality issue. We've produced an interface that makes it hard for our users to complete a common task. Clearly the solution is not to make session items in the planner selected by default. But what if a user wants to delete all their sessions to create a new plan? We can make this task easier by including a 'select all' button, which sets all items in the plan as selected. The user can then use the 'delete selected' button to remove the items.

Testing the content

We also need to test that our site's content is formatted clearly, easily readable, scannable and ultimately meets the needs of our users. We can use a similar task test that we used in developing an Information Architecture to get our test users to confirm that the content meets their needs.

It's important at this stage to have some test users accessing the site using a modem connection so any issues with download times or streaming content can be identified.

Here are the results of our testing:

Task	Responses
Looking for a venue map	Our testers easily found the venue map in the venue section of the **Venue, Travel and Hotels** section of the site. The map was found to be clear and was easily printed off for reference.
Register for the conference	All testers easily found the **Registration** section and as noted in our navigation testing found the registration form easy to use and complete.
Find out about the keynote speakers	Our testers easily found information on the keynote speakers in the **Speakers** section of the site. Users found the video/audio interface intuitive to use and had no issues with viewing the content.
Find out information on the cost of the conference	Users easily found out the cost of the conference from the home page.

The main site loaded within twenty seconds for users accessing the site using a modem. However the audio and video content download was fairly slow over a modem connection. While the content did stream in, users found that it sometimes paused as more data was being downloaded. Some suggested that they'd rather have a text version of the interview.

We raised the concept of a text version of our interviews when we previously discussed accessibility. Clearly it will be worthwhile providing a transcript of the video and audio interviews, as this will raise the accessibility of this content and will satisfy the needs of some modem users.

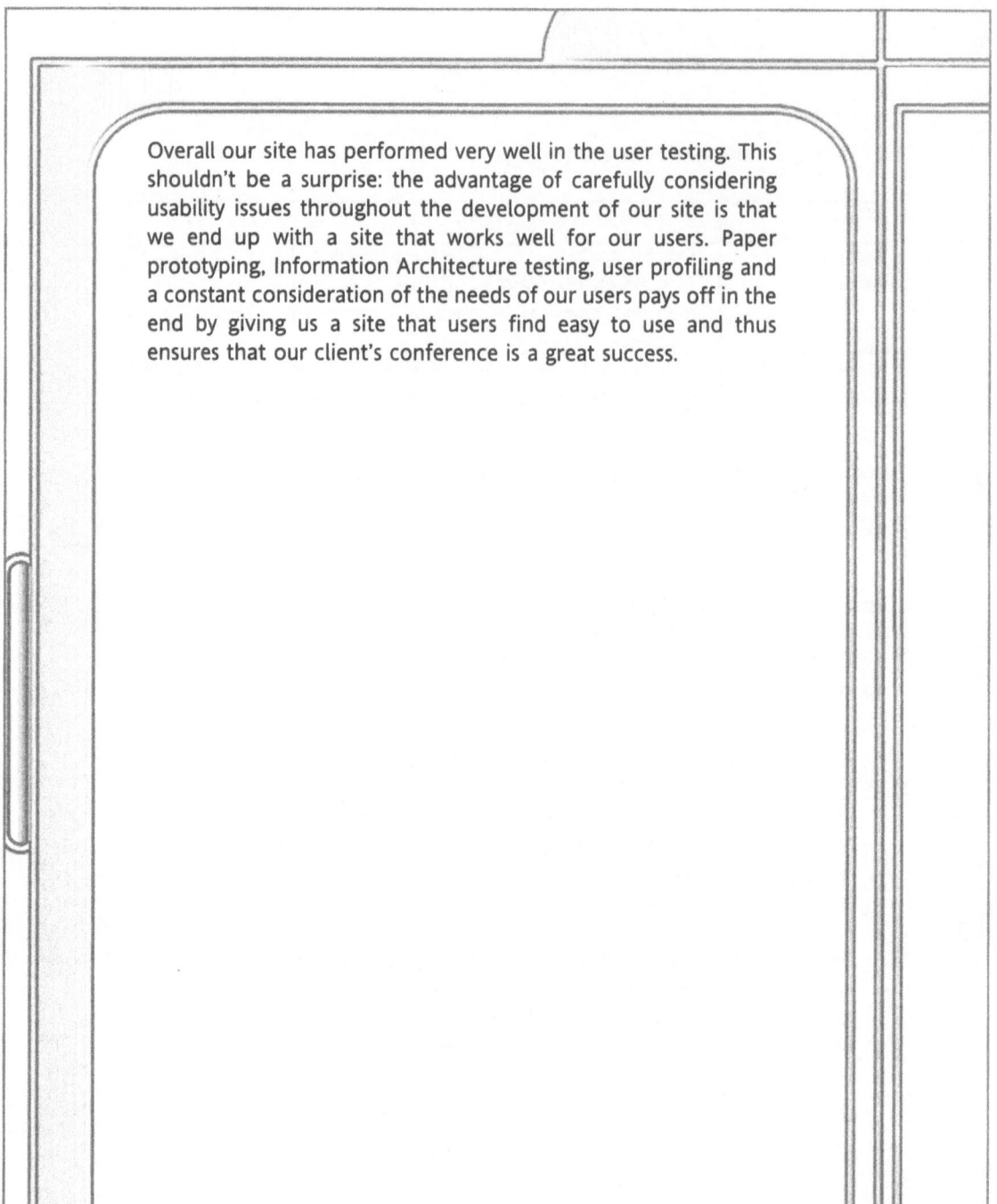

Overall our site has performed very well in the user testing. This shouldn't be a surprise: the advantage of carefully considering usability issues throughout the development of our site is that we end up with a site that works well for our users. Paper prototyping, Information Architecture testing, user profiling and a constant consideration of the needs of our users pays off in the end by giving us a site that users find easy to use and thus ensures that our client's conference is a great success.

Summary

User testing encompasses a huge range of processes – there's only one solid, for-sure recommendation I can make: **do it!** And keep doing it. Bring your results back to your team, process the data, and use the information that you learn to make your site better.

Remember that an informal (and invaluable) way to test your site after launch is simply to ask your users for feedback and ***listen to what they have to say***. There will always be someone out there with too much time on his or her hands, who'll gladly write you a forty-page report on *everything* that's wrong with your site. You can ignore those if you want.

Those that write with comments about how they interact (or can't interact) with your site are always valuable though. You might discover workarounds for a persistent navigation problem prompted by a user suggestion, or come up with questions and scenarios for your next project's user testing opportunity.

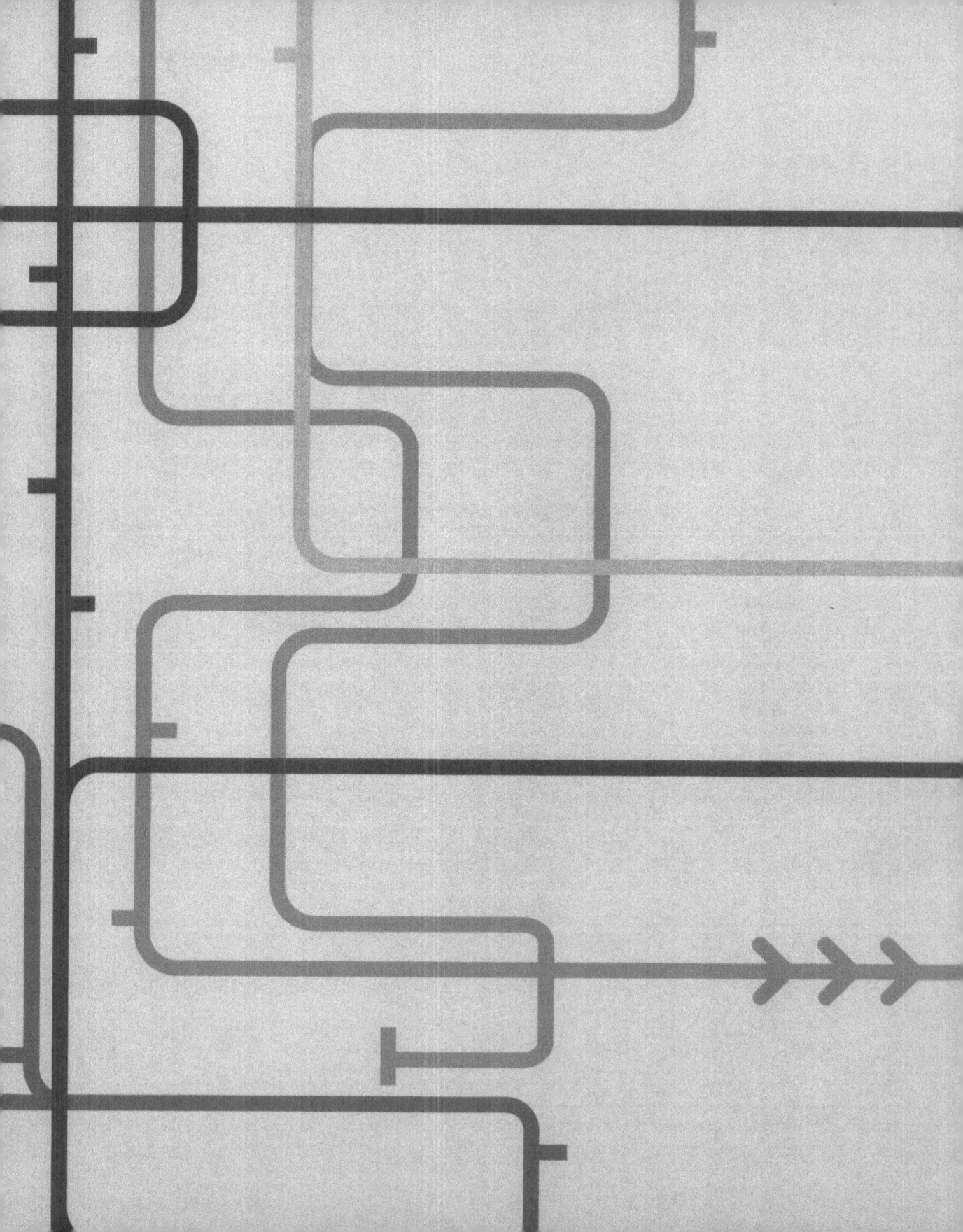

Appendix: Resources and Articles on the Web

Web sites

Macromedia Flash: Usability. Macromedia's resource for information on Flash usability.

http://www.macromedia.com/software/flash/productinfo/usability/

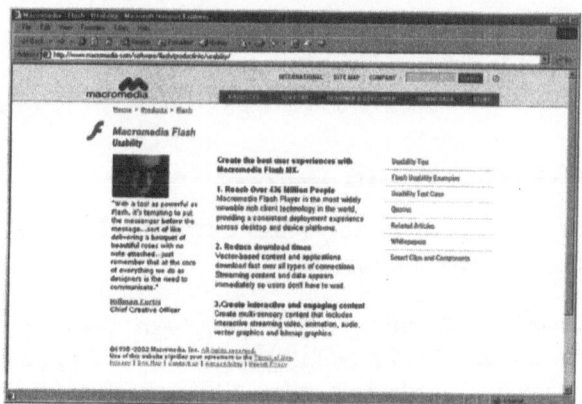

Flazoom.com. CHris MacGregor's own web log, covering Flash usability issues.

http://www.flazoom.com/

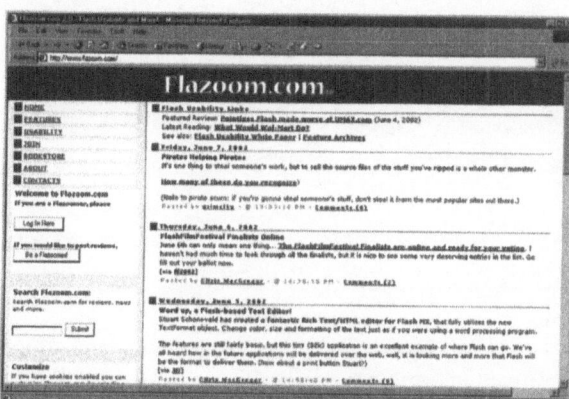

Flash99%Good. The companion site to Osborne's Flash usability book "Flash: 99% Good".
http://www.Flash99good.com/

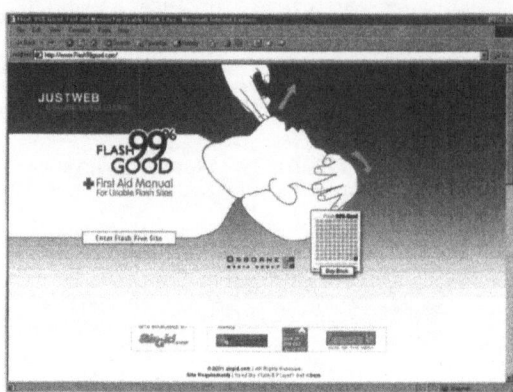

Reports and white papers

Developing User-Friendly Flash Content (*Chris MacGregor*).
http://www.flazoom.com/usability/

Macromedia Flash™: A New Hope for Web Applications (*Christine Perfetti and Jared M. Spool, User Interface Engineering*).
http://www.macromedia.com/resources/business/solutions/user_centric/flash _web_apps.pdf

Making the Best with Flash™– Five Best Practices for Creating Engaging Content with Macromedia® Flash™ (*Christine Perfetti and Matthew Klee, User Interface Engineering – $34.99*).
http://www.uie.com/flash.htm

Articles

Tipping Jakob's Ladder (*Julie Meloni*). A fantastic article about the 'Flash is 99% Bad' debacle of late 2000 (you can find Jakob Nielsen's original piece at http://www.useit.com/alertbox/20001029.html). She goes through his article like a hot knife through butter, and serves up what is left on toast.
http://hotwired.lycos.com/webmonkey/templates/print_template.htmlt?meta
=/webmonkey/01/26/index1a_meta.html

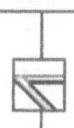

Criticism of Flash grows with its popularity (*Stefanie Olsen – CNET News.com*). Looking at the criticism Flash has received from certain usability pundits.
http://news.cnet.com/news/0-1005-200-5772284.html

Flash Usability (*Meryl K. Evans*). This article outlines a number of good steps that developers should take when developing usable Flash content.
http://www.digital-web.com/tutorials/tutorial_2002-01.shtml

Consider It Before You Build It (*Samuel Granato*). The author shares his experiences designing for the color blind and examines what Flash developers can do to help.
http://www.stumede.com/flashkit/pope/green/green2.html

Guidelines For Multimedia on the Web (*Jakob Nielsen*).
http://www.useit.com/alertbox/9512.html

Repent From Flash Sins (*Tim Kennedy*).
http://smw.internet.com/symm/voices/flashsins/

Usability vs. Interactivity on the Web (*Keran McKenzie*).
http://www.virtual-fx.net/articles/usability.htm

Create a Usable Flash Site (*Aaron West*).
http://www.iboost.com/build/design/articles/pageview/603.htm

The Flash Usability Guide

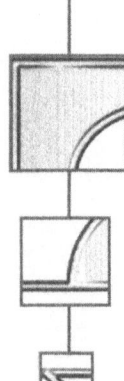

Flash is Evil (*dack.com*).
http://www.dack.com/web/flash_evil.html

Flash vs. HTML: A Usability Test (*dack.com*).
http://www.dack.com/web/flashVhtml/

Introduction to Flash Usability (*Jeremy Riga*).
http://www.flashkit.com/tutorials/Tips_And_Techniques/Introduc-Jeremy_R-161/index.shtml

Flash: Interface Usability (*Merien Q. Kunst*).
http://www.quintus.org/use/article01.asp

Flash Usability (*Tom Wheeler*).
http://www.stlwebdev.org/resources/articles/flash_usability.shtml

The Flash Usability Challenge (*John S. Rhodes – WebWord.com*).
http://webword.com/flashusability.html

Response to the Flash Usability Challenge (*Jason Kottke*).
http://www.kottke.org/plus/misc/flashusability_response.html

Flash Usability: 25 Tips for Better Websites (*Keran McKenzie & David Emberton*).
http://www.studiowhiz.com/_publications/_fk01/_emberton.php

A usable future for Flash? (*Chris Rourke – User Vision*).
http://www.uservision.co.uk/Articles/FlashArticle.html

Accessibility

Flash News Flash: It's Accessible (*Lisa Delgado*). This article looks at a groundbreaking tool that now makes Flash captioning practical, opening up Flash movies to a whole new audience.

http://www.wired.com/news/culture/0,1284,51638,00.html

Flash Access: Unclear on the Concept (*Joe Clark*). This article explores accessibility in-depth, examines the major obstacles involved, and spanks hotshot designers on general principles.
http://www.alistapart.com/stories/unclear/

A Call to Action: Making Flash Accessible (*Jim Heid*).
http://www.heidsite.com/archives/flashaccess.html

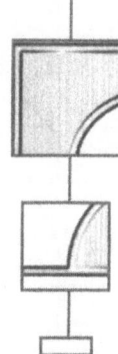

Usable web applications

Flash MX: From fluff to serious application builder? (*Lamont Adams*). A good overview of Flash MX's application-building powers.
http://builder.com.com/article.jhtml?id=u00220020312adm01.htm

Build Rich Front Ends to Your Web Applications (*Shawn Morton*). A good look at the debate whether to use Flash or HTML for web content.
http://builder.com.com/article.jhtml?id=u00420020507shm01.htm

Flash's Got a Brand New Bag (*Michael Cardenas*). Consumers love shopping. Designers love Flash. You do the math. Developer Michael Cardenas shares tips to help you get started building Flash-based e-commerce sites.
http://www.alistapart.com/stories/flashbag/

Components and Conformity (*David Doull*). An excellent overview of Flash MX's new UI components. The author takes a look at why they are useful, how they change the model of application development in Flash, as well as some of the issues with component development and use.
http://www.urbanev.com/components.html

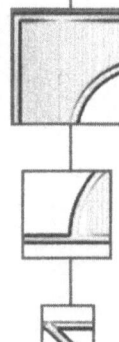

Search Engine Strategies

Flash – Search Engine Roadblock Solutions (*Andrew Gerhart*). If you're deploying Flash sites on the Web, and want them to be found via a search engine, this article is for you. The author moderates the Search Engine Promotion forum at Webmaster World, and here he gives a great introduction to search engine issues that face Flash developers.
http://www.promotionbase.com/article/568

Avoid Search Engine Roadblocks in Macromedia Flash MX (*Andrew Gerhart*). An article on search engine strategies for Flash MX developers. It lists many of the problems with search engines and Flash, and suggests ways to get around them. The solution that they offer, to create an HTML version of the site, is actually a very good idea for both search engine performance and accessibility.
http://www.traffick.com/article.asp?aID=74

Designing for Search Engines and Stars (*Shirley E. Kaiser, M.A.*). A must-read for anyone creating commercial sites, this article explains SEO (Search Engine Optimization), and features a special section on Flash about halfway down.
http://www.digital-web.com/tutorials/tutorial_2001-4.shtml

Miscellaneous

Size Matters: Small Is Good (*Erik Sherman, Newsweek*). This article is really more about how businesses use the Web than about Flash itself. However, it raises key issues and still makes for a good read.
http://www.msnbc.com/news/747698.asp

Flash + Information Visualization = Great User Experiences (*Matthew Klee, User Interface Engineering*). Not so much about Flash as it is about changing the way that web designers and user experience folks *think about* Flash. It shows concrete example of Flash's ability to improve the user's experience.

http://world.std.com/~uieweb/Articles/info_visualization.htm

SWF Is Not Flash (and Other Vectored Thoughts) (*Jacek Artymiak*). A good, level-headed look at the differences between SWF, SVG, FLA, and the overall Flash picture on the Web.
http://www.oreillynet.com/pub/a/javascript/2002/05/24/swf_not_flash.html

It May Flash, But It Doesn't Streak and **Flash Forward: A Year Later** (*Sean Carton*). Written twelve months apart, two takes from one guy on the state of Flash usability on the Web.
http://www.clickz.com/tech/lead_edge/article.php/997021

Beyond the Banner (*Verne Kopytoff, San Francisco Chronicle*). This article looks at the market for floating Flash ads, and also considers the reaction from users.
http://www.sfgate.com/cgi-bin/article.cgi? file=/c/a/2002/04/02
➥/BU98776.DTL

Flash 99% Good (*Michael Truese*). This article debunks some of the myths surrounding Flash and its use on the Web.
http://www.webmasterbase.com/article.php?aid=374

Is Flash Too Flash? (*Frank Gaine*).
http://infocentre.frontend.com/servlet/Infocentre?access=no&page=article&
➥rows=5&id=97

Beyond the Bells and Whistles: A Practical Look at Macromedia's Flash and Its Usability for Libraries (*Heidi N. Abbey*).
http://www.bates.edu/acrlnec/sigs/itig/tc_july_aug2000.htm

Empire of the Disconnected (*D. Keith Robinson*).
http://www.alistapart.com/stories/empire/index.html

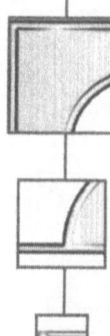

The Flash Usability Guide

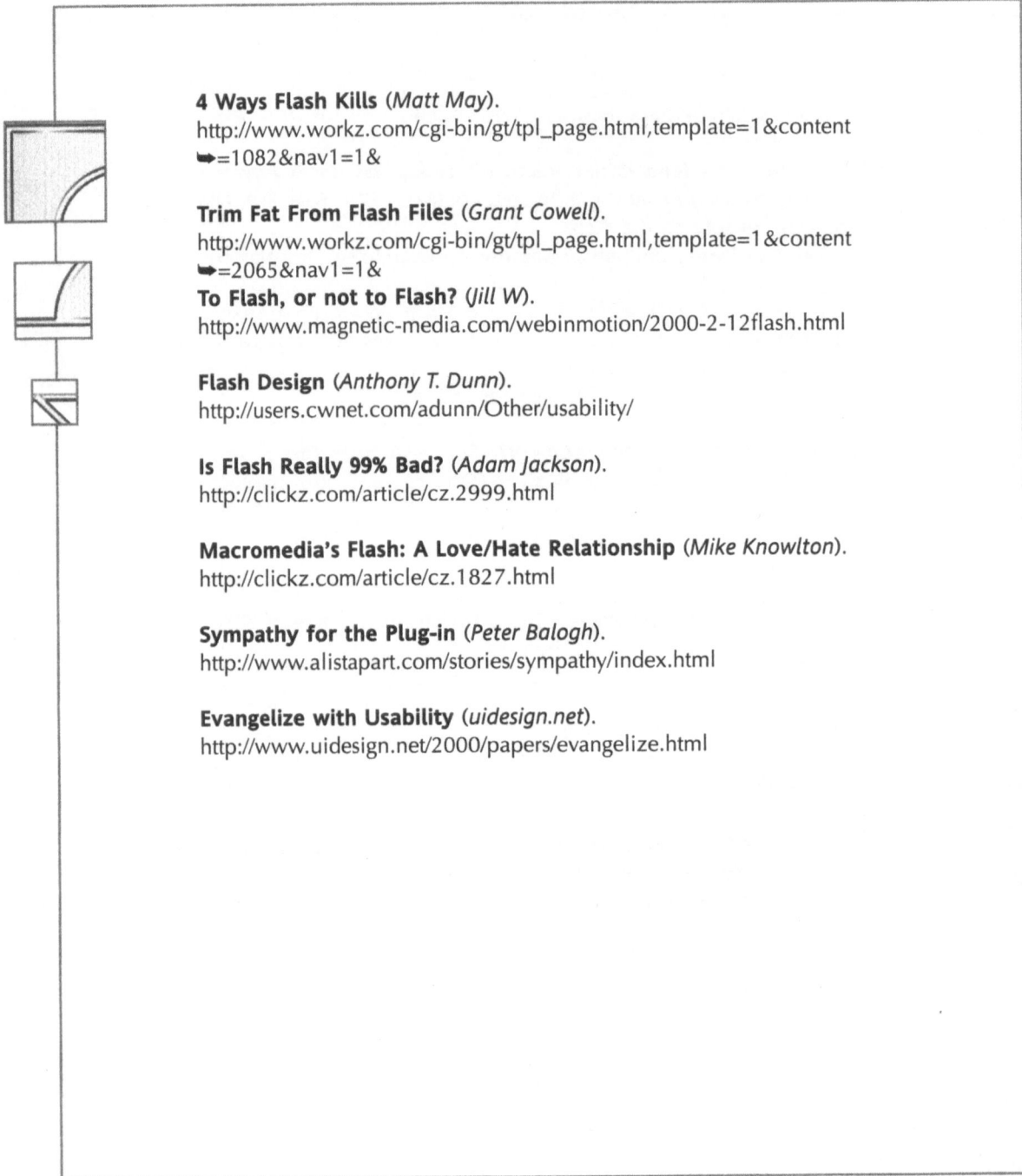

4 Ways Flash Kills (*Matt May*).
http://www.workz.com/cgi-bin/gt/tpl_page.html,template=1&content
➡=1082&nav1=1&

Trim Fat From Flash Files (*Grant Cowell*).
http://www.workz.com/cgi-bin/gt/tpl_page.html,template=1&content
➡=2065&nav1=1&

To Flash, or not to Flash? (*Jill W*).
http://www.magnetic-media.com/webinmotion/2000-2-12flash.html

Flash Design (*Anthony T. Dunn*).
http://users.cwnet.com/adunn/Other/usability/

Is Flash Really 99% Bad? (*Adam Jackson*).
http://clickz.com/article/cz.2999.html

Macromedia's Flash: A Love/Hate Relationship (*Mike Knowlton*).
http://clickz.com/article/cz.1827.html

Sympathy for the Plug-in (*Peter Balogh*).
http://www.alistapart.com/stories/sympathy/index.html

Evangelize with Usability (*uidesign.net*).
http://www.uidesign.net/2000/papers/evangelize.html

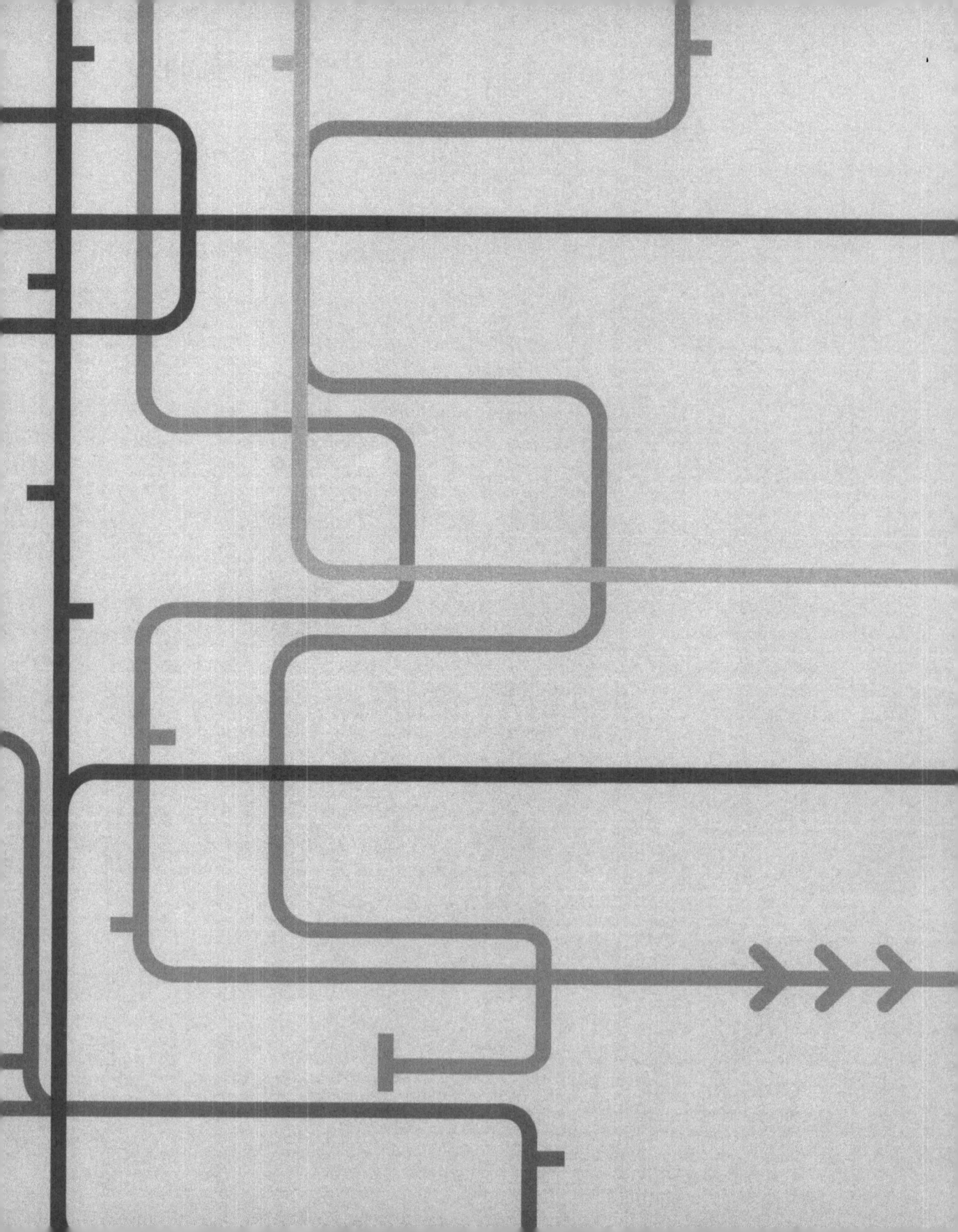

Index

The index is arranged hierarchically, in alphabetical order, with symbols preceding the letter A. Many second-level entries also occur as first-level entries. This is to ensure that users will find the information they require however they choose to search for it.

The Flash Usability Guide

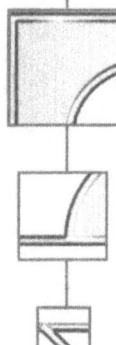

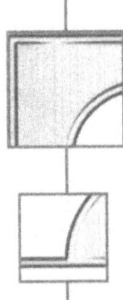

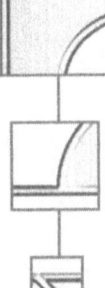

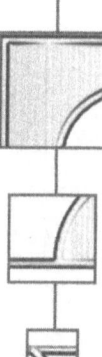

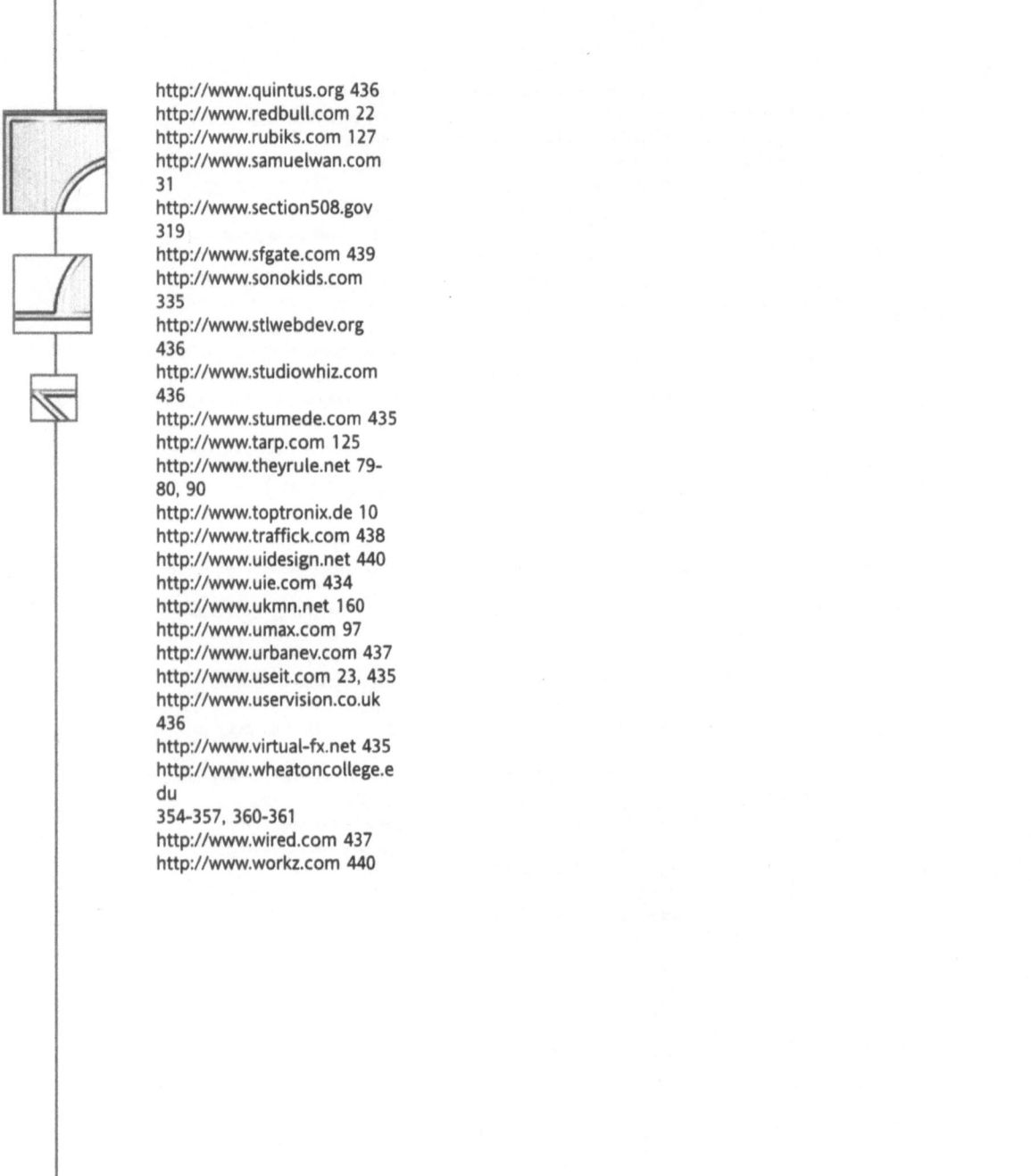

Notes